The
Wadleigh Chronicle

Donald E. Wadleigh

HERITAGE BOOKS
AN IMPRINT OF HERITAGE BOOKS, INC.

Books, CDs, and more—Worldwide

For our listing of thousands of titles see our website
at
www.HeritageBooks.com

Published 2007 by
HERITAGE BOOKS, INC.
Publishing Division
65 East Main Street
Westminster, Maryland 21157-5026

International Standard Book Number: 978-1-55613-712-5

INTRODUCTION

One Thanksgiving when I was in grade school my mother mentioned that I was descended from the Pilgrims of Plymouth Rock as my great-great-great, I forget how many, great-grandfather was the minister on the Mayflower, that my father was mostly English and that she was all German. Some years later, I remember her writing to several cousins asking for information, she said it was for this relative in Montana.

After I was grown and married, she sent several copies of a hard-bound book written by this relative in Montana. On page 58 was a listing for Donald Elvin Wadleigh, his wife and two children. Right there in black and white it showed that I was not only a descendant of Elder William Brewster, but of John Wadleigh who left from Bristol, England in 1630 and landed at Saco, Maine. The bait was taken and the hook set.

I began with an effort to trace the roots of my immediate family. The starting point was that small book from the relative in Montana, The Descendants of Edwin Flavel Brewster, 1822-1911 by William Keven Armstrong. I began asking questions. I read local New England histories. Other family members sent me copies of work done years ago. I found people with similar interests.

Soon, I found and got to know some truly fascinating individuals like Robert[2] Wadleigh who pleaded a case before the King of England, Charles Edwin[8] Wadleigh who fought under Grant at Vicksburg and then spent the rest of the Civil War vacationing (my word for it) on the Texas Gulf Coast. He later became a breeder of fine Morgan horses in Missouri.

Later, I was introduced to even more interesting people who were not in my direct ancestry like Susan (Wadleigh) Pillsbury, mother of
the first Governor of Minnesota and founder of
the Pillsbury Flour.   And there was Senator
Bainbridge Wadleigh from New Hampshire, Lydia
F. Wadleigh the longtime Supt. of New York
Female Normal Academy, Judge Robert Wadleigh
whose family founded Wadleigh's Hill outside
Sutton, N.H., Enos Dole Wadley who changed the
spelling of the name and moved to Georgia where
he built a plantation and where his grandson
grew to become a high official in the Confederate States government and later president of
the Southern Pacific Railroad.

There are some equally interesting, but
tragic figures as well.   There was Moses Wadleigh who made a habit of getting drunk on
weekends until one night he left the pub with a
new friend and his body was found the next day.
The number of children who died in infancy or
adolescence is sometimes staggering.   One
family who fled to Canada to avoid the Revolutionary War were wiped out by a fever, except
for the youngest son who returned alone to his
home in New Hampshire.   There are documented
instances of wife- and child-abuse.   The one I
was particularly touched by was a woman in the
late 1600's who was weekly tied to a high post
in her front yard and beaten with a horse-whip
by her husband.   She had such a lovely name,
Argentine Cram.

There are Wadleigh's of every political
persuasion, including Loyalists.   Several
families left New Hampshire in the mid 1700's
for Quebec.   One family moved to Hatley, Quebec, and all of their children moved back once
they were grown.

As I learned more about the Wadleigh family
and the history of New England, I set some
goals.   One was to develop a complete North
American Ancestry of my children.   The second
is to compile a genealogy of each first genera-

tion settler and the third is to make this information available, readable, and above all interesting to the widest possible audience. Obviously, these goals will never be reached completely.

This book is but one step towards those goals. It contains a genealogy of the Wadleigh descendants, compiled from a variety of sources. By no means complete, it is a complete compilation of data available to me as of the date of publication. Future volumes, if they can be developed, will contain selected genealogies of associated families, possibly the Libbys, the Brewsters, the Pluckers, the Robisons, the Harts, the Wittes, the Treworgies, the Shapleighs, or others. Future volumes may also contain updates of this work as additional data is incorporated.

I find that most genealogical books and local history accounts with genealogies are written and re-written many times over but mostly they are extremely cryptic as the writer or compiler tries to pack the most information into the smallest space. As a result, trying to find information is more like trying to crack a secret code than researching history.

In the Wadleigh Chronicle, I have tried to display information so that it is easily followed and enjoyed by the casual or novice reader while still being a usable and effective reference for the serious researcher. The genealogy of John Wadleigh forms the body of this book. It is preceded by a listing of each family unit in the genealogy and the page on which it is located and is followed by several Appendices:

* Appendix A contains an indexed listing of each descendant and the page on which they can be found.

* Appendix B contains an indexed list of all towns, major institutions or significant

organizations mentioned in the genealogy.

*   Appendix C contains an indexed list of all surnames found in the genealogy including the surnames of all spouses and their families.

*   Following Appendix C is a list of references from which all the data herein was developed. All references are cited by reference number (Ref. #) that identifies which source in this list is used.

The genealogical information is displayed in a generation by generation format closely akin to the New England Genealogical Society Standard. Each entry contains, at a minimum, the basic information listed below. If any items are not known, a blank is provided. The sequential identifier starts with "1" for the family immigrant. Each child is given a sequential number beginning with the eldest. The numbering system continues sequentially from the youngest child to the firstborn of the eldest to begin the next generation.

*   Sequential identifier.
*   Name with a generational indicator
*   Lineage to John Wadleigh
*   Birth Date
*   Death Date
*   Source(s)

This is a typical basic entry:

276- <u>Thomas</u>^{6} <u>Wadleigh</u>, (Dean^5, John^4, John^3, Robert^2, John^1), b. February 25, 1757, d. March 18, 1803 in Kensington, N.H. (Ref. 3)

When additional specific information is known, it is added at a logical point as in this illustration:

263- <u>Mary</u>^{6} <u>Wadleigh</u>, (Benjamin^5, Joseph^4, John^3, Robert^2, John^1), b. February 23, 1743 in Salisbury, Mass., d. March 25, 1798 in (presum.) Salisbury. unmarried. (Ref. 3)

Occasionally, additional lineage information is known about an individual leading to other North American immigrants. Within limits, this additional lineage data is shown following the Wadleigh lineage.

When an individual is married, additional basic information is shown concerning the marriage and the spouse as in the following example. Second and third marriages are shown in the same manner.

317- <u>Elizabeth</u>^{6} <u>Wadleigh</u>, (Edward^5, Philip^4, Robert^3, Robert^2, John^1), bpt. June 10, 1753 in Exeter, N.H. m. (presum.) June 15, 1786 Reuben Smith, no additional data. (Ref. 6)

Children are listed following the basic entry with each child's sequential identifier. These sequential identifiers are the keys used to track persons from one generation to their parents or offspring in other generations.

357- <u>John</u>^{6} <u>Wadleigh</u>, (James^5, Joseph^4, Henry^3, Robert^2, John^1), b. August 10, 1753 (twin) in Epping, N.H., d. 1842 (or 1848). m. Molly Fox, b. 1757, d. 1827. Res. Epping and Meredith, N.H. (Ref. 3)

608 - Dearborn	612 - Nancy
609 - Polly	613 - Caroline
610 - Betsey	614 - Sally
611 - Hannah	615 - Cyrene

The basic entries for siblings are gathered in family groups based on parentage. Thus, it is possible to track a family line through the text by following the sequential identifier back with the parental reference and forward with the listing of offspring. The following is an example of a complete family listing.

Issue of 218- Ebenezer[5] Wadleigh, and Love (Huntress) Wadleigh:

368- <u>Dorothy</u>[6] <u>Wadleigh</u>, (Ebenezer[5], John[4], Daniel[3], John[2], John[1]), b. in South Berwick, Me. no additional data. (Ref. 3)

369- <u>Albra</u>[6] <u>Wadleigh</u>, (Ebenezer[5], John[4], Daniel[3], John[2], John[1]), b. November 12, 1804 in South Berwick, Me., Grad. Harvard 1854, Priest of Philadelphia Protestant Episcopal Church, d. July 23, 1864 in Philadelphia, Pa. m. January 24, 1826 Eliza Payson Brewster, d. of William Brewster and Izette (Noble) Brewster, b. March 31, 1809 in Portsmouth, N.H., d. in Brookline, Mass. (Ref. 3)
   635 - Mary Rice   636 - Frances Wentworth

For those who wish to check references and pursue their own family histories, most of the sources cited in Appendix have been available through local library loan sources. Where possible, I have included the individual data entries the page number within the source document where the information could be found.

As I said above, this document is nowhere near a complete genealogy, nor is it intended to be. I feel that genealogies should be living and growing endeavors where people of like interests can cooperate, study and above all enjoy working with each other to learn more about themselves and the cultures, both past and present, that shape the way we think, act, interact, behave and exist in the world in which we find ourselves.

WADLEIGH CHRONICLE
WADLEIGH GENEALOGY   FAMILY LISTING

WADLEIGH GENEALOGY   FAMILY LISTING

Fifth Generation Families:

Sixth Generation Families:

- x -

Seventh Generation Families:

Eighth Generation Families:

WADLEIGH GENEALOGY   FAMILY LISTING

Ninth Generation Families:

veye # WADLEIGH GENEALOGY   FAMILY LISTING

Eleventh Generation Families:

Twelfth Generation Families:

WADLEIGH GENEALOGY   FAMILY LISTING

Thirteenth Generation Families:

Family Emigrant:

1- John[1] Wadleigh, b. ca. 1600 in England
(presum. Bristol, Devonshire), d. previous to
September. 16, 1671 (presum. in Wells Me.),
arr. Saco Me. 1632. m. Mary, b. ca. 1600 in
England (presum. Bristol, Devonshire), d. 1671.
Occ. Planter, Vinter. Res. Saco Me., Kittery
Me., Wells Me. (by November 20, 1645)
Selectman in 1647 and 1648. (Ref. 2, 3, 10-
379, 24, 36-183, 38-707)

2 - Robert	4 - Joanna
3 - Mary	5 - John

Issue of 1- John[1] Wadleigh and Mary Wadleigh:

2- Robert[2] Wadleigh, (John[1]), b. 1627 Bristol,
Devonshire, England, d. 1708/9, arr. Saco Me.
m. ca. 1650 Sarah Smith(?), b. ca. 1632, (alive
in 1698). Res. Saco, Wells, Kittery, & Dover
Me. and Exeter, N.H. (Ref. 2, 3, 38-707, 49,
S4) Note: Ref. 49 states h. alive in 1714.

6 - Sarah	10 - Mary
7 - John	11 - Henry
8 - Robert	12 - Jonathan
9 - Joseph	

3- Mary[2] Wadleigh, (John[1]), b. ca. 1629 in
Bristol, Devonshire, England, arr. Saco Me.
m. Thomas[1] Mills of Wells Me. b. Excester,

England, d. in (presum.) England.   (Ref. 2, 3, 24)

        13 - John   15 - Sarah
        14 - Mary   16 - Martha

4- <u>Joanna^2 Wadleigh</u>, (John^1), b. ca. 1632.   m. 1st Jonathan Thing, b. ca. 1620/21, d. April 29, 1674. m. 2nd Bartholomew Tipping. (Ref. 24, 38-707, 49)

        17 - Jonathan   20 - Samuel
        18 - Elizabeth   21 - Mary
        19 - John

5- <u>John^2 Wadleigh</u>, (John^1), b. in Wells Me. (presum.). m. an unknown person. no additional data. (Ref. 2, 3)

        22 - William   24 - Mary
        23 - Daniel   25 - John

WADLEIGH CHRONICLE
WADLEIGH GENEALOGY   THIRD GENERATION

Issue of 2- Robert^2 Wadleigh and Sarah Wadleigh:

6- <u>Sarah^3 Wadleigh</u>, (Robert^2, John^1), b. June 15, 1655 in (presum.) Wells, Me. m. 1st February 1671/2 John Young of Lampriel River, N.H., d. June 9, 1697 killed by Indians.   m. 2nd Mr. Robinson of Exeter, N.H. no additional data. (Ref. 2, 3)

        26 - Daniel

7- <u>John^3 Wadleigh</u>, (Robert^2, John^1), b. December 7, 1657 in (presum.) Wells, Me. d. November 7, 1727. m. Abigail Marston, d. of John Marston, Marblehead, Mass. no additional

data. Res. Exeter N.H. & Salisbury, Mass.
prior to 1694, Occ. Millwright, imprisoned in
Gove Rebellion in 1693 pardoned. (Ref. 2, 3,
4, S4)

27 - Abigail	30 - Alice
28 - Joseph	31 - Ephriam
29 - John	32 - Ruth

8- <u>Robert[3]</u> Wadleigh, (Robert[2], John[1]), b.
December 29, 1659 in (presum.) Wells, Me. m.
September 8, 1696 Sarah[3] Nelson, (Phillip[2],
Thomas[1]) of Rowley, Me., d. of Capt. Phillip
and Elizabeth (Lowell) Nelson. no additional
data. Occ. Farmer. (Ref. 2, 3, 4, 11) (Ref.
11 says 38- Joseph was 4th son)

33 - Robert	36 - Abigail
34 - Benjamin	37 - Jonathan
35 - Philip	38 - Joseph

9- <u>Joseph[3]</u> Wadleigh, (Robert[2], John[1]), b.
December 3, 1660 in (presum.) Wells or Kittery,
Me., d. 1683/4 in prison for Gove's Rebellion,
unmarried.

10- <u>Mary[3]</u> Wadleigh, (Robert[2], John[1]), b. ca.
1664 in (presum.) Kittery, Me., d. December 24,
1727. m. 1693 John[3] Cram (Benjamin[2], John[1]) of
Hampton, N.H. (Ref. S4 says March 1690), s. of
Benjamin[2] and Argentine (Cromwell) Cram, b.
April 6, 1665 at Hampton Falls, N.H., d.
January 1728 at Hampton Falls, N.H. (Ref. 2,
3, S4)

39 - Argentine	43 - Jonathan
40 - Abigail	44 - John
41 - Benjamin	45 - Mary
42 - Wadleigh	

NOTE: Benjamin[2] Cram is son of John[1] and
Hester Cram. He m. Argentine Cromwell on
November 28, 1662. She was possibly widow of
Thomas Cromwell. (Ref. S4) 9 Children:
    a. Sarah, b. September 19, 1663, m. March

27, 1708 Jacob Basford.

    b.   John, see above.

    c.   Benjamin, b. December 30, 1666, m. Mary.

    d.   Mary, b. August 6, 1669.

    e.   Joseph, b. April 12, 1671, m. May 17, 1700 Jane Philbrick.

    f.   Hannah, b. August 22, 1673, m. William Fifield.

    g.   Esther, b. October 16, 1675.

    h.   Jonathan, April 26, 1678, unmarried.

    i.   Elizabeth, January 3, 1681, m. Samuel Melcher.

NOTE: John[1] Cram died March 5, 1682. His wife, Hester, died May 16, 1677. (Ref. S4) 5 Children:

    a.   Joseph, b. ca. 1633, d. June 24, 1648.

    b.   Benjamin, see above.

    c.   Thomas, m. December 20, 1681 Elizabeth Weare.

    d.   Mary, m. January 25, 1666 Abraham Tilton.

    e.   Lydia, b. July 27, 1648.

11- Henry[3] Wadleigh, (Robert[2], John[1]), b. May 16, 1666 in (presum.) Kittery, Me., d. August 2, 1732 in Exeter, N.H. m. December 3, 1693 Elizabeth[3] (Gilman) Ladd, (Gilman: John[2], Edward[1]), d. of John[2] Gilman, Esq. and Elizabeth (Treworgie) Gilman (Treworgie: James[1]), (d. of James[1] Treworgie and Catherine (Shapleigh) Treworgie), widow of Nathaniel[2] Ladd, (Daniel[1]), b. August 16, 1661 in Haverhill, Mass., d. 1733/4 in Exeter, N.H. Occ. Millwright. Res. Kittery, Me. and Exeter N.H. (Ref. 2, 3, 25, 35-69, 38-707)

      46 - Sarah   49 - Martha
      47 - Abigail   50 - Benjamin
      48 - Joseph

12- Jonathan[3] Wadleigh, (Robert[2], John[1]), b. between 1666-1670 in (presum.) Lee, N.H., d. 1755/6 in Exeter, N.H., m. 1st Abigail

Eastman, d. of Peter Eastman. m. 2nd December
21, 1665 in Exeter Ann (Wilson) Hilton, widow
of Col. Winthrop Hilton, d. of Humphrey and
Judith (Hershey or Herswy) Wilson. no
additional data. March 8, 1743/4, (Ref. 2, 3,
4)

          51 - Hannah   54 - Thomas
          52 - Mary   55 - Elizabeth
          53 - Jonathan

Issue of Thomas[1] Mills, and 3- Mary (Wadleigh) Mills:

13- John[2] Mills, (Wadleigh: Mary[2], John[1];
Mills: Thomas[1]). no additional data. (Ref.
3)

14- Mary[2] Mills, (Wadleigh: Mary[2], John[1];
Mills: Thomas[1]). no additional data. (Ref.
3)

15- Sarah[2] Mills, (Wadleigh: Mary[2], John[1];
Mills: Thomas[1]). no additional data. (Ref.
3)

16- Martha[2] Mills, (Wadleigh: Mary[2], John[1];
Mills: Thomas[1]), b. June 18, 1653 in Saco, Me.
m. 1st James Smith of Saco, Me. m. 2nd
Christopher Grant. no additional data. (Ref.
3) 56 - 57 by 1st h.
          56 - John   57 - James

Issue of Jonathan Thing, and 4- Joanna (Wadleigh) Thing:

17- Capt. Jonathan Thing, (Wadleigh: Joanna[2],
John[1]), b. ca. 1654, d. October 30, 1694. m.
1st July 26, 1677 Mary[3] Gilman, (John[2],
Edward[1]), d. of John[2] Gilman, and Elizabeth

(Treworgye) Gilman, b. September 10, 1658 in
Exeter, N.H., d. August 1691. m. 2nd Martha
Wiggin. no additional data. Killed by
accidental gun discharge while riding with 20-
Samuel Thing and Peter Folsom. 58 - 64 by 1st
w., 65 - by 2nd w. (Ref. 24, 35-69, 40-6, 49,
37-300, 47-88))

58 - Jonathan	62 - Elizabeth
59 - John	63 - Benjamin
60 - Bartholomew	64 - Josiah
61 - Joseph	65 - Daniel

18- Elizabeth Thing, (Wadleigh: Joanna[2],
John[1]). no additional data. (Ref. 24)

19- John Thing, (Wadleigh: Joanna[2], John[1]).
no additional data. (Ref. 24)

20- Samuel Thing, (Wadleigh: Joanna[2], John[1]),
b. June 3, 1667, d. before January 1748/9. m.
July 8, 1696 Abigail[3] Gilman, (John[2], Edward[1]),
b. November 3, 1674 at Exeter, N.H., d.
November 7, 1725. (Ref. 24, 35-70, 40-7, S4)

66 - Joanna	72 - Deborah
67 - Samuel	73 - Catherine
68 - Abigail	74 - Josiah
69 - Elizabeth	75 - John
70 - Sarah	76 - Mary
71 - Lydia	77 - Alice

21- Mary Thing, (Wadleigh: Joanna[2], John[1]), b.
d. (Ref. 24) {NOTE: a Mary Thing of Salisbury
m. Stephen Dudley of Exeter -- Ref. 4-141}

Issue of 5- John[2] Wadleigh:

22- William[3] Wadleigh, (John[2], John[1]), b. ca.
1662 in (presum.) Berwick, Me. m. 1st in
(presum.) 1686 Abigail Belcher. m. 2nd
Elizabeth. no additional data. Res. Berwick,

Me.   (Ref. 3, 26)   78- by 1st wife, 79 - 83 by
2nd wife.

78 - John	81 - Ebenezer
79 - Sarah	82 - Moses
80 - Mary	83 - Patience

23- <u>Daniel</u>[3] Wadleigh, (John[2], John[1]), b. ca.
1664 in (presum.) Berwick, Me. m. Hannah. no
additional data. Note: Ref. 26 has spelling
Wadlin. (Ref. 3, 26)

84 - William	89 - Mary
85 - Daniel	90 - Elizabeth
86 - Ebenezer	91 - Hannah
87 - Sarah	92 - Daniel
88 - John	

24- <u>Mary</u>[3] Wadleigh, (John[2], John[1]), b. ca.
1666. (Ref. 3)

25- <u>John</u>[3] Wadleigh, (John[2], John[1]), b. ca.
1668. (Ref. 3)

93 - Daniel	96 - Abigail
94 - Moses	97 - Mary
95 - John	

Issue of John Young and 6- Sarah (Wadleigh)
Young:

26- <u>Daniel</u> Young, (Wadleigh: Sarah[3], Robert[2],
John[1]). m. 62- Elizabeth (Thing) Stevens,
(Wadleigh: Jonathan[3], Joanna[2], John[1]; Gilman:
Mary[3], John[2], Edward[1]), b. ca. 1686 at Exeter,
N.H. (Ref. 49)

    98 - Mary

Issue of 7- John[3] Wadleigh and Abigail (Marston) Wadleigh:

27- Abigail[4] Wadleigh, (John[3], Robert[2], John[1]), b. March 30, 1684 in Exeter, N.H., d. May 28, 1728 in Salisbury, Mass.   m. January 22, 1704 Capt. Ezekiel[3] Morrill, (Morrill: Jacob[2], Abraham[1]), b. September 20, 1675 in Salisbury, d. October 11, 1732 in Salisbury. (h. m. 2nd March 25, 1732 Sarah (Roobe) Clough, wid. of Samuel[3] Clough, (Thomas[2], John[1]),). Res. Salisbury, Mass., and Southampton and Canterbury N.H.   (Ref. 3, 4-256)

99 - Jonathan	105 - Ephriam
100 - Ezekiel	106 - Abigail
101 - Abner	107 - Ruth
102 - Hannah	108 - Susanna
103 - John	109 - David
104 - Thomas	110 - Sarah

28- Joseph[4] Wadleigh, (John[3], Robert[2], John[1]), b. March 7 1686 in (presum.) Exeter, N.H., d. November 25, 1727 in Salisbury, Mass. m. January 9, 1711 in Salisbury, Abigail[3] Allen, (William[2], William[1]) of Salisbury, d. of William and Mary (Harris) Allen of Salisbury, Mass. b. July 2, 1683 in Salisbury, Mass., bpt. August 7, 1687, d. May 28, 1762. (Ref. 3, 4-33, 4-339)

111 - Joseph	114 - John
112 - Benjamin	115 - Mary
113 - William	116 - William

29- John[4] Wadleigh, (John[3], Robert[2], John[1]), b. August 14, 1691 in (presum.) Exeter, N.H., d. February 10, 1776 in Salisbury, Mass. m. February 7, 1719 Mary (Dean) Caruthers, widow of David Caruthers of Boston, Mass., d. of Thomas and Mary (Scammon) Dean, b. August 20, 1692 in Boston, Mass., d. June 10, 1736 in Salisbury. (Ref 3)

    117 - Dean

30- Alice[4] Wadleigh, (John[3], Robert[2], John[1]),
b. August 27, 1693 in Salisbury, Mass., bpt.
December 25, 1698. m. December 10, 1718,
William Daniels. (Ref. 3, 4-339)

31- Ephriam[4] Wadleigh, (John[3], Robert[2], John[1]),
b. May 25, 1697 in Salisbury, Mass., d. March
14, 1774 in Salisbury. m. June 28, 1720/21 at
Amesbury, Mass. Sarah Adams, d. of Achelius and
Sarah (Marsh) Adams, b. January 22, 1698 in
Amesbury. d. February 16, 1776. (Ref. 3, 4)

118 - Susan	122 - Enoch
119 - Moses	123 - Enoch
120 - Adams	124 - Abel
121 - Jonathan	

32- Ruth[4] Wadleigh, (John[3], Robert[2], John[1]), b.
June 28, 1700 in Salisbury, Mass., died in
childhood. (Ref. 3)

**Issue of 8- Robert[3] Wadleigh and Sarah
(Nelson) Wadleigh:**

33- Robert[4] Wadleigh, (Robert[3], Robert[2],
John[1]), b. ca. 1697 in Exeter, N.H. d. August
1773 in Stratham, N.H. m. December 16, 1718
Deborah Smith, d. of Israel and Hannah Smith of
Stratham, N.H. no additional data. Res.
Stratham, N.H. (Ref. 3, 38-708)

125 - John	129 - Deborah
126 - Robert	130 - Sarah
127 - Mary	131 - Meriable
128 - Marcia	

34- Benjamin[4] Wadleigh, (Robert[3], Robert[2],
John[1]), b. ca. 1699 in Exeter, N.H. m.
December 24, 1722 Judith[3] Clough, (Thomas[2],
John[1]) of Salisbury, Mass., d. of Thomas[2] and
Ruth[2] (Connor) Clough, (Connor: Cornelius[1]),
b. October 1, 1700 in Salisbury. (Ref. 3, 4-
724)

132 - Benjamin   137 - Love
133 - Hanna   138 - John
134 - Thomas   139 - Judith
135 - Sarah   140 - Ruth
136 - John

35- Philip[4] Wadleigh, (Robert[3], Robert[2], John[1]), b. ca. 1702 in Exeter, N.H., d. prior to July 29, 1767. m. 198- Mary Stevens, (Wadleigh: Elizabeth[4], Jonathan[3], Joanna[2], John[1]), b. September 1705. (Ref. 3, 35-69)

141 - Edward   143 - Sarah
142 - _____

36- Abigail[4] Wadleigh, (Robert[3], Robert[2], John[1]), b. ca. 1605 in Exeter, N.H. (Ref. 3)

37- Jonathan[4] Wadleigh, (Robert[3], Robert[2], John[1]), b. 1709 in Exeter, N.H., d. 1756 in Brentwood, N.H. m. 1st Joanna Moody, a widow. m. 2nd Sarah. no additional data. (Ref. 3, 38-708)

144 - Jonathan   147 - Anna
145 - John   148 - Rachel
146 - Robert

38- Joseph[4] Wadleigh, (Robert[3], Robert[2], John[1]), b. September 7, 1711 in Exeter, N.H., d. January 23, 1792 at Brentwood, N.H. now part of Exeter, N.H. bur. Wadleigh Cemetary on Brentwood Road from Great Hill.   m. January 7, 1737/8 Ann Swain, d. of Caleb and Hannah (Brown) Swain of Hampton, N.H., b. October 18, 1710 in Hampton Falls, d. February 10, 1777 in Brentwood. Deacon of Congregational Church in Brentwood. (Ref. 3, 11)

149 - Hannah   152 - Anna
150 - Sarah   153 - Rachel
151 - Joseph   154 - Mary

Issue of John[3] Cram and 10- Mary (Wadleigh) Cram:

39- Argentine[4] Cram, (Wadleigh: Mary[3], Robert[2], John[1]; Cram: John[3], Benjamin[2], John[1]), b. December 20, 1693 in Hampton, N.H., d. June 19, 1771. m. February 6, 1718 Abraham Brown, s. of Jacob Brown, b. 1689, d. 1789. (Ref. 3, 30, S4)

155 - Abraham	157 - Elizabeth
156 - Levi	

40- Abigail[4] Cram, (Wadleigh: Mary[3], Robert[2], John[1]; Cram: John[3], Benjamin[2], John[1]), b. September 10, 1695 in Hampton, N.H., d. February 25, 1773 at Kensington, N.H. m. December 30, 1714 in Hampton, Deacon John[5] Batchelder, (Nathaniel[4], Nathaniel[3], Nathaniel[2], Stephen[1]), s. of Nathaniel[4] and Elizabeth (Foss) Batchelder, b. July 28, 1692 at Kensington, (Ref. S4 says Hampton), d. March 16, 1753 at Kensington. Chosen Constable of Kensington April 18, 1737. (Ref. 3, 21, 30, S4)

158 - Mary	164 - Hannah
159 - Elizabeth	165 - Ruth
160 - John	166 - Nathan
161 - Joshua	167 - Daniel
162 - Abigail	168 - Eunice
163 - Deborah	169 - Benjamin

NOTE: Nathaniel[4] Batchelder, (Nathaniel[3], Nathaniel[2], Stephen[1]), m. Elizabeth Foss of Dover, N.H. ca. 1685. Mr. Batchelder was b. December 24, 1659 at Hampton, N.H. He died in 1745. Miss Foss was born to John Foss and Mary (Berry) Foss in 1666 and died in 1746. (Ref. S4) They had 9 children:
     a. Deborah, b. April 9, 1686 in Hampton, N.H., m. 1st David Tilton on January 8, 1708, m. 2nd Deacon Jonathan Fellows on June 14, 1733.
     b. Nathaniel, b. February 19, 1690 in Hampton, N.H., d. ca. 1724. m. Sarah Robie on

February 24, 1717.

    c. John, above.

    d. Elizabeth, b. 1694 in Hampton, N.H., d. January 21, 1753, m. Richard Sanborn on January 21, 1713.

    e. Josiah, b. July 1, 1695 in Hampton, N.H., d. October 9, 1759 in Chichester, N.H., m. Sarah Page in 1722.

    f. Jethro, b. January 2, 1698 in Hampton, N.H., d. May 1723, m. Dorothy Sanborn on May 15, 1721.

    g. Nathan, b. July 3, 1700 in Hampton, N.H., d. March 17, 1755. m. Mary Tilton on February 25, 1724.

    h. Phineas, b. November 1, 1701 in Kingston, N.H., d. January 16, 1793 in E. Kingston, N.H., m. Elizabeth Gilman.

    i. Ebenezer, b. December 10, 1710 in E. Kingston, N.H., d. 1784 in E. Kingston, N.H., m. Dorothy Boynton on February 10, 1733.

NOTE: Nathaniel[3] Batchelder, (Nathaniel[2], Stephen[1]), m. 1st Deborah Smith on December 10, 1656 in Hampton, N.H. who was dau. of John Smith. She died (probably in childbirth) March 8, 1676. On October 31, 1676, Nathaniel m. Mrs. Mary (Carter) Wyman, dau. of Rev. Thomas Carter. He later married Mrs. Elizabeth Knill, wid. of John Knill, who survivied him. Nathaniel was b. ca. 1630 in England and d. January 17, 1710. His father did not come with him to America, but rather stayed in Engl., see below. (Ref. S4) Nathaniel and Deborah had 9 children:

    a. Deborah, b. October 12, 1657, m. Joseph Palmer on January 25, 1677.

    b. Nathaniel, above.

    c. Ruth, b. May 9, 1662, d. January 11, 1752, m. Deacon James Blake.

    d. Esther, b. February 22, 1665, d. January 24, 1715, m. Samuel Shaw.

    e. Abigail, b. December 28, 1667, d. November 13, 1736. m. John Dearborn on November 4, 1689.

    f. Jane, b. January 8, 1670, m. Benjamin Lamprey on November 10, 1687.

g. Stephen, b. July 31, 1672, d. December 7 1718.

h. Benjamin, b. September 19, 1673 in Hampton, N.H., d. January 12, 1718, m. Susanna Page on December 25, 1696.

i. Stephen, b. March 8, 1676, d. September 19, 1748, m. Mary Dearborn on August 25, 1698.

Nathaniel[3] and Mary had 8 children:

a. Mercy, b. December 11, 1677, m. Samuel Dearborn on July 12, 1694.

b. Mary, b. September 18, 1679, d. young.

c. Samuel, b. January 10 1681 in Hampton, N.H., m. Elizabeth Davis on April 1, 1706.

d. Jonathan, b. 1683 in Hampton, N.H., m. Sarah Blake on December 2, 1708.

e. Thoedate, b. 1684, m. Morris Hobbs on November 18, 1703.

f. Thomas, b. ca. 1685/6, d. February 10, 1764, m. 1st Mary Moulton in 1712, m. 2nd Sarah Tuck with whom he had 9 children.

g. Joseph, b. August 9, 1687 in Hampton, N.H., d. October 26 1750, m. Mehetabel Marston.

h. Mary, b. October 17, 1688, d. in infancy.

Nathaniel[3] and Elizabeth had no children.

NOTE: Nathaniel[2] Bachiler (Batchelder) did not come to America. Rather, he stayed in England. He was b. ca. 1590 and m. Hester Mercer. (Ref. S4). They had 5 children.

a. Stephen.

b. Anna, d. after 1661, m. Daniel DuCornet.

c. Francis.

d. Nathaniel, above.

e. Benjamin.

NOTE: Stephen[1] Bachiler (Batchelder) was born ca. 1561 in England and d. in England in 1660. He came to America in 1632 and founded the town of Hampton, N.H. in 1638 where he was the first pastor of the church and minister of the town. Only dau. Theodate is known to have come to Hampton with him. His first wife is unknown. He m. 2nd Helen who died in 1642 and in 1648 m.

Mary. (Ref. S4) He is known to have 6
children:
    a. Nathaniel, above.
    b. Deborah, b. 1592, m. Ref. John Wing.
    c. Stephen, b. ca. 1594, d. ca. 1630.
    d. Theodate, b. 1596, d. October 16, 1649
in Hampton, N.H., m. Capt. Christopher Hussey.
    e. Ann, b. ca. 1601, d. 1631 as a widow in
Engl., m. John Sanborn.
    f. Samuel, d. in Holland.

41- Benjamin[4] Cram, (Wadleigh: Mary[3], Robert[2],
John[1]; Cram: John[3], Benjamin[2], John[1]), b. March
16, 1699 in Hampton, N.H. m. December 28, 1721
Abigail Dearborn. no additional data. (Ref.
3, S4)
        170 - Elizabeth

42- Wadleigh[4] Cram, (Wadleigh: Mary[3], Robert[2],
John[1]; Cram: John[3], Benjamin[2], John[1]), b.
October 12, 1702 in Hampton, N.H. m. 1st
October 24, 1723 Hannah Marston, d. of Samuel
Marston of Hampton. m. 2nd April 18, 1725
Ruth[4] Gilman of Exeter, N.H., (James[3], Moses[2],
Edward[1]). no additional data. (Ref. 3, 30,
38-263, S4)

43- Jonathan[4] Cram, (Wadleigh: Mary[3], Robert[2],
John[1]; Cram: John[3], Benjamin[2], John[1]), b.
August 22, 1706 in Hampton, N.H., d. May 3,
1760. m. November 28, 1728 (Ref. 3: May 3)
Elizabeth Heath, d. of Nehemiah Heath and a
Miss Gove or Johanna Dow. no additional data.
(Ref. 3, 30, S4)
        171 - Nehemiah

44- John[4] Cram, (Wadleigh: Mary[3], Robert[2],
John[1]; Cram: John[3], Benjamin[2], John[1]), b. May
16, 1710 in Hampton, N.H., d. ca. 1773. m.
January 13, 1730 Mary Sanborn, d. of Jabez
Sanborn. no additional data. (Ref. 3, S4)

45- Mary[4] Cram, (Wadleigh: Mary[3], Robert[2], John[1]; Cram: John[3], Benjamin[2], John[1]), b. July 23, 1713 in Hampton, N.H. m. Samuel Cram. no additional data. (Ref. 3, S4)

Issue of 11- Henry[3] Wadleigh and Elizabeth (Gilman) (Ladd) Wadleigh:

46- Sarah[4] Wadleigh, (Henry[3], Robert[2], John[1]) b. September 3, 1694 in Exeter, N.H. m. John Scribner. no additional data. (Ref. 2, 3, 35-69)

47- Abigail[4] Wadleigh, (Henry[3], Robert[2], John[1]) b. September 2, 1696 in Exeter, N.H. m. Samuel Magoon. no additional data. (Ref. 2, 3, 35-69)

48- Joseph[4] Wadleigh, (Henry[3], Robert[2], John[1]) b. b. September 1698 in Exeter, N.H., d. April 14, 1779 in Kensington, N.H. m. 1st ca. 1720 Lydia Smith, d. of Theophilus Smith of Exeter and Mary (Stanyan) Smith of Hampton Falls, N.H. (d. of John and Mary (Bradbury) Stanyon, (Bradbury: Thomas[1]) of Hampton Falls), d. 1723/4. m. 2nd Mary Fogg, d. of James Fogg of Hampton, b. January 5, 1697, d. August 30, 1774. m. 3rd Esther Fogg, d. of Seth Fogg of Hampton, b. March 16, 1697. Res. Exeter and Kensington, N.H. (Ref. 2, 3, 4-69, 4-1009, 35-69)   172 - 174 by 1st wife, 175 - 179 by 2nd wife.

172	- Theophilis	176	- James
173	- Joseph	177	- John
174	- Lydia	178	- Mary
175	- Benjamin	179	- Sarah

49- Martha[4] Wadleigh, (Henry[3], Robert[2], John[1]) b. September 1700/1 in Exeter, N.H. m. Ephriam Philbrick. no additional data. (Ref. 3, 35-69)

180 - Benjamin   183 - Martha
181 - Joseph   184 - Trueworthy
182 - Elizabeth   185 - John

50- Benjamin[4] Wadleigh, (Henry[3], Robert[2],
John[1]) b. 1703, d. 1716. died in childhood.
(Ref. 3, 35-69)

**Issue of 12- Jonathan[3] Wadleigh and Ann
(Wilson) Wadleigh:**

Compiler's Note: Ref. 3 cites 9 children,
seven of which are recorded in Exeter Town
Records, i.e. sans seventh (Ann) and eighth
(Martha), but only lists 5 offspring.

51- Hannah[4] Wadleigh, (Jonathan[3], Robert[2],
John[1]), b. in Exeter N.H. m. before 1716
Joseph Noyes of Newberry, Mass. no additional
data. (Ref. 3, 38-708)
        186 - Jonathan   190 - Parker
        187 - Elizabeth   191 - Hannah
        188 - Thomas   192 - Mary
        189 - Hannah

52- Mary[4] Wadleigh, (Jonathan[3], Robert[2],
John[1]), b. in Exeter N.H. m. Joseph Leavitt.
no additional data. (Ref. 3)
        193 - Mary

53- Jonathan[4] Wadleigh, (Jonathan[3], Robert[2],
John[1]), b. in Exeter N.H. (Ref. 3)

54- Thomas[4] Wadleigh, (Jonathan[3], Robert[2],
John[1]), b. in Exeter N.H. (Ref. 3)

55- Elizabeth[4] Wadleigh, (Jonathan[3], Robert[2],
John[1]), b. in Exeter N.H. m. Mr. Hopkins. no
additional data. (Ref. 3)
        194 - Elizabeth

WADLEIGH GENEALOGY   FOURTH GENERATION

Issue of James Smith and 16- Martha (Mills) Smith:

Compiler's Note: Ref. 3 cites James Smith's Will naming four children.

56- John Smith, (Wadleigh: Martha[3], Mary[2], John[1]), b. before May 3, 1693 (bpt. date) (presum. August 1685) in Berwick, Me., was captured in war on March 18, 1690 and kept as endentured servant by Mr. Dargenteuil, a French Marine Lieutenant. After redemption m. Elizabeth. no additional data. (Ref. 3)

57- James Smith, (Wadleigh: Martha[3], Mary[2], John[1]). m. Martha Bragdon, d. of Thomas Bragdon. no additional data. (Ref. 36-182)
    195 - John

Issue of 17- Jonathan Thing and Mary[3] (Gilman) Thing:

58- Jonathan Thing, (Wadleigh: Jonathan[3], Joanna[2], John[1]; Gilman: Mary[3], John[2], Edward[1]), b. September 21, 1678 at Exeter, N.H., d. ca. 1735. m. Abigail[4] Gilman, (Edward[3], Edward[2], Edward[1]), d. of Edward and Abigail (Maverick) Gilman of Exeter, N.H. no additional data. (Ref. 35-69, 38-263)

59- John Thing, (Wadleigh: Jonathan[3], Joanna[2], John[1]; Gilman: Mary[3], John[2], Edward[1]), b. June 1680 at Exeter, N.H. m. 1st Mehitable Stevens. m. 2nd Mrs. Wentworth, wid. of Thomas Wentworth. no additional data. 196 - by 1st w. (Ref. 35-69)
    196 - Mary

60- Bartholomew Thing, (Wadleigh: Jonathan[3], Joanna[2], John[1]; Gilman: Mary[3], John[2], Edward[1]), b. February 1681 at Exeter, N.H., d. April

1738. m. 1st Abigail Coffin. m. 2nd Sarah
(Little) Kent. no additonal data. 197- by 2nd
w. (Ref. 35-69)
     197 - Mary

61- Joseph Thing, (Wadleigh: Jonathan[3],
Joanna[2], John[1]; Gilman: Mary[3], John[2], Edward[1]),
b. March 1684 at Exeter, N.H. m. Mary Folsom.
no additional data. (Ref. 35-69)

62- Elizabeth Thing, (Wadleigh: Jonathan[3],
Joanna[2], John[1]; Gilman: Mary[3], John[2], Edward[1]),
b. ca. 1686 at Exeter, N.H. m. 1st Edward
Stevens. m. 2nd 26- Daniel Young, (Wadleigh:
Sarah[3], Robert[2], John[1]). no additional data.
(Ref. 3, 35-69, 49) 198- by 1st h. For issue
by 2nd h. see 26- Daniel Young.
     198 - Mary

63- Benjamin Thing, (Wadleigh: Jonathan[3],
Joanna[2], John[1]; Gilman: Mary[3], John[2], Edward[1]),
b. November 12, 1688 at Exeter, N.H. m.
1st in 1711 Pernel Coffin. m. 2nd
Deborah (Hilton) Thing, wid. of 67- Samuel
Thing. no additional data. (Ref. 35-69) 199
- 200 by 1st w., 201 - 204 by 2nd w.

199 - Coffin	203 - Mary
200 - Deborah	204 - Anna
201 - Pernel	205 - Samuel
202 - Winthrop	206 - Elizabeth

64- Josiah Thing, (Wadleigh: Jonathan[3],
Joanna[2], John[1]; Gilman: Mary[3], John[2], Edward[1]),
b. ca. 1690, died in infancy. (Ref. 35-69)

**Issue of 17- Jonathan Thing and Martha
(Wiggin) Thing:**

65- Daniel Thing, (Wadleigh: Jonathan[3],
Joanna[2], John[1]). no additional data. (Ref.
35-69)

Issue of 20- Samuel Thing and Abigail (Gilman) Thing:

66- Joanna Thing, (Wadleigh: Samuel[3], Joanna[2], John[1]; Gilman: Abigail[3], John[2], Edward[1]), b. 1697, d. November 16, 1727. m. January 27, 1714/5 Andrew[4] Gilman, (Jeremiah[3], Moses[2], Edward[1]), s. of Jeremiah and Mary (Wiggin) Gilman, b. 1690, d. ca. 1756 at Brentwood, N.H. h. m. 2nd Bridget Hilton. h. m. 3rd Jemima (Storer) Preble. (Ref. 35-70, 38-263) Ref. 38 notes 5 children.

67- Samuel Thing, (Wadleigh: Samuel[3], Joanna[2], John[1]; Gilman: Abigail[3], John[2], Edward[1]), b. 1699, d. 1723. m. Deborah Hilton. no additional data. (Ref. 35-70)

68- Abigail Thing, (Wadleigh: Samuel[3], Joanna[2], John[1]; Gilman: Abigail[3], John[2], Edward[1]), b. 1700. m. Capt. John Gilman. no additional data. (Ref. 35-70)

69- Elizabeth Thing, (Wadleigh: Samuel[3], Joanna[2], John[1]; Gilman: Abigail[3], John[2], Edward[1]), b. 1702. m. Benjamin[4] Gilman, (Jeremiah[3], Moses[2], Edward[1]). no additional data. (Ref. 35-70, 38-263)
        207 - Jonathan

70- Sarah Thing, (Wadleigh: Samuel[3], Joanna[2], John[1]; Gilman: Abigail[3], John[2], Edward[1]), b. 1704. m. Mr. Wormall. no additional data. (Ref. 35-70)

71- Lydia Thing, (Wadleigh: Samuel[3], Joanna[2], John[1]; Gilman: Abigail[3], John[2], Edward[1]), b. 1708 (twin). m. Antipas Gilman. no additional data. (Ref. 35-70)

72- <u>Deborah Thing</u>, (Wadleigh: Samuel[3], Joanna[2], John[1]; Gilman: Abigail[3], John[2], Edward[1]), b. February 14, 1708 (twin), d. before 1748. m. Isreal[4] Gilman, (Jeremiah[3], Moses[2], Edward[1]). no additional data. (Ref. 35-70, 38-263)

73- <u>Catherine Thing</u>, (Wadleigh: Samuel[3], Joanna[2], John[1]; Gilman: Abigail[3], John[2], Edward[1]), b. May 19, 1711, d. February 10, 1773 at Belmont, N.H. m. February 10, 1733 Edward[4] Ladd, (Gilman: Nathaniel[4], Elizabeth[3], John[2], Edward[1]; Ladd: Nathaniel[3], Nathaniel[2], Daniel[1]), b. June 22, 1707 at Exeter, N.H., d. July 5, 1787 at Belmont. (Ref. 26, 35-69, 35-70, 39, S4)

208 - Abigail	212 - Samuel
209 - Edward	213 - John
210 - Thing	214 - Abigail
211 - Nathaniel	

74- <u>Josiah Thing</u>, (Wadleigh: Samuel[3], Joanna[2], John[1]; Gilman: Abigail[3], John[2], Edward[1]), b. 1713. m. Hannah Dudley. no additional data. (Ref. 35-70)

215 - Abigail	217 - Hannah
216 - John	

75- <u>John Thing</u>, (Wadleigh: Samuel[3], Joanna[2], John[1]; Gilman: Abigail[3], John[2], Edward[1]), b. 1716. (Ref. 35-70)

76- <u>Mary Thing</u>, (Wadleigh: Samuel[3], Joanna[2], John[1]; Gilman: Abigail[3], John[2], Edward[1]), b. 1718. (Ref. 35-70)

77- <u>Alice Thing</u>, (Wadleigh: Samuel[3], Joanna[2], John[1]; Gilman: Abigail[3], John[2], Edward[1]), b. 1722. m. Mr. Ladd. no additional data. (Ref. 35-70)

Issue of 22- William[3] Wadleigh and Abigail (Belcher) Wadleigh:

78- John[4] Wadleigh, (William[3], John[2], John[1]), b. in Berwick Me. (Ref. 3)

Issue of 22- William[3] Wadleigh and Elizabeth Wadleigh:

79- Sarah[4] Wadleigh, (William[3], John[2], John[1]), b. in Berwick, Me., bpt. October 25, 1716 at South Berwick. Note: Ref. 26 has spelling Wadlin. (Ref. 3, 26)

80- Mary[4] Wadleigh, (William[3], John[2], John[1]), b. in Berwick Me., bpt. October 25, 1716 at South Berwick, Me. m. July 14, 1726 John Rowell. no additional data. Note: Ref. 26 has spelling Wadlin. (Ref. 3, 26)

81- Ebenezer[4] Wadleigh, (William[3], John[2], John[1]), bpt. October 25, 1716 at South Berwick, Me. Note: Ref. 26 has spelling Wadlin. (Ref. 3, 26)

82- Moses[4] Wadleigh, (William[3], John[2], John[1]), bpt. October 25, 1716 at South Berwick, Me. Note: Ref. 26 has spelling Wadlin. (Ref. 3, 26)

83- Patience[4] Wadleigh, (William[3], John[2], John[1]) b. bpt. October 25, 1716 at South Berwick, Me. Note: Ref. 26 has spelling Wadlin. (Ref. 3, 26)

Issue of 23- Daniel[3] Wadleigh and Hannah Wadleigh:

84- William[4] Wadleigh, (Daniel[3] John[2], John[1]),
b. bpt. June 1, 1736. Note: Ref. 26 has
spelling Wadlin. (Ref. 3, 26)

85- Daniel[4] Wadleigh, (Daniel[3] John[2], John[1]),
bpt. June 1, 1736. Note: Ref. 26 has spelling
Wadlin. (Ref. 3, 26)

86- Ebenezer[4] Wadleigh, (Daniel[3] John[2], John[1]),
bpt. June 1, 1736 Note: Ref. 26 has spelling
Wadlin. (Ref. 3, 26)

87- Sarah[4] Wadleigh, (Daniel[3] John[2], John[1]),
bpt. June 1, 1736. Note: Ref. 26 has spelling
Wadlin. (Ref. 3, 26)

88- John[4] Wadleigh, (Daniel[3] John[2], John[1]),
bpt. 1739 in Berwick, Me., d. 1815.   m.
Patience. no additional data. (Ref. 3)
        218 - Ebenezer   220 - Hannah
        219 - Elisah

89- Mary[4] Wadleigh, (Daniel[3] John[2], John[1]), b.
bpt. November 14, 1742. m. December 30, 1761
Timothy Ramsdel of York, Me. no additional
data. Note: Ref. 26 has spelling Wadlin.
(Ref. 3, 26)

90- Elizabeth[4] Wadleigh, (Daniel[3] John[2],
John[1]), bpt. February 12, 1744/5. m. July 26,
1764 Daniel Ramsdel of York, Me. no additional
data. Note: Ref. 26 has spelling Wadlin.
(Ref. 3, 26)

91- Hannah[4] Wadleigh, (Daniel[3] John[2], John[1]),
bpt. April 3, 1750. Note: Ref. 26 has
spelling Wadlin. (Ref. 3, 26)

92- Daniel[4] Wadleigh, (Daniel[3] John[2], John[1]),
bpt. 1753. Note: Ref. 26 has spelling Wadlin.
(Ref. 3, 26)

Issue of 25- John[3] Wadleigh:

93- Daniel[4] Wadleigh, (John[3], John[2], John[1]), b.
in Berwick, Me. (Ref. 3)

94- Moses[4] Wadleigh, (John[3], John[2], John[1]),
bpt. October 26, 1741 in Berwick, Me. m. July
13, 1760 Patience Grant. no additional data.
(Ref. 3)

95- John[4] Wadleigh, (John[3], John[2], John[1]), bpt.
October 26, 1741 in Berwick, Me. (Ref. 3)

96- Abigail[4] Wadleigh, (John[3], John[2], John[1]),
bpt. October 26, 1741 in Berwick, Me. (Ref. 3)

97- Mary[4] Wadleigh, (John[3], John[2], John[1]), bpt.
October 26, 1741 in Berwick, Me. (Ref. 3)

Issue of 26- Daniel Young and 62- Elizabeth (Thing) (Stevens) Young:

98- Mary Young, (Wadleigh: Elizabeth[4], Jonathan[3], Joanna[2], John[1]; Gilman: Elizabeth[4], Mary[3], John[2], Edward[1]). m. November 17, 1739 Jonathan Dolloff, s. of Richard and Catherine[2] (Bean) Dolloff, (Bean: John[1] Bean, Donald[1A] MacBean, Aaron[2A] MacBean), b. October 17, 1710 at Exeter, N.H., d. June 14, 1746 in R.I. Militia, possibly at Cape Brenton. (Ref. 49)
        221 - Richard

Issue of Ezekiel[3] Morrill and 27- Abigail (Wadleigh) Morrill:

99- Jonathan[4] Morrill, (Wadleigh: Abigail[4], John[3], Robert[2], John[1]; Morrill: Ezekiel[3], Jacob[2], Abraham[1]), b. in Salisbury, Mass., d. 1706 in Salisbury, Mass. died in childhood. (Ref. 3, 4-256)

100- Ezekiel[4] Morrill, (Wadleigh: Abigail[4], John[3], Robert[2], John[1]; Morrill: Ezekiel[3], Jacob[2], Abraham[1]), b. September 3, 1707 in Salisbury, Mass. m. June 19, 1731 Jemima[4] Morrill, (Abraham[3], Issac[2], Abraham[1]) of Salisbury, d. of Abraham and Elizabeth (Sargent) Morrill, (Sargent: William[2], William[1]). no additional data. Res. Salisbury, Mass. and South Hampton (adm. to church 1742) and Canterbury, N.H. (trans. church mem. 1750) {Poss. m. 2nd Joanna Gilman} (Ref. 3, 4-777)

222 - Abigail		230 - Ezekiel
223 - David		231 - Ezekiel
224 - Abigail		232 - unnamed
225 - Reuben		233 - Masten
226 - Elizabeth		234 - Sargent
227 - Laban		235 - Abraham

228 - Susanna   236 - Susanna
229 - Mary

101- Abner[4] Morrill, (Wadleigh: Abigail[4],
John[3], Robert[2], John[1]; Morrill: Ezekiel[3],
Jacob[2], Abraham[1]), b. July 12, 1709 in
Salisbury, Mass. m. January 7, 1731 Lydia
Greeley of Salisbury. no additional data.
(Ref. 3, 4-256)
            237 - Ezekiel   242 - Lydia
            238 - Philip   243 - Jeremiah
            239 - Miriam   244 - Joseph
            240 - Abel   245 - Mary
            241 - Abigail

102- Hannah[4] Morrill, (Wadleigh: Abigail[4],
John[3], Robert[2], John[1]; Morrill: Ezekiel[3],
Jacob[2], Abraham[1]), b. June 24, 1711 in
Salisbury, Mass., d. at Hampstead, N.H. m.
June 24, 1731 Samuel[4] Currier, (Samuel[3],
Thomas[2], Richard[1]) of Salisbury. s. of Samuel
and Dorothy (Foot) Currier of Salisbury, b.
February 1, 1709, d. September 24, 1766. Res.
Hampstead, and West Hampstead (after 1760),
N.H. (Ref. 3, 4-122, 20)
            246 - Samuel   248 - Samuel
            247 - Ezekiel   249 - Dorothy

103- John[4] Morrill, (Wadleigh: Abigail[4], John[3],
Robert[2], John[1]; Morrill: Ezekiel[3], Jacob[2],
Abraham[1]), b. March 28, 1713 in Salisbury,
Mass. m. Judith Morrill, d. of Jacob and
Elizabeth (Sterns) Morrill. no additional
data. Res. Londonderry, N.H.   (Ref. 3)
                  - OR -
103- John[4] Morrill, (Wadleigh: Abigail[4], John[3],
Robert[2], John[1]; Morrill: Ezekiel[3], Jacob[2],
Abraham[1]), b. March 28, 1713 in Salisbury,
Mass., living in 1732. m. 1st. Abigail
Flanders. m. 2nd Edith. Res. Londonderry,
N.H. (Ref. 3, 4-256)
            250 - Jonathan   251 - Micajah

104- Thomas[4] Morrill, (Wadleigh: Abigail[4], John[3], Robert[2], John[1]; Morrill: Ezekiel[3], Jacob[2], Abraham[1]), b. September 19, 1715 in Salisbury, Mass. m. (per Ref. 3) Elizabeth Severance. -OR- m. (per Ref. 4) June 24, 1740 Elizabeth Stevens. no additional data. (Ref. 3, 4-256)

105- Ephriam[4] Morrill, (Wadleigh: Abigail[4], John[3], Robert[2], John[1]; Morrill: Ezekiel[3], Jacob[2], Abraham[1]), b. December 9, 1717 in Salisbury, Mass. (Ref. 3, 4-256)

106- Abigail[4] Morrill, (Wadleigh: Abigail[4], John[3], Robert[2], John[1]; Morrill: Ezekiel[3], Jacob[2], Abraham[1]), b. January 27, 1719 in Salisbury, Mass. m. Henry Lunt, Jr. of Newbury, Conn. no additional data. (Ref. 3, 4-256)

107- Ruth[4] Morrill, (Wadleigh: Abigail[4], John[3], Robert[2], John[1]; Morrill: Ezekiel[3], Jacob[2], Abraham[1]), b. November 9, 1721 in Salisbury, Mass. m. January 5, 1748 Jabez Tucker of Salisbury. (Ref. 3, 4-256)

108- Susanna[4] Morrill, (Wadleigh: Abigail[4], John[3], Robert[2], John[1]; Morrill: Ezekiel[3], Jacob[2], Abraham[1]), b. January 10, 1723 in Salisbury, Mass., d. October 5, 1806. m. November 17, 1748 Nathaniel[5] Currier, (Jacob[4], Samuel[3], Thomas[2], Richard[1]), s. of Jacob[4] and Mary[4] (Barnard) Currier, (Barnard: Joseph[3], Thomas[2], Thomas[1]), b. November 10, 1924, d. December 23, 1776. Owned land in Poplin and Warner N.H. (Ref. 3, 4-702, 4-911, 4-925)

         252 - Anna   255 - David
         253 - Dorothy   256 - Hannah
         254 - Susanna   257 - Molly

109- David[4] Morrill, (Wadleigh: Abigail[4], John[3], Robert[2], John[1]; Morrill: Ezekiel[3], Jacob[2], Abraham[1]), b. 1724 in Salisbury, Mass., died in childhood. (Ref. 3)

110- Sarah[4] Morrill, (Wadleigh: Abigail[4], John[3], Robert[2], John[1]; Morrill: Ezekiel[3], Jacob[2], Abraham[1]), b. April 20, 1728 in Salisbury, Mass. (Ref. 3)

Issue of 28- Joseph[4] Wadleigh and Abigail (Allen) Wadleigh:

111- Joseph[5] Wadleigh, (Joseph[4], John[3], Robert[2], John[1]), b. November 16, 1712 in Salisbury, N.H., d. at sea 1781/2 as shipmaster. m. Mary (Tyers) Jones in England. no additional data. (Ref. 3)
     258 - Joseph   259 - Benjamin

112- Benjamin[5] Wadleigh, (Joseph[4], John[3], Robert[2], John[1]), b. November 16, 1712 in Salisbury, Mass., d. January 21, 1787 in Salisbury. m. 1st (unknown), m. 2nd February 3, 1737 Judith[4] Morrill, (Daniel[3], Isaac[2], Abraham[1]), d. of Daniel Morrill b. October 8, 1715, d. October 22, 1769 in Salisbury. (Ref. 3, 4-256)

260 - Eleanor	265 - Elizabeth
261 - Abigail	266 - Anne
262 - Hannah	267 - Joseph
263 - Mary	268 - Lois
264 - Merriam	269 - Judith
/Miriam	270 - Daniel

113- William[5] Wadleigh, (Joseph[4], John[3], Robert[2], John[1]), b. April 26, 1718 (twin) in Salisbury, Mass. d. 1718. died in childhood. (Ref. 3)

114- John[5] Wadleigh, (Joseph[4], John[3], Robert[2], John[1]), b. April 26, 1718 (twin) in Salisbury, Mass. d. 1718. died in childhood. (Ref. 3)

115- Mary[5] Wadleigh, (Joseph[4], John[3], Robert[2], John[1]), b. December 22, 1719 in Salisbury, Mass. m. January 24, 1745 Josiah Dow. no additional data. (Ref. 3)

116- William[5] Wadleigh, (Joseph[4], John[3], Robert[2], John[1]), b. November 20, 1723 in Salisbury, Mass. d. 1724. died in childhood. (Ref. 3)

Issue of 29- John[4] Wadleigh and Mary (Dean) Wadleigh:

117- Dean[5] Wadleigh, (John[4], John[3], Robert[2], John[1]), b. May 17, 1724 in Salisbury, Mass. m. Margaret[5] Morrill, (Morrill: Benjamin[4], Isaac[3], Issac[3], Abraham[1]), d. of Benjamin Morrill and Ruth[4] (Allen) Morrill, (Allen: Stillson[3], William[2], William[1]), b. January 19, 1724 in Salisbury. Res. Salisbury, Mass. and Candia, N.H. (Ref. 3, 4)

271 - Mary	276 - Thomas
272 - Ruth	277 - Benjamin
273 - John	278 - Dean
274 - Albra	279 - Dorothy
275 - Benjamin	

Issue of 31- Ephriam[4] Wadleigh and Sarah (Adams) Wadleigh:

118- Sarah[5] Wadleigh, (Ephriam[4], John[3], Robert[2], John[1]), b. February 6, 1722 in Salisbury, Mass. m. April 15, 1742 Moses Barnes[4] Morrill, (William Barnes[3], Moses[2], Abraham[1]) of Amesbury, s. of William Barnes[3] and Lydia (Pillsbury) Morrill, b. March 9, 1717/8 in Salisbury. (Ref. 3, 4-253, 4-769, 4-782) Note: Ref. 3 also refers to Sarah[5]

Wadleigh as Susan Wadleigh.

280 - Ephriam		284 - Jonathan
281 - Adams		285 - Mary
282 - Elizabeth		286 - Molly
283 - Abel		

119- Moses[5] Wadleigh, (Ephriam[4], John[3], Robert[2], John[1]), b. February 26, 1724 in Salisbury, Mass., d. February 28, 1781 in Salisbury, m. May 24, 1746 Susan[6] Rowell, (Philip[5], Jacob[4], Philip[3], Valentine[2], Thomas[1]) d. of Philip and Elizabeth[4] (Purrington) Rowell, (Purrington: James[3], John[2], George[1]), b. ca. 1727 d. June 12, 1815. (Ref. 3 also says January 12, 1815). (Ref. 3, 4-306)

287 - Rhoda	290 - Philip
288 - Adams	291 - Sarah
289 - Philip	292 - Ephriam

120- Adams[5] Wadleigh, (Ephriam[4], John[3], Robert[2], John[1]), b. July 13, 1726 in Salisbury, Mass., died in childhood. (Ref. 3)

121- Jonathan[5] Wadleigh, (Ephriam[4], John[3], Robert[2], John[1]), b. September 8, 1730 in Salisbury, Mass. d. 1735. died in childhood. (Ref. 3)

122- Enoch[5] Wadleigh, (Ephriam[4], John[3], Robert[2], John[1]), b. July 12, 1733 in Salisbury, Mass., d. 1736. died in childhood. (Ref. 3)

123- Enoch[5] Wadleigh, (Ephriam[4], John[3], Robert[2], John[1]), b. January 10, 1736 in Salisbury, Mass., d. 1738. died in childhood. (Ref. 3)

124- Abel[5] Wadleigh, (Ephriam[4], John[3], Robert[2], John[1]), b. in Salisbury, Mass. (Ref. 3)

Issue of 33- Robert[4] Wadleigh and Deborah
(Smith) Wadleigh:

125- John[5] Wadleigh, (Robert[4], Robert[3],
Robert[2], John[1]), b. ca. 1719 in Stratham, N.H.
m. Hannah Sanborn. no additional data. (Ref.
3)

126- Robert[5] Wadleigh, (Robert[4], Robert[3],
Robert[2], John[1]), b. in Stratham, N.H. m. Miss
Roby. no additional data. (Ref. 3)

127- Mary[5] Wadleigh, (Robert[4], Robert[3],
Robert[2], John[1]), b. in Stratham, N.H. (Ref. 3)

128- Marcia[5] Wadleigh, (Robert[4], Robert[3],
Robert[2], John[1]), b. in Stratham, N.H. (Ref. 3)

129- Deborah[5] Wadleigh, (Robert[4], Robert[3],
Robert[2], John[1]), b. in Stratham, N.H. (Ref. 3)

130- Sarah[5] Wadleigh, (Robert[4], Robert[3],
Robert[2], John[1]), b. in Stratham, N.H. (Ref. 3)

131- Meriable[5] Wadleigh, (Robert[4], Robert[3],
Robert[2], John[1]), b. in Stratham, N.H. (Ref. 3)

Issue of 34- Benjamin[4] Wadleigh and Judith
(Clough) Wadleigh:

132- Benjamin[5] Wadleigh, (Benjamin[4], Robert[3],
Robert[2], John[1]), b. September 29, 1725 in
Kingston, N.H. (Ref. 3)

133- Hanna[5] Wadleigh, (Benjamin[4], Robert[3],
Robert[2], John[1]), b. November 5, 1727, d.
December 1760 of smallpox. m. at Kingston,
N.H. April 7, 1747/8 John[4] Davis, (Jonathan[3],

John[2], John[1]), s. of Jonathan[3] and Martha (Dow)
Davis of West Amesbury, b. February 7, 1725/6
at Amesbury. Occ. Yeoman. (Ref. 3, 4-721, 4-
724)

293 - Elenor	296 - Juda
294 - Jonathan	297 - Phinehas
295 - Jonathan	298 - John

(NOTE: Martha (Dow) Davis m. 2nd August 21,
1746 at Amesbury Benjamin Wadleigh, Ref. 4-721)

134- Thomas[5] Wadleigh, (Benjamin[4], Robert[3],
Robert[2], John[1]), b. 1723, bpt. November 5, 1727
in Kingston, N.H., d. September 9, 1787 in
Hampstead, N.H. m. September 22, 1748 Margaret
Rowen of Kingston, d. of Andrew and Elizabeth
(Stevens) Rowen of Plastow N.H., d. 1790 in
Hampstead, Res. Kingston, Hampstead and Sutton
N.H. Soldier in French, and Indian War. (Ref.
3, 25-37 & 967)

299 - Benjamin	305 - Betty/Betsey
300 - Jonathan	306 - Moses
301 - Joseph	307 - Aaron
302 - Thomas	308 - Ephriam
303 - John	309 - Henry
304 - Judith	310 - Susanna

135- Sarah[5] Wadleigh, (Benjamin[4], Robert[3],
Robert[2], John[1]), b. March 30, 1729 in Kingston,
N.H. m. February 17, 1746 Obadiah Clough of
Kingston, N.H. no additional data. (Ref 3)

136- John[5] Wadleigh, (Benjamin[4], Robert[3],
Robert[2], John[1]), b. April 4, 1731 in Kingston,
N.H., d. May 18, 1734. died in childhood.
(Ref. 3)

137- Love[5] Wadleigh, (Benjamin[4], Robert[3],
Robert[2], John[1]), b. September 1, 1734. (Ref.
3)

138- <u>John</u>[5] <u>Wadleigh</u>, (Benjamin[4], Robert[3], Robert[2], John[1]), b. May 16, 1736. m. December 27, 1757 Mary Dent of Kingston, N.H. no additional data. (Ref. 3)

311 - Daniel	314 - Martha
312 - Mary	315 - Nancy
313 - Ashsah	316 - Lovey

139- <u>Judith</u>[5] <u>Wadleigh</u>, (Benjamin[4], Robert[3], Robert[2], John[1]), b. August 30, 1738. (Ref. 3)

140- <u>Ruth</u>[5] <u>Wadleigh</u>, (Benjamin[4], Robert[3], Robert[2], John[1]), b. March 2, 1739. m. July 12, 1764 Timothy Jewel of Newton, N.H. no additional data. (Ref. 3)

Issue of 35- Philip[4] Wadleigh and 198- Mary (Stevens) Wadleigh:

141- <u>Edward</u>[5] <u>Wadleigh</u>, (Philip[4], Robert[3], Robert[2], John[1]), b. ca. 1725 in Exeter, N.H. m. Mary Gilman. no additional data. (Ref. 3)

317 - Elizabeth	320 - Abraham
318 - John	321 - Lydia
319 - Mary	322 - Sarah

142- _____[5] <u>Wadleigh</u>, (Philip[4], Robert[3], Robert[2], John[1]), b. ca. 1727 in Exeter, N.H. m. a Scribner. no additional data. (Ref. 3)

143- <u>Sarah</u>[5] <u>Wadleigh</u>, (Philip[4], Robert[3], Robert[2], John[1]), b. ca. 1729 in Exeter, N.H. m. Mr. Gilman. no additional data. (Ref. 3)

Issue of 37- Jonathan[4] Wadleigh and Sarah Wadleigh:

144- <u>Jonathan</u>[5] <u>Wadleigh</u>, (Jonathan[4], Robert[3], Robert[2], John[1]), b. ca. 1730 in Exeter, N.H. (Ref. 3)

145- <u>John</u>[5] <u>Wadleigh</u>, (Jonathan[4], Robert[3], Robert[2], John[1]), b. ca. 1733 in Exeter, N.H. (Ref. 3)

146- <u>Robert</u>[5] <u>Wadleigh</u>, (Jonathan[4], Robert[3], Robert[2], John[1]), b. ca. 1735 in Exeter, N.H. (Ref. 3)

147- <u>Anna</u>[5] <u>Wadleigh</u>, (Jonathan[4], Robert[3], Robert[2], John[1]), b. ca. 1737 in Exeter, N.H. (Ref. 3)

148- <u>Rachel</u>[5] <u>Wadleigh</u>, (Jonathan[4], Robert[3], Robert[2], John[1]), b. ca. 1740 in Exeter, N.H. (Ref. 3)

Issue of 38- Joseph[4] Wadleigh and Ann (Swain) Wadleigh:

149- <u>Hannah</u>[5] <u>Wadleigh</u>, (Joseph[4], Robert[3], Robert[2], John[1]), b. August 1, 1739 in Exeter, N.H., d. after 1787. m. Caleb Smith of Raymond N.H. no additional data. (Ref. 3, 11)
      323 - Hannah   324 - Caleb

150- <u>Sarah</u>[5] <u>Wadleigh</u>, (Joseph[4], Robert[3], Robert[2], John[1]), b. November 29, 1741 in Exeter, N.H. m. Mr. Chase of West Newbury, Mass. no additional data. (Ref. 3)

151- Joseph[5] Wadleigh, (Joseph[4], Robert[3], Robert[2], John[1]), b. November 3, 1743 in Exeter, N.H., d. April 5, 1821 in Brentwood, N.H., m. February 9, 1775 Elizabeth[4] Dole (Benjamin[3], William[2], Richard[1]) of Newbury, Mass., d. of Benjamin and Sarah (Clark) Dole, b. March 2, 1744 in Salisbury, Mass., d. April 12, 1826 in Brentwood. Fought in the Revolutionary War at Saratoga against Burgoyne in 1776. Res. in Brentwood, N.H. (Ref. 3, 11)

325	- Benjamin	330	- Enos Dole
326	- Joseph	331	- David
327	- Moses	332	- Annie
328	- Daniel	333	- Rachel
329	- Sarah	334	- Mary

152- Anna[5] Wadleigh, (Joseph[4], Robert[3], Robert[2], John[1]), b. January 17, 1745 in Exeter, N.H., d. April 25, 1830. m. May 24, 1779 Joseph Woodman of Kingston, N.H., d. April 6, 1829. (Ref. 3, 11)

153- Rachel[5] Wadleigh, (Joseph[4], Robert[3], Robert[2], John[1]), b. February 3, 1747 in Exeter, N.H., d. April 13, 1821. m. February 14, 1788 Joshua/Joseph Smith of Raymond, N.H. no additional data. (Ref. 3)

154- Mary[5] Wadleigh, (Joseph[4], Robert[3], Robert[2], John[1]), b. ca. 1749. (Ref. 3)

Issue of Abraham Brown and 39- Argentine[4] (Cram) Brown:

155- Abraham Brown, (Wadleigh: Mary[4], Robert[3], Robert[2], John[1]). m. Judith Runnells of Hampton Falls, N.H. no additional data. (Ref. 30)

335	- Noah	337	- Joseph
336	- Mary	338	- Levi

156- Levi Brown, (Wadleigh: Mary[4], Robert[3], Robert[2], John[1]). no data. (Ref. 30)

157- Elizabeth Brown, (Wadleigh: Mary[4], Robert[3], Robert[2], John[1]). m. Daniel Leavitt of Hampton Falls, N.H. no data. (Ref. 30)

Issue of Deacon John[5] Batchelder and 40-Abigail[4] (Cram) Batchelder:

158- Mary[6] Batchelder, (Wadleigh: Abigail[4], Mary[3], Robert[2], John[1]; Batchelder: John[5], Nathaniel[4], Nathaniel[3], Nathaniel[2], Stephen[1]; Cram: Abigail[4], John[3], Benjamin[2], John[1]), b. December 25, 1715 at Kensington, N.H., d. May 18, 1790. m. February 13, 1735 Capt. Jonathan Sanborn. no additional data. (Ref. S4)

159- Elizabeth[6] Batchelder, (Wadleigh: Abigail[4], Mary[3], Robert[2], John[1]; Batchelder: John[5], Nathaniel[4], Nathaniel[3], Nathaniel[2], Stephen[1]; Cram: Abigail[4], John[3], Benjamin[2], John[1]), b. April 8, 1717 at Kensington, N.H., d. 1736. m. January 22, 1734 Joseph Shaw. no additional data. (Ref. S4)

160- John[6] Batchelder, (Wadleigh: Abigail[4], Mary[3], Robert[2], John[1]; Batchelder: John[5], Nathaniel[4], Nathaniel[3], Nathaniel[2], Stephen[1]; Cram: Abigail[4], John[3], Benjamin[2], John[1]), b. October 5, 1719 at Kensington, N.H., d. September 25, 1792 at Raymond, N.H. m. Esther Pettingell. no additional data. (Ref. S4)

161- Joshua[6] Batchelder, (Wadleigh: Abigail[4], Mary[3], Robert[2], John[1]; Batchelder: John[5], Nathaniel[4], Nathaniel[3], Nathaniel[2], Stephen[1]; Cram: Abigail[4], John[3], Benjamin[2], John[1]), b. 1720 at Kensington, N.H., d. at Kensington. m. January 15, 1745 Mary Connor. no data. (Ref. S4)

162- Abigail[6] Batchelder, (Wadleigh: Abigail[4], Mary[3], Robert[2], John[1]; Batchelder: John[5], Nathaniel[4], Nathaniel[3], Nathaniel[2], Stephen[1]; Cram: Abigail[4], John[3], Benjamin[2], John[1]), b. July 28, 1721 at Kensington, N.H., d. February 2, 1810 at Kensington. m. January 20, 1742 Caleb Shaw, b. May 9, 1719 at Kensington, d. December 20, 1791 at Kensington. (Ref. S4)
        339 - Hannah

163- Deborah[6] Batchelder, (Wadleigh: Abigail[4], Mary[3], Robert[2], John[1]; Batchelder: John[5], Nathaniel[4], Nathaniel[3], Nathaniel[2], Stephen[1]; Cram: Abigail[4], John[3], Benjamin[2], John[1]), b. January 13, 1723 at Kensington, N.H. m. Mr. Sherburne. no additional data. (Ref. S4)

164- Hannah[6] Batchelder, (Wadleigh: Abigail[4], Mary[3], Robert[2], John[1]; Batchelder: John[5], Nathaniel[4], Nathaniel[3], Nathaniel[2], Stephen[1]; Cram: Abigail[4], John[3], Benjamin[2], John[1]), b. October 26, 1725 at Kensington, N.H. (Ref. S4)

165- Ruth[6] Batchelder, (Wadleigh: Abigail[4], Mary[3], Robert[2], John[1]; Batchelder: John[5], Nathaniel[4], Nathaniel[3], Nathaniel[2], Stephen[1]; Cram: Abigail[4], John[3], Benjamin[2], John[1]), b. November 23, 1727. (Ref. S4)

166- Nathan[6] Batchelder, (Wadleigh: Abigail[4], Mary[3], Robert[2], John[1]; Batchelder: John[5], Nathaniel[4], Nathaniel[3], Nathaniel[2], Stephen[1]; Cram: Abigail[4], John[3], Benjamin[2], John[1]), b. July 28, 1729 at Kensington, N.H., d. January 23, 1765. m. December 27, 1752 Elizabeth Page, b. ca. 1719, d. June 18, 1764. (Ref. S4)

167- Daniel[6] Batchelder, (Wadleigh: Abigail[4], Mary[3], Robert[2], John[1]; Batchelder: John[5], Nathaniel[4], Nathaniel[3], Nathaniel[2], Stephen[1]; Cram: Abigail[4], John[3], Benjamin[2], John[1]), b.

May 6, 1731 at Kensington, N.H., d. November
27, 1758. m. February 6, 1754 Mary Fogg. no
additional data. (Ref. S4)

168- Eunice[6] Batchelder, (Wadleigh: Abigail[4],
Mary[3], Robert[2], John[1]; Batchelder; John[5],
Nathaniel[4], Nathaniel[3], Nathaniel[2], Stephen[1];
Cram: Abigail[4], John[3], Benjamin[2], John[1]), b.
ca. 1733 at Kensington, N.H., d. October 1,
1799. (Ref. S4)

169- Benjamin[6] Batchelder, (Wadleigh: Abigail[4],
Mary[3], Robert[2], John[1]; Batchelder; John[5],
Nathaniel[4], Nathaniel[3], Nathaniel[2], Stephen[1];
Cram: Abigail[4], John[3], Benjamin[2], John[1]), b.
October 20, 1735 at Candia, N.H., d. 1813 at
Andover, N.H. m. 1762 Dorothy Prescott. no
additional data. (Ref. S4)

Issue of 41- Benjamin[4] Cram and Abigail (Dearborn) Cram:

170- Elizabeth[5] Cram, (Wadleigh: Benjamin[4],
Mary[3], Robert[2], John[1]; Cram: Benjamin[4], John[3],
Benjamin[2], John[1]), b. ca. 1679, d. 1765. m.
May 16, 1700 Samuel[2] Melcher, (Melcher: (?)[1]),
b. ca. 1667, d. 1754. (Ref. 3)
     340 - Samuel

Issue of 43- Jonathan[4] Cram and Elizabeth (Heath) Cram:

171- Nehemiah[5] Cram, (Wadleigh: Jonathan[4],
Mary[3], Robert[2], John[1]; Cram: Jonathan[4], John[3],
Benjamin[2], John[1]). no data. (Ref. 30)

Issue of 48- Joseph[4] Wadleigh and Lydia (Smith) Wadleigh:

172- Theophilus[5] Wadleigh, (Joseph[4], Henry[3],
Robert[2], John[1]) b. July 30, 1721 in Kingston

(or Kensington) N.H. m. June 13, 1742 (or June 3) in Kensington, Abigail Bean of Exeter, N.H. no additional data. (Ref. 2, 3)

341 - Elizabeth   342 - Theophilus

173- Joseph[5] Wadleigh, (Joseph[4], Henry[3], Robert[2], John[1]), b. September 1722 in Kensington, N.H., d. December 31, 1808, m. 1st January 11, 1749 Anne[4] Dearborn, (John[3], John[2], Godfrey[1]), d. of John[3] Dearborn, of Hampton, N.H., b. December 17, 1725, d. February 19, 1786 in Kensington. m. 2nd December 14, 1786 Jane Buffum of Salem, Mass., a widow. no additional data. (Ref. 2, 3) 343 - 347 by 1st wife, 348 - 350 by 2nd wife.

343 - Anne	347 - Ruth
344 - Joseph	348 - Jane
345 - Mary	349 - William Henry
346 - John	350 - Mary Anna

174- Lydia[5] Wadleigh, (Joseph[4], Henry[3], Robert[2], John[1]), b. 1723/4 in Kensington, N.H. m. Mr. Robinson of Exeter, N.H. no data. (Ref. 2, 3)

Issue of 48- Joseph[4] Wadleigh and Mary (Fogg) Wadleigh:

175- Benjamin[5] Wadleigh, (Joseph[4], Henry[3], Robert[2], John[1]), b. January 18, 1728 in Kensington, N.H. m. October 29, 1752 Hannah[5] Dearborn, (Simon[4], John[3], John[2], Godfrey[1]) of Hampton Falls, N.H., d. of Simon[4] and Sarah (Marston) Dearborn, b. October 29, 1729. (Ref. 2, 3)

351 - Mary	354 - Sarah
352 - Simon Dearborn	355 - James Marston
353 - Elijah	

176- James[5] Wadleigh, (Joseph[4], Henry[3], Robert[2], John[1]), b. September 20, 1730 in Kensington, N.H. m. November 16, 1752 Mary

Dearborn, of Hampton, N.H. d. of John and Anna
(Sanborn) Dearborn, b. August 1, 1732. (Ref.
2, 3)

356 - James	360 - Dearborn
357 - John	361 - Simeon
358 - William	362 - Enoch
359 - Joseph	363 - Joseph

177- John[5] Wadleigh, (Joseph[4], Henry[3], Robert[2],
John[1]), b. November 26, 1732 in Kensington,
N.H., d. August 30, 1762. (Ref. 2, 3)

178- Mary[5] Wadleigh, (Joseph[4], Henry[3], Robert[2],
John[1]), b. December 22, 1734 in Kensington,
N.H., d. between September 25, 1758, and May
20, 1761, m. December 26, 1757 Enoch Coffin of
Exeter, N.H. no additional data. (Ref. 2, 3)

364 - Sarah	365 - Mary

179- Sarah[5] Wadleigh, (Joseph[4], Henry[3],
Robert[2], John[1]). no data. (Ref. 2, 3)

**Issue of Ephriam Philbrick and 49- Martha[4]
(Wadleigh) Philbrick:**

180- Benjamin Philbrick, (Wadleigh: Martha[4],
Henry[3], Robert[2], John[1]), b. July 16, 1721 in
Exeter, N.H. m. 1st October 6, 1743 at
Amesbury, Mass., Hannah Currier, d. of William and
Hannah (Harvey) Currier of Amesbury. m. 2nd
Lydia Colcord. no data. (Ref. 3, 4-701)

181- Joseph Philbrick, (Wadleigh: Martha[4],
Henry[3], Robert[2], John[1]), b. in Exeter. (Ref. 3)

182- Elizabeth Philbrick, (Wadleigh: Martha[4],
Henry[3], Robert[2], John[1]), b. in Exeter, N.H. m.
Ichabod Thurston. no data. (Ref. 3)

183- <u>Martha</u> <u>Philbrick</u>, (Wadleigh: Martha[4], Henry[3], Robert[2], John[1]), b. in Exeter, N.H. m. William Moore. no additional data. (Ref. 3)

184- <u>Trueworthy</u> <u>Philbrick</u>, (Wadleigh: Martha[4], Henry[3], Robert[2], John[1]). no data. (Ref. 3)

185- <u>John</u> <u>Philbrick</u>, (Wadleigh: Martha[4], Henry[3], Robert[2], John[1]). m. an unknown person. no additional data. (Ref. 3)

Issue of Jonathan Noyes and 51- Hannah (Wadleigh) Noyes:

186- <u>Jonathan</u> <u>Noyes</u>, (Wadleigh: Hannah[4], Jonathan[3], Robert[2], John[1]), b. July 23, 1717 in (presum.) Exeter, N.H. (Ref. 3)

187- <u>Elizabeth</u> <u>Noyes</u>, (Wadleigh: Hannah[4], Jonathan[3], Robert[2], John[1]), b. March 12, 1719 in Exeter, N.H. m. 1st 1735 John Hopkins. m. 2nd Stephen Illsley. no data. (Ref. 3)

188- <u>Thomas</u> <u>Noyes</u>, (Wadleigh: Hannah[4], Jonathan[3], Robert[2], John[1]), b. July 20, 1721 in (presum.) Exeter, N.H. m. Ann Follansbee. no additional data. (Ref. 3)

189- <u>Hannah</u> <u>Noyes</u>, (Wadleigh: Hannah[4], Jonathan[3], Robert[2], John[1]), b. March 23, 1723 in Exeter, N.H., died in childhood. (Ref. 3)

190- <u>Parker</u> <u>Noyes</u>, (Wadleigh: Hannah[4], Jonathan[3], Robert[2], John[1]), b. September 15, 1724 in (presum.) Exeter, N.H., died in childhood. (Ref. 3)

191- <u>Hannah Noyes</u>, (Wadleigh: Hannah[4],
Jonathan[3], Robert[2], John[1]), b. September 25,
1726 in (presum.) Exeter, N.H. m. Nicholas
Short. no additional data. (Ref. 3)

192- <u>Mary Noyes</u>, (Wadleigh: Hannah[4], Jonathan[3],
Robert[2], John[1]), b. October 22, 1730 in
(presum.) Exeter, N.H. m. Samuel Jacques. no
additional data. (Ref. 3)

**Issue of Joseph Leavitt and 52- Mary
(Wadleigh) Leavitt:**

193- <u>Mary Leavitt</u>, (Wadleigh: Mary[4],
Jonathan[3], Robert[2], John[1]). no additional
data. (Ref. 3)

**Issue of Mr. Hopkins, and 55- Elizabeth
(Wadleigh) Hopkins:**

194- <u>Elizabeth Hopkins</u>, (Wadleigh: Elizabeth[4],
Jonathan[3], Robert[2], John[1]). no additional
data. (Ref. 3)

**Issue of 57- James Smith and Martha (Bragdon)
Smith:**

195- <u>John Smith</u>, (Wadleigh: James[4], Martha[3],
Mary[2], John[1]). m. Judith Thompson. no
additional data. (Ref. 36-182)
          366 - Thomas

**Issue of 59- John Thing and Mehitable
(Stevens) Thing:**

196- <u>Mary Thing</u>, (Wadleigh: John[4], Jonathan[3],
Joanna[2], John[1]). m. 1st John Gilman. m. 2nd
1724 Peter[4] Gilman, (John[3], John[2], Edward[1]), s.
of John[3] and Elizabeth (Coffin) Gilman, b.
1705, d. 1788. (Ref. 35-69, 37)

Issue of Jonathan Dolloff and 98- Mary (Young) Dolloff:

221- <u>Richard Dolloff</u>, (Wadleigh: Mary[5], Elizabeth[4], Jonathan[3], Joanna[2], John[1]; Gilman: [5], Elizabeth[4], Mary[3], John[2], Edward[1]). m. Ms. Wells. no additional data. Res. Mt. Vernon, Me. (1788) (Ref. 49)

      379 - David   382 - John
      380 - Sally   383 - Ruth
      381 - Betty

Issue of 100- Ezekiel[4] Morrill and Jemima (Morrill) Morrill:

222- <u>Abigail[5] Morrill</u>, (Wadleigh: Ezekiel[5], Abigail[4], John[3], Robert[2], John[1]; Morrill: Ezekiel[4], Ezekiel[3], Jacob[2], Abraham[1]), b. August 4, 1732 in Salisbury, Mass., d. March 8, 1733 in Salisbury. died in childhood. (Ref. 4-777)

223- <u>David[5] Morrill</u>, (Wadleigh: Ezekiel[5], Abigail[4], John[3], Robert[2], John[1]; Morrill: Ezekiel[4], Ezekiel[3], Jacob[2], Abraham[1]), b. January 4, 1734 in Salisbury, Mass. Res. (prob.) Canterbury, N.H. (Ref. 4-777)

224- <u>Abigail[5] Morrill</u>, (Wadleigh: Ezekiel[5], Abigail[4], John[3], Robert[2], John[1]; Morrill: Ezekiel[4], Ezekiel[3], Jacob[2], Abraham[1]), b. October 6, 1735 in Salisbury, Mass. (Ref. 4-777)

225- <u>Reuben[5] Morrill</u>, (Wadleigh: Ezekiel[5], Abigail[4], John[3], Robert[2], John[1]; Morrill:

Ezekiel[4], Ezekiel[3], Jacob[2], Abraham[1]), b. May 5, 1737 in Salisbury, Mass., bpt. June 5, 1737 in Salisbury. (Ref. 4-777)

226- **Elizabeth**[5] Morrill, (Wadleigh: Ezekiel[5], Abigail[4], John[3], Robert[2], John[1]; Morrill: Ezekiel[4], Ezekiel[3], Jacob[2], Abraham[1]), b. March 2, 1739 in Salisbury, Mass. (Ref. 4-777)

227- **Laban**[5] Morrill, (Wadleigh: Ezekiel[5], Abigail[4], John[3], Robert[2], John[1]; Morrill: Ezekiel[4], Ezekiel[3], Jacob[2], Abraham[1]), b. September 25, 1740 in Salisbury, Mass., bpt. September 28, 1740 in Salisbury, d. 1812. m. Sarah Ames of Canterbury, N.H. no additional data. (Ref. 4-777)

228- **Susanna**[5] Morrill, (Wadleigh: Ezekiel[5], Abigail[4], John[3], Robert[2], John[1]; Morrill: Ezekiel[4], Ezekiel[3], Jacob[2], Abraham[1]), b. May 21, 1742 in Salisbury, Mass., d. November 3, 1744 in Salisbury. died in childhood. (Ref. 4-777)

229- **Mary**[5] Morrill, (Wadleigh: Ezekiel[5], Abigail[4], John[3], Robert[2], John[1]; Morrill: Ezekiel[4], Ezekiel[3], Jacob[2], Abraham[1]), b. March 6, 1744 in South Hampton, N.H., bpt. March 11, 1744 in South Hampton. m. Mr. Miles. no additional data. (Ref. 4-777)

230- **Ezekiel**[5] Morrill, (Wadleigh: Ezekiel[5], Abigail[4], John[3], Robert[2], John[1]; Morrill: Ezekiel[4], Ezekiel[3], Jacob[2], Abraham[1]), b. January 27, 1746 in South Hampton, N.H., bpt. February 2, 1746 in South Hampton, d. February 27, 1747. died in childhood. (Ref. 4-777)

231- **Ezekiel**[5] Morrill, (Wadleigh: Ezekiel[5], Abigail[4], John[3], Robert[2], John[1]; Morrill:

Ezekiel[4], Ezekiel[3], Jacob[2], Abraham[1]), b. November 4, 1747 in South Hampton, N.H., bpt. November 8, 1747 in South Hampton, d. November 17, 1794 at Enfield Community. m. Miss Tilton, no issue. no additional data. Res. Canterbury and Enfield Shaker Comm. (Ref. 4-777)

232- unnamed child[5] Morrill, (Wadleigh: Ezekiel[5], Abigail[4], John[3], Robert[2], John[1]; Morrill: Ezekiel[4], Ezekiel[3], Jacob[2], Abraham[1]), b. ca. 1750, d. when 2 days old. (Ref. 4-777)

233- Masten[5] Morrill, (Wadleigh: Ezekiel[5], Abigail[4], John[3], Robert[2], John[1]; Morrill: Ezekiel[4], Ezekiel[3], Jacob[2], Abraham[1]), b. March 29, 1751 in Canterbury, N.H. Res. Loudon, N.H. (Ref. 4-777)

234- Sargent[5] Morrill, (Wadleigh: Ezekiel[5], Abigail[4], John[3], Robert[2], John[1]; Morrill: Ezekiel[4], Ezekiel[3], Jacob[2], Abraham[1]), b. June 24, 1754 in Canterbury, N.H. m. September 16, 1777 Ruth[6] Hoyt. no additional data. Res. Canterbury, N.H. and Wheelock, Vt. (Ref. 4-759)

235- Abraham[5] Morrill, (Wadleigh: Ezekiel[5], Abigail[4], John[3], Robert[2], John[1]; Morrill: Ezekiel[4], Ezekiel[3], Jacob[2], Abraham[1]), b. January 1, 1756. m. March 24, 1785 Sarah[6] Hoyt, (Thomas[5], Thomas[4], Thomas[3], Thomas[2], John[1]). no additional data. Res. Canterbury, N.H., Wheelock, Vt., and N.Y. state. (Ref. 4-209, 4-777)

236- Susanna[5] Morrill, (Wadleigh: Ezekiel[5], Abigail[4], John[3], Robert[2], John[1]; Morrill: Ezekiel[4], Ezekiel[3], Jacob[2], Abraham[1]), b. March 1, 1758. m. February 6, 1778 Joshua Weeks. no additional data. (Ref. 4-777)

Issue of 101- Abner[4] Morrill and Lydia (Greeley) Morrill:

237- Ezekiel[5] Morrill, (Wadleigh: Abner[5], Abigail[4], John[3], Robert[2], John[1]; Morrill: Abner[4], Ezekiel[3], Jacob[2], Abraham[1]), b. February 17, 1733 in Salisbury, Mass., bpt. March 4, 1732/3 in Salisbury. m. Sarah. no additional data. Res. South Hampton, N.H. (Ref. 4-778)

384 - Joanna	386 - Molly
385 - Sarah	387 - Philip

238- Philip[5] Morrill, (Wadleigh: Abner[5], Abigail[4], John[3], Robert[2], John[1]; Morrill: Abner[4], Ezekiel[3], Jacob[2], Abraham[1]), b. November, 1734 in Salisbury, Mass., d. February 23, 1735. died in childhood. (Ref. 4-778)

239- Miriam[5] Morrill, (Wadleigh: Abner[5], Abigail[4], John[3], Robert[2], John[1]; Morrill: Abner[4], Ezekiel[3], Jacob[2], Abraham[1]), b. November 24, 1736 in Salisbury, Mass. (Ref. 4)

240- Abel[5] Morrill, (or Abner[5]) (Wadleigh: Abner[5], Abigail[4], John[3], Robert[2], John[1]; Morrill: Abner[4], Ezekiel[3], Jacob[2], Abraham[1]), b. May 8, 1742, bpt. September 11, 1743 in South Hampton, N.H. (Ref. 4-778)

241- Abigail[5] Morrill, (Wadleigh: Abner[5], Abigail[4], John[3], Robert[2], John[1]; Morrill: Abner[4], Ezekiel[3], Jacob[2], Abraham[1]), b. January 25, 1745 in South Hampton, N.H., bpt. March 3, 1746 in South Hampton. (Ref. 4-778)

242- Lydia[5] Morrill, (Wadleigh: Abner[5], Abigail[4], John[3], Robert[2], John[1]; Morrill: Abner[4], Ezekiel[3], Jacob[2], Abraham[1]), b. January 9, 1749 in South Hampton, N.H., bpt. February. 5, 1749 in South Hampton. (Ref. 4-778)

243- <u>Jeremiah</u>[5] Morrill, (Wadleigh: Abner[5], Abigail[4], John[3], Robert[2], John[1]; Morrill: Abner[4], Ezekiel[3], Jacob[2], Abraham[1]), bpt. March 31, 1751 in South Hampton, N.H. (Ref. 4-778)

244- <u>Joseph</u>[5] Morrill, (Wadleigh: Abner[5], Abigail[4], John[3], Robert[2], John[1]; Morrill: Abner[4], Ezekiel[3], Jacob[2], Abraham[1]), (twin), bpt. July 29, 1753. (Ref. 4-778)

245- <u>Mary</u>[5] Morrill, (Wadleigh: Abner[5], Abigail[4], John[3], Robert[2], John[1]; Morrill: Abner[4], Ezekiel[3], Jacob[2], Abraham[1]), (twin), bpt. July 29, 1753. (Ref. 4-778)

Issue of Samuel[4] Currier and 102-Hannah (Morrill) Currier:

246- <u>Samuel</u>[5] Currier, (Wadleigh: Hannah[5], Abigail[4], John[3], Robert[2], John[1]; Currier: Samuel[4], Samuel[3], Thomas[2] Richard[1]), bpt. November 4, 1744 in South Hampton, N.H. died young. (Ref. 20)

247- <u>Ezekiel</u>[5] Currier, (Wadleigh: Hannah[5], Abigail[4], John[3], Robert[2], John[1]; Currier: Samuel[4], Samuel[3], Thomas[2] Richard[1]). m. Susanna Emerson. no data. (Ref. 20)

248- <u>Samuel</u>[5] Currier, (Wadleigh: Hannah[5], Abigail[4], John[3], Robert[2], John[1]; Currier: Samuel[4], Samuel[3], Thomas[2] Richard[1]), bpt. January 17, 1747. m. Mary Rowell, b. 1750 in Kingston, N.H., d. of Daniel and Anne (Currier) Rowell. no additional data. (Ref. 20)

249- <u>Dorothy</u>[5] Currier, (Wadleigh: Hannah[5], Abigail[4], John[3], Robert[2], John[1]; Currier: Samuel[4], Samuel[3], Thomas[2] Richard[1]), bpt. November 5, 1752. (Ref. 20)

NOTE: History of Hampstead states that John[4] Morrill married Judith[4] Morrill while Ref. 4 states that John[4] Morrill married 1st Abigail Flanders, and 2nd Edith (unknown).

Issue of 103- John[4] Morrill and Abigail (Flanders) Morrill:

250- <u>Jonathan[5] Morrill</u>, (Wadleigh: John[5], Abigail[4], John[3], Robert[2], John[1]; Morrill: John[4], Ezekiel[3], Jacob[2], Abraham[1]), b. October 28, 1737 in South Hampton, N.H. m. Rachel. no additional data. (Ref. 4-778, 4-790)

        388 - Abigail   390 - John
        389 - Anne   391 - Sarah

251- <u>Micajah[5] Morrill</u>, (Wadleigh: John[5], Abigail[4], John[3], Robert[2], John[1]; Morrill: John[4], Ezekiel[3], Jacob[2], Abraham[1]), b. April 28, 1741 in South Hampton, N.H. (Ref. 4-778)

Issue of Nathaniel[5] Currier and 108- Susanna (Morrill) Currier:

252- <u>Anna[6] Currier</u>, (Wadleigh: Susanna[5], Abigail[4], John[3], Robert[2], John[1]; Currier: Jacob[4], Samuel[3], Thomas[2], Richard[1]; Morrill: Susanna[4], Ezekiel[3], Jacob[2], Abraham[1]), b. June 11, 1749 at Salisbury, Mass. m. June 9, 1768 Ephriam Morrill. no additional data. (Ref. 4-925)

253- <u>Dorothy[6] Currier</u>, (Wadleigh: Susanna[5], Abigail[4], John[3], Robert[2], John[1]; Currier: Jacob[4], Samuel[3], Thomas[2], Richard[1]; Morrill: Susanna[4], Ezekiel[3], Jacob[2], Abraham[1]), b. March 19, 1750 in Salisbury, Mass., d. June 1788 at Salisbury. m. December 1769 Joshua Follansbee. no additional data. (Ref. 4-925)

254- Susanna[6] Currier, (Wadleigh: Susanna[5],
Abigail[4], John[3], Robert[2], John[1]; Currier:
Jacob[4], Samuel[3], Thomas[2], Richard[1]; Morrill:
Susanna[4], Ezekiel[3], Jacob[2], Abraham[1]), b. March
29, 1753 at Salisbury, Mass. m. Nathaniel
Bean. no additional data. (Ref. 4-925)

255- David[6] Currier, (Wadleigh: Susanna[5],
Abigail[4], John[3], Robert[2], John[1]; Currier:
Jacob[4], Samuel[3], Thomas[2], Richard[1]; Morrill:
Susanna[4], Ezekiel[3], Jacob[2], Abraham[1]), b. April
16, 1755 at Salisbury, Mass., d. October 16,
1823 at Salisbury. m. 1st July 19/21, 1781
Sarah Chase, b. ca. 1764, d. November 26, 1802.
m. 2nd September 13, 1806 Hannah Riggs, b. ca.
1756, d. April 20, 1842. (Ref. 4-925, 4-931)
392 - 400 by 1st w.

392 - Nathaniel	397 - Susanna
393 - David	398 - James
394 - Elizabeth	399 - James
395 - Moses	400 - Thomas
396 - Jacob	

256- Hannah[6] Currier, (Wadleigh: Susanna[5],
Abigail[4], John[3], Robert[2], John[1]; Currier:
Jacob[4], Samuel[3], Thomas[2], Richard[1]; Morrill:
Susanna[4], Ezekiel[3], Jacob[2], Abraham[1]), b.
September 5, 1757 at Salisbury, Mass. (Ref. 4-
925)

257- Molly[6] Currier, (Wadleigh: Susanna[5],
Abigail[4], John[3], Robert[2], John[1]; Currier:
Jacob[4], Samuel[3], Thomas[2], Richard[1]; Morrill:
Susanna[4], Ezekiel[3], Jacob[2], Abraham[1]), b. May
20, 1760 at Salisbury, Mass. (Ref. 4-925)

**Issue of 111- Joseph[5] Wadleigh and Mary
(Tyers) (Jones) Wadleigh:**

258- Joseph[6] Wadleigh, (Joseph[5], Joseph[4],
John[3], Robert[2], John[1]), b. September 3, 1752 in

England, d. 1787 (or 1808 both dates in Ref. 3)
in Salisbury, Mass., bur. Amesbury, Mass. m.
October 22, 1779 Elizabeth[5] Morrill (or Betty),
(John[4], John[3], Isaac[2], Abraham[1]), d. of John[4]
Morrill, and Betty (Clough) Morrill (or
Elizabeth), b. February 6, 1754, d. October 9
1822, bur. Amesbury. (Ref. 3, 4-775)

401 -	Elijah	405 -	Joseph
402 -	Mary	406 -	Joseph
403 -	Elizabeth	407 -	James
404 -	Anna	408 -	Benjamin Harrod

259- Benjamin[6] Wadleigh, (Joseph[5], Joseph[4],
John[3], Robert[2], John[1]), d. June 1813 in
Salisbury, Mass., bur. Amesbury, Mass. m.
October 5, 1783, 419- Hannah Goodwin,
(Wadleigh: Hannah[6], Benjamin[5], Joseph[4], John[3],
Robert[2], John[1]), d. of Eleazer and 262- Hannah
(Wadleigh) Goodwin, d. October 15, 1807 in
Salisbury, bur. Amesbury. (Ref. 3)

409 -	Hannah	414 -	Mary
410 -	Joseph	415 -	Lois
411 -	Benjamin	416 -	Elener
412 -	Robert	417 -	Eleazer
413 -	Edward		

**Issue of 112- Benjamin[5] Wadleigh and Judith
(Morrill) Wadleigh:**

260- Eleanor[6] Wadleigh, (Benjamin[5], Joseph[4],
John[3], Robert[2], John[1]), b. April 17, 1737 in
Salisbury, Mass. m. November 10, 1758 Joseph
Clifford of Salisbury. no additional data.
(Ref. 3, 4-463)

261- Abigail[6] Wadleigh, (Benjamin[5], Joseph[4],
John[3], Robert[2], John[1]), b. November 4, 1738 in
Salisbury, Mass. m. March 15, 1764 in
Salisbury John[5] Currier, (Ezekiel[4], Thomas[3],
Thomas[2], Richard[1]), b. January, 27, 1740, d.
July 14, 1770 at Salisbury. Occ. Blacksmith.
(Ref. 3, 4-919)

418 - Benjamin

262-[3]Hannah[6] Wadleigh, (Benjamin[5], Joseph[4], John[3], Robert[2], John[1]), b. April 22, 1740 in Salisbury, Mass. m. December 16, Eleazor Goodwin. (Ref. 3)

419 - Hannah

263-[3]Mary[6] Wadleigh, (Benjamin[5], Joseph[4], John[3], Robert[2], John[1]), b. February 23, 1743 in Salisbury, Mass., d. March 25, 1798 in (presum.) Salisbury. unmarried. (Ref. 3)

264- Merriam[6] (or Miriam) Wadleigh, (Benjamin[5], Joseph[4], [3]John[3], Robert[2], John[1]), b. March 24, 1745 in Salisbury, Mass., d. in Candia, N.H. m. June 8, 1766 (or 1767) in Salisbury, Moses[5] Martin, (Jonathan[4], John[3], Richard[2], George[1]), s. of Jonathan[4] and Deborah[3] (Worthen) Martin, b. March 10, 1743, bpt. May 8, 1743 at Amesbury, d. in Candia. Res. Salisbury, Mass., and Candia, N.H. (Ref. 3, 4-762)

265-[3]Elizabeth[6] Wadleigh, (Benjamin[5], Joseph[4], John[3], Robert[2], John[1]), b. September 15, 1747 in Salisbury, Mass. m. Elias Pike. no additional data. (Ref. 3)

266-[3]Anne[6] Wadleigh, [1](Benjamin[5], Joseph[4], John[3], Robert[2], John[1]), b. December 23, 1749 in Salisbury, Mass. m. April 23, 1770 Simeon Lowell. no additional data. (Ref. 3)

267-[3]Joseph[6] Wadleigh, (Benjamin[5], Joseph[4], John[3], Robert[2], John[1]), b. June 19, 1752 in Salisbury, Mass., d. 1799. m. June 24, 1779 Anna Stevens. no additional data. (Ref. 3)

268-[3]Lois[6] Wadleigh, [1](Benjamin[5], Joseph[4], John[3], Robert[2], John[1]), b. June 23, 1755 in Salisbury, Mass. (Ref. 3)

269- Judith[6] Wadleigh, (Benjamin[5], Joseph[4], John[3], Robert[2], John[1]), b. November 12, 1757, d. 1760. died in childhood. (Ref. 3)

270- Daniel[6] Wadleigh, (Benjamin[5], Joseph[4], John[3], Robert[2], John[1]), b. March 19, 1760 in Salisbury, Mass. (Ref. 3)

Issue of 117- Dean[5] Wadleigh and Margaret (Morrill) Wadleigh:

271- Mary[6] Wadleigh, (Dean[5], John[4], John[3], Robert[2], John[1]), b. January 31, 1747 in Salisbury, Mass. (Ref. 3)

272- Ruth[6] Wadleigh, (Dean[5], John[4], John[3], Robert[2], John[1]), b. February 22, 1748 in Salisbury, Mass. m. May 5, 1768 David[6] Graves of Unity, N.H., (James[5], Samuel[4], Abraham[3], Mark[2], Samuel[1]), s. of James[5] and Sarah (Roberts) Graves of South Hampton, N.H., b. June 1, 1742, d. July 25, 1813. (Ref. 3, 12)
    420 - James

273- John[6] Wadleigh, (Dean[5], John[4], John[3], Robert[2], John[1]), b. March 25, 1751 in Salisbury, Mass. m. Rachel Phillips. no additional data. (Ref. 3)

274- Albra[6] Wadleigh, (Dean[5], John[4], John[3], Robert[2], John[1]), b. February 6, 1753 in Salisbury, Mass. (Ref. 3)

275- Benjamin[6] Wadleigh, (Dean[5], John[4], John[3], Robert[2], John[1]), b. November 20, 1754, died in childhood. (Ref. 3)

276- <u>Thomas</u>[6] <u>Wadleigh</u>, (Dean[5], John[4], John[3], Robert[2], John[1]), b. February 25, 1757. (Ref. 3)

277- <u>Benjamin</u>[6] <u>Wadleigh</u>, (Dean[5], John[4], John[3], Robert[2], John[1]), b. June 16, 1759 in Salisbury, Mass., d. November 14, 1807 in Candia, N.H. m. May 15, 1788 Sarah Patten of Candia, gr. dau. of Deacon Robert Patten from Edinburgh, Scotland, d. in Candia. Res. Boston, Mass., and Candia, N.H. (Ref. 3)

421 - Polly	425 - Samuel
422 - Ira	426 - Sarah
423 - Moses	427 - Ruth
424 - Jesse	

278- <u>Dean</u>[6] <u>Wadleigh</u>, (Dean[5], John[4], John[3], Robert[2], John[1]), b. April 27, 1762 in Salisbury, Mass., d. 1843. Had a son by Anna Colby (1767-1836), d. of Reuben Colby, and Elizabeth Colby of Salisbury, Mass. m. Allie, b. ca. 1763, d. April 23, 1826. Res. Salisbury, Mass. and Mt. Vernon, Me. (Ref. 3, 24) 428 by Anna Colby, 429 - 433 by w.

428 - Benjamin Dean	431 - John
429 - William	432 - Mahitable
430 - Sarah	433 - Dorothy

279- <u>Dorothy</u>[6] <u>Wadleigh</u>, (Dean[5], John[4], John[3], Robert[2], John[1]), b. June 16, 1764 in Salisbury, Mass. (Ref. 3)

Issue of Moses Barnes[4] Morrill and 118-Susan[5] (Wadleigh) Morrill:

280- <u>Ephriam</u>[5] <u>Morrill</u>, (Wadleigh: Susan[5], Ephriam[4], John[3], Robert[2], John[1]; Morrill: Moses Barnes[4], William Barnes[3], Moses[2], Abraham[1]), b. February 25, 1743 at Amesbury, Mass. (Ref. 4-782)

281- Adams[5] Morrill, (Wadleigh: Susan[5],
Ephriam[4], John[3], Robert[2], John[1]; Morrill: Moses
Barnes[4], William Barnes[3], Moses[2], Abraham[1]), b.
August 16, 1745 at Amesbury, Mass., bpt.
December 1, 1745 at Amesbury. (Ref. 4-782)

282- Elizabeth[5] Morrill, (Wadleigh: Susan[5],
Ephriam[4], John[3], Robert[2], John[1]; Morrill: Moses
Barnes[4], William Barnes[3], Moses[2], Abraham[1]), b.
February 21, 1748 at Amesbury, Mass., bpt.
April 23, 1749 at Amesbury. (Ref. 4-782)

283- Abel[5] Morrill, (Wadleigh: Susan[5],
Ephriam[4], John[3], Robert[2], John[1]; Morrill: Moses
Barnes[4], William Barnes[3], Moses[2], Abraham[1]),
bpt. August 1, 1753 at Amesbury, Mass. (Ref.
4-782)

284- Jonathan[5] Morrill, (Wadleigh: Susan[5],
Ephriam[4], John[3], Robert[2], John[1]; Morrill: Moses
Barnes[4], William Barnes[3], Moses[2], Abraham[1]), b.
August 4, 1754, bpt. October 20, 1754 at
Amesbury, Mass. (Ref. 4-782)

285- Mary[5] Morrill, (Wadleigh: Susan[5],
Ephriam[4], John[3], Robert[2], John[1]; Morrill: Moses
Barnes[4], William Barnes[3], Moses[2], Abraham[1]),
bpt. June 4, 1758 at Amesbury, Mass. prob.
died young. (Ref. 4-782)

286- Molly[5] (or Polly) Morrill, (Wadleigh:
Susan[5], Ephriam[4], John[3], Robert[2], John[1];
Morrill: Moses Barnes[4], William Barnes[3],
Moses[2], Abraham[1]), b. 1761, bpt. August 2, 1761
at Amesbury, Mass., d. April 1854. (Ref. 4-
782)

Issue of 119- Moses[5] Wadleigh and Susan (Rowell) Wadleigh:

287- Rhoda[6] Wadleigh, (Moses[5], Ephriam[4], John[3], Robert[2], John[1]), b. November 8, 1746 in Salisbury, Mass. m. 1st August 24, 1766 Rev. Benjamin Pigeon. m. 2nd August 1, 1782 Henry (or Hendry) Nowell, d. May 1, 1839. Res. Salisbury and Amesbury, Mass. (Ref. 3, 4)

288- Adams[6] Wadleigh, (Moses[5], Ephriam[4], John[3], Robert[2], John[1]), b. July 12, 1750 (or July 27) in Salisbury, Mass., d. January 28, 1822 in Salisbury, m. 1st February 3, 1774 Sarah Greeley, d. of Samuel and Judith Greeley of Salisbury, d. May 4, 1795 in Salisbury. m. 2nd Naomi (Blaisdell) Wadleigh, (Blaisdell: Daniel[5], Daniel[4], Jonathan[3], Henry[2], Ralph[1]), wid. of Edward Wadleigh, b. August 22, 1758 at Salisbury, d. September 20, 1832 in Salisbury, (Ref. 3, 4-633)   434 - 442 by 1st wife.

434 - Jonathan	439 - Philip
435 - Sarah	440 - Peter
436 - Elizabeth	441 - Judith
437 - Hannah	442 - William
438 - Enoch	

289- Philip[6] Wadleigh, (Moses[5], Ephriam[4], John[3], Robert[2], John[1]), b. April 27, 1752 in Salisbury, Mass., d. 1753. died in childhood. (Ref. 3)

290- Philip[6] Wadleigh, (Moses[5], Ephriam[4], John[3], Robert[2], John[1]), b. December 20, 1753 in Salisbury, Mass., d. January 9 1822 in Salisbury. m. February 2, 1777 Sarah Kimball, d. of Samuel and Hannah (Elliott) Kimball of Salisbury, d. December 12, 1820. (Ref. 3)

443 - Moses	447 - John
444 - Samuel	448 - Rhoda
445 - Ephriam	449 - Philip
446 - Henry	450 - Hannah

291- Sarah[6] Wadleigh, (Moses[5], Ephriam[4], John[3], Robert[2], John[1]), b. January 28, 1756 in Salisbury, Mass., d. 1759. died young. (Ref. 3)

292- Ephriam[6] Wadleigh, (Moses[5], Ephriam[4], John[3], Robert[2], John[1]), (Major), b. April 14, 1762 in Salisbury, Mass., d. July 30, 1823 in Salisbury, bur. Amesbury, Mass. m. February 11, 1784 Molly (or Mary) Barnard, d. August 10, 1823 in Salisbury, bur. Amesbury. (Ref. 3)

451	- Eliphalet	457	- Ezekiel
452	- Sally	458	- Moses
453	- Ephriam	459	- Pauline
454	- Elizabeth	460	- Charloi
455	- Polly	461	- Ebenezer
456	- Nancy	462	- Jonathan

Issue of John[4] Davis and 133- Hannah (Wadleigh) Davis:

293- Elenor[5] Davis, (Wadleigh: Hannah[5], Benjamin[4], Robert[3], Robert[2], John[1]; Davis: John[4], Jonathan[3], John[2], John[1]), b. June 30, 1748 at Kingston, N.H., bpt. August 7, 1748 at Amesbury, Mass. (Ref. 4-724)

294- Jonathan[5] Davis, (Wadleigh: Hannah[5], Benjamin[4], Robert[3], Robert[2], John[1]; Davis: John[4], Jonathan[3], John[2], John[1]), bpt. March 4, 1749/50 at Amesbury, Mass. died young. (Ref. 4-724)

295- Jonathan[5] Davis, (Wadleigh: Hannah[5], Benjamin[4], Robert[3], Robert[2], John[1]; Davis: John[4], Jonathan[3], John[2], John[1]), b. March 20, 1751 at Kingston, N.H. (Ref. 4-724)

296- Juda[5] Davis, (Wadleigh: Hannah[5], Benjamin[4], Robert[3], Robert[2], John[1]; Davis: John[4], Jonathan[3], John[2], John[1]), b. April 7, 1752 at Kingston. (Ref. 4-724)

297- <u>Phinehas</u>[5] <u>Davis</u>, (Wadleigh: Hannah[5], Benjamin[4], Robert[3], Robert[2], John[1]; Davis: John[4], Jonathan[3], John[2], John[1]), b. March 25, 1754 at Kingston, N.H. (Ref. 4-724)

298- <u>John</u>[5] <u>Davis</u>, (Wadleigh: Hannah[5], Benjamin[4], Robert[3], Robert[2], John[1]; Davis: John[4], Jonathan[3], John[2], John[1]), b. July 16, 1759 at Kingston, N.H. (Ref. 4-724)

Issue of 134- Thomas[5] Wadleigh and Margaret (Rowen) Wadleigh:

299- <u>Benjamin</u>[6] <u>Wadleigh</u>, (Thomas[5], Benjamin[4], Robert[3], Robert[2], John[1]), b. March 26, 1749 in Hampstead, N.H., bpt. February 6, 1752, d. August 9, 1817 of a slight accidental injury to the knee, resulting in "mortification". m. 1769 Hannah Kezar of Hampstead, d. of Ebenezer Kezar, and Hannah (Moulton) Kezar of (presum.) Hampstead, b. 1750, d. 1836. Occ. shoemaker, and tanner. Res. Hampstead, and "Wadleigh's Hill" outside Sutton, N.H. (Ref. 3, 4, 25)

463	Mehitible	469	Benjamin
464	Hannah	470	Eliphalet
465	Dolly	471	Judith
466	Jesse	472	Simeon
467	Eliphalet	473	Ebenezer
468	John	474	Susanna

Note from Ref. 25: Among the descendants of Thomas Wadleigh are Senator Bainbridge Wadleigh, George A. Pillsbury, and Governor John S. Pillsbury of Minneapolis, Minn., (Compiler's note: Founder of Pillsbury Flour, and Milling Co.) Gilbert Wadleigh of Milford, Edward D. Burnham of Hopkinson, state concillor Thomas Wadleigh Pillsbury, Benjamin E. Badger, Dr. Moses Wadleigh Russell, John E. Robinson, and the widow of Hon. J. V. Mugridge, all of Concord, N.H. Benjamin E. Porter of Lynn, Mass. Hon. Thomas Wadleigh Harvey,

Plainsville, Ohio. George A. Wadleigh, and
Corliss Wadleigh, merchants of Boston, Mass.
Lydia F. Wadleigh, Lady Supt., of New York
Female Normal College.

300- <u>Jonathan</u>[6] <u>Wadleigh</u>, (Thomas[5], Benjamin[4],
Robert[3], Robert[2], John[1]), b. March 26, 1751 in
Hampstead, N.H., bpt. February 6, 1752, d. ca
1833 in Gilmanton, N.H. m. 1st ca. 1770 Miss
Miles of Salisbury, Mass., d. 1779. m. 2nd ca.
1779 Abigail Eastman, d. of Peter Eastman of
Hampstead, b. June 9, 1756, d. ca. 1780. m.
3rd in Northfield, N.H. Susanna (Russell)
Little, no additional data. Served in
Revolutionary War at Bunker Hill with brothers
John, and Thomas. Served one term in
Legislature as a Representative. Res.
Hampstead, Canterbury, and Gilmanton, N.H.
(Ref. 3, 4, 20, 25)   475 by 1st wife, 476 by
2nd wife, 477 - 484 by 3rd wife.

475 - Thomas Miles		480 - John
476 - Jonathan Eastman		481 - Ebenezer
477 - Peter		482 - Abigail
478 - Benjamin		483 - Patsy
479 - Susan		484 - Betsy

NOTE: Ref. 3 and Ref. 25 carry slightly
conflicting information which, taken as a
whole, leads to the information presented here.

301- <u>Joseph</u>[6] <u>Wadleigh</u>, (Thomas[5], Benjamin[4],
Robert[3], Robert[2], John[1]), b. March 27, 1753 in
Hampstead, N.H. m. 1st ca. 1773 Betty/Betsey
Ingalls, d. in Sutton, N.H. m. 2nd an unknown
woman. no additional data. Res. Northfield,
Gilmanton, and Sutton N.H., and Blackwater,
N.Y. (Ref. 3, 4, 20, 25) 485 - 496 by 1st
wife, had 9 additional children by 2nd wife.

485 - John		491 - Betsey
486 - Margaret		492 - Moses
487 - Joseph		493 - Joshua
488 - Thomas		494 - Sally
489 - James		495 - Nathaniel
490 - Samuel		496 - Amos

302- <u>Thomas</u>[6] <u>Wadleigh</u>, (Thomas[5], Benjamin[4], Robert[3], Robert[2], John[1]), b. March 29, 1755 in Hampstead, N.H., d. Feb. 26, 1827. m. December 11, 1783 Miriam Atwood, d. of John and Ruth (Whittaker) Atwood of Hampstead, b. January 18, 1763, d. 1843. Served in Revolutionary War at Bunker Hill. (Ref. 3, 4, 25)

497	Ruth	504	Mehitibel
498	Miriam	505	Patty
499	Daniel	506	Thomas
500	Elizabeth	507	David
501	Lucretia	508	Susanna
502	Polly	509	James Madison
503	Sarah		

303- <u>John</u>[6] <u>Wadleigh</u>, (Thomas[5], Benjamin[4], Robert[3], Robert[2], John[1]), b. March 14, 1759 in Hampstead, N.H. living with the Shakers at Enfield Community, Canterbury, N.H. in 1848 (at age 92). Served in Revolutionary War at Bunker Hill. (Ref. 3, 4, 25)

304- <u>Judith</u>[6] <u>Wadleigh</u>, (Thomas[5], Benjamin[4], Robert[3], Robert[2], John[1]), b. March 31, 1761 in Hampstead, N.H. m. April 13, 1781 (or February 2, 1783- also cited in Ref. 3) Moses Atwood of Hampstead or Hill, N.H., s. of John and Ruth (Whittaker) Atwood of Hampstead, d. in Alexander, N.H. Res. Hampstead, and (after 1800) Alexander, Grafton Co., N.H. (Ref. 3, 25)

510	Betsey	514	Moses
511	William	515	Joseph
512	Nancy	516	Polly
513	Thomas	517	Samuel

305- <u>Betty/Betsey</u>[6] <u>Wadleigh</u>, (Thomas[5], Benjamin[4], Robert[3], Robert[2], John[1]), b. May 14, 1766 in Hampstead, N.H., d. at age 75. m. 1st John Kent of Canterbury, N.H. m. 2nd Mr. Lovering of Loudon, N.H. no additional data. (Ref. 3, 25)

306- Moses[6] Wadleigh, (Thomas[5], Benjamin[4],
Robert[3], Robert[2], John[1]), b. March 1, 1763 in
Hampstead, N.H., d. 1839 in Sutton, N.H. m.
August 9, 1790 at Deerfield, N.H. Elizabeth Dow
of Atkinson, N.H., d. March 20, 1867. Res.
Hampstead, Atkinson, and Sutton, N.H. (Ref. 3,
25)

518	William	522	Elizabeth
519	Moses Dow	523	Benjamin Evans
520	Sally Dow	524	Thomas J.
521	John Dow	525	Anna Dow

307- Aaron[6] Wadleigh, (Thomas[5], Benjamin[4],
Robert[3], Robert[2], John[1]), b. 1769 in Hampstead,
N.H., bpt. July 31, 1769, d. 1848 in
Starksboro, Vt. m. April 1, 1790 (or April 3)
Abigail Simon of Hampstead. no additional
data. (Ref. 3, 25)
      526 - Thomas

308- Ephriam[6] Wadleigh, (Thomas[5], Benjamin[4],
Robert[3], Robert[2], John[1]), b. March 8, 1770 in
Hampstead, N.H., bpt. April 20, 1770, d.
January 30, 1852 at age 82. m. August 30, 1793
Alice Little, s. of Deacon Ezekiel Little, b.
May 2, 1773 in Sutton, N.H., d. February 21,
1852. In 1801 moved to Hatley, Quebec, Canada
settling on No. 10, 2nd Range. (Ref. 3, 25)

527	Samuel	531	Thomas
528	Elizabeth	532	Ruth
529	Mary	533	Roxanna
530	Taylor	534	Luke

309- Henry[6] Wadleigh, (Thomas[5], Benjamin[4],
Robert[3], Robert[2], John[1]), b. 1773 in Hampstead,
N.H., bpt. August 23, 1778, d. 1857 in Newport,
N.H. m. Hannah Stevens. no additional data.
(Ref. 3, 25)

310- Susanna[6] Wadleigh, (Thomas[5], Benjamin[4],
Robert[3], Robert[2], John[1]), b. March 1774 in
Hampstead, N.H., d. April 20, 1848. m.

Benjamin Evans of Warner, N.H. no additional
data. (Ref. 3, 25)

535 - Abigail	539 - Sarah
536 - Susan	540 - Sophronia
537 - Susan	541 - Hannah
538 - Lucinda	542 - Benjamin

Issue of 138- John[5] Wadleigh and Mary (Dent) Wadleigh:

311- Daniel[6] Wadleigh, (John[5], Benjamin[4],
Robert[3], Robert[2], John[1]), b. September 21, 1758
in Kingston, N.H., d. January 30, 1819 in
Kingston, m. March 30, 1788 Dolly Bartlett of
Kingston, b. June 16, 1751 in Kingston, d.
September 30, 1843 in Kingston. Occ. Attorney
(Ref. 3)

543 - John	545 - Daniel
544 - Joseph	546 - Hannah

312- Mary[6] Wadleigh, (John[5], Benjamin[4],
Robert[3], Robert[2], John[1])c b. September 24, 1760
(Ref. 3 also cites August 13, 1763) in
Kingston, N.H. m. February 20, 1780 Peter
Sweatt of Hawks, N.H. no additional data.
(Ref. 3)

313- Achsah[6] Wadleigh, (John[5], Benjamin[4],
Robert[3], Robert[2], John[1]), b. February 16, 1763
in Kingston, N.H. m. Jonathan Povear. no
additional data. (Ref. 3)

314- Martha[6] Wadleigh, (John[5], Benjamin[4],
Robert[3], Robert[2], John[1]), b. May 5, 1765 in
Kingston, N.H. (Ref. 3)

315- Nancy[6] Wadleigh, (John[5], Benjamin[4],
Robert[3], Robert[2], John[1]), b. 1767 in Kingston,
N.H., d. April 5, 1837. m. John Rowe, s. of
Nathan and Lydia (Page) Rowe. no additional
data. (Ref. 3)

316- Lovey[6] Wadleigh, (John[5], Benjamin[4], Robert[3], Robert[2], John[1]). m. Peter Sweatt as 2nd wife. no additional data. (Ref. 3)

Issue of 141- Edward[5] Wadleigh and Mary (Gilman) Wadleigh:

317- Elizabeth[6] Wadleigh, (Edward[5], Philip[4], Robert[3], Robert[2], John[1]), bpt. June 10, 1753 in Exeter, N.H. m. June 15, 1786 Reuben Smith. no additional data. (Ref. 6)

318- John[6] Wadleigh, (Edward[5], Philip[4], Robert[3], Robert[2], John[1]), bpt. July 30, 1755 in Exeter, N.H. m. (presum.) March 3, 1784 Elizabeth Daniels. no additional data. (Ref. 3)

319- Mary[6] Wadleigh, (Edward[5], Philip[4], Robert[3], Robert[2], John[1]), bpt. July 30, 1757 in Exeter, N.H. m. (presum.) February 23, 1777 Charles Hilton. (Ref. 3)

320- Abraham[6] Wadleigh, (Edward[5], Philip[4], Robert[3], Robert[2], John[1]), bpt. April 29, 1759. (Ref. 3)

321- Lydia[6] Wadleigh, (Edward[5], Philip[4], Robert[3], Robert[2], John[1]), bpt. August 3, 1760. (Ref. 3)

322- Sarah[6] Wadleigh, (Edward[5], Philip[4], Robert[3], Robert[2], John[1]), bpt. December 12, 1762. m. (presum.) October 29, 1788 Benjamin Cilly of Hawks, N.H. no additional data. (Ref. 3)

**Issue of Caleb Smith and 149- Hannah
(Wadleigh) Smith:**

323- Hannah Smith, (Wadleigh: Hannah[5], Joseph[4],
Robert[3], Robert[2], John[1]), b. in Raymond, N.H.
(Ref. 3)

324- Caleb Smith, (Wadleigh: Hannah[5], Joseph[4],
Robert[3], Robert[2], John[1]), b. in Raymond, N.H.
m. 1788, Sarah Wadleigh. no additional data.
(Ref. 3)

**Issue of 151- Joseph[5] Wadleigh and Elizabeth
(Dole) Wadleigh:**

325- Benjamin[6] Wadleigh, (Joseph[5], Joseph[4],
Robert[3], Robert[2], John[1]), b. 1776 in Brentwood,
N.H., d. April 14, 1837. m. September 29, 1803
Hannah Colcord of Brentwood. no additional
data. (Ref. 3, 11)

326- Joseph[6] Wadleigh, (Joseph[5], Joseph[4],
Robert[3], Robert[2], John[1]), b. 1778 in Brentwood,
N.H., d. June 20, 1828 in Brentwood, bur. in
Small Cemetery at Kingston Plaines. m.
November 3, 1806 Hannah Stevens of Brentwood.
no additional data. (Ref. 3, 11)
547 - Hiram	551 - Sarah Frances
548 - Betsey	552 - Susan Dole
549 - Oliver	553 - Nancy Currier
550 - Calvin	

327- Moses[6] Wadleigh, (Joseph[5], Joseph[4],
Robert[3], Robert[2], John[1]), b. November 11, 1781
in Brentwood, N.H., d. May 10, 1864. (Ref. 3,
11)

328- Daniel[6] Wadleigh, (Joseph[5], Joseph[4],
Robert[3], Robert[2], John[1]), b. 1781 in Brentwood,
N.H., d. 1810. unmarried. (Ref. 3)

329- <u>Sarah</u>[6] Wadleigh, (Joseph[5], Joseph[4], Robert[3], Robert[2], John[1]), b. in Brentwood, N.H. (Ref. 3)

330- <u>Enos Dole</u>[6] Wadleigh, (Joseph[5], Joseph[4], Robert[3], Robert[2], John[1]), b. October 19, 1783 in Brentwood, N.H., d. June 6, 1826 in Brentwood. m. February 1, 1812 in Kingston, N.H. Sarah Colcord, d. of John and Lydia (Morrill) Colcord of Brentwood, b. August 14, 1791, d. July 12, 1862 at "Oakland", Onachita Parish, Monroe, La. (Oakland is presumed to be a plantation). Changed spelling of name to "Wadley". Occ. Blacksmith. Res. Brentwood, Dover and Nashua, N.H. (Ref. 3, 11)

    554 - William Morrill   557 - David Richard
    555 - Satura Dole   558 - Moses
    556 - Lydia Colcord   559 - Dole

331- <u>David</u>[6] Wadleigh, (Joseph[5], Joseph[4], Robert[3], Robert[2], John[1]), b. ca. 1786 in Brentwood, N.H., d. Feb. 22, 1815. (Ref. 11)

332- <u>Annie</u>[6] Wadleigh, (Joseph[5], Joseph[4], Robert[3], Robert[2], John[1]), b. in Brentwood, N.H. (Ref. 3)

333- <u>Rachel</u>[6] Wadleigh, (Joseph[5], Joseph[4], Robert[3], Robert[2], John[1]), b. in Brentwood, N.H. (Ref. 3)

334- <u>Mary</u>[6] Wadleigh, (Joseph[5], Joseph[4], Robert[3], Robert[2], John[1]), b. in Brentwood, N.H. (Ref. 3)

Issue of 155- Abraham Brown and Judith (Runnells) Brown:

335- Noah Brown, (Wadleigh: Abraham[5], Mary[4], Robert[3], Robert[2], John[1]). no data. Res. Hampton Falls, N.H., did not marry. (Ref. 30)

336- Mary Brown, (Wadleigh: Abraham[5], Mary[4], Robert[3], Robert[2], John[1]). no data. Res. Hampton Falls, N.H., did not marry. (Ref. 30)

337- Joseph Brown, (Wadleigh: Abraham[5], Mary[4], Robert[3], Robert[2], John[1]). m. 1st Susan Holman. m. 2nd Mercy West. no additional data. Res. Hampton Falls, N.H., (Ref. 30)
    560 - daughter   561 - daughter

338- Levi Brown, (Wadleigh: Abraham[5], Mary[4], Robert[3], Robert[2], John[1]). no data. (Ref. 30)
    562 - Frederick   564 - Levi
    563 - Polly   565 - Sewell

Issue of Caleb Shaw and 162- Abigail (Batchelder) Shaw:

339- Hannah Shaw, (Wadleigh: Abigail[5], Abigail[4], Mary[3], Robert[2], John[1]; Batchelder: John[5], Nathaniel[4], Nathaniel[3], Nathaniel[2], Stephen[1]), b. September 22, 1742. m. 209- Edward Ladd, (Wadleigh: Catherine[4], Samuel[3], Joanna[2], John[1]), b. April 13, 1736, d.   For issue, see 209- Edward Ladd. (Ref. S4)

Issue of Samuel[2] Melcher and 170- Elizabeth (Cram) Melcher:

340- Samuel[3] Melcher, (Wadleigh: Elizabeth[5], Benjamin[4], Mary[3], Robert[2], John[1]; Melcher: Samuel[2], (?)[1]), b. ca. 1708, d. 1802. m. 1735

Esther Green, d. of Benjamin Green, b. ca. 1710, d. 1797. Res. Melcher Homestead in Hampton Falls, N.H. (Ref. 30)
          566 - Samuel

Issue of 172- Theophilus[5] Wadleigh and Abigail (Bean) Wadleigh:

341- Elizabeth[6] Wadleigh, (Theophilus[5], Joseph[4], Henry[3], Robert[2], John[1]), bpt. June 20, 1743 in Kensington, N.H. (Ref. 3)

342- Theophilus[6] Wadleigh, (Theophilus[5], Joseph[4], Henry[3], Robert[2], John[1]), bpt. March 10, 1745 in Kensington, N.H. (Ref. 3)

Issue of 173- Joseph[5] Wadleigh and Anne (Dearborn) Wadleigh:

343- Anne[6] Wadleigh, (Joseph[5], Joseph[4], Henry[3], Robert[2], John[1]), b. November 11, 1749 in Kensington, N.H., d. April 19, 1776. (Ref. 2, 3)

344- Joseph[6] Wadleigh, (Joseph[5], Joseph[4], Henry[3], Robert[2], John[1]), b. September 3, 1751 in Kensington, N.H., d. May 11, 1817 in Kensington. m. January 29, 1777 Betsey[5] Longfellow, (Nathan[4], Nathan[3], William[2], William[1]) of Machias, Me., d. of Nathan[4] Longfellow and Susan (Ellis) Longfellow, b. ca. 1761, d. April 15, 1841 in Kensington. h.-w. bur. in Old Cemetery of Universalist Church. (Ref. 2, 3)

567 - Nancy	572 - Joseph Dearborn
568 - Susanna	573 - Ruth
569 - Betsey	574 - Jeremiah
570 - John	575 - Mark
571 - Betsey	576 - Sewall

345- Mary[6] Wadleigh, (Joseph[5], Joseph[4], Henry[3], Robert[2], John[1]), b. January 25, 1754 in Kensington, N.H., d. January 10, 1789. Did not marry. (Ref. 2, 3)

346- John[6] Wadleigh, (Joseph[5], Joseph[4], Henry[3], Robert[2], John[1]), b. May 13, 1759 (Ref. 3 also cites May 15) in Kensington, N.H., d. June 10, 1795 in Hampton Falls, N.H. m. June 5, 1781 Hannah Prescott of Epping, N.H., d. of John and Hannah (Rundlett) Prescott of Epping, N.H. no additional data. Note: Hannah (Prescott) Wadleigh m. 2nd ca. 1800 Abner[5] Sanborn, (Timothy[4], Abner[3], John[2], John[1]). (Ref. 2, 3)

    577 - Hannah   580 - Joseph
    578 - Leah Prescott   581 - Hannah
    579 - Joseph

347- Ruth[6] Wadleigh, (Joseph[5], Joseph[4], Henry[3], Robert[2], John[1]), b. November 12, 1761 in Kensington, N.H., d. April 17, 1790 at Hampton Falls, N.H., m. October 4, 1787 Simeon Prescott, b. September 18, 1764. (Ref. 2, 3)

    582 - Joseph

Issue of 173- Joseph[5] Wadleigh and Jane (Buffum) Wadleigh:

348- Jane[6] Wadleigh, (Joseph[5], Joseph[4], Henry[3], Robert[2], John[1]), b. November 12, 1787 in Kensington, N.H. m. Ezra Chase of Kensington. no additional data. (Ref. 2, 3)

349- William Henry[6] Wadleigh, (Joseph[5], Joseph[4], Henry[3], Robert[2], John[1]), b. August 23, 1788 or August 23, 1789 or August 25, 1789 in Kensington, N.H., d. October 30, 1828 in Kensington. m. June 25, 1810 or August 25, 1810 or August 23, 1810 Abigail Stockbridge, d. of John Stockbridge of (presum.) Stratham,

N.H., b. March 4, 1794, d. June 25, 1873 in
Rutland, Ill. (Ref. 2, 3)

  583 - William Henry   587 - Emery Leland
  584 - Daniel Foster   588 - Leully
  585 - Sarah Jane   589 - John H.
  586 - Joseph Dearborn

350- Mary Ann[6] Wadleigh, (Joseph[5], Joseph[4],
Henry[3], Robert[2], John[1]), b. (presum.) November
19 1791 in Kensington, N.H., d. December 30,
1843. m. January 22, 1818 Abraham Rowe of
Kensington, b. ca. 1798, d. January 15, 1873.
(Ref. 2, 3)

**Issue of 175- Benjamin[5] Wadleigh and Hannah[5]
(Dearborn) Wadleigh:**

351- Mary[6] Wadleigh, (Benjamin[5], Joseph[4],
Henry[3], Robert[2], John[1]), b. February 11, 1753
in Epping, N.H. m. April 25, 1780 David
Marston. no additional data. (Ref. 3)

352- Simon Dearborn[6] Wadleigh, (Benjamin[5],
Joseph[4], Henry[3], Robert[2], John[1]), b. July 14,
1754 in Epping N.H. m. January 5, 1779 Dorothy
Rowe of Canterbury, N.H. no additional data.
(Ref. 3)

    590 - Parmala   593 - Life
    591 - John   594 - Simon Dearborn
    592 - Newell

353- Elijah[6] Wadleigh, (Benjamin[5], Joseph[4],
Henry[3], Robert[2], John[1]), b. March 18, 1757 in
Epping, N.H. m. April 23, 1790 Patty Saunders.
no additional data. (Ref. 3)

    595 - George   597 - Benjamin
    596 - Henry

354- Sarah[6] Wadleigh, (Benjamin[5], Joseph[4],
Henry[3], Robert[2], John[1]), b. January 1, 1759 in
Epping, N.H. (Ref. 3)

355- James Marston[6] Wadleigh, (Benjamin[5], Joseph[4], Henry[3], Robert[2], John[1]), b. 1762 in Epping N.H., d. 1843. m. 1813 Nancy Neal of (presum.) Meredith, N.H., d. of Joseph "Red Oak" Neal and Nancy (Perkins) Neal. no additional data. (Ref. 3)

      598 - John Calvin   599 - Nathan B.

Issue of 176- James[5] Wadleigh and Mary (Dearborn) Wadleigh:

356- James[6] Wadleigh, (James[5], Joseph[4], Henry[3], Robert[2], John[1]), b. August 10, 1753 (twin) in Epping, N.H. m. June 5, 1781 Molly/Mary Blake of Epping, N.H. no additional data. (Ref. 3)

600 - James		604 - John
601 - Joseph		605 - Betsey
602 - Nancy		606 - Sally
603 - Polly		607 - Asa

357- John[6] Wadleigh, (James[5], Joseph[4], Henry[3], Robert[2], John[1]), b. August 10, 1753 (twin) in Epping, N.H., d. 1842 (or 1848). m. Molly Fox, b. 1757, d. 1827. Res. Epping and Meredith, N.H. (Ref. 3)

608 - Dearborn		612 - Nancy
609 - Polly		613 - Caroline
610 - Betsey		614 - Sally
611 - Hannah		615 - Cyrene

358- William[6] Wadleigh, (James[5], Joseph[4], Henry[3], Robert[2], John[1]). no data. (Ref. 3)

359- Joseph[6] Wadleigh, (James[5], Joseph[4], Henry[3], Robert[2], John[1]), b. January 1759 in Epping, N.H., d. July 10, 1851 in Sanbornton, N.H. m. 1st May 3, 1787 Molly/Polly[5] Weeks, d. of Cole[4] Weeks, (John[3], Samuel[2], Leonard[1]), b. 1766 in Epping N.H., d. August 13, 1825. m. 2nd December 28, 1825 Mary P. Sanborn of

Chichester, N.H., (Ref. 3 also says Sanbornton
or Sanbornville), N.H. a widow, d. January
1852. (Ref. 3) 616 - 623 by 1st wife.

616 - Eunice	621 - Joseph
617 - Huldah	622 - unnamed
618 - James Dearborn	623 - Chase Weeks
619 - Molly	624 - Simon Hayes
620 - Newell	

360- Dearborn[6] Wadleigh, (James[5], Joseph[4],
Henry[3], Robert[2], John[1]), b. 1761 in Epping,
N.H. m. March 1793 Judith Roby of Deerfield,
N.H. no additional data. (Ref. 3)

361- Simeon[6] Wadleigh, (James[5], Joseph[4],
Henry[3], Robert[2], John[1]), b. 1762 in Epping,
N.H., d. 1843. m. March 27, 1785 Abigail Hayes
of Epping, d. of William Hayes and Mary
(Plummer) Hayes of Epping, d. 1849. Res.
Epping and the "Wadleighboro" section of
Meredith, N.H. (Ref. 3)

625 - William P.	627 - Stephen G.
626 - John	

362- Enoch[6] Wadleigh, (James[5], Joseph[4], Henry[3],
Robert[2], John[1]), b. 1766 in Epping, N.H., d.
June 6, 1838. m. August 6 (or 5), 1782 Hannah
Morrill of Epping, b. 1772, d. March 14, 1815.
(Ref. 3)

628 - William	631 - daughter
629 - Enoch	632 - daughter
630 - Eliza	

363- Joseph/Josiah[6] Wadleigh, (James[5], Joseph[4],
Henry[3], Robert[2], John[1]), b. 1771 in Epping,
N.H., d. 1822 in Meredith, N.H. m. Sally
Chapman, d. of (presum.) Joseph and Phebe
Chapman. no additional data. Res. Epping and
on Province Road near Meredith where built part
of "Ballard House". (Ref. 3)

633 - Betsey	634 - Dexter

Issue of Enoch Coffin and 178- Mary (Wadleigh) Coffin:

364- Sarah Coffin, (Wadleigh: Mary[5], Joseph[4], Henry[3], Robert[2], John[1]), b. September 24, 1758 (twin-?). m. Richard Dow. no additional data. (Ref. 3)

365- Mary Coffin, (Wadleigh: Mary[5], Joseph[4], Henry[3], Robert[2], John[1]), b. September 25, 1758 (twin-?). m. Daniel Barber. no additional data. (Ref. 3)

Issue of 195- John Smith and Judith (Thompson) Smith:

366- Thomas Smith, (Wadleigh: John[5], James[4], Martha[3], Mary[2], John[1]). m. Rhoda Rounds. no additional data. (Ref. 36-182)

Issue of 209- Edward[5] Ladd and 339- Hannah (Shaw) Ladd:

367- Nathaniel[6] Ladd, (Wadleigh: Edward[5], Catherine[4], Samuel[3], Joanna[2], John[1]; Ladd: Edward[5], Edward[4], Nathaniel[3], Nathaniel[2], Daniel[1]), b. February 8, 178_. (Ref. S4)

Issue of 218- Ebenezer[5] Wadleigh and Love (Huntress) Wadleigh:

368- Dorothy[6] Wadleigh, (Ebenezer[5], John[4], Daniel[3], John[2], John[1]), b. in South Berwick, Me. (Ref. 3)

369- Albra[6] Wadleigh, (Ebenezer[5], John[4], Daniel[3], John[2], John[1]), b. November 12, 1804 in South Berwick, Me., d. July 23, 1864 in

WADLEIGH GENEALOGY   SIXTH GENERATION

Philadelphia, Pa. m. January 24, 1826 Eliza
Payson Brewster, d. of William Brewster and
Izette (Noble) Brewster, b. March 31, 1809 in
Portsmouth, N.H., d. in Brookline, Mass. Ed.
Harvard 1854. Occ. Priest of Philadelphia
Protestant Episcopal Church. (Ref. 3)
    635 - Mary Rice   636 - Frances Wentworth

Issue of 219- Elisha⁵ Wadleigh and Sally
(Smith) Wadleigh:

370- John⁶ Wadleigh, (Elisha⁵, John⁴, Daniel³,
John², John¹), b. October 7, 1792 in South
Berwick (or Parsonfield), Me., d. February 27,
1856. m. November 10, 1817 Sally Burbank. no
additional data. (Ref. 3)
        637 - Elisha   640 - John
        638 - Jesse   641 - William
        639 - Eliza   642 - Sarah

371- James⁶ Wadleigh, (Elisha⁵, John⁴, Daniel³,
John², John¹), b. November 1, 1794 in South
Berwick (or Parsonfield), Me. m. November 10
1817 Rachel Dearborn. no additional data.
(Ref. 3)
        643 - James Dearborn   648 - Hannah M.
        644 - George W.   649 - Mahala
        645 - Mary   650 - Eliza F.
        646 - Sarah J.   651 - Jacob D.
        647 - Caroline D.   652 - Elisha B.

372- Livina⁶ Wadleigh, (Elisha⁵, John⁴,
Daniel³, John², John¹), b. December 20, 1796 in
South Berwick, Me., d. April 17, 1853. m.
April 9, 1818 Thomas Wedgewood. no additional
data. (Ref. 3)

373- Daniel⁶ Wadleigh, (Elisha⁵, John⁴,
Daniel³, John², John¹), b. November 11, 1799 in
Parsonfield, Me., d. January 12, 1864/8 in

WADLEIGH - 71

Brewster, Me. m. Mary Footman. no additional
data. (Ref. 3)

374- Elisha[6] Wadleigh, (Elisha[5], John[4],
Daniel[3], John[2], John[1]), b. September 29, 1801
in Parsonfield, Me., d. August 4, 1875, m.
Mary A. Burbank, d. of Caleb Burbank of
Parsonfield, Me. no additional data. (Ref. 3)
      653 - Caleb   655 - Sally B.
      654 - Elisha   656 - Lemuel M.

375- Sally S.[6] Wadleigh, (Elisha[5], John[4],
Daniel[3], John[2], John[1]), b. August 5, 1803 in
Parsonfield, Me., d. May 18, 1850. m. John
Dearborn. no additional data. (Ref. 3)

376- Catherine[6] Wadleigh, (Elisha[5], John[4],
Daniel[3], John[2], John[1]), b. October 1, 1805 in
Parsonfield, Me. m. December 2, 1834 Stephen
Wedgewood. no additional data. Res.
Parsonfield and Newport, Me. (Ref. 3)

INTRODUCING:

377- Henry Wadleigh, b. in Rye, N.Y. m.
October 14, 1800 Sally Weeks, d. of Benjamin
and Sarah (Weed) Weeks, b. December 3, 1779.
Res. Rye, N.Y. and Gilford, N.H. Occ.
Blacksmith (Ref. 3)
      657 - Benjamin   659 - Catherine E.
      658 - William H.   660 - Isabelle

378- Nathaniel Wadleigh, d. April 4, 1834. m.
1st Betsey (Elizabeth) Ray. m. 2nd December
21, 1819 Polly H. Ray of Meredith, N.H., d. of

William and Eliza (Neal) Ray. m. 3rd. December
9, 1827 Nancy Pickering. no additional data.
(Ref. 3)   661 - 663 by 1st wife, 664 - 666 by
2nd wife, 667 - 670 by 3rd wife.

661 - Sally		666 - Issac
662 - Abigail		667 - Almira Jane
663 - Betsey		668 - Andrew
664 - Mary Robinson		669 - Mary Ann
665 - Eliza		670 - John

Issue of 221- Richard Dolloff and Mrs.
(Wells) Dolloff:

379- David Dolloff, (Wadleigh: Richard[6],
Mary[5], Elizabeth[4], Jonathan[3], Joanna[2], John[1];
Gilman: Mary[5], Elizabeth[4], Mary[3], John[2],
Edward[1]). no additional data. (Ref. 49)

380- Sally Dolloff, (Wadleigh: Richard[6], Mary[5],
Elizabeth[4], Jonathan[3], Joanna[2], John[1]; Gilman:
Richard[6], Mary[5], Elizabeth[4], Mary[3], John[2],
Edward[1]). no additional data. m. Waldron[5]
Smith, (John W.[4], Jonathan[3], Jonathan[2],
Robert[1]), b. 1767, d. 1846. (Ref. 49)
        672 - Henry M.

381- Betty Dolloff, (Wadleigh: Richard[6], Mary[5],
Elizabeth[4], Jonathan[3], Joanna[2], John[1]; Gilman:
Richard[6], Mary[5], Elizabeth[4], Mary[3], John[2],
Edward[1]). m. Nathan Smith. no additional
data. (Ref. 49)

382- John Dolloff, (Wadleigh: Richard[6], Mary[5],
Elizabeth[4], Jonathan[3], Joanna[2], John[1]; Gilman:
Richard[6], Mary[5], Elizabeth[4], Mary[3], John[2],
Edward[1]). no additional data. (Ref. 49)

383- Ruth Dolloff, (Wadleigh: Richard[6], Mary[5],
Elizabeth[4], Jonathan[3], Joanna[2], John[1]; Gilman:
Richard[6], Mary[5], Elizabeth[4], Mary[3], John[2],
Edward[1]). m. Smith Cram. no additional data.
(Ref. 49)

Issue of 237- Ezekiel[5] Morrill and Sarah Morrill:

384- Joanna[6] Morrill, (Wadleigh: Ezekiel[6], Abner[5], Abigail[4], John[3], Robert[2], John[1]; Morrill: Ezekiel[6], Abner[4], Ezekiel[3], Jacob[2], Abraham[1]), bpt. December 3, 1758. (Ref. 4-778)

385- Sarah[6] Morrill, (Wadleigh: Ezekiel[6], Abner[5], Abigail[4], John[3], Robert[2], John[1]; Morrill: Ezekiel[6], Abner[4], Ezekiel[3], Jacob[2], Abraham[1]), bpt. October 7, 1759. (Ref. 4-778)

386- Molly[6] Morrill, (Wadleigh: Ezekiel[6], Abner[5], Abigail[4], John[3], Robert[2], John[1]; Morrill: Ezekiel[6], Abner[4], Ezekiel[3], Jacob[2], Abraham[1]), bpt. July 17, 1762. (Ref. 4-778)

387- Philip[6] Morrill, (Wadleigh: Ezekiel[6], Abner[5], Abigail[4], John[3], Robert[2], John[1]; Morrill: Ezekiel[6], Abner[4], Ezekiel[3], Jacob[2], Abraham[1]), bpt. November 17, 1765. (Ref. 4-778)

Issue of 250- Jonathan[5] Morrill and Rachel Morrill:

388- Abigail[6] Morrill, (Wadleigh: Jonathan[6], John[5], Abigail[4], John[3], Robert[2], John[1]; Morrill: Jonathan[5], John[4], Ezekiel[3], Jacob[2], Abraham[1]), b. January 12, 1762 at South Hampton, N.H. bpt. June 20, 1762. (Ref. 4-790)

389- Anne[6] Morrill, (Wadleigh: Jonathan[6], John[5], Abigail[4], John[3], Robert[2], John[1]; Morrill: Jonathan[5], John[4], Ezekiel[3], Jacob[2], Abraham[1]), b. August 4, 1763 at South Hampton, N.H. bpt. September 25, 1763 at South Hampton. (Ref. 4-790)

390- John[6] Morrill, (Wadleigh: Jonathan[6], John[5], Abigail[4], John[3], Robert[2], John[1]; Morrill: Jonathan[5], John[4], Ezekiel[3], Jacob[2], Abraham[1]), b. September 25, 1766 at South Hampton. (Ref. 4-790)

391- Sarah[6] Morrill, (Wadleigh: Jonathan[6], John[5], Abigail[4], John[3], Robert[2], John[1]; Morrill: Jonathan[5], John[4], Ezekiel[3], Jacob[2], Abraham[1]), b. September 11, 1769 at East Kingston. (Ref. 4-790)

Issue of 255- David[6] Currier and Sarah (Chase) Currier:

392- Nathaniel[7] Currier, (Wadleigh: David[6], David[5], Susanna[5], Abigail[4], John[3], Robert[2], John[1]; Currier: David[6], David[5], Jacob[4], Samuel[3], Thomas[2], Richard[1]; Morrill: David[6], David[5], Susanna[4], Ezekiel[3], Jacob[2], Abraham[1]), b. July 2, 1782, d. October 16, 1805 at Salisbury, Mass. (Ref. 4-932)

393- David[7] Currier, (Wadleigh: David[6], David[5], Susanna[5], Abigail[4], John[3], Robert[2], John[1]; Currier: David[6], David[5], Jacob[4], Samuel[3], Thomas[2], Richard[1]; Morrill: David[6], David[5], Susanna[4], Ezekiel[3], Jacob[2], Abraham[1]), b. July 21, 1784, d. January 30, 1823 at Salisbury, Mass. m. Betsey. no additional data. (Ref. 4-932)

394- Elizabeth[7] Currier, (Wadleigh: David[6], David[5], Susanna[5], Abigail[4], John[3], Robert[2], John[1]; Currier: David[6], David[5], Jacob[4], Samuel[3], Thomas[2], Richard[1]; Morrill: David[6], David[5], Susanna[4], Ezekiel[3], Jacob[2], Abraham[1]), b. July 11, 1786. m. August 13, 1806 in Salisbury, Mass., Capt. Samuel Brown. no additional data. (Ref. 4-932)

395- <u>Moses</u>[7] <u>Currier</u>, (Wadleigh: David[6], David[5], Susanna[5], Abigail[4], John[3], Robert[2], John[1]; Currier: David[6], David[5], Jacob[4], Samuel[3], Thomas[2], Richard[1]; Morrill: David[6], David[5], Susanna[4], Ezekiel[3], Jacob[2], Abraham[1]), b. November 9, 1788 at Salisbury, Mass. m. November 7, 1809 Nancy Stevens. no additional data. (Ref. 4-932)

396- <u>Jacob</u>[7] <u>Currier</u>, (Wadleigh: David[6], David[5], Susanna[5], Abigail[4], John[3], Robert[2], John[1]; Currier: David[6], David[5], Jacob[4], Samuel[3], Thomas[2], Richard[1]; Morrill: David[6], David[5], Susanna[4], Ezekiel[3], Jacob[2], Abraham[1]), b. January 31, 1792 at Salisbury, Mass. m. December 24, 1817 at Salisbury, Ruth Osgood. no additional data. (Ref. 4-932)

397- <u>Susanna</u>[7] <u>Currier</u>, (Wadleigh: David[6], David[5], Susanna[5], Abigail[4], John[3], Robert[2], John[1]; Currier: David[6], David[5], Jacob[4], Samuel[3], Thomas[2], Richard[1]; Morrill: David[6], David[5], Susanna[4], Ezekiel[3], Jacob[2], Abraham[1]), b. August 3, 1794, d. July 16, 1795. died in infancy. (Ref. 4-932)

398- <u>James</u>[7] <u>Currier</u>, (Wadleigh: David[6], David[5], Susanna[5], Abigail[4], John[3], Robert[2], John[1]; Currier: David[6], David[5], Jacob[4], Samuel[3], Thomas[2], Richard[1]; Morrill: David[6], David[5], Susanna[4], Ezekiel[3], Jacob[2], Abraham[1]), b. June 24, 1796, d. April 15, 1797. died in infancy. (Ref. 4-932)

399- <u>James</u>[7] <u>Currier</u>, (Wadleigh: David[6], David[5], Susanna[5], Abigail[4], John[3], Robert[2], John[1]; Currier: David[6], David[5], Jacob[4], Samuel[3], Thomas[2], Richard[1]; Morrill: David[6], David[5], Susanna[4], Ezekiel[3], Jacob[2], Abraham[1]), b. April 27, 1798, d. November 16, 1801. died in childhood. (Ref. 4-932)

400- Thomas[7] Currier, (Wadleigh: David[6], David[5], Susanna[5], Abigail[4], John[3], Robert[2], John[1]; Currier: David[6], David[5], Jacob[4], Samuel[3], Thomas[2], Richard[1]; Morrill: David[6], David[5], Susanna[4], Ezekiel[3], Jacob[2], Abraham[1]), b. August 9, 1800, d. February 28, 1802. died in infancy. (Ref. 4-932)

Issue of 258- Joseph[6] Wadleigh and Elizabeth (Morrill) Wadleigh:

401- Elijah[7] Wadleigh, (Joseph[6], Joseph[5], Joseph[4], John[3], Robert[2], John[1]), b. September 3, 1780 in Salisbury, Mass., d. December 6, in Salisbury. m. August 4, 1800 Rhoda Smith, d. December 1867 in Salisbury. (Ref. 3, 4)

>   673 - Mary Ann   675 - Elijah
>   674 - George

402- Mary[7] Wadleigh, (Joseph[6], Joseph[5], Joseph[4], John[3], Robert[2], John[1]), b. January 22, 1782 in Salisbury, Mass. (Ref. 3)

403- Elizabeth[7] Wadleigh, (Joseph[6], Joseph[5], Joseph[4], John[3], Robert[2], John[1]), b. October 1, 1784 in Salisbury, Mass., d. September 26, 1790 in Salisbury. died in childhood. (Ref. 3)

404- Anna[7] Wadleigh, (Joseph[6], Joseph[5], Joseph[4], John[3], Robert[2], John[1]), b. January 20, 1787 in Salisbury, Mass. m. September 16, 180? Samuel Adams. no additional data. (Ref. 3)

405- Joseph[7] Wadleigh, (Joseph[6], Joseph[5], Joseph[4], John[3], Robert[2], John[1]), b. October 31, 1788 in Salisbury, Mass., d. 1789. died in childhood. (Ref. 3)

406- <u>Joseph</u>[7] <u>Wadleigh</u>, (Joseph[6], Joseph[5], Joseph[4], John[3], Robert[2], John[1]), b. March 18, 1791 in Salisbury, Mass. m. October 2, 1813 Jane Carson. no additional data. Res. Salisbury, Mass. and Boscawin, N.H. (Ref. 3)

407- <u>James</u>[7] <u>Wadleigh</u>, (Joseph[6], Joseph[5], Joseph[4], John[3], Robert[2], John[1]), b. January 18, 1793 in Salisbury, Mass. m. Miss Ayers. no additional data. (Ref. 3)

408- <u>Benjamin Harrod</u>[7] <u>Wadleigh</u>, (Joseph[6], Joseph[5], Joseph[4], John[3], Robert[2], John[1]), b. September 19, 1794 in Salisbury, Mass. m. December 24, 1822 Judith Clough. no additional data. (Ref. 3)

Issue of 259- Benjamin[6] Wadleigh and 419-Hannah (Goodwin) Wadleigh:

409- <u>Hannah</u>[7] <u>Wadleigh</u>, (Benjamin[6], Joseph[5], Joseph[4], John[3], Robert[2], John[1]), b. October 25, 1785 in Salisbury, Mass. (Ref. 3)

410- <u>Joseph</u>[7] <u>Wadleigh</u>, (Benjamin[6], Joseph[5], Joseph[4], John[3], Robert[2], John[1]), b. October 12, 1787 in Salisbury, Mass. (Ref. 3)

411- <u>Benjamin</u>[7] <u>Wadleigh</u>, (Benjamin[6], Joseph[5], Joseph[4], John[3], Robert[2], John[1]), b. November 12, 1789 in Salisbury, Mass. (Ref. 3)

412- <u>Robert</u>[7] <u>Wadleigh</u>, (Benjamin[6], Joseph[5], Joseph[4], John[3], Robert[2], John[1]), b. March, 27, 1792 in Salisbury, Mass. (Ref. 3)

413- Edward[7] Wadleigh, (Benjamin[6], Joseph[5], Joseph[4], John[3], Robert[2], John[1]), b. January 1795 in Salisbury, Mass. (Ref. 3)

414- Mary[7] Wadleigh, (Benjamin[6], Joseph[5], Joseph[4], John[3], Robert[2], John[1]), b. July, 9 1798 in Salisbury, Mass. (Ref. 3)

415- Lois[7] Wadleigh, (Benjamin[6], Joseph[5], Joseph[4], John[3], Robert[2], John[1]), b. July, 31, 1800 in Salisbury, Mass. (Ref. 3)

416- Elener[7] Wadleigh, (Benjamin[6], Joseph[5], Joseph[4], John[3], Robert[2], John[1]), b. January 6, 1802 in Salisbury, Mass. (Ref. 3)

417- Eleazer[7] Wadleigh, (Benjamin[6], Joseph[5], Joseph[4], John[3], Robert[2], John[1]), b. September 4, 1807 in Salisbury, Mass., d. December 10, 1840 in Salisbury. m. January 17, 1829 Sally P. Wells, (from Tombstone: "Relict of Eleazer Wadleigh and wife of Jonathan French"), d. January 12, 1887. (Ref. 3)

    676 - Charlotte   678 - Lois A.
    677 - Sarah   679 - Horace

Issue of John[5] Currier and 261- Abigail (Wadleigh) Currier:

418- Benjamin[6] Currier, (Wadleigh; John[6], Benjamin[5], Joseph[4], John[3], Robert[2], John[1]; Currier; John[5], Ezekiel[4], Thomas[3], Thomas[2], Richard[1]), b. December 19, 1764/5, d. June 22, 1817 at Salisbury, Mass. m. December 28, 1787 at Amesbury Rhoda Jewell, d. October 24, 1849 at Salisbury. (Ref. 4-919)

    680 - Abigail

Issue of Elezor Goodwin and 262- Hannah (Wadleigh) Goodwin:

419- <u>Hannah Goodwin</u>, (Wadleigh: Hannah[6], Benjamin[5], Joseph[4], John[3], Robert[2], John[1]), d. October 15, 1807 in Salisbury, Mass., bur. Amesbury, Mass. m. October 5, 1783, 259- Benjamin[6] Wadleigh, (Joseph[5], Joseph[4], John[3], Robert[2], John[1]), d. June 1813 in Salisbury, Mass., bur. Amesbury, Mass. For issue, See: 259- Benjamin[6] Wadleigh,

Issue of David[6] Graves and 272- Ruth (Wadleigh) Graves:

420- <u>James[7] Graves</u>, (Wadleigh: Ruth[6], Dean[5], John[4], John[3], Robert[2], John[1]; Graves: James[5], Samuel[4], Abraham[3], Mark[2], Samuel[1]), b. October 25, 1771, d. December 30, 1856. m. April 25, 1794 Polly Gilman, d. of Caleb Gilman. no additional data. Res. Elizabethtown, N.Y. (Ref. 12)
    681 - John

Issue of 277- Benjamin[6] Wadleigh and Sarah (Patten) Wadleigh:

421- <u>Polly[7] Wadleigh</u>, (Benjamin[6], Dean[5], John[4], John[3], Robert[2], John[1]), b. June 20, 1791 in Candia, N.H., d. June 27, 1846. m. Reuben Boyce. no additional data. (Ref. 3)
    682 - Reuben   684 - Ruth Fairbanks
    683 - Ira Wadleigh

422- <u>Ira[7] Wadleigh</u>, (Benjamin[6], Dean[5], John[4], John[3], Robert[2], John[1]), b. June 22, 1794 in Candia, N.H., d. August 27, 1875 in Candia, N.H. m. Theodosia Sargent. no additional data. Res. Oldtown, Me. (Ref. 3)
    685 - Theodosia B.   686 - Susan A.

423- Moses[7] Wadleigh, (Benjamin[6], Dean[5], John[4], John[3], Robert[2], John[1]), b. May 2, 1796 in Candia, N.H., d. June 10 1847.   (Ref. 3)

424- Jesse[7] Wadleigh, (Benjamin[6], Dean[5], John[4], John[3], Robert[2], John[1]), b. September 18, 1798 in Candia, N.H., d. January 11, 1877. m. Susan Grant. no additional data. Res. Oldtown, Me. (Ref. 3)
>   687 - Carria

425- Samuel[7] Wadleigh, (Benjamin[6], Dean[5], John[4], John[3], Robert[2], John[1]), b. August 6, 1800 in Candia, N.H., d. August 1847. Res. Oldtown, Me. (Ref. 3)

426- Sarah[7] Wadleigh, (Benjamin[6], Dean[5], John[4], John[3], Robert[2], John[1]), b. December 23, 1802 in Candia, N.H., d. January 10, 1847. m. Mr. Dearborn. no additional data. (Ref. 3)

427- Ruth[7] Wadleigh, (Benjamin[6], Dean[5], John[4], John[3], Robert[2], John[1]), b. June 3, 1805 in Candia, N.H., d. August 4, 1848 in Candia. m. September 18, 1823 Rufus Sargent, b. April 3, 1778 in Candia, d. April 29, 1857 in Candia. (Ref. 3)
>   688 - Frank Wadleigh   689 - Theodosia

Issue of 278- Dean[6] Wadleigh by Anna Colby (unmarried):

428- Benjamin Dean[7] Wadleigh, (Dean[6], Dean[5], John[4], John[3], Robert[2], John[1]), b. 1784 in Salisbury, Mass., d. March 15, 1855 in Salisbury. m. 1810 Lois Edwards, b. 1789 in Salisbury, d. 1832 in Salisbury. (Ref. 3)
>   690 - Enoch Hunt   694 - Benjamin Dean
>   691 - Benjamin   695 - Philip
>   692 - Mary Jane   696 - Ephriam S.
>   693 - Anna W.   697 - David E.

Issue of 278- Dean[6] Wadleigh and Allie Wadleigh:

429- William[7] Wadleigh, (Dean[6], Dean[5], John[4], John[3], Robert[2], John[1]). no additional data. (Ref. 24)

430- Sarah[7] Wadleigh, (Dean[6], Dean[5], John[4], John[3], Robert[2], John[1]). m. Joseph Clifford. no additional data. (Ref. 24)

431- John[7] Wadleigh, (Dean[6], Dean[5], John[4], John[3], Robert[2], John[1]). m. Olive Cram. no additional data. (Ref. 24)

432- Mahitable[7] Wadleigh, (Dean[6], Dean[5], John[4], John[3], Robert[2], John[1]). m. Shadrach Cram. no additional data. (Ref. 24)

433- Dorothy[7] Wadleigh, (Dean[6], Dean[5], John[4], John[3], Robert[2], John[1]). m. Sampson Woods. no additional data. (Ref. 24)

Issue of 288- Adams[6] Wadleigh and Sarah (Greeley) Wadleigh:

434- Jonathan[7] Wadleigh, (Adams[6], Moses[5], Ephriam[4], John[3], Robert[2], John[1]), b. September 20, 1774 in Salisbury, Mass. (Ref. 3)

435- Sarah[7] Wadleigh, (Adams[6], Moses[5], Ephriam[4], John[3], Robert[2], John[1]), b. November 2 (or 24), 1776 in Salisbury, Mass., d. March 15, 1798 in Amesbury, Mass. m. November 5, 1794 William Swett in Amesbury. no additional data. (Ref. 3)
     698 - Mary

436- <u>Elizabeth</u>[7] <u>Wadleigh</u>, (Adams[6], Moses[5], Ephriam[4], John[3], Robert[2], John[1]), b. February 27, 1779 (twin) in Salisbury, Mass. no additional data. (Ref. 3)

437- <u>Hannah</u>[7] <u>Wadleigh</u>, (Adams[6], Moses[5], Ephriam[4], John[3], Robert[2], John[1]), b. February 27, 1779 (twin) in Salisbury, Mass. m. William Swett, widower of 435- Sarah[7] Wadleigh, as his 2nd wife. no additional data. (Ref. 3)
        699 - William   701 - Hannah
        700 - Benjamin   702 - Judith

438- <u>Enoch</u>[7] <u>Wadleigh</u>, (Adams[6], Moses[5], Ephriam[4], John[3], Robert[2], John[1]). b. July 2, 1781 in Salisbury, Mass. m. October 26, 1809 Elizabeth Fowler, d. of Elijah, and Hannah (Abbot) Fowler. no additional data. (Ref. 3)
        703 - Adrines   705 - Elizabeth
        704 - Adams

439- <u>Philip</u>[7] <u>Wadleigh</u>, (Adams[6], Moses[5], Ephriam[4], John[3], Robert[2], John[1]), b. July 7, 1783 in Salisbury, Mass. (Ref. 3)

440- <u>Peter</u>[7] <u>Wadleigh</u>, (Adams[6], Moses[5], Ephriam[4], John[3], Robert[2], John[1]), b. June 22, 1786 in Salisbury, Mass., d. October 26, 1815 in Salisbury. m. 455- Polly[7] Wadleigh, (Ephriam[6], Moses[5], Ephriam[4], John[3], Robert[2], John[1]), d. of 292- Ephriam[6] and Molly/Mary (Barnard) Wadleigh of Salisbury. b. August 9, 1793 in Salisbury. d. August 10, 1823 in Salisbury. (Ref. 3, 4)
        706 - Sophronia

441- <u>Judith</u>[7] <u>Wadleigh</u>, (Adams[6], Moses[5], Ephriam[4], John[3], Robert[2], John[1]), b. December 11, 1788 (or 1786) in Salisbury, Mass., d. August 11, 1833. m. May 31 (or 21), 1809 Capt. Joseph[1] Guest, b. December 8, 1782 in Dublin,

Ireland, d. June 6, 1833 in Tampico, Mexico.
(Ref. 3)

707 - Sarah	709 - Marcia A.
708 - Elizabeth	710 - Marcia Ann

442- <u>William</u>[7] Wadleigh, (Adams[6], Moses[5],
Ephriam[4], John[3], Robert[2], John[1]), b. September
15, 1791 in Salisbury, Mass., d. August 30,
1852 in Salisbury. (Ref. 3)

**Issue of 290- Philip[6] Wadleigh and Sarah
(Kimball) Wadleigh:**

443- <u>Moses</u>[7] Wadleigh, (Philip[6], Moses[5],
Ephriam[4], John[3], Robert[2], John[1]), b. September
3, 1777 in Salisbury, Mass. died young. (Ref.
3)

444- <u>Samuel</u>[7] Wadleigh, (Philip[6], Moses[5],
Ephriam[4], John[3], Robert[2], John[1]), b. December
11, 1778 in Salisbury, Mass., d. June 19, 1862
in Salisbury, Mass. m. November 10, 1813 (or
1815) Miriam Gordon Webster, d. October 22,
1865 in Salisbury. (Ref. 3)

711 - Samuel	712 - Benjamin

445- <u>Ephriam</u>[7] Wadleigh, (Philip[6], Moses[5],
Ephriam[4], John[3], Robert[2], John[1]), b. February
16, 1781 in Salisbury, Mass. m. Sarah Farlie
of Salem, Mass. no additional data. (Ref. 3)

713 - Eliza Ann	714 - Mary Ann

446- <u>Henry</u>[7] Wadleigh, (Philip[6], Moses[5],
Ephriam[4], John[3], Robert[2], John[1]), b. December
1, 1782 in Salisbury, Mass., d. August 1842 in
Salisbury. m. December 1811 Sally Titcomb of
Kensington, N.H., d. December 24, 1877 in
Salisbury. (Ref. 3)

715 - William	718 - Henry K.
716 - Sarah	719 - Clarissa
717 - Susanna	720 - Andrew J.

447- John[7] Wadleigh, (Philip[6], Moses[5], Ephriam[4], John[3], Robert[2], John[1]), b. September 1784 in Salisbury, Mass., d. January 7, 1871. m. November 26, 1812 Miriam Tuxbury, d. October 20, 1854. (Ref. 3)

721 - John	725 - John Bergin
722 - Frederick A.	726 - M. Louisa
723 - Mary	727 - Caroline T.
724 - Hannah	

448- Rhoda[7] Wadleigh, (Philip[6], Moses[5], Ephriam[4], John[3], Robert[2], John[1]), b. November 25, 1788 in Salisbury, Mass. m. Stephen Greeley. no additional data. (Ref. 3)

449- Philip[7] Wadleigh, (Philip[6], Moses[5], Ephriam[4], John[3], Robert[2], John[1]), b. December 30, 1794 in Salisbury, Mass. d. September 27, 1840 in Salisbury. m. December 30, 1824 Annie Morrill, b. in Salisbury, d. April 24, 1874 in Salisbury. (Ref. 3)
    728 - Joseph Guest

450- Hannah[7] Wadleigh, (Philip[6], Moses[5], Ephriam[4], John[3], Robert[2], John[1]), b. in Salisbury, Mass. m. 1817 Philip Webster of Salisbury. no additional data. (Ref. 3)

729 - Hannah	732 - infant
730 - Eliza	733 - Mary Ann
731 - infant	

Issue of 292- Ephriam[6] Wadleigh and Molly/Mary (Barnard) Wadleigh:

451- Eliphalet[7] Wadleigh, (Ephriam[6], Moses[5], Ephriam[4], John[3], Robert[2], John[1]), b. May 8, 1784 in Salisbury, Mass., d. May 10, 1870 in Salisbury. m. April 10, 1814 Elizabeth Currier, d. in Salisbury. (Ref. 3)

734 - Abigail	736 - Ephriam
735 - Joseph	

452- <u>Sally</u>[7] Wadleigh, (Ephriam[6], Moses[5], Ephriam[4], John[3], Robert[2], John[1]), b. March 11, 1786 in Salisbury, Mass. m. Enoch Currier. no additional data. (Ref. 3)

453- <u>Ephriam</u>[7] Wadleigh, (Ephriam[6], Moses[5], Ephriam[4], John[3], Robert[2], John[1]), b. July 1, 1786 in Salisbury, Mass., d. December 12, 1826 in Salisbury. m. March 11, 1812 Lydia Leonard, d. June 15, 1861 in Salisbury. (Ref. 3)

    737 - Ethelinda   739 - George
    738 - Mary   740 - Lydia

454- <u>Elizabeth</u>[7] Wadleigh, (Ephriam[6], Moses[5], Ephriam[4], John[3], Robert[2], John[1]), b. January 30, 1791 in Salisbury, Mass., d. September 24, 1875 in Salisbury. m. April 15, 1811 Samuel Hoyt, d. August 24, 1841 in Salisbury. (Ref. 3)

    741 - Ebenezer   744 - Mary
    742 - Charles   745 - Elizabeth
    743 - Mary

455- <u>Polly</u>[7] Wadleigh, (Ephriam[6], Moses[5], Ephriam[4], John[3], Robert[2], John[1]), b. August 9, 1793 in Salisbury, Mass., d. August 10, 1823 in Salisbury. m. 1st 440- Peter[7] Wadleigh, (Adams[6], Moses[5], Ephriam[4], John[3], Robert[2], John[1]), b. June 22, 1786 in Salisbury, d. October 26, 1815 in Salisbury, m. a 2nd time. no additional data. (Ref. 3) For issue by 1st h., see: 440- Peter[7] Wadleigh

456- <u>Nancy</u>[7] Wadleigh, (Ephriam[6], Moses[5], Ephriam[4], John[3], Robert[2], John[1]), b. July 14, 1796 in Salisbury, Mass. m. Edward Flanders. no additional data. (Ref. 3)

457- <u>Ezekiel</u>[7] Wadleigh, (Ephriam[6], Moses[5], Ephriam[4], John[3], Robert[2], John[1]), b. November 29, 1798 in Salisbury, Mass. m. Elizabeth[8]

Blaisdell, (Samuel[7], Stephen[6], Samuel[5], Ephraim[4], Ebenezer[3], Henry[2], Ralph[1]), d. of Samuel[7] and Ruth Blaisdell of Amesbury and Newburyport, Mass., b. January 21, 1797 in Salisbury, (Ref. 4: June in Amesbury). (Ref. 3, 4-640)

746 - Polly	748 - Eben Pearson
747 - Charles T. P.	749 - Hannah

458- <u>Moses</u>[7] <u>Wadleigh</u>, (Ephriam[6], Moses[5], Ephriam[4], John[3], Robert[2], John[1]), b. March 10, 1802 in Salisbury, Mass. d. in Alabama. unmarried. Res. Salisbury, Mass. and Alabama. (Ref. 3)

459- <u>Pauline</u>[7] <u>Wadleigh</u>, (Ephriam[6], Moses[5], Ephriam[4], John[3], Robert[2], John[1]), b. September 17, 1804 in Salisbury, Mass. m. 1825 David Carr. no additional data. (Ref. 3)

460- <u>Charloi</u>[7] <u>Wadleigh</u>, (Ephriam[6], Moses[5], Ephriam[4], John[3], Robert[2], John[1]), b. February 17, 1807 in Salisbury, Mass., d. 1810 in Alabama. unmarried. Res. Salisbury, Mass. and Alabama. (Ref. 3)

461- <u>Ebenezer</u>[7] <u>Wadleigh</u>, (Ephriam[6], Moses[5], Ephriam[4], John[3], Robert[2], John[1]), b. September 12, 1809 in Salisbury, Mass., d. January 3, 1810 in Salisbury. died in childhood. (Ref. 3)

462- <u>Jonathan</u>[7] <u>Wadleigh</u>, (Ephriam[6], Moses[5], Ephriam[4], John[3], Robert[2], John[1]), b. January 7, 1812 in Salisbury, Mass. m. 1st Mary Leach, wid. of Mr. Lowell. m. 2nd Elizabeth Blumbley, a widow. no additional data. (Ref. 3)

Issue of 299- Benjamin[6] Wadleigh and Hannah (Kezar) Wadleigh:

463- <u>Mehitible</u>[7] <u>Wadleigh</u>, (Benjamin[6], Thomas[5], Benjamin[4], Robert[3], Robert[2], John[1]), b. March 4, 1770 in Hampstead, N.H., d. December 8, 1846 in Sutton, N.H. m. December 30, 1793 Jonathan Carr of Canaan, N.H. no additional data. w. became noted and influential leader in Calvinist Church. (Ref. 25-39 & 968 & 990)

    750 - Sally   751 - Daniel

464- <u>Hannah</u>[7] <u>Wadleigh</u>, (Benjamin[6], Thomas[5], Benjamin[4], Robert[3], Robert[2], John[1]), b. September 6, 1772 in Sutton N.H., d. April 11, 1841. m. December 29, 1796 Joseph Bean. no additional data. Possibly moved to Hatley, Quebec, Canada. (Ref. 3, 25-35 & 38 & 969)

    752 - Daniel   754 - Hannah
    753 - William

465- <u>Dolly</u>[7] <u>Wadleigh</u>, (Benjamin[6], Thomas[5], Benjamin[4], Robert[3], Robert[2], John[1]), b. February 8, 1775 in Sutton, N.H., d. November 19, 1797 in Sutton. (Ref. 3, 25-969)

466- <u>Jesse</u>[7] <u>Wadleigh</u>, (Benjamin[6], Thomas[5], Benjamin[4], Robert[3], Robert[2], John[1]), b. January 6, 1777 in Sutton N.H. m. Lucy Turner. no additional data. Res. Sutton, N.H. and Canada in 1797. (Ref. 3, 25-969)

467- <u>Eliphalet</u>[7] <u>Wadleigh</u>, (Benjamin[6], Thomas[5], Benjamin[4], Robert[3], Robert[2], John[1]), b. April 19, 1779 in Sutton, N.H., d. March 4, 1780 in Sutton. died in childhood. (Ref. 3-969)

468- <u>John</u>[7] <u>Wadleigh</u>, (Benjamin[6], Thomas[5], Benjamin[4], Robert[3], Robert[2], John[1]), b. July 10, 1781 in Sutton, N.H., d. April 25, 1843 in Hatley, Quebec, Canada. m. 1808 Judith Emery,

d. 1859 in Hatley. Res. Sutton, N.H. and
Hatley, Quebec. (Ref. 3, 25-969)
    755 - Amasa   756 - Lydia

469- <u>Benjamin</u>[7] <u>Wadleigh</u>, (Benjamin[6], Thomas[5],
Benjamin[4], Robert[3], Robert[2], John[1]), b. October
8, 1783 in Sutton, N.H., d. June 24, 1864 in
Sutton. m. August 21, 1803 Polly Marston, d.
of Jacob and Lydia (Gile) Marston, b. ca. 1781,
d. December 17, 1857 in Sutton. Known as
"Judge Wadleigh" acting as arbitrator by mutual
consent over considerable time and area. (Ref.
3, 25-38 & 969 & 982)
    757 - David   762 - Amanda
    758 - Eliphalet   763 - Hannah
    759 - Luther   764 - Lydia F.
    760 - Erastus   765 - Benjamin
    761 - Milton   766 - Gilbert

470- <u>Eliphalet</u>[7] <u>Wadleigh</u>, (Benjamin[6], Thomas[5],
Benjamin[4], Robert[3], Robert[2], John[1]), b. July
28, 1785 in Sutton, N.H., d. March 19, 1787 in
Sutton. died in childhood. (Ref. 3, 25-969)

471- <u>Judith</u>[7] <u>Wadleigh</u>, (Benjamin[6], Thomas[5],
Benjamin[4], Robert[3], Robert[2], John[1]), b. in
Sutton, N.H. m. Ebenezer Fowler, (or Towle).
no additional data. Res. Sutton, N.H. and
Canada. (Ref. 3, 25-39 & 969)

472- <u>Simeon</u>[7] <u>Wadleigh</u>, (Benjamin[6], Thomas[5],
Benjamin[4], Robert[3], Robert[2], John[1]), b. April
15, 1789 in Sutton, N.H., d. April 21, 1798 in
Sutton. died in childhood. (Ref. 3, 25-969)

473- <u>Ebenezer</u>[7] <u>Wadleigh</u>, (Benjamin[6], Thomas[5],
Benjamin[4], Robert[3], Robert[2], John[1]), b. May
1(13), 1791 in Sutton, N.H., d. December 15,
1791 in Sutton. died in childhood. (Ref. 3,
25-969)

474- <u>Susanna</u>[7] Wadleigh, (Benjamin[6], Thomas[5], Benjamin[4], Robert[3], Robert[2], John[1]), b. March 23, 1793 in Sutton, N.H., d. May 2, 1876 in Sutton. m. April 2, 1811 Capt. John[6] Pillsbury, (Micajah[5], Caleb[4], Caleb[3], Moses[2], William[1]) of Amesbury, Mass. s. of Micajah and Sarah (Sargent) Pillsbury, b. May 24, 1789 in Amesbury, Mass., d. October 11, 1856 in Sutton. h. became prominent in Sutton, served as selectman, as Legislator and as Justice. Occ. Joiner. Res. South Village of Sutton. (Ref. 3, 25-39 & 969, 50-22)

767 - Simon W.	770 - John Sargent
768 - George Alfred	771 - Benjamin F.
769 - Dolly Wadleigh	

Issue of 300- Jonathan[6] Wadleigh and Mrs. (Miles) Wadleigh:

475- <u>Thomas Miles</u>[7] Wadleigh, (Jonathan[6], Thomas[5], Benjamin[4], Robert[3], Robert[2], John[1]), b. November 21, 1774 in Kingston, N.H. m. June 16, 1808 Rachel Gile of Northfield, N.H. no additional data. Mother died while an infant, taken by his uncle 302- Thomas Wadleigh to her relatives in Salisbury or Northfield, Mass. (Ref. 3, 25)

    772 - Horace

Issue of 300- Jonathan[6] Wadleigh and Abigail (Eastman) Wadleigh:

476- <u>Jonathan Eastman</u>[7] Wadleigh, (Jonathan[6], Thomas[5], Benjamin[4], Robert[3], Robert[2], John[1]), b. March 17, 1777 in Northfield, N.H. m. March 28, 1801 Sally Buswell of Hampstead, N.H. no additional data. (Ref. 3)

773 - infant	776 - Jonathan
774 - Abigail	777 - Ebenezer Stevens
775 - Sally Sargent	

Issue of 307- Aaron[6] Wadleigh and Abigail (Simon) Wadleigh:

526- Thomas[7] Wadleigh, (Aaron[6], Thomas[5], Benjamin[4], Robert[3], Robert[2], John[1]), b. January 22, 1791 in Sutton, N.H., died in childhood by thrown stone. (Ref. 3)

Issue of 308- Ephriam[6] Wadleigh and Alice (Little) Wadleigh:

527- Samuel[7] Wadleigh, (Ephriam[6], Thomas[5], Benjamin[4], Robert[3], Robert[2], John[1]), b. January 17, 1794 in Sutton, N.H. m. 1st Polly Marsh. m. 2nd Polly Evans. no additional data. (Ref. 3, 25-968)

528- Elizabeth[7] Wadleigh, (Ephriam[6], Thomas[5], Benjamin[4], Robert[3], Robert[2], John[1]), b. October 7, 1796 in Sutton, N.H. m. Moses Colburn. no additional data. (Ref. 3, 25-968)

529- Mary[7] Wadleigh, (Ephriam[6], Thomas[5], Benjamin[4], Robert[3], Robert[2], John[1]), b. December 20, 1798 in Sutton, N.H. m. Nathaniel Batchelder. no additional data. (Ref. 3, 25-968)

530- Taylor[7] Wadleigh, (Ephriam[6], Thomas[5], Benjamin[4], Robert[3], Robert[2], John[1]), b. December 8, 1799 in Fisherfield, N.H., d. November 29, 1866 in Hatley, Quebec, Canada. m. ca. 1819 Melinda Hovey of Hatley, d. July 26, 1864. Occ. Farmer and politician. Was in the rebellion of 1837-39 and jailed in Montreal Jail in 1837 for High Treason and released. moved to Canada ca. 1802. (Ref. 3, 25-968)

```
813 - Horace          816 - Everett Frederick
814 - Malinda         817 - Elen
815 - Alice C.
```

531- Thomas[7] Wadleigh, (Ephriam[6], Thomas[5], Benjamin[4], Robert[3], Robert[2], John[1]), b. April 15, 1802 in Hatley, Quebec, Canada, d. September 4, 1850. m. Hannah N. Little, d. of Deacon Ezekiel Little, b. March 20, 1808, d. September 21, 1879. (Ref. 3, 25-968)

532- Ruth[7] Wadleigh, (Ephriam[6], Thomas[5], Benjamin[4], Robert[3], Robert[2], John[1]), b. September 13, 1806 in Hatley, Quebec, Canada. m. 1st Thomas Paradis. m. 2nd John Belden. no additional data.   (Ref. 3, 25-968)

533- Roxanna[7] Wadleigh, (Ephriam[6], Thomas[5], Benjamin[4], Robert[3], Robert[2], John[1]), b. May 16, 1808 in Hatley, Quebec, Canada. m. Chauncy Kezar. no additional data. (Ref. 3, 25-968)

534- Luke[7] Wadleigh, (Ephriam[6], Thomas[5], Benjamin[4], Robert[3], Robert[2], John[1]), b. August 10, 1810 in Hatley, Quebec, Canada. m. Phebe Rowell. no additional data. (Ref. 3, 25-968)

Issue of Benjamin Evans and 310- Susanna (Wadleigh) Evans:

535- Abigail Evans, (Wadleigh: Susanna[6], Thomas[5], Benjamin[4], Robert[3], Robert[2], John[1]), b. April 30, 1796 in Sutton, N.H., d. July 29, 1882. m. August 24, 1813, Hon. Reuben Porter. no additional data. (Ref. 3, 25-697 & 979)

536- Susan Evans, (Wadleigh: Susanna[6], Thomas[5], Benjamin[4], Robert[3], Robert[2], John[1]). died young. no additional data. (Ref. 25-697)

537- Susan Evans, (Wadleigh: Susanna[6], Thomas[5], Benjamin[4], Robert[3], Robert[2], John[1]). m. Dr. Leonard Eaton. no additional data. (Ref. 25-697 & 979)

538- <u>Lucinda Evans</u>, (Wadleigh: Susanna[6], Thomas[5], Benjamin[4], Robert[3], Robert[2], John[1]), b. February 18, 1803 in Sutton, N.H. m. Nathan S. Colby of Warner, N.H. no additional data. (Ref. 3, 25-697 & 979)

| 818 - Charles | 820 - Walter |
| 819 - Walter | 821 - Elizabeth |

539- <u>Sarah Evans</u>, (Wadleigh: Susanna[6], Thomas[5], Benjamin[4], Robert[3], Robert[2], John[1]). m. Harrison D. Robertson. no additional data. (Ref. 25-697 & 979)

| 822 - Lucinda | 824 - John |
| 823 - Sarah | |

540- <u>Sophronia Evans</u>, (Wadleigh: Susanna[6], Thomas[5], Benjamin[4], Robert[3], Robert[2], John[1]), b. April 1, 1807 in Sutton, N.H. m. Stephen C. Badger. no additional data. (Ref. 3, 25-979)

825 - Benjamin E.   826 - William

541- <u>Hannah Evans</u>, (Wadleigh: Susanna[6], Thomas[5], Benjamin[4], Robert[3], Robert[2], John[1]), d. May 26, 1885. m. as 2nd w. Abner Woodman. no additional data. (Ref. 25-697)

542- <u>Benjamin Evans</u>, (Wadleigh: Susanna[6], Thomas[5], Benjamin[4], Robert[3], Robert[2], John[1]), died in childhood. (Ref. 25-697)

Issue of 311- Daniel[6] Wadleigh and Dolly (Bartlett) Wadleigh:

543- <u>John[7] Wadleigh</u>, (Daniel[6], John[5], Benjamin[4], Robert[3], Robert[2], John[1]), b. January 10, 1789 in Kingston, N.H., d. May 25, 1845 in Kingston. m. Susan, d. January 11, 1831 in Kingston, h. and w. bur. in South Kingston Cemetery. (Ref. 3)

544- <u>Joseph</u>[7] <u>Wadleigh</u>, (Daniel[6], John[5], Benjamin[4], Robert[3], Robert[2], John[1]), b. October 30, 1790 in Kingston, N.H., d. April 21, 1826 in Kingston, bur. in Kingston Plaines Cemetery. m. December 7, 1815 Anna Sleeper of Kingston, d. of Jonathan and Mary (Clark) Sleeper, b. 1798, d. 1883 in Kingston, bur. in West Kingston Cemetery. (Ref. 3)

  827 - Jonathan S. 830 - Nancy
  828 - Daniel   831 - Daniel
  829 - Hannah

545- <u>Daniel</u>[7] <u>Wadleigh</u>, (Daniel[6], John[5], Benjamin[4], Robert[3], Robert[2], John[1]), b. August 14, 1783 in Kingston, N.H., d. July 31, 1862 in Kingston, bur. in South Kingston Cemetery. m. April 11, 1839 Sally Davis of Hampstead, N.H., d. of John and Betty (Kimball) Davis, b. March 12, 1808. Occ. blacksmith (Ref. 3)

  832 - Elizabeth 833 - Joseph Bartlett

546- <u>Hannah</u>[7] <u>Wadleigh</u>, (Daniel[6], John[5], Benjamin[4], Robert[3], Robert[2], John[1]), b. June 26, 1797 in Kingston, N.H., d. September. 12, 1800 in Kingston, bur. in Kingston Plaines Cemetery. (Ref. 3)

Issue of 326- Joseph[6] Wadleigh and Hannah (Stevens) Wadleigh:

547- <u>Hiram</u>[7] <u>Wadleigh</u>, (Joseph[6], Joseph[5], Joseph[4], Robert[3], Robert[2], John[1]), b. June 8, 1808 in Brentwood, N.H., d. May 13, 1833. (Ref. 3)

548- <u>Betsey</u>[7] <u>Wadleigh</u>, (Joseph[6], Joseph[5], Joseph[4], Robert[3], Robert[2], John[1]), b. June 9, 1809 in Brentwood, N.H., d. March 4, 1891. m. Abraham Smith Sanborn. no additional data. Res. Fremont, N.H. (Ref. 3)

549- <u>Oliver</u>[7] <u>Wadleigh</u>, (Joseph[6], Joseph[5], Joseph[4], Robert[3], Robert[2], John[1]), b. 1811 in Brentwood, N.H., d. October 6, 1885 in Brentwood. m. Marcia M. Holbrook, d. 1902. (Ref. 3)

    834 - Eliza Ann   835 - Elwell

550- <u>Calvin</u>[7] <u>Wadleigh</u>, (Joseph[6], Joseph[5], Joseph[4], Robert[3], Robert[2], John[1]), b. 1813 in Brentwood, N.H. m. Lucy Tarr. no additional data. (Ref. 3)

551- <u>Sarah</u> <u>Frances</u>[7] <u>Wadleigh</u>, (Joseph[6], Joseph[5], Joseph[4], Robert[3], Robert[2], John[1]), b. March 1, 1815 in Brentwood, N.H. m. Timothy Tilton of Fremont, N.H. no additional data. (Ref. 3)

552- <u>Susan</u> <u>Dole</u>[7] <u>Wadleigh</u>, (Joseph[6], Joseph[5], Joseph[4], Robert[3], Robert[2], John[1]), b. December 29, 1817 in Brentwood, N.H., d. December 3, 1894. (Ref. 3)

553- <u>Nancy</u> <u>Currier</u>[7] <u>Wadleigh</u>, (Joseph[6], Joseph[5], Joseph[4], Robert[3], Robert[2], John[1]), b. October 1821 in Brentwood, N.H., d. May 8, 1886 in Kingston, N.H. (Ref. 3)

Issue of 330- Enos Dole[6] Wadley and Sarah (Colcord) Wadley:

554- <u>William</u> <u>Morrill</u>[7] <u>Wadley</u>, (Enos Dole[6], Joseph[5], Joseph[4], Robert[3], Robert[2], John[1]), b. November 12, 1813 in Brentwood, N.H., d. August 10, 1882 at Saratoga, N.Y., bur. in Old Cemetery at Great Hill Plantation, Bolingbroke, Ga. m. November 12, 1840 Rebecca Barnard Everingham, d. of John and Sarah Weber (Barnard) Everingham of Savannah, Ga., b. May 12, 1819, d. June 4, 1905 at Great Hill

Plantation, bur. in Old Cemetery at Great Hill.
Occ. Blacksmith, Superintendant of
Transportation for Adjutant-General Dept. with
Confederate States of America and President of
Central Railroad from 1866-1882. Res.
Brentwood, N.H.; Savannah, Georgia (1834),
Saratoga, N.Y., and owner of Great Hill
Plantation, Ga. (Ref. 3, 11)

836	- William Oconius	841	- Loring Reynolds
837	- Sarah Lois	842	- George Dole
838	- John Dole	843	- John Everingham
839	- Mary Millen		
840	- Rebecca Everingham		

555- <u>Satura</u> <u>Dole</u>[7] <u>Wadley</u>, (Enos Dole[6], Joseph[5],
Joseph[4], Robert[3], Robert[2], John[1]), b. November
19, 1815 in Brentwood, N.H., d. Sept. 2, 1881.
m. 1841 Lucian M. Pike of Newmarket, N.H. no
additional data. (Ref. 3, 11)

556- <u>Lydia</u> <u>Colcord</u>[7] <u>Wadley</u>, (Enos Dole[6],
Joseph[5], Joseph[4], Robert[3], Robert[2], John[1]), b.
January 22, 1818 in Brentwood, N.H., d. July
22, 1860. m. 1843 David Josselyn. no
additional data. (Ref. 3, 11)

557- <u>David</u> <u>Richard</u>[7] <u>Wadley</u>, (Enos Dole[6],
Joseph[5], Joseph[4], Robert[3], Robert[2], John[1]), b.
November 11, 1819 in Brentwood, N.H., d.
December 20, 1883 in Atlanta, Ga. m. 1848 Mary
Gossyevert, d. June 7, 1899, bur. in Old
Cemetery at Great Hill Plantation, Bolingbroke,
Ga. (Ref. 3, 11)

558- <u>Moses</u>[7] <u>Wadley</u>, (Enos Dole[6], Joseph[5],
Joseph[4], Robert[3], Robert[2], John[1]), b. April 29,
1822 in Brentwood, N.H., d. January 6, 1884 in
Augusta, Ga. m. 1860 Mary Jane Clark. no
additional data. (Ref. 3, 11)

559- Dole[7] Wadley, (Enos Dole[6], Joseph[5], Joseph[4], Robert[3], Robert[2], John[1]), b. July 24, 1824 in Brentwood, N.H., d. April 9, 1891. m. 1861 Elizabeth Carroll Pierce, d. of Elbridge Gerry and Sarah Jane (Gorham) Pierce, b. July 13, 1806 in Hollowell, Me., d. 1881. Moved to Georgia in 1844. (Ref. 3, 11, 12)
    844 - Sarah Pierce 845 - George

NOTE: Elbridge Gerry Pierce was b. December 1, 1801 in Hollowell, Me. and s. of Ebenezer and Charity (Hinds) Pierce of Hollowell.   Sarah Jane[6] Gorham, (Gorham: Barnabas[5], Stephen[4], Josiah[3], Joseph[2], John[1]), was b. July 13, 1806 in Hollowell and is d. of Barnabas[5] and Jane (Johnson) Gorham of Hollowell, Jane Johnson (June 21, 1784 - September 5, 1837) is d. of Benjamin Johnson of Hollowell.

Issue of 337- Joseph Brown and Susan (Holman) Brown:

560- Miss Brown, (Wadleigh: Joseph[6], Abraham[5], Mary[4], Robert[3], Robert[2], John[1]). m. Harvey D. Parker. Founder of Parker House of Boston. no additional data. Res. Boston, Mass. (Ref. 30)

561- Miss Brown, (Wadleigh: Joseph[6], Abraham[5], Mary[4], Robert[3], Robert[2], John[1]), d. after 1900. m. Mr. Bickford. no additional data. Res. Exeter, N.H. (Ref. 30)

Issue of 338- Levi Brown and Sarah (Drake) Brown:

562- Frederick Brown, (Wadleigh: Levi[6], Abraham[5], Mary[4], Robert[3], Robert[2], John[1]). no additional data. did not marry. (Ref. 30)

563- <u>Polly Brown</u>, (Wadleigh: Levi[6], Abraham[5], Mary[4], Robert[3], Robert[2], John[1]). no additional data. did not marry. (Ref. 30)

564- <u>Levi Brown</u>, (Wadleigh: Levi[6], Abraham[5], Mary[4], Robert[3], Robert[2], John[1]), d. 1869. m. Miss Robinson of North Hampton, N.H. No additional data. (Ref. 30)
    846 - George H.   847 - Alice

565- <u>Sewell Brown</u>, (Wadleigh: Levi[6], Abraham[5], Mary[4], Robert[3], Robert[2], John[1]), d. 1867. m. Miss Robinson of North Hampton, N.H. No additional data. Occ. Shoemaker. (Ref. 30)
    848 - son   850 - Mary E.
    849 - son   851 - Martha

Issue of 340- Samuel[3] Melcher and Esther (Green) Melcher:

566- <u>Samuel[4] Melcher</u>, (Wadleigh: Samuel[6], Elizabeth[5], Benjamin[4], Mary[3], Robert[2], John[1]; Melcher: Samuel[3], Samuel[2], (?)[1]), b. ca. 1737, d. 1823. m. January 1, 1763, Elizabeth Hilliard, d. of Jonathan Hilliard, b. ca. 1742, d. 1826. Res. Melcher Homestead in Hampton Falls, N.H., (Ref. 30)
    852 - Joseph   854 - Hannah
    853 - Levi

Issue of 344- Joseph[6] Wadleigh and Betsey (Longfellow) Wadleigh:

567- <u>Nancy[7] Wadleigh</u>, (Joseph[6], Joseph[5], Joseph[4], Henry[3], Robert[2], John[1]), b. March 31, 1777 in Kensington, N.H., d. January 6, 1801. m. Jesse[6] Tuck, (Jesse[5], Edward[4], John[3], Edward[2], Robert[1] Tuck), b. 1773/4 in Kensington, N.H., bpt. March 17, 1774. h. lived in Maine after w.'s death. (Ref. 3)

568- <u>Susanna</u>[7] <u>Wadleigh</u>, (Joseph[6], Joseph[5], Joseph[4], Henry[3], Robert[2], John[1]), b. June 20, 1779 in Kensington, N.H., d. March 10 (or 25), 1826. m. November 30, 1803 Josiah Rowe of Kensington, N.H. no additional data. (Ref. 3)

569- <u>Betsey</u>[7] <u>Wadleigh</u>, (Joseph[6], Joseph[5], Joseph[4], Henry[3], Robert[2], John[1]), b. December 24, 1781 in Kensington, N.H., d. September 2, 1783. died in childhood. (Ref. 3)

570- <u>John</u>[7] <u>Wadleigh</u>, (Joseph[6], Joseph[5], Joseph[4], Henry[3], Robert[2], John[1]), b. March 25, 1784 in Kensington, N.H., d. February 19, 1822 (apparently murdered, verdict against John Blaisdell was "guilty of manslaughter"). m. November 16, 1804 Mary Call of Kensington, b. d. October 27, 1839. (Ref. 3, 21)
      855 - Mark John

571- <u>Betsey</u>[7] <u>Wadleigh</u>, (Joseph[6], Joseph[5], Joseph[4], Henry[3], Robert[2], John[1]), b. March 28, 1786 in Kensington, N.H., d. December 5, 1867 in East Kingston, N.H. m. September 10, 1817 Levi Tilton of East Kingston, d. in East Kingston. Res. East Kingston and Middle Road, site 50 Kensington after 1832. (Ref. 3, 21)
      856 - Martha F. Shaw   857 - Nathan

572- <u>Joseph Dearborn</u>[7] <u>Wadleigh</u>, (Joseph[6], Joseph[5], Joseph[4], Henry[3], Robert[2], John[1]), b. March 3, 1788 in Kensington, N.H., d. July 11, 1839. m. December 23, 1807 Sarah Patten of Kensington, d. March 3, 1861. (Ref. 3)
      858 - Nancy   861 - Mary
      859 - James   862 - Jonathan B.
      860 - Sally   863 - Joseph Plummer

573- <u>Ruth</u>[7] <u>Wadleigh</u>, (Joseph[6], Joseph[5], Joseph[4], Henry[3], Robert[2], John[1]), b. June 13, 1790 in Kensington, N.H., d. May 10, 1877. m.

May 8, 1843 Jonathan Rowe of Kensington, N.H.
s. of Nancy Rowe of Kensington, d. October 15,
1869. Killed in action in Civil War, mother
rec'd $8.00 per month pension. (Ref. 3, 21)

574- Jeremiah[7] Wadleigh, (Joseph[6], Joseph[5],
Joseph[4], Henry[3], Robert[2], John[1]), b. November
17, 1792 in Kensington, N.H., d. June 12, 1872
in Kensington, N.H.   m. in Hampton Falls, N.H.
May 7, 1843 Elizabeth B. Blake of Kensington,
sis. to Ira Blake, d. April 13, 1875 in
Kensington. (Ref. 3)

      864 - son   867 - son
      865 - George   868 - Ann Eliza
      866 - Ellery Channing

575- Mark[7] Wadleigh, (Joseph[6], Joseph[5],
Joseph[4], Henry[3], Robert[2], John[1]), b. December
20, 1794 in Kensington, N.H., d. May 2, 1862 in
Kensington. m. 1st August 12, 1818 Sarah
Bullock, d. March 9, 1837 in Kensington. m.
2nd March 14, 1838 Louisa (Ladd) Gove, wid. of
Mr. Gove, d. September 7, 1872 in Kensington.
Occ. sea captain, sailed the "Citizen" owned by
John Wills of Newbury under Nathaniel S.
Osgood, ship's master; later ship's master for
same owners.   (Ref. 3) 869 - 874 by 1st wife.

      869 - Mark   872 - George J.
      870 - Alwin C.   873 - Ruth Ann
      871 - Sarah E.   874 - Sarah Coffin

576- Sewall[7] Wadleigh, (Joseph[6], Joseph[5],
Joseph[4], Henry[3], Robert[2], John[1]), b. July 10,
1797 in Kensington, N.H., d. April 12, 1829 in
Kensington, N.H. m. February 26, 1820 Susan
Sanborn, d. of Jewett and Susan (Prescott)
Sanborn of Kensington, (Susan Prescott is d. of
Jonathan Prescott and Rachel (Clifford)
Prescott), d. April 30, 1881 in Kensington.
Veteran of War of 1812. Note: Ref. 21 cites
Susan Wadleigh, a widow of the War of 1812
recieving a Federal pension of $8.00 per month
as published on December 14, 1883. (Ref. 3)

875 - Harriett   877 - Cyrus Dearborn
876 - Sewall   878 - Susan W.

Issue of 346- John[6] Wadleigh and Hannah (Prescott) Wadleigh:

577- Hannah[7] Wadleigh, (John[6], Joseph[5], Joseph[4], Henry[3], Robert[2], John[1]), b. August 1782 in Hampton Falls, N.H., died in childhood. (Ref. 3)

578- Leah Prescott[7] Wadleigh, (John[6], Joseph[5], Joseph[4], Henry[3], Robert[2], John[1]), b. August 29, 1785 in Hampton Falls, N.H. m. February 8, 1806 Horatio Gates Prescott of Gilmanton, N.H. no additional data. (Ref. 3)

579- Joseph[7] Wadleigh, (John[6], Joseph[5], Joseph[4], Henry[3], Robert[2], John[1]), b. in Hampton Falls, N.H., died in childhood. (Ref. 3)

580- Joseph[7] Wadleigh, (John[6], Joseph[5], Joseph[4], Henry[3], Robert[2], John[1]), b. in Hampton Falls, N.H. (Ref. 3)

581- Hannah[7] Wadleigh, (John[6], Joseph[5], Joseph[4], Henry[3], Robert[2], John[1]), b. in Hampton Falls, N.H. (Ref. 3)

Issue of Simeon Prescott and 347- Ruth (Wadleigh) Prescott:

582- Joseph Prescott, (Ruth[6], Joseph[5], Joseph[4], Henry[3], Robert[2], John[1]), b. October 1, 1788, d. November 24, 1809. (Ref. 2, 3)

Issue of 349- William Henry[6] Wadleigh and Abigail (Stockbridge) Wadleigh:

583- William Henry[7] Wadleigh, (William Henry[6], Joseph[5], Joseph[4], Henry[3], Robert[2], John[1]), b. November 28, 1810 in Kensington, N.H. on the old Wadleigh farm near Tuck's Corner (also called Five Corners), d. July 3, 1901 in Kensington. m. September 26, 1843 Mehitible Ann (Masters) Mallon of Hampton Falls, N.H., wid. of Mr. Mallon, d. of the Rev. Otis Wing of Hampton Falls, b. November 25, 1816, d. January 13, 1884. Res. Kensington, N.H. (Ref. 2, 3, 21)

879 - Lucy Jane	882 - Anna Marshall
880 - Frank Lawrence	883 - Charles Fremont
881 - Ellen Foster	

NOTE: Mehitible Mallon had two sons, James and John, by Mr. Mallon. James was killed in Civil War in 1865 at Wilmington, N.C. John lived with Mr. Wadleigh until age 13, became a merchant seaman sailing around the world and fishing off Labrador. He then became a cabinet maker in Exeter. Enlisted and served the entire Civil War. He was the first to decorate C.W. veterans graves during a visit, with other soldiers, in 1878.

584- Daniel Foster[7] Wadleigh, (William Henry[6], Joseph[5], Joseph[4], Henry[3], Robert[2], John[1]), b. March 20, 1814 in Kensington, N.H. on the old Wadleigh farm near Tuck's Corner (also called Five Corners), d. April 12, 1898 in Green Ridge, Pettis Co., Mo., m. December 16, 1842 on farm near Epsom, N.H. Lucinda[7] Libby, (Libby: David[6], Jethro[5], Reuben[4], Isaac[3], Anthony[2], John[1]), d. of David and Martha (Dolbeer) Libby of Epsom and (prev.) Rye, N.H., (David Libby is s. of Jethro Libby of Epsom, N.H.), b. July 14, 1815, d. August 12, 1873 in Green Ridge. Occ. Farmer. Res. Kensington, N.H., Grundy Co. Ill., and Green Ridge, Pettis Co. Mo. In 1838 joined to build new Unitarian/Universalist Union Meeting house, purchased pew in 1840. (Ref. 1, 2, 3, 16)

884 - Charles Edwin   888 - Everett
885 - Helen Maria   889 - Clara Eugenia
886 - Maaura   890 - Henry Libby
887 - Abbie Jane

585- <u>Sarah Jane</u>[7] <u>Wadleigh</u>, (William Henry[6], Joseph[5], Joseph[4], Henry[3], Robert[2], John[1]), b. May 10, 1816 or April 14, 1816 in Kensington, N.H. on the old Wadleigh farm near Tuck's Corner (also called Five Corners), d. June 7, 1899 in Peoria, Ill, bur. Rutland, Ill. m. 1837 John Frances Gove of Hampton Falls, N.H., b. 1815, d. January 1895 in Peoria, bur. Rutland. Res. Kensington, N.H., Rutland, Ill. (Ref. 2, 3)

891 - Aaron   893 - Francis
892 - Frank

586- <u>Joseph Dearborn</u>[7] <u>Wadleigh</u>, (William Henry[6], Joseph[5], Joseph[4], Henry[3], Robert[2], John[1]), b. May 10, 1818 in Kensington, N.H. on the old Wadleigh farm near Tuck's Corner (also called Five Corners), d. February 23, 1904 in Green Ridge, Mo. m. May 24, 1843, (or May 28,) 1843 Frances Esther Prescott of Kensington, b. February 13, 1826 in Exeter, N.H., d. September 10, 1877 in Green Ridge. Res. Kensington and Exeter N.H., Rutland, Ill., and Green Ridge, Mo. (Ref., 2, 3)

894 - Joseph Brazure   896 - Caroline Russell
895 - George Henry   897 - Jennie Russell

587- <u>Emery Leland</u>[7] <u>Wadleigh</u>, (William Henry[6], Joseph[5], Joseph[4], Henry[3], Robert[2], John[1]), b. July 10, 1822 (or July 19, 1822) in Kensington, N.H. on the old Wadleigh farm near Tuck's Corner (also called Five Corners), d. December 28, 1895 in Green Ridge, Mo., m. September 25, 1851 in Concord, N.H. Harriet Marsh of Concord, b. June 28, 1832 in Concord, d. August 29, 1890 in Green Ridge. Res. Kensington, Rutland, Ill., and Green Ridge, Mo. (Ref. 2, 3)

WADLEIGH GENEALOGY   SEVENTH GENERATION

588- <u>Leully</u>[7] <u>Wadleigh</u>, (William Henry[6],
Joseph[5], Joseph[4], Henry[3], Robert[2], John[1]), b.
June 25, 1825 in Kensington, N.H. on the old
Wadleigh farm near Tuck's Corner (also called
Five Corners), d. November 23, 1827. died in
childhood. (Ref. 3)

589- <u>John H.</u>[7] <u>Wadleigh</u>, (William Henry[6],
Joseph[5], Joseph[4], Henry[3], Robert[2], John[1]), b.
October 20, (or October 30,) 1827 in
Kensington, N.H. on the old Wadleigh farm near
Tuck's Corner (also called Five Corners), d.
November 15, 1900 in Rutland, Ill. m. June 13,
1852 Pauline P. Kimball of Kensington, b.
January 8, 1833, d. October 8, 1908 in Rutland.
Res. Kensington, N.H. and Rutland, Ill.
Officer in Civil War, Battlefield prom. to Col.
(Ref. 2, 3, 21)
        898 - Inez Menerva   900 - Laura D.
        899 - Mary A.   901 - William H.

**Issue of 352- Simon Dearborn[6] Wadleigh and
Dorothy (Rowe) Wadleigh:**

590- <u>Parmala</u>[7] <u>Wadleigh</u>, (Simon Dearborn[6],
Benjamin[5], Joseph[4], Henry[3], Robert[2], John[1]), b.
January 16, 1780 in Hanover, N.H. (Ref. 3)

591- <u>John</u>[7] <u>Wadleigh</u>, (Simon Dearborn[6],
Benjamin[5], Joseph[4], Henry[3], Robert[2], John[1]), b.
November 4, 1781 in Hanover, N.H. m. June 17,
1804 Betsey Cole of Hill, N.H., d. of Nathan
Flint Cole who was born in Antrim, N.H. (Ref.
3)
        902 - John   905 - Joseph
        903 - Achsah   906 - Levi C.
        904 - Mary

592- <u>Newell</u>[7] <u>Wadleigh</u>, (Simon Dearborn[6],
Benjamin[5], Joseph[4], Henry[3], Robert[2], John[1]), b.
February 16, 1784 in Hanover, N.H. m. October

26, 1807 Filey Chatterton of Bolton, Quebec, Canada. no additional data. Res. Hanover and Acworth, N.H. and Bolton, Quebec. (Ref. 3)
    907 - Permelia   909 - Frank H. Newell
    908 - Hiram Gilmore

592- **Life**[7] **Wadleigh**, (Simon Dearborn[6], Benjamin[5], Joseph[4], Henry[3], Robert[2], John[1]), b. June 12, 1786 in Hanover, N.H. (Ref. 3)

594- **Simon Dearborn**[7] **Wadleigh**, (Simon Dearborn[6], Benjamin[5], Joseph[4], Henry[3], Robert[2], John[1]). m. November 27, 1826 Nancy D. Smith of Gilmanton, N.H. no additional data. (Ref. 3)

Issue of 353- Elijah[6] Wadleigh and Patty (Saunders) Wadleigh:

595- **George**[7] **Wadleigh**, (Elijah[6], Benjamin[5], Joseph[4], Henry[3], Robert[2], John[1]), b. January 10, 1791 in Hanover, N.H. (Ref. 3)

596- **Henry**[7] **Wadleigh**, (Elijah[6], Benjamin[5], Joseph[4], Henry[3], Robert[2], John[1]), b. May 25, 1795 in Hanover, N.H. (Ref. 3)

597- **Benjamin**[7] **Wadleigh**, (Elijah[6], Benjamin[5], Joseph[4], Henry[3], Robert[2], John[1]), b. June 13, 1796 in Hanover, N.H. (Ref. 3)

Issue of 355- James Marston[6] Wadleigh and Nancy (Neal) Wadleigh:

598- **John Calvin**[7] **Wadleigh**, (James Marston[6], Benjamin[5], Joseph[4], Henry[3], Robert[2], John[1]), b. in Meredith, N.H. m. 1st Mary Nealley. m. 2nd Sarah Way. no additional data. (Ref. 3)

599- <u>Nathan B.</u>[7] <u>Wadleigh</u>, (James Marston[6], Benjamin[5], Joseph[4], Henry[3], Robert[2], John[1]). m. 1857 Sarah (Lang) Whidden. no additional data. (Ref. 3)

Issue of 356- James[6] Wadleigh and Molly/Mary (Blake) Wadleigh:

600- <u>James</u>[7] <u>Wadleigh</u>, (James[6], James[5], Joseph[4], Henry[3], Robert[2], John[1]), b. December 15, 1781 in Epping, N.H., d. August (or September) 8, 1836. m. November 25, 1802, Eunice Farnham, d. of Barachias W. Farnham of Sanbornton, N.H., b. February 25, 1782, d. August 15, 1870 in Sanbornton, N.H. (Ref. 3)
   910 - Hannah Piper   912 - Esther
   911 - James C.   913 - Nathaniel Farnham

601- <u>Joseph</u>[7] <u>Wadleigh</u>, (James[6], James[5], Joseph[4], Henry[3], Robert[2], John[1]), b. January 11, 1784 in Sanbornton, N.H., d. May 1, 1867. m. July 3, 1802 Phebe Dustin, d. of David Dustin, d. March 12, 1872. (Ref. 3)
   914 - Lydia Dustin 917 - Benjamin Mason
   915 - Warren   918 - Joseph Dustin
   916 - Shadrach

602- <u>Nancy</u>[7] <u>Wadleigh</u>, (James[6], James[5], Joseph[4], Henry[3], Robert[2], John[1]) (twin), b. February 6, 1786 in Sanbornton, N.H., d. August 4, 1822. m. March 26, 1812 Ebenezer[6] Lane, (Samuel[5], John[4]). no additional data. (Ref. 3)

603- <u>Polly</u>[7] <u>Wadleigh</u>, (James[6], James[5], Joseph[4], Henry[3], Robert[2], John[1]) (twin), b. February 6, 1786 in Sanbornton, N.H., d. July 19, 1827. m. February 18, 1808 Benjamin[3] Marston (Ward[2], Edward[1]). no additional data. (Ref. 3)

604- John[7] Wadleigh, (James[6], James[5], Joseph[4], Henry[3], Robert[2], John[1]) b. June 24, 1788 in Sanbornton, N.H., d. August 29, 1850 on family homestead near Sanbornton, N.H.   m. March 3, 1824 Sarah Taylor of Sanbornton, N.H., d. of Jonathan Taylor of Sanbornton, N.H., d. May 8, 1858 in Sanbornton, N.H.   (Ref. 3)
  919 - Molly Blake   923 - Elizabeth Malcher
  920 - Molly Blake   924 - John Blake
  921 - Jonathan Taylor 925 - Daniel Taylor
  922 - Sarah Ann Bartlett

605- Betsey[7] Wadleigh, (James[6], James[5], Joseph[4], Henry[3], Robert[2], John[1]) b. April 30, 1791 in Sanbornton, N.H., d. July 1, 1850. (Ref. 3)

606- Sally[7] Wadleigh, (James[6], James[5], Joseph[4], Henry[3], Robert[2], John[1]) b. August 11, 1793 in Sanbornton, N.H.   m. November 28, 1821 Thomas Morrison.   no additional data.   (Ref. 3)

607- Asa[7] Wadleigh, (James[6], James[5], Joseph[4], Henry[3], Robert[2], John[1]) b. June 24, 1801 in Sanbornton, N.H., d. July 16, 1880.   m. 1st March 30, 1826 Lucy Woodman of Tamworth, N.H., d. December 27, 1852.   m. 2nd November 11, 1856 Jannet Eastman, d. of Thomas Eastman.   no additional data.   (Ref. 3)   926 - 928 by 1st wife.
      926 - James Monroe   928 - Mary Mason
      927 - Jacob Woodman

Issue of 357- John[6] Wadleigh and Molly (Fox) Wadleigh:

608- Dearborn[7] Wadleigh, (John[6], James[5], Joseph[4], Henry[3], Robert[2], John[1]), b. 1778 in Epping, N.H., d. 1853.   m. Polly Hayes of Epping N.H., d. of William Hayes and Mary (Plummer) Hayes of Epping, N.H.   no additional

data. (Ref. 3)
     929 - John

609- <u>Polly</u>[7] <u>Wadleigh</u>, (John[6], James[5], Joseph[4], Henry[3], Robert[2], John[1]), b. 1780 in Meredith, N.H. m. Gordon Lawrence. no additional data. (Ref. 3)

610- <u>Betsey</u>[7] <u>Wadleigh</u>, (John[6], James[5], Joseph[4], Henry[3], Robert[2], John[1]), b. 1782 in Meredith, N.H. m. John Neal, b. of Joseph "White Oak" Neal. no additional data. (Ref. 3)

611- <u>Hannah</u>[7] <u>Wadleigh</u>, (John[6], James[5], Joseph[4], Henry[3], Robert[2], John[1]), b. 1784 in Meredith, N.H. m. Daniel Cass. no additional data. (Ref. 3)

612- <u>Nancy</u>[7] <u>Wadleigh</u>, (John[6], James[5], Joseph[4], Henry[3], Robert[2], John[1]), b. 1787 in Meredith, N.H. m. Noah Robinson. no additional data. (Ref. 3)

613- <u>Caroline</u>[7] <u>Wadleigh</u>, (John[6], James[5], Joseph[4], Henry[3], Robert[2], John[1]), b. 1791 in Meredith, N.H. m. John Tilton. no additional data. (Ref. 3)

614- <u>Sally</u>[7] <u>Wadleigh</u>, (John[6], James[5], Joseph[4], Henry[3], Robert[2], John[1]), b. 1793 in Meredith, N.H. m. Abraham Tilton. no additional data. (Ref. 3)

615- <u>Cyrene</u>[7] <u>Wadleigh</u>, (John[6], James[5], Joseph[4], Henry[3], Robert[2], John[1]), b. 1799 in Meredith, N.H. m. Jonathan Cram Sanborn, b. March 29, 1797 in Meredith, N.H. Res. Meredith and Oxford, N.H. (Ref. 3)

Issue of 359- Joseph[6] Wadleigh and Molly/Polly (Weeks) Wadleigh:

616- Eunice[7] Wadleigh, (Joseph[6], James[5], Joseph[4], Henry[3], Robert[2], John[1]), b. October 5, 1788 in Sanbornton, N.H. m. Richard. no additional data. (Ref. 3)

617- Huldah[7] Wadleigh, (Joseph[6], James[5], Joseph[4], Henry[3], Robert[2], John[1]), b. March 28, 1790 in Sanbornton, N.H. m. 1st July 11, 1811 Thomas Cawley, Jr., b. August 31, 1789. m. 2nd A. S. Jud_ins. no additional data. (Ref. 3)

618- James Dearborn[7] Wadleigh, (Joseph[6], James[5], Joseph[4], Henry[3], Robert[2], John[1]), b. February 8, 1792 in Sanbornton, N.H. m. February 27, 1816 Phebe Chase, d. of Jonathan Chase. no additional data. Occ. Farmer and Carpenter. Res. Sanbornton and Franklin, N.H. (until 1853/4) and Wisconsin. (Ref. 3)
    930 - Polly   932 - Maranda
    931 - Charles Joseph

619- Molly[7] Wadleigh, (Joseph[6], James[5], Joseph[4], Henry[3], Robert[2], John[1]), b. September 4, 1797 in Sanbornton, N.H. m. April 1816 Nathaniel[2] Buswell, (Noah[1]), b. January 12, 1794. (Ref. 3)

620- Newell[7] Wadleigh, (Joseph[6], James[5], Joseph[4], Henry[3], Robert[2], John[1]), b. September 3, 1799 in Sanbornton, N.H. m. Mrs. Wadleigh. no additional data. Res. Lowell and Dracut, Mass. (Ref. 3)
    933 - daughter   934 - Joseph

621- Joseph[7] Wadleigh, (Joseph[6], James[5], Joseph[4], Henry[3], Robert[2], John[1]), b. February 16, 1802 in Sanbornton, N.H., d. May 12, 1874 in Hill, N.H. m. 1st October 14, 1824 Sally

Quimby of Sanbornton, N.H., d. of Harper Quimby
of Meredith, N.H., d. January 12, 1852 (or
1856). m. 2nd Hannah Sanborn, d. of Benjamin
Sanborn of Meredith, N.H. no additional data.
Occ. Carpenter known as "Joseph W. 3rd". Res.
Sanbornton and Hill, N.H. (Ref. 3) 935 - 947
by 1st wife.

935	Nathaniel Read	942	Sarah
936	Harper Quimby	943	Albert Prescott
937	Nancy Morrill	944	Martha Ellen
938	G_rish	945	Clarissa Weeks
939	Hiram Porter	946	George Eli
940	Gustave Bartlett	947	Lucy
941	Fannie		

622- <u>unamed</u>[7] Wadleigh, (Joseph[6], James[5],
Joseph[4], Henry[3], Robert[2], John[1]), b. September
1803. (Ref. 3.)

623- <u>Chase Weeks</u>[7] Wadleigh, (Joseph[6], James[5],
Joseph[4], Henry[3], Robert[2], John[1]), b. September
23, 1805 in Sanbornton, N.H., d. June 6, 1877.
m. May 7, 1831 Marcia A. Whitcher, d. of Reuben
Whitcher of Hill, N.H., b. May 7, 1831. Occ.
merchant marine sailor, shoemaker. Res. New
Hampton and Clark's Corner, N.H. (Ref. 3)

948	Alonzo	950	Melissa Colby
949	Melissa		

624- <u>Simon Hayes</u>[7] Wadleigh, (Joseph[6], James[5],
Joseph[4], Henry[3], Robert[2], John[1]), b. June 2,
1809 in Sanbornton, N.H. m. April 13, 1834
Jane B. Sleeper of Bristol, N.H. no additional
data. Occ. teamster. (Ref. 3)

951	George Weston	953	Mary Ellen
952	John Hayes	954	Anna T.

Issue of 361- Simeon[6] Wadleigh and Abigail (Hayes) Wadleigh:

NOTE: discrepancy within Ref. 3. At one point, oldest son is called "Joseph[7] Wadleigh", in another is called "William P.". Opinion of compiler is that the latter is correct. Also, John Wadleigh married to Betsey Sanborn is shown in both 7th and 8th generations. Opinion of the compiler is that the 7th generation is correct.

625- William P.[7] Wadleigh, (Simeon[6], James[5], Joseph[4], Henry[3], Robert[2], John[1]), b. September 17, 1786 in Meredith, N.H., d. January 6, 1855. m. Lydia Neal, d. of Joseph "Red Oak" Neal and Nancy (Perkins) Neal. no additional data. (Ref. 3)

955 - Joseph	958 - William H.
956 - Simeon F.	959 - Nancy
957 - William S.	960 - Mary Jane

626- John[7] Wadleigh, (Simeon[6], James[5], Joseph[4], Henry[3], Robert[2], John[1]), b. 1787/8 in Meredith, N.H. m. Betsey Sanborn. no additional data. (Ref. 3)

627- Stephen G.[7] Wadleigh, (Simeon[6], James[5], Joseph[4], Henry[3], Robert[2], John[1]), b. 1789 in Meredith, N.H., d. 1863. m. 1st Polly Neal, b. 1794, d. 1825. m. 2nd Olive Neal, sister to Polly, b. 1802, d. 1885. (Ref. 3) 961 - 963 by 1st w., 964 - 966 by 2nd w.

961 - Charles	964 - Polly
962 - Abigail	965 - Jane
963 - Edward F.	966 - Olive

Issue of 362- Enoch[6] Wadleigh and Hannah (Morrill) Wadleigh:

628- William[7] Wadleigh, (Enoch[6], James[5], Joseph[4], Henry[3], Robert[2], John[1]), b. December 12, 1793 in Epping, N.H., d. June 27, 1867 in Exeter, N.H. m. February 29, 1844 Emily A. Dearborn of Exeter, N.H. no additional data. (Ref. 3)

967 - George W.	970 - Ada Margaret
968 - John M.	971 - Frank H.
969 - Emma Josephine	972 - Minnie Cora

629- Enoch[7] Wadleigh, (Enoch[6], James[5], Joseph[4], Henry[3], Robert[2], John[1]), b. 1794 in Epping, N.H., d. 1830 in Epping, N.H. m. February 13, 1816 Sally Sanborn of Epping, N.H. no additional data. (Ref. 3)

630- Eliza[7] Wadleigh, (Enoch[6], James[5], Joseph[4], Henry[3], Robert[2], John[1]), b. August 7, 1807 in Epping, N.H. m. Mary Burley. no additional data. (Ref. 3)

631- daughter[7] Wadleigh, (Enoch[6], James[5], Joseph[4], Henry[3], Robert[2], John[1]). no additional data. (Ref. 3)

632- daughter[7] Wadleigh, (Enoch[6], James[5], Joseph[4], Henry[3], Robert[2], John[1]). no additional data. (Ref. 3)

Issue of 363- Joseph/Josiah[6] Wadleigh and Sally (Chapman) Wadleigh:

633- Betsey[7] Wadleigh, (Joseph or Josiah[6], James[5], Joseph[4], Henry[3], Robert[2], John[1]), b. ca. 1800 in Meredith, N.H., d. 1867. m. Nathaniel Maloon, b. 1810, d. 1874. Occ. Carpenter in Boston, Mass. before coming to

Meredith, N.H. (Ref. 3)
    973 - Sophia

634- Dexter[7] Wadleigh, (Joseph or Josiah[6], James[5], Joseph[4], Henry[3], Robert[2], John[1]), b. ca. 1800 in Meredith, N.H. (Ref. 3)
    974 - Dexter E.

Issue of 369- Albra[6] Wadleigh and Eliza Payson (Brewster) Wadleigh:

635- Mary Rice[7] Wadleigh, (Albra[6], Ebenezer[5], John[4], Daniel[3], John[2], John[1]), bpt. July 24, 1827 in Portsmouth N.H. (Ref. 3)

636- Frances Wentworth[7] Wadleigh, (Albra[6], Ebenezer[5], John[4], Daniel[3], John[2], John[1]), b. July 24, 1846 in Boston, Mass., d. March 13, 1927 in Brookline, Mass. m. June 23, 1868 Alfred Love Stokes of Philadelphia, Pa., s. of Edward D. and Esther S. Stokes of Philadelphia. no additional data. (Ref. 3)
    975 - Mary Wadleigh

Issue of 370- John[6] Wadleigh and Sally (Burbank) Wadleigh:

637- Elisha[7] Wadleigh, (John[6], Elisha[5], John[4], Daniel[3], John[2], John[1]), b. in Parsonfield, Me., d. in Lyman, Me. m. Lydia Banks. no additional data. (Ref. 3)

638- Jesse[7] Wadleigh, (John[6], Elisha[5], John[4], Daniel[3], John[2], John[1]), b. in Parsonfield, Me., d. in New York. m. Charlotte Hall. no additional data. (Ref. 3)

WADLEIGH GENEALOGY   SEVENTH GENERATION

639- Eliza[7] Wadleigh, (John[6], Elisha[5], John[4], Daniel[3], John[2], John[1]), b. in Parsonfield, Me., d. in Saco, Me. m. Edward Leavitt. no additional data. (Ref. 3)

640- John[7] Wadleigh, (John[6], Elisha[5], John[4], Daniel[3], John[2], John[1]), b. in Parsonfield, Me. m. Melessa. no additional data. (Ref. 3)
    976 - daughter

641- William[7] Wadleigh, (John[6], Elisha[5], John[4], Daniel[3], John[2], John[1]), b. in Parsonfield, Me., d. in North Parsonfield. Me. m. Harriet Newell. no additional data. (Ref. 3)

642- Sarah[7] Wadleigh, (John[6], Elisha[5], John[4], Daniel[3], John[2], John[1]), b. in Parsonfield, Me., d. in Saco, Me. m. Milton Goodwin. no additional data. (Ref. 3)

Issue of 371- James[6] Wadleigh and Rachel (Dearborn) Wadleigh:

643- James Dearborn[7] Wadleigh, (James[6], Elisha[5], John[4], Daniel[3], John[2], John[1]), b. in Parsonfield, Me., d. in Gorham, Me. m. December 12, 1848 Harriet Moore. no data. Res. Parsonfield and Gorham, Me. (Ref. 3)

644- George W.[7] Wadleigh, (James[6], Elisha[5], John[4], Daniel[3], John[2], John[1]), b. 1820 in Parsonfield, Me. m. August 26, 1847 Abigail Edgecomb, b. August 29, 1821, d. March 31, 1889. Res. Kezar Falls, N.H. (Ref. 3)
    977 - Clarence   979 - Ernest W.
    978 - George W.   980 - Fred

645- Mary[7] Wadleigh, (James[6], Elisha[5], John[4], Daniel[3], John[2], John[1]), b. ca. 1823 in

Parsonfield, Me. m. 1846 Joseph Thompson of
Parsonfield, Me. no additional data. (Ref. 3)

646- <u>Sarah J.</u>[7] <u>Wadleigh</u>, (James[6], Elisha[5],
John[4], Daniel[3], John[2], John[1]), b. 1825 in
Parsonfield, Me., d. 1842. died in
adolescence. (Ref. 3)

647- <u>Caroline D.</u>[7] <u>Wadleigh</u>, (James[6], Elisha[5],
John[4], Daniel[3], John[2], John[1]), b. 1827 in
Parsonfield, Me. m. 1846, Woodbury Gooch of
Biddeford, Me. no additional data. (Ref. 3)

648- <u>Hannah M.</u>[7] <u>Wadleigh</u>, (James[6], Elisha[5],
John[4], Daniel[3], John[2], John[1]), b. 1829 in
Parsonfield, Me. m. 1848 John S. Hidden. no
additional data. Res. (presum.) Karsas, Me.
(Ref. 3)

649- <u>Mahala</u>[7] <u>Wadleigh</u>, (James[6], Elisha[5], John[4],
Daniel[3], John[2], John[1]), b. 1831 in Parsonfield,
Me. m. Edward Blimmer of Biddeford, Me. no
additional data. (Ref. 3)

650- <u>Eliza F.</u>[7] <u>Wadleigh</u>, (James[6], Elisha[5],
John[4], Daniel[3], John[2], John[1]), b. 1833 in
Parsonfield, Me. m. Elijah P. Lewis. no
additional data. Res. Portland, Me. (Ref. 3)

651- <u>Jacob D.</u>[7] <u>Wadleigh</u>, (James[6], Elisha[5],
John[4], Daniel[3], John[2], John[1]), b. 1836 in
Parsonfield, Me. m. 1853 Arvilla Hobson. no
data. Res. Sebago Lake, Me. (Ref. 3)

652- <u>Elisha B.</u>[7] <u>Wadleigh</u>, (James[6], Elisha[5],
John[4], Daniel[3], John[2], John[1]), b. 1839 in
Parsonfield, Me. m. 18_7 Jennie Eastman. no
data. Res. North Parsonfield, Me. (Ref. 3)

Issue of Waldron[5] Smith and 380- Sally (Dolloff) Smith:

672- Henry M.[6] Smith, (Wadleigh: Sally[7], Richard[6], Mary[5], Elizabeth[4], Jonathan[3], Joanna[2], John[1]; Gilman: Sally[7], Richard[6], Mary[5], Elizabeth[4], Mary[3], John[2], Edward[1]; Smith: Waldron[5], John W.[4], Jonathan[3], Jonathan[2], Robert[1]). m. Hannah Hurd. no additional data. (Ref. 49)
   991 - Isaiah Waldron

Issue of 401- Elijah[7] Wadleigh and Rhoda (Smith) Wadleigh:

673- Mary Ann[8] Wadleigh, (Elijah[7], Joseph[6], Joseph[5], Joseph[4], John[3], Robert[2], John[1]), b. December 9, 1805 in Salisbury, Mass. m. Timothy S. Robinson. no additional data. (Ref. 3)

674- George[8] Wadleigh, (Elijah[7], Joseph[6], Joseph[5], Joseph[4], John[3], Robert[2], John[1]), b. December 21, 1807 in Salisbury, Mass., d. August 12, 1885. m. May 7, 1840 Sarah H. Gilman, d. of James and Betsey Gilman of Meredith, N.H., b. in Meredith. Occ. Printer, published newspaper in Dover, N.H. (Ref. 3)

675- Elijah[8] Wadleigh, Jr., (Elijah[7], Joseph[6], Joseph[5], Joseph[4], John[3], Robert[2], John[1]), b. August 6, 1812 in Salisbury, Mass. (Ref. 3)

WADLEIGH GENEALOGY   EIGHTH GENERATION

Issue of 417- Eleazer[7] Wadleigh and Sally P. (Wells) Wadleigh:

676- <u>Charlotte</u>[8] <u>Wadleigh</u>, (Eleazer[7], Benjamin[6], Joseph[5], Joseph[4], John[3], Robert[2], John[1]), b. 1829 in Salisbury, Mass. m. Charles Blake. no additional data. (Ref. 3)

677- <u>Sarah</u>[8] <u>Wadleigh</u>, (Eleazer[7], Benjamin[6], Joseph[5], Joseph[4], John[3], Robert[2], John[1]), b. December 20, 1831 in Salisbury, Mass., d. in Chicago, Ill. did not marry. (Ref. 3)

678- <u>Lois A.</u>[8] <u>Wadleigh</u>, (Eleazer[7], Benjamin[6], Joseph[5], Joseph[4], John[3], Robert[2], John[1]), b. January 13, 1834 in Salisbury, Mass. Res. in Boston, Mass. did not marry. (Ref. 3)

679- <u>Horace</u>[8] <u>Wadleigh</u>, (Eleazer[7], Benjamin[6], Joseph[5], Joseph[4], John[3], Robert[2], John[1]), b. 1838 in Salisbury, Mass. (Ref. 3)

Issue of 418- Benjamin[6] Currier and Rhoda (Jewell) Currier:

680- <u>Abigail</u>[7] <u>Currier</u>, (Wadleigh: Benjamin[7], John[6], Benjamin[5], Joseph[4], John[3], Robert[2] John[1]; Currier: Benjamin[6], John[5], Ezekiel[4], Thomas[3], Thomas[2], Richard[1]), b. January 6, 1791. (Ref. 4-919)

Issue of 420- James[7] Graves and Polly (Gilman) Graves:

681- <u>John</u>[8] <u>Graves</u>, (Wadleigh: James[7], Ruth[6], Dean[5], John[4], John[3], Robert[2], John[1]; Graves: James[7], David[6], James[5], Samuel[4], Abraham[3], Mark[2], Samuel[1]), b. May 27, 1808, d. May 13, 1902. m. August 27, 1834 Merial Mason, d. of

Jacob and Abigail Marcy Mason. no additional
data. Occ. Minister. Res. Saratoga Springs,
N.Y. (Ref. 12)
     992 - David Haslem

**Issue of Reuben Boyce and 421- Polly[7]
(Wadleigh) Boyce:**

682- <u>Reuben Boyce</u>, (Wadleigh: Polly[7],
Benjamin[6], Dean[5], John[4], John[3], Robert[2],
John[1]). no additional data. (Ref. 3)

683- <u>Ira Wadleigh Boyce</u>, (Wadleigh: Polly[7],
Benjamin[6], Dean[5], John[4], John[3], Robert[2],
John[1]). m. Mrs. Wadleigh. no additional data.
(Ref. 3)
     993 - Jesse Wadleigh

684- <u>Ruth Fairbanks Boyce</u>, (Wadleigh: Polly[7],
Benjamin[6], Dean[5], John[4], John[3], Robert[2],
John[1]). no additional data. (Ref. 3)

**Issue of 422- Ira[7] Wadleigh and Theodosia
(Sargent) Wadleigh:**

685- <u>Theodosia B.[8] Wadleigh</u>, (Ira[7], Benjamin[6],
Dean[5], John[4], John[3], Robert[2], John[1]). m. Mr.
Moor. no additional data. (Ref. 3)

686- <u>Susan A.[8] Wadleigh</u>, (Ira[7], Benjamin[6],
Dean[5], John[4], John[3], Robert[2], John[1]). m. Mr.
Hoskins. no additional data. (Ref. 3)

Issue of 424- Jesse[7] Wadleigh and Susan
(Grant) Wadleigh:

687- Carria[8] Wadleigh, (Benjamin[6], Dean[5],
John[4], John[3], Robert[2], John[1]). m. Mr. Bacon.
no additional data. (Ref. 3)

Issue of Rufus Sargent and 427- Ruth[7]
(Wadleigh) Sargent:

688- Frank Wadleigh Sargent, (Wadleigh: Ruth[7],
Benjamin[6], Dean[5], John[4], John[3], Robert[2],
John[1]), b. in Candia, N.H. m. Mrs. Sargent.
no additional data. (Ref. 3)
        994 - Paul E.

689- Theodisia Sargent, (Wadleigh: Ruth[7],
Benjamin[6], Dean[5], John[4], John[3], Robert[2],
John[1]). no additional data. (Ref. 3)

Issue of 428- Benjamin Dean[7] Wadleigh and
Lois (Edwards) Wadleigh:

690- Enoch Hunt[8] Wadleigh, (Benjamin Dean[7],
Dean[6], Dean[5], John[4], John[3], Robert[2], John[1]), b.
December 2, 1810 in Salisbury, Mass., d. 1847
in N.H. (Ref. 3)

691- Benjamin[8] Wadleigh, (Benjamin Dean[7],
Dean[6], Dean[5], John[4], John[3], Robert[2], John[1]), b.
1811 in Salisbury, Mass., d. 1815. died in
childhood. (Ref. 3)

692- Mary Jane[8] Wadleigh, (Benjamin Dean[7],
Dean[6], Dean[5], John[4], John[3], Robert[2], John[1]), b.
May 6, 1813 in Salisbury, Mass., d. 1849.
(Ref. 3)

693- Anna W.[8] Wadleigh, (Benjamin Dean[7], Dean[6], Dean[5], John[4], John[3], Robert[2], John[1]), b. March 21, 1817 in Salisbury, Mass., d. 1877. (Ref. 3)

694- Benjamin Dean[8] Wadleigh, (Benjamin Dean[7], Dean[6], Dean[5], John[4], John[3], Robert[2], John[1]), b. May 2, 1820 in Salisbury, Mass., d. 1895. m. Sarah Goodrich. no additional data. (Ref. 3)
     995 - John   997 - Jane
     996 - Nellie

695- Philip[8] Wadleigh, (Benjamin Dean[7], Dean[6], Dean[5], John[4], John[3], Robert[2], John[1]), b. 1822 in Salisbury, Mass., d. 1893. (Ref. 3)

696- Ephriam S.[8] Wadleigh, (Benjamin Dean[7], Dean[6], Dean[5], John[4], John[3], Robert[2], John[1]), b. April 17, 1824 in Salisbury, Mass., d. 1893 (or 1902). (Ref. 3)

697- David E.[8] Wadleigh, (Benjamin Dean[7], Dean[6], Dean[5], John[4], John[3], Robert[2], John[1]), b. February 7, 1828 in Salisbury, Mass. m. December 31, 1853 Mehitable Currier. no additional data. (Ref. 3)
     998 - David   999 - Porter

Issue of William Swett and 435- Sarah (Wadleigh) Swett:

698- Mary Swett, (Wadleigh: Sarah[7], Adams[6], Moses[5], Ephriam[4], John[3], Robert[2], John[1]), b. in Amesbury, Mass. m. Eliphalet Swett, a cousin. no additional data. (Ref. 3)

Issue of William Swett and 437- Hannah (Wadleigh) Swett:

699- William Swett, (Wadleigh: Hannah[7], Adams[6], Moses[5], Ephriam[4], John[3], Robert[2], John[1]), b. in Amesbury, Mass. (Ref. 3)

700- Benjamin Swett, (Wadleigh: Hannah[7], Adams[6], Moses[5], Ephriam[4], John[3], Robert[2], John[1]), b. in Amesbury, Mass. (Ref. 3)

701- Hannah Swett, (Wadleigh: Hannah[7], Adams[6], Moses[5], Ephriam[4], John[3], Robert[2], John[1]), b. in Amesbury, Mass. (Ref. 3)

702- Judith Swett, (Wadleigh: Hannah[7], Adams[6], Moses[5], Ephriam[4], John[3], Robert[2], John[1]), b. in Amesbury, Mass. (Ref. 3)

Issue of 438- Enoch[7] Wadleigh and Elizabeth (Fowler) Wadleigh:

703- Adrines[8] Wadleigh, (Enoch[7], Adams[6], Moses[5], Ephriam[4], John[3], Robert[2], John[1]), b. July in Salisbury, Mass., d. July 1810. (Ref. 3)

704- Adams[8] Wadleigh, (Enoch[7], Adams[6], Moses[5], Ephriam[4], John[3], Robert[2], John[1]), b. in Salisbury, Mass., d. July 1810. (Ref. 3)

705- Elizabeth[8] Wadleigh, (Enoch[7], Adams[6], Moses[5], Ephriam[4], John[3], Robert[2], John[1]), b. July 26, 1812 in Salisbury, Mass. m. 1st Mr. Jordan. m. 2nd Thomas Leavitt. no additional data. (Ref. 3)

Issue of 440- Peter[7] Wadleigh and 455- Polly (Wadleigh) Wadleigh:

706- Sophronia[8] Wadleigh, (Peter[7], Adams[6], Moses[5], Ephriam[4], John[3], Robert[2], John[1]), b. November 25, 1813 in Salisbury, Mass., d. January 26, 1825. (Ref. 3)

Issue of Joseph[1] Guest and 441- Judith (Wadleigh) Guest:

707- Sarah[2] Guest, (Wadleigh: Judith[7], Adams[6], Moses[5], Ephriam[4], John[3], Robert[2], John[1]; Guest: Joseph[1]), b. October 13, 1810 in Salisbury, Mass. m. November 19, 1832 Francis Keniston. no additional data. (Ref. 3)

708- Elizabeth[2] Guest, (Wadleigh: Judith[7], Adams[6], Moses[5], Ephriam[4], John[3], Robert[2], John[1]; Guest: Joseph[1]), b. August 7, 1814 in Salisbury, Mass. m. October 1837 Elbridge Wood. no additional data. (Ref. 3)

709- Marcia A.[2] Guest, (Wadleigh: Judith[7], Adams[6], Moses[5], Ephriam[4], John[3], Robert[2], John[1]; Guest: Joseph[1]), b. April 23, 1824 in Salisbury, Mass., d. July 17, 1825. died in infancy. (Ref. 3)

710- Marcia Ann[2] Guest, (Wadleigh: Judith[7], Adams[6], Moses[5], Ephriam[4], John[3], Robert[2], John[1]; Guest: Joseph[1]), b. February 27, 1827 in Salisbury, Mass. m. Rev. George Price. no additional data. (Ref. 3)

Issue of 444- Samuel[7] Wadleigh and Meriam Gordon (Webster) Wadleigh:

711- Samuel[8] Wadleigh, (Samuel[7], Philip[6], Moses[5], Ephriam[4], John[3], Robert[2], John[1]), b. September 26, 1816 in Salisbury, Mass., d. 1905. m. January 1850 Mary A. Morrill, d. of James and Mary (Smith) Morrill, b. 1810, d. 1904. (Ref. 3)
        1000 - Orrin

712- Benjamin[8] Wadleigh, (Samuel[7], Philip[6], Moses[5], Ephriam[4], John[3], Robert[2], John[1]), b. May 22, 1822 in Salisbury, Mass. m. 1st April 7, 1847 Sarah A. Morrill. m. 2nd January 1849 Hannah Healey. no additional data. (Ref. 3)

Issue of 445- Ephriam[7] Wadleigh and Sarah (Farlie) Wadleigh:

713- Eliza Ann[8] Wadleigh, (Ephriam[7], Philip[6], Moses[5], Ephriam[4], John[3], Robert[2], John[1]), b. February 8, 1808 in Salisbury, Mass. m. May 13, 1833 Joseph Flanders, b. February 14, 1814 in Salisbury, Mass., d. July 17, 1899. (Ref. 3)

714- Mary Ann[8] Wadleigh, (Ephriam[7], Philip[6], Moses[5], Ephriam[4], John[3], Robert[2], John[1]), b. in Salisbury, Mass. m. George Morrill. no additional data. (Ref. 3)

Issue of 446- Henry[7] Wadleigh and Sally (Titcomb) Wadleigh:

715- William[8] Wadleigh, (Henry[7], Philip[6], Moses[5], Ephriam[4], John[3], Robert[2], John[1]), b. April 11, 1811 in Salisbury, Mass. (Ref. 3)

716- <u>Sarah</u>[8] Wadleigh, (Henry[7], Philip[6], Moses[5], Ephriam[4], John[3], Robert[2], John[1]), b. January 22, 1813 in Salisbury, Mass. (Ref. 3)

717- <u>Susanna</u>[8] Wadleigh, (Henry[7], Philip[6], Moses[5], Ephriam[4], John[3], Robert[2], John[1]), b. October 24, 1815 in Salisbury, Mass. m. October 8, 1836 Soloman Garland. no additional data. (Ref. 3)

718- <u>Henry K.</u>[8] Wadleigh, (Henry[7], Philip[6], Moses[5], Ephriam[4], John[3], Robert[2], John[1]), b. October 5, 1822 in Salisbury, Mass. (Ref. 3)

719- <u>Clarissa</u>[8] Wadleigh, (Henry[7], Philip[6], Moses[5], Ephriam[4], John[3], Robert[2], John[1]), b. September 2, 1824 in Salisbury, Mass. m. 1844 Ira Brown. no additional data. (Ref. 3)

720- <u>Andrew J.</u>[8] Wadleigh, (Henry[7], Philip[6], Moses[5], Ephriam[4], John[3], Robert[2], John[1]), b. March 10, 1829 in Salisbury, Mass., d. January 23, 1873. m. May 15, 1860 Hannah J. Yorke. no additional data. Awarded Medal for Gallantry on the field of Chancellorville, Va. on February 16, 1864. (Ref. 3)

Issue of 447- John[7] Wadleigh and Meriam (Tuxbury) Wadleigh:

721- <u>John</u>[8] Wadleigh, (John[7], Philip[6], Moses[5], Ephriam[4], John[3], Robert[2], John[1]). no additional data. (Ref. 3)

722- <u>Frederick A.</u>[8] Wadleigh, (John[7], Philip[6], Moses[5], Ephriam[4], John[3], Robert[2], John[1]), b. May 21, 1814, d. March 25, 1884 in Enosbury Falls, Vt. mention of 2 marriages. (Ref. 3)
     1001 - Abby Elizabeth   1007 - Edna Blanche

1002 - John Frederick   1008 - Frederick Paul
1003 - George Hutchinson
1004 - Mary Louisa
1005 - Bertha Katherine
1006 - Katherine Grace

723- Mary[8] Wadleigh, (John[7], Philip[6], Moses[5], Ephriam[4], John[3], Robert[2], John[1]). no data. (Ref. 3)

724- Hannah Maria[8] Wadleigh, (John[7], Philip[6], Moses[5], Ephriam[4], John[3], Robert[2], John[1]), b. November 27, 1816 in South Hampton, N.H. m. October 15, 1846 George Carlton of Bradford, N.H. no additional data. (Ref. 3)
        1009 - Ida Marie   1011 - Henrietta
        1010 - Anna   1012 - John Herbert

725- John Bergin[8] Wadleigh, (John[7], Philip[6], Moses[5], Ephriam[4], John[3], Robert[2], John[1]), b. November 12, 1819 in South Hampton, N.H., d. 1850. (Ref. 3)

726- M. Louisa[8] Wadleigh, (John[7], Philip[6], Moses[5], Ephriam[4], John[3], Robert[2], John[1]), b. 1826 in South Hampton, N.H., d. 1907. (Ref. 3)

727- Caroline T.[8] Wadleigh, (John[7], Philip[6], Moses[5], Ephriam[4], John[3], Robert[2], John[1]), b. 1827 in South Hampton, N.H., d. 1828. died in childhood. (Ref.3)

Issue of 449- Philip[7] Wadleigh and Annie (Morrill) Wadleigh:

728- Joseph Guest[8] Wadleigh, (Philip[7], Philip[6], Moses[5], Ephriam[4], John[3], Robert[2], John[1]), b. July 14, 1829 in Salisbury, Mass., d. August 2, 1831. died in childhood. (Ref. 3)

Issue of Philip Webster and 450- Hannah (Wadleigh) Webster:

729- <u>Hannah Webster</u>, (Wadleigh: Hannah[7], Philip[6], Moses[5], Ephriam[4], John[3], Robert[2], John[1]), b. 1820 in Salisbury, Mass. m. Amos Morrill. no additional data. (Ref. 3)

730- <u>Eliza Webster</u>, (Wadleigh: Hannah[7], Philip[6], Moses[5], Ephriam[4], John[3], Robert[2], John[1]), b. 1822 in Salisbury, Mass. m. S. S. Colby. no additional data. (Ref. 3)

731- <u>child Webster</u>, (Wadleigh: Hannah[7], Philip[6], Moses[5], Ephriam[4], John[3], Robert[2], John[1]). no additional data. (Ref. 3)

732- <u>child Webster</u>, (Wadleigh: Hannah[7], Philip[6], Moses[5], Ephriam[4], John[3], Robert[2], John[1]). no additional data. (Ref. 3)

733- <u>Mary Ann Webster</u>, (Wadleigh: Hannah[7], Philip[6], Moses[5], Ephriam[4], John[3], Robert[2], John[1]), b. 1827 in Salisbury, Mass. m. Elijah Davis. no additional data. (Ref. 3)

Issue of 451- Eliphalet[7] Wadleigh and Elizabeth (Currier) Wadleigh:

734- <u>Abigail[8] Wadleigh</u>, (Eliphalet[7], Ephriam[6], Moses[5], Ephriam[4], John[3], Robert[2], John[1]), b. September 14, 1814 in Salisbury, Mass. m. John Coffin. no additional data. (Ref. 3)

735- <u>Joseph[8] Wadleigh</u>, (Eliphalet[7], Ephriam[6], Moses[5], Ephriam[4], John[3], Robert[2], John[1]), b. December 22, 1818 in Salisbury, Mass., d. in New Orleans, La. (Ref. 3)

736- Ephriam[8] Wadleigh, (Eliphalet[7], Ephriam[6], Moses[5], Ephriam[4], John[3], Robert[2], John[1]), b. January 31, 1830 in Salisbury, Mass. m. Abbie Eaton. no additional data. (Ref. 3)
    1013 - Mae Warren

Issue of 453- Ephriam[7] Wadleigh and Lydia (Leonard) Wadleigh:

737- Ethelinda[8] Wadleigh, (Ephriam[7], Ephriam[6], Moses[5], Ephriam[4], John[3], Robert[2], John[1]), b. June 29, 1812 in Salisbury, Mass., d. 1896. m. Ebenezer Tucker, b. 1807, d. 188_. (Ref. 3)

738- Mary[8] Wadleigh, (Ephriam[7], Ephriam[6], Moses[5], Ephriam[4], John[3], Robert[2], John[1]), b. October 21, 1815 in Salisbury, Mass. (Ref. 3)

739- George[8] Wadleigh, (Ephriam[7], Ephriam[6], Moses[5], Ephriam[4], John[3], Robert[2], John[1]), b. May 11, 1820 in Salisbury, Mass. (Ref. 3)

740- Lydia[8] Wadleigh, (Ephriam[7], Ephriam[6], Moses[5], Ephriam[4], John[3], Robert[2], John[1]), b. July 12, 1823 in Salisbury, Mass. (Ref. 3)

Issue of Samuel Hoyt and 454- Elizabeth (Wadleigh) Hoyt:

741- Ebenezer Hoyt, (Wadleigh: Elizabeth[7], Ephriam[6], Moses[5], Ephriam[4], John[3], Robert[2], John[1]), b. June 1814 in Salisbury, Mass. (Ref. 3)

742- Charles Hoyt, (Wadleigh: Elizabeth[7], Ephriam[6], Moses[5], Ephriam[4], John[3], Robert[2], John[1]), b. February 1817 in Salisbury, Mass. (Ref. 3)

743- <u>Mary Hoyt</u>, (Wadleigh: Elizabeth[7],
Ephriam[6], Moses[5], Ephriam[4], John[3], Robert[2],
John[1]), b. August 1819 in Salisbury, Mass.
died in childhood. (Ref. 3)

744- <u>Mary Hoyt</u>, (Wadleigh: Elizabeth[7],
Ephriam[6], Moses[5], Ephriam[4], John[3], Robert[2],
John[1]), b. January 1823 in Salisbury, Mass. m.
Charles Fowler. no additional data. (Ref. 3)

745- <u>Elizabeth Hoyt</u>, (Wadleigh: Elizabeth[7],
Ephriam[6], Moses[5], Ephriam[4], John[3], Robert[2],
John[1]), b. November 1825 in Salisbury, Mass.
(Ref. 3)

**Issue of 457- Ezekiel[7] Wadleigh and Elizabeth
(Blaisdell) Wadleigh:**

746- <u>Polly[8] Wadleigh</u>, (Ezekiel[7], Ephriam[6],
Moses[5], Ephriam[4], John[3], Robert[2], John[1]), b.
February 9, 1823 in Salisbury, Mass., d.
February 23, 1865. m. Eben P. Fowler, b.
1815/6 in Salisbury. d. January 14, 1894 in
Salisbury. (Ref. 3)
        1014 - Lizzie A.

747- <u>Charles T. P.[8] Wadleigh</u>, (Ezekiel[7],
Ephriam[6], Moses[5], Ephriam[4], John[3], Robert[2],
John[1]), b. April 22, 1825 in Salisbury, Mass.,
d. July 9, 1916. m. June 1851 Hannah P.
Corliss, d. December 6, 1886 in Amesbury, Mass.
(Ref. 3)
        1015 - Jonathan C.

748- <u>Eben Pearson[8] Wadleigh</u>, (Ezekiel[7],
Ephriam[6], Moses[5], Ephriam[4], John[3], Robert[2],
John[1]), b. November 23, 1829 in Salisbury,
Mass., d. March 26, 1906. m. Jane Kendrick.
no additional data. Res. Amesbury, Mass. Occ.
Ships carpenter in Newburyport, and Salisbury

shipyards. (Ref. 3)
     1016 - Cyrus Pearson   1018 - Willie
     1017 - Sarah Jane   1019 - Charles William

749- Hannah[8] Wadleigh, (Ezekiel[7], Ephriam[6], Moses[5], Ephriam[4], John[3], Robert[2], John[1]), b. July 26, 1837 in Salisbury, Mass., d. January 4, 1909. m. Novemeber 3, 1857 George T. Williams, d. lost at sea. (Ref. 3)
     1020 - George T.

Issue of Jonathan Carr and 463- Mehitable (Wadleigh) Carr:

750- Sally Carr, (Wadleigh: Mehitable[7], Benjamin[6], Thomas[5], Benjamin[4], Robert[3], Robert[2], John[1]), b. June 14, 1794, d. July 3, 1796. died in childhood. (Ref. 25-969)

751- Daniel Carr, (Wadleigh: Mehitable[7], Benjamin[6], Thomas[5], Benjamin[4], Robert[3], Robert[2], John[1]), b. January 11, 1796, d. April 11, 1797. died in childhood. (Ref. 25-969)

Issue of Joseph Bean and 464- Hannah (Wadleigh) Bean:

752- Daniel Bean, (Wadleigh: Hannah[7], Benjamin[6], Thomas[5], Benjamin[4], Robert[3], Robert[2], John[1]), b. November 2, 1797. m. Clarissa Pressey. no additional data. (Ref. 25-969)

753- William Bean, (Wadleigh: Hannah[7], Benjamin[6], Thomas[5], Benjamin[4], Robert[3], Robert[2], John[1]), b. November 8, 1800. m. Jane McQuesten. no additional data. (Ref. 25-969)

754- <u>Hannah Bean</u>, (Wadleigh: Hannah[7], Benjamin[6], Thomas[5], Benjamin[4], Robert[3], Robert[2], John[1]), b. July 27, 1808. m. Winthrop Pressey. no additional data. (Ref. 25-969)

Issue of 468- John[7] Wadleigh and Judith (Emery) Wadleigh:

755- <u>Amasa</u>[8] Wadleigh, (John[7], Benjamin[6], Thomas[5], Benjamin[4], Robert[3], Robert[2], John[1]), b. July 27, 1809 in Hatley, Quebec, Canada. m. Zelphia P. Jones. no additional data. (Ref. 3)
    1021 - Viola   1022 - John R.

756- <u>Lydia</u>[8] Wadleigh, (John[7], Benjamin[6], Thomas[5], Benjamin[4], Robert[3], Robert[2], John[1]), b. in Hatley, Quebec, Canada. m. 1st Joseph Fletcher. m. 2nd Samuel Kezar. no additional data. (Ref. 3)

Issue of 469- Benjamin[7] Wadleigh and Polly (Marston) Wadleigh:

757- <u>David</u>[8] Wadleigh, (Benjamin[7], Benjamin[6], Thomas[5], Benjamin[4], Robert[3], Robert[2], John[1]), b. November 22, 1804 in Sutton, N.H., died in childhood. (Ref. 3, 25-969)

758- <u>Eliphalet</u>[8] Wadleigh, (Benjamin[7], Benjamin[6], Thomas[5], Benjamin[4], Robert[3], Robert[2], John[1]), b. November 22, 1804 in Sutton, N.H, d. October 1864. m. 1st Ruth M. Pressey, d. of William and Polly (Chadwick) Pressey, d. April 1, 1839. m. 2nd Susan D. Flanders, b. June 14, 1803 in North Sutton, N.H., d. March 29, 1854. (Ref. 3, 25-969)
1023 - 1026 by 1st wife.
       1023 - Alonzo   1025 - Mary Mianda
       1024 - Benjamin F. 1026 - Corliss

759- <u>Luther</u>[8] <u>Wadleigh</u>, (Benjamin[7], Benjamin[6], Thomas[5], Benjamin[4], Robert[3], Robert[2], John[1]), b. July 11, 1806 in Sutton, N.H., d. July 25, 1873. m. September 29, 1831 Eliza Little, d. of Deacon Ezekiel Little, b. April 25, 1810, d. June 7, 1880. Res. Sutton, N.H., and East Corinth, Me. prominent citizen of East Corinth. (Ref. 3, 25-970)

1027	- Benjamin F.	1031	- George B.
1028	- Alonzo K.	1032	- Eliza A.
1029	- Carlos B.	1033	- Maria
1030	- Mary N.	1034	- Addie

760- <u>Erastus</u>[8] <u>Wadleigh</u>, (Benjamin[7], Benjamin[6], Thomas[5], Benjamin[4], Robert[3], Robert[2], John[1]), b. April 27, 1808 in Sutton, N.H., d. May 21, 1881. m. 1st February 21, 1839 Elvina Challis, d. of Timothy Challis, b. Oct. 23, 1815, d. July 14, 1842. m. 2nd January 5, 1848 Mary W. Flanders, b. April 17, 1808, d. May 4, 1865. m. 3rd as 3rd husb. Olive (Holmes) (Shattuck) Davis, d. November 1, 1880. Occ. Teacher, School Administrator and local historian, author of first history of Sutton N.H. Res. Sutton. (Ref. 3, 25-969)

1035 - Milton B.	1037	- Mary Elvira
1036 - B. Frank		

761- <u>Milton</u>[8] <u>Wadleigh</u>, (Benjamin[7], Benjamin[6], Thomas[5], Benjamin[4], Robert[3], Robert[2], John[1]), b. February 13, 1810 in Sutton, N.H., d. in Galena, Ill. Ed. Norwich Univ. 1837 as Civil Engineer. City Engineer for Galena, Ill. and Surveyor for Jo Davies Co. Ill. (Ref. 3-969 & 976)

762- <u>Amanda</u>[8] <u>Wadleigh</u>, (Benjamin[7], Benjamin[6], Thomas[5], Benjamin[4], Robert[3], Robert[2], John[1]), b. December 18, 1811 in Sutton, N.H., died in childhood. (Ref. 3)

763- Hannah[8] Wadleigh, (Benjamin[7], Benjamin[6], Thomas[5], Benjamin[4], Robert[3], Robert[2], John[1]), b. November 22, 1814 in Sutton, N.H., d. November 8, 1853. m. Col. Nathaniel A. Davis, s. of David and Polly Ambrose Davis of Sutton, N.H. no additional data. (Ref. 3, 25-40 & 66)

NOTE: David Davis was s. of Jonathan Davis and was b. in Sutton, N.H. and was 92 yrs. old when he died. He married Polly, eldest dau. of Rev. Samuel Ambrose. (Ref. 25-40)

764- Lydia F.[8] Wadleigh, (Benjamin[7], Benjamin[6], Thomas[5], Benjamin[4], Robert[3], Robert[2], John[1]), b. February 8, 1817 in Sutton, N.H., d. October 27, 1888 in New York City, N.Y. bur. at Wadleigh Homestead in Sutton, N.H. V.P. and Prof. of Ethics at Normal College in City of New York. Also Prof. at Georgetown Univ. in D.C. Active in Baptist Church in New Hampton and University Place Pres. Church in New York. did not marry. (Ref. 25-969 & 983)

765- Benjamin[8] Wadleigh, (Benjamin[7], Benjamin[6], Thomas[5], Benjamin[4], Robert[3], Robert[2], John[1]), b. July 5, 1819 in Sutton, N.H., d. November 8, 1868 in Newport, N.H. m. August 31, 1848 Hannah P. Young, d. of William Young of Sunapee, N.H. no additional data. Occ. merchant in Newport. (Ref. 3, 25-969 & 976)
    1038 - Arthur Edison   1041 - Gilbert H.
    1039 - William Young   1042 - May Helene
    1040 - Benjamin F.

766- Gilbert[8] Wadleigh, (Benjamin[7], Benjamin[6], Thomas[5], Benjamin[4], Robert[3], Robert[2], John[1]), b. May 27, 1821 in Sutton, N.H., d. March 7, 1886. unmarried. Ed. New London Academy and Dartmouth (1847). Occ. teacher in Milford, N.H. had a law practice and was a banker. Was a paymaster in the army during Civil War. (Ref. 3, 25-969 & 976)

Issue of Capt. John[6] Pillsbury and 474-
Susanna (Wadleigh) Pillsbury:

767- <u>Simon</u> W.[7] <u>Pillsbury</u>, (Wadleigh: Susanna[7],
Benjamin[6], Thomas[5], Benjamin[4], Robert[3],
Robert[2], John[1]; Pillsbury: John[6], Micajah[5],
Caleb[4], Caleb[3], Moses[2], William[1]), b. June 22,
1812 in Sutton, N.H., d. January 27, 1836 in
Minnesota. Res. Sutton, N.H., and St.
Anthony Falls, Minn. (Ref. 3, 50-23)

768- <u>George Alfred</u>[7] <u>Pillsbury</u>, (Wadleigh:
Susanna[7], Benjamin[6], Thomas[5], Benjamin[4],
Robert[3], Robert[2], John[1]; Pillsbury: John[6],
Micajah[5], Caleb[4], Caleb[3], Moses[2], William[1]), b.
August 29, 1816 in Sutton, N.H., d. July 17,
1898 in Minneapolis, Minn. m. May 9, 1841 in
Sutton, N.H. Margaret Sprague Carleton of
Bucksport, Me., d. of Henry and Polly (Greeley)
Carleton, b. September 20, 1817 in Bucksport,
d. March 16, 1901 in Minneapolis. Mfd. stoves
and sheet iron in partnership with cousin John
C. Pillsbury, merchant in Warner, N.H. and
Concord, N.H., became purchasing agent for
Concord Railroad Corp and organizer and
president of First National Bank of Concord and
the First Savings Bank of Concord. Became a
philantropist contributing library building to
Sutton, hospital to Warner, and large sums to
orphanages and homes for the aged. At age 62
moved to Minneapolis to join 770- John Sargent[7]
Pillsbury and 1043- Charles Alfred[8] Pillsbury
in the C. A. Pillsbury Flour Co., became Mayor
of Minneapolis, pres. of Minneapolis City
Council, the Board of Trade, the Chamber of
Commerce, a Hospital, the Pillsbury and
Hurlburt Elevator Co., St. Paul and Minneapolis
Baptist Union, the American Baptist Missionary
Union, Northwestern National Bank and V.P. of
Minnesota Loan & Trust Co. He gave a woman's
dormitory and academy building to the Pillsbury
Academy at Owatonna, Minn. (Ref. 3, 50-23)
      1043 - Charles Alfred 1045 - Fred Carleton
      1044 - Mary A.

769- Dolly Wadleigh[7] Pillsbury, (Wadleigh:
Susanna[7], Benjamin[6], Thomas[5], Benjamin[4],
Robert[3], Robert[2], John[1]; Pillsbury: John[6],
Micajah[5], Caleb[4], Caleb[3], Moses[2], William[1]), b.
September 6, 1818 in Sutton, N.H., d. December
8, 1858 in Sutton. m. January 14, 1838 in
Sutton Enoch P. Cummings of Concord, N.H.
(Ref. 3, 25-39, 50-23)
    1046 - Alfred Pillsbury   1047 - Charles E.

770- John Sargent[7] Pillsbury, (Wadleigh:
Susanna[7], Benjamin[6], Thomas[5], Benjamin[4],
Robert[3], Robert[2], John[1]; Pillsbury: John[6],
Micajah[5], Caleb[4], Caleb[3], Moses[2], William[1]), b.
July 29, 1827 in Sutton N.H., d. October 18,
1901 in Minneapolis, Minn. m. November 3, 1856
in Warner, N.H. Mahala Fisk, d. of Capt. John
and Sarah (Goodhue) Fisk, b. May 7, 1832 in
Springfield, N.H., d. June 23, 1910 in
Minneapolis. Occ. painter, businessman,
merchant and politician. Was clerk for 768-
George Alfred[7] Pillsbury at store in Warner,
N.H. and later entered business partnership
with Walter Harriman who became Gov. of N.H.
After becoming merchant in Concord, moved to
St. Anthony Falls, Minnesota. Became hardware
merchant in St. Anthony Falls until destroyed
by fire in 1857 but reorganized and continued
until 1875 when joined with 1043- Charles
Alfred[8] Pillsbury to form C. A. Pillsbury Flour
Co. Elected state senator and later Governor
of Minnesota, serving three successive terms,
resigning by his own choice. Appointed in 1863
Pres. of the then non-existant University of
Minnesota, guiding it to national prominence by
the time of his death. As a philantropist gave
Pillsbury Hall to the University of Minnesota,
the Town Hall of Sutton, the Pillsbury Library
Building in Minneapolis, established the Mahala
Fisk Pillsbury Home for Girls in Minneapolis
and others. Attended faithfully the
Congregational Church, but not a member. (Ref.
3, 50-25)
        1048 - Addie Eva   1050 - Sarah Belle
        1049 - Susan M.   1051 - Alfred Fisk

771- <u>Benjamin F.</u>[7] <u>Pillsbury</u>, (Wadleigh:
Susanna[7], Benjamin[6], Thomas[5], Benjamin[4],
Robert[3], Robert[2], John[1]; Pillsbury: John[6],
Micajah[5], Caleb[4], Caleb[3], Moses[2], William[1]), b.
March 29, 1831 in Sutton, N.H, d. October 1890
in Granite Falls, Minn. m. March 27, 1872
Susan Wright. no additional data. (Ref. 3,
50-23)

**Issue of 475- Thomas Miles[7] Wadleigh and
Rachel (Gile) Wadleigh:**

772- <u>Horace</u>[8] <u>Wadleigh</u>, (Thomas Miles[7],
Jonathan[6], Thomas[5], Benjamin[4], Robert[3],
Robert[2], John[1]), b. in Northfield, N.H., m.
Sally Wright of Belmont Village, N.H., d. 1893
in Belmont Village. no children. (Ref. 3)

**Issue of 476- Jonathan Eastman[7] Wadleigh and
Sally (Buswell) Wadleigh:**

773- <u>child</u> <u>Wadleigh</u>, (Jonathan Eastman[7],
Jonathan[6], Thomas[5], Benjamin[4], Robert[3],
Robert[2], John[1]). no additional data. (Ref. 3)

774- <u>Abigail</u>[8] <u>Wadleigh</u>, (Jonathan Eastman[7],
Jonathan[6], Thomas[5], Benjamin[4], Robert[3],
Robert[2], John[1]), b. September 21, 1804 in
Hampstead, N.H. (Ref. 3)

775- <u>Sally Sargent</u>[8] <u>Wadleigh</u>, (Jonathan
Eastman[7], Jonathan[6], Thomas[5], Benjamin[4],
Robert[3], Robert[2], John[1]), b. June 30, 1807 in
Hampstead, N.H. (Ref. 3)

776- <u>Jonathan</u>[8] <u>Wadleigh</u>, (Jonathan Eastman[7],
Jonathan[6], Thomas[5], Benjamin[4], Robert[3],
Robert[2], John[1]), b. August 2, 1809 in
Hampstead, N.H. (Ref. 3)

777- Ebenezer Stevens[8] Wadleigh, (Jonathan
Eastman[7], Jonathan[6], Thomas[5], Benjamin[4],
Robert[3], Robert[2], John[1]), b. November 11, 1811
in Hampstead, N.H. (Ref. 3)

**Issue of 477- Peter[7] Wadleigh and Jane
(Smith) (Gorrell) Wadleigh:**

778- Ephriam[8] Wadleigh, (Peter[7], Jonathan[6],
Thomas[5], Benjamin[4], Robert[3], Robert[2], John[1]),
b. June 23, 1803 in Northfield, N.H., d. June
1, 1883. m. November 8, 1823 Mary Elizabeth
Smith, d. September 1904. (Ref. 3)
    1052 - Oliva Alice   1054 - Smith Glidden
    1053 - Adelaide Phillips

779- Mary[8] Wadleigh, (Peter[7], Jonathan[6],
Thomas[5], Benjamin[4], Robert[3], Robert[2], John[1]),
b. May 3, 1805 in Northfield, N.H., d. April 8,
1878 in Columbia, N.H. m. March 1826 John W.
Morrill, d. September 2, 1879 in Columbia, N.H.
Res. East Northfield, and Columbia, N.H. (Ref.
3)

780- Charles Joseph[8] Wadleigh, (Peter[7],
Jonathan[6], Thomas[5], Benjamin[4], Robert[3],
Robert[2], John[1]), b. February 27, 1816 in
Northfield, N.H., d. January 14, 1864 in
Northfield. m. October 19, 1847 Janette Ramsey
of Sutton, N.H., d. 1902 in New Hampton, N.H.
(Ref. 3)

**Issue of 481- Ebenezer[7] Wadleigh and Huldah
Elkins (Ewer) Wadleigh:**

781- Ebenezer Eastman[8] Wadleigh, (Ebenezer[7],
Jonathan[6], Thomas[5], Benjamin[4], Robert[3],
Robert[2], John[1]), b. in Northfield, N.H., m.
Miss Elkins. no additional data. (Ref. 3)
    1055 - Elkins

782- Curtis Elkins[8] Wadleigh, (Ebenezer[7], Jonathan[6], Thomas[5], Benjamin[4], Robert[3], Robert[2], John[1]). no additional data. (Ref. 3)

Issue of 499- Daniel[7] Wadleigh and Nancy (Champlin) Wadleigh:

783- Horace[8] Wadleigh, (Daniel[7], Thomas[6], Thomas[5], Benjamin[4], Robert[3], Robert[2], John[1]), died young. (Ref. 25-980)

784- Sylvia[8] Wadleigh, (Daniel[7], Thomas[6], Thomas[5], Benjamin[4], Robert[3], Robert[2], John[1]), died young. (Ref. 25-980)

785- Juliana[8] Wadleigh, (Daniel[7], Thomas[6], Thomas[5], Benjamin[4], Robert[3], Robert[2], John[1]), b. March 1, 1814. m. October 25, 1836, Timothy H. Loverin of Sutton, N.H. no additional data. (Ref. 25-980)
    1056 - Adeline   1058 - Julia
    1057 - Charles

786- Philip S. Harvey[8] Wadleigh, (Daniel[7], Thomas[6], Thomas[5], Benjamin[4], Robert[3], Robert[2], John[1]), b. October 1, 1815, d. after 1902. m. Rhoda W. Kendrick of Sutton, N.H. no additional data. 1875. (Ref. 25-980)
    1059 - Julia A.

787- Thomas H.[8] Wadleigh, (Daniel[7], Thomas[6], Thomas[5], Benjamin[4], Robert[3], Robert[2], John[1]), b. September 4, 1817, d. 1824. died in childhood. (Ref. 25-980)

788- Adeline[8] Wadleigh, (Daniel[7], Thomas[6], Thomas[5], Benjamin[4], Robert[3], Robert[2], John[1]), b. May 16, 1819, d. after 1902. m. 1st Amos Blood, d. before 1902. m. 2nd Benjamin F.

Shelton, d. before 1902.   Res. Iona, Mich.
(Ref. 25-980)

789- Augusta[8] Wadleigh, (Daniel[7], Thomas[6], Thomas[5], Benjamin[4], Robert[3], Robert[2], John[1]), b. July 12, 1822. d. April 1817. m. December 28, 1841, Charles Bean of Warner, N.H. no additional data. Res. Iona, Mich. no issue. (Ref. 25-981)

Issue of Edward Dodge and 502- Polly (Wadleigh) Dodge:

790- Thomas W. Dodge, (Wadleigh: Polly[7], Thomas[6], Thomas[5], Benjamin[4], Robert[3], Robert[2], John[1]), b. October 25, 1818, d. February 12, 1819. died in infancy. (Ref. 25-981)

791- Sarah Williams Dodge, (Wadleigh: Polly[7], Thomas[6], Thomas[5], Benjamin[4], Robert[3], Robert[2], John[1]), b. June 1, 1820. (Ref. 25-981)

792- Edward W. Dodge, (Wadleigh: Polly[7], Thomas[6], Thomas[5], Benjamin[4], Robert[3], Robert[2], John[1]), b. June 15, 1822. m. March 18, 1850 Eliza N. Jones of Washington, N.H. no additional data. (Ref. 25-981)
    1060 - Susan Maria   1061 - Jennie Greeley

Issue of Thomas Cheney and 504- Mehitibel (Wadleigh) Cheney:

793- Miriam W. Cheney, (Wadleigh: Mehitibel[7], Thomas[6], Thomas[5], Benjamin[4], Robert[3], Robert[2], John[1]), d. May 20, 1825. died in childhood. (Ref. 25-981)

794- <u>Nathaniel Cheney</u>, (Wadleigh: Mehitibel[7], Thomas[6], Thomas[5], Benjamin[4], Robert[3], Robert[2], John[1]), b. July, 1822. m. Rebecca Goodrich. no additional data. (Ref. 25-981)
    1062 - Emma   1063 - Flora

Issue of 506- Thomas[7] Wadleigh and Hannah (Roby) Wadleigh:

795- <u>Miriam</u>[8] <u>Wadleigh</u>, (Thomas[7], Thomas[6], Thomas[5], Benjamin[4], Robert[3], Robert[2], John[1]), b. December 15, 1824, d. December 19, 1827. died in childhood. (Ref. 25-981)

796- <u>Sally</u>[8] <u>Wadleigh</u>, (Thomas[7], Thomas[6], Thomas[5], Benjamin[4], Robert[3], Robert[2], John[1]), b. July 13, 1827. m. Jabez Townsend of Dublin, N.H. no additional data. (Ref. 25-981)
    1064 - Sarah

797- <u>Thomas</u>[8] <u>Wadleigh</u>, (Thomas[7], Thomas[6], Thomas[5], Benjamin[4], Robert[3], Robert[2], John[1]), b. May 19, 1829. m. in Concord, N.H., Abbie Prescott. no additional data. (Ref. 25-981)
    1065 - Prescott T.   1066 - Sarah

798- <u>Robert</u>[8] <u>Wadleigh</u>, (Thomas[7], Thomas[6], Thomas[5], Benjamin[4], Robert[3], Robert[2], John[1]), b. May 4, 1832. m. December 24, 1856 Hannah Porter. no additional data. (Ref. 25-981)

Issue of 506- <u>Thomas</u>[7] <u>Wadleigh</u> and Polly/Mary (Kimball) Wadleigh:

799- <u>Hannah</u>[8] <u>Wadleigh</u>, (Thomas[7], Thomas[6], Thomas[5], Benjamin[4], Robert[3], Robert[2], John[1]), b. 1841, d. March 13, 1845. died in childhood. (Ref. 25-981)

Issue of John Burnham and 508- Susanna (Wadleigh) Burnham:

800- <u>James M. Burnham</u>, (Wadleigh: Susanna[7], Thomas[6], Thomas[5], Benjamin[4], Robert[3], Robert[2], John[1]). m. Emma F. Marston. no additional data. (Ref. 25-981)
1067 - Walter M.   1068 - John C.

801- <u>John F. Burnham</u>, (Wadleigh: Susanna[7], Thomas[6], Thomas[5], Benjamin[4], Robert[3], Robert[2], John[1]). m. 1st Satrica W. Peabody. m. 2nd Frances E. Richmond. no additional data. (Ref. 25-981) 1069 - 1072 by 1st w., 1073 by 2nd w.
        1069 - Herbert B.   1072 - Mary E.
        1070 - Susan W.   1073 - Clara B.
        1071 - Addie L.

802- <u>Edward D. Burnham</u>, (Wadleigh: Susanna[7], Thomas[6], Thomas[5], Benjamin[4], Robert[3], Robert[2], John[1]). m. Georgie B. Davis. no additional data. (Ref. 25-982)
        1074 - Nathan D.   1077 - Frank P.
        1075 - Grace L.   1078 - Charles D.
        1076 - Fred T.

Issue of 519- Moses Dow[7] Wadleigh and Judith F. (Adams) Wadleigh:

803- <u>Franklin Adams</u>[8] <u>Wadleigh</u>, (Moses Dow[7], Moses[6], Thomas[5], Benjamin[4], Robert[3], Robert[2], John[1]), b. June 15, 1822 in Bradford, N.H. (Ref. 3)

804- <u>George Adams</u>[8] <u>Wadleigh</u>, (Moses Dow[7], Moses[6], Thomas[5], Benjamin[4], Robert[3], Robert[2], John[1]), b. June 14, 1824 in Bradford, N.H. (Ref. 3)

WADLEIGH GENEALOGY   EIGHTH GENERATION

805- Sarah Louise[8] Wadleigh, (Moses Dow[7], Moses[6], Thomas[5], Benjamin[4], Robert[3], Robert[2], John[1]), b. March 23, 1826 in Bradford, N.H. (Ref. 3)

806- Martha Jane[8] Wadleigh, (Moses Dow[7], Moses[6], Thomas[5], Benjamin[4], Robert[3], Robert[2], John[1]), b. December 23, 1828 in Bradford, N.H. (Ref. 3)

807- Harriet Elizabeth[8] Wadleigh, (Moses Dow[7], Moses[6], Thomas[5], Benjamin[4], Robert[3], Robert[2], John[1]), b. September 4, 1829 in Bradford, N.H. (Ref. 3)

808- Emily H.[8] Wadleigh, (Moses Dow[7], Moses[6], Thomas[5], Benjamin[4], Robert[3], Robert[2], John[1]), b. March 24, 1838 in Bradford, N.H. (Ref. 3)

Issue of 521- John Dow[7] Wadleigh and Huldah (Gillingham) Wadleigh:

809- Bainbridge[8] Wadleigh, (John Dow[7], Moses[6], Thomas[5], Benjamin[4], Robert[3], Robert[2], John[1]), b. June 14, 1831 in Bradford, N.H., d. January 24, 1891 in Boston, Mass. bur. Milford, N.H. m. January 6, 1853 Ann Marie Putnam of Boston, d. of Daniel and Elizabeth (Hale) Putnam, b. August 20, 1834 in Boston, d. November 29, 1879 in Boston. Attended common schools and Kimball Union Academy at Plainfield, N.H. practiced law in Milford, Hillsborough Co., N.H. Member N.H. House of Representatives 1855, 1856, 1859, 1860 and 1869-72. Elected U.S. Senate 1872 (Republican), served one term. (Ref. 3, 44)
    1079 - Caroline   1081 - Helen Putnam
    1080 - child

810- Lydia[8] Wadleigh, (John Dow[7], Moses[6], Thomas[5], Benjamin[4], Robert[3], Robert[2], John[1]), b. June 30, 1837 in Bradford, N.H. (Ref. 3)

Issue of 523- Benjamin Evans[7] Wadleigh and Olive Wadleigh:

811- Lucinda[8] Wadleigh, (Benjamin Evans[7], Moses[6], Thomas[5], Benjamin[4], Robert[3], Robert[2], John[1]), b. October 2, 1843 in Bradford, N.H. (Ref. 3)

812- Martha Jane[8] Wadleigh, (Benjamin Evans[7], Moses[6], Thomas[5], Benjamin[4], Robert[3], Robert[2], John[1]), b. May 24, 1836 in Bradford, N.H. (Ref. 3)

Issue of 530- Taylor[7] Wadleigh and Melinda (Hovey) Wadleigh:

813- Horace[8] Wadleigh, (Taylor[7], Ephriam[6], Thomas[5], Benjamin[4], Robert[3], Robert[2], John[1]), b. February 1820 in Hatley, Quebec, Canada. m. Matilda Gould. no additional data. (Ref. 3)

814- Malinda[8] Wadleigh, (Taylor[7], Ephriam[6], Thomas[5], Benjamin[4], Robert[3], Robert[2], John[1]), b. August 19, 1822 in Hatley, Quebec, Canada. m. Edward Hawes. no additional data. (Ref. 3)

815- Alice C.[8] Wadleigh, (Taylor[7], Ephriam[6], Thomas[5], Benjamin[4], Robert[3], Robert[2], John[1]), b. June 7, 1830 in Hatley, Quebec, Canada. (Ref. 3)

816- Everett Frederick[8] Wadleigh, (Taylor[7], Ephriam[6], Thomas[5], Benjamin[4], Robert[3], Robert[2], John[1]), b. August 23, 1832 in Hatley, Quebec,

Canada.   m. Addie Brooks, d. of George W. Brooks. no additional data. (Ref. 3)

817- Elen[8] Wadleigh, (Taylor[7], Ephriam[6], Thomas[5], Benjamin[4], Robert[3], Robert[2], John[1]), b. August 19, 1844 in Hatley, Quebec, Canada. (Ref. 3)

Issue of Nathan S. Colby and 538- Lucinda (Evans) Colby:

818- Charles Colby, (Wadleigh: Lucinda[7], Susanna[6], Thomas[5], Benjamin[4], Robert[3], Robert[2], John[1]). m. H. Clement. no additional data. (Ref. 25-979)
    1082 - Sarah   1084 - Fred
    1083 - Nathan

819- Walter Colby, (Wadleigh: Lucinda[7], Susanna[6], Thomas[5], Benjamin[4], Robert[3], Robert[2], John[1]), died young. no data. (Ref. 25-979)

820- Walter Colby, (Wadleigh: Lucinda[7], Susanna[6], Thomas[5], Benjamin[4], Robert[3], Robert[2], John[1]). no data. (Ref. 25-979)

821- Elizabeth Colby, (Wadleigh: Lucinda[7], Susanna[6], Thomas[5], Benjamin[4], Robert[3], Robert[2], John[1]). no data. (Ref. 25-979)

Issue of Harrison D. Robertson and 539- Sarah (Evans) Robertson:

822- Lucinda Robertson, (Wadleigh: Sarah[7], Susanna[6], Thomas[5], Benjamin[4], Robert[3], Robert[2], John[1]). m. John Putney. no additional data. (Ref. 25-979)
    1085 - Susie

823- <u>Sarah Robertson</u>, (Wadleigh: Sarah[7], Susanna[6], Thomas[5], Benjamin[4], Robert[3], Robert[2], John[1]). no data. (Ref. 25-979)

824- <u>John Robertson</u>, (Wadleigh: Sarah[7], Susanna[6], Thomas[5], Benjamin[4], Robert[3], Robert[2], John[1]). m. Mattie Page. no additional data. (Ref. 25-979)
  1086 - Sarah   1088 - Sadie
  1087 - Carl

Issue of Stephen C. Badger and 540- Sophronia (Evans) Badger:

825- <u>Benjamin E. Badger</u>, (Wadleigh: Sophronia[7], Susanna[6], Thomas[5], Benjamin[4], Robert[3], Robert[2], John[1]). m. Rachel Eastman. no additional data. (Ref. 25-979)
  1089 - Gertrude 1091 - Estella
  1090 - William

826- <u>William Badger</u>, (Wadleigh: Sophronia[7], Susanna[6], Thomas[5], Benjamin[4], Robert[3], Robert[2], John[1]). m. Fannie. no additional data. (Ref. 25-979)
  1092 - Walter   1093 - Sadie

Issue of 544- Joseph[7] Wadleigh and Anna (Sleeper) Wadleigh:

827- <u>Jonathan S.</u>[8] <u>Wadleigh</u>, (Joseph[7], Daniel[6], John[5], Benjamin[4], Robert[3], Robert[2], John[1]), b. March 10, 1817 in Kingston, N.H., d. 1875 in Kingston, N.H., bur. in West Kingston Cemetary. m. Harriett, d. February 4, 1854 in Kingston, N.H. (Ref. 3)

828- <u>Daniel</u>[8] <u>Wadleigh</u>, (Joseph[7], Daniel[6], John[5], Benjamin[4], Robert[3], Robert[2], John[1]), b.

1818 in Kingston, N.H., d. February 12, 1821.
died in childhood. (Ref. 3)

829- Hannah[8] Wadleigh, (Joseph[7], Daniel[6],
John[5], Benjamin[4], Robert[3], Robert[2], John[1]), b.
September 10, 1820 in Kingston, N.H. (Ref. 3)

830- Nancy[8] Wadleigh, (Joseph[7], Daniel[6], John[5],
Benjamin[4], Robert[3], Robert[2], John[1]), b. March
18, 1822 in Kingston, N.H., d. April 1836 in
Kingston, N.H. (Ref. 3)

831- Daniel[8] Wadleigh, (Joseph[7], Daniel[6],
John[5], Benjamin[4], Robert[3], Robert[2], John[1]), b.
March 8, 1824 in Kingston, N.H. m. December
24, 1854 Marie R. Hoyt. no additional data.
(Ref. 3)

**Issue of 545- Daniel[7] Wadleigh and Sally
(Davis) Wadleigh:**

832- Elizabeth[8] Wadleigh, (Daniel[7], Daniel[6],
John[5], Benjamin[4], Robert[3], Robert[2], John[1]), b.
in Kingston, N.H., d. (presum.) June 13, 1874.
m. William Davis of Hampstead, N.H. no
additional data. (Ref. 3)

833- Joseph Bartlett[8] Wadleigh, (Daniel[7],
Daniel[6], John[5], Benjamin[4], Robert[3], Robert[2],
John[1]), b. January 8, 1844 in Kingston, N.H.,
d. 1909. m. March 13, 1885 Edith E. Geneney
(or Gemery) in Junction City, Colo. (or Kans.).
no additional data. (Ref. 3)
    1094 - Joseph Bartlett 1095 - Clarence B.

Issue of 549- Oliver[7] Wadleigh and Marcia M.
(Holbrook) Wadleigh:

834- Eliza Ann[8] Wadleigh, (Oliver[7], Joseph[6],
Joseph[5], Joseph[4], Robert[3], Robert[2], John[1]), b.
1848 in Brentwood, N.H. (Ref. 3)

835- Elwell[8] Wadleigh, (Oliver[7], Joseph[6],
Joseph[5], Joseph[4], Robert[3], Robert[2], John[1]), b.
1853 in Brentwood, N.H. m. Ella F. no
additional data. (Ref. 3)
     1096 - Percy   1097 - daughter

Issue of 554- William Morrill[7] Wadley and
Phebe (Everingham) Wadley:

836- William Oconius[8] Wadley, (William
Morrill[7], Enos Dole[6], Joseph[5], Joseph[4],
Robert[3], Robert[2], John[1]), b. October 29, 1841
in Washington Co., Ga., d. February 4, 1903.
m. January 8, 1851 Anna Eliza Winship Hancock.
no additional data. (Ref. 11)

837- Sarah Lois[8] Wadley, (William Morrill[7],
Enos Dole[6], Joseph[5], Joseph[4], Robert[3], Robert[2],
John[1]), b. November 26, 1844 in Newmarket,
N.H., d. December 7, 1920. (Ref. 11)

838- John Dole[8] Wadley, (William Morrill[7], Enos
Dole[6], Joseph[5], Joseph[4], Robert[3], Robert[2],
John[1]), b. November 6, 1846 at Oakland,
Washington Co., Ga., d. February 2, 1847. died
in infancy. (Ref. 11)

839- Mary Millen[8] Wadley, (William Morrill[7],
Enos Dole[6], Joseph[5], Joseph[4], Robert[3], Robert[2],
John[1]), b. March 4, 1848 at Oakland, Washington
Co., Ga. m. October 27, 1868 William Green
Raoul. no additional data. (Ref. 11)

840- <u>Rebecca</u> <u>Everingham</u>[8] <u>Wadley</u>, (William
Morrill[7], Enos Dole[6], Joseph[5], Joseph[4],
Robert[3], Robert[2], John[1]), b. April 29, 1850 at
Savannah, Ga. m. June 23, 1886 Stephen N.
Noble. no additional data. (Ref. 11)

841- <u>Loring</u> <u>Reynolds</u>[8] <u>Wadley</u>, (William
Morrill[7], Enos Dole[6], Joseph[5], Joseph[4],
Robert[3], Robert[2], John[1]), b. May 4, 1853 at
Oakland, Washington Co., Ga., d. August 20,
1885. (Ref. 11)

842- <u>George</u> <u>Dole</u>[8] <u>Wadley</u>, (William Morrill[7],
Enos Dole[6], Joseph[5], Joseph[4], Robert[3], Robert[2],
John[1]), b. November 15, 1857 at Oakland,
Washington Co., Ga., d. January 16, 1930. m.
June 27, 1883 Georgia Eliza Tracy. no
additional data. (Ref. 11)

843- <u>John</u> <u>Everingham</u>[8] <u>Wadley</u>, (William
Morrill[7], Enos Dole[6], Joseph[5], Joseph[4],
Robert[3], Robert[2], John[1]), b. April 6, 1860 at
Vicksburg, Miss. m. February 2, 1886 Henrietta
Lane. no additional data. (Ref. 11)

**Issue of 559- Dole[7] Wadley and Elizabeth
(Gorham) (Pierce) Wadley:**

844- <u>Sara</u> <u>Pierce</u>[8] <u>Wadley</u>, (Dole[7], Enos Dole[6],
Joseph[5], Joseph[4], Robert[3], Robert[2], John[1]), b.
July 14, 1861 at Pikes Peak Plantation,
Screvens County, Ga. m. Edward Everett
Capehart, s. of Henry Capehart of Bridgeport,
Ohio, b. February 18, 1859, d. February 20,
1917. Occ. U.S. Navy (Ref. 3, 11)
   1098 - Wadleigh Pierce   1099 - Everett Dole

845- <u>George</u>[8] <u>Wadley</u>, (Dole[7], Enos Dole[6],
Joseph[5], Joseph[4], Robert[3], Robert[2], John[1]). no
data. (Ref. 3)

WADLEIGH GENEALOGY   EIGHTH GENERATION

Issue of 564- Levi Brown and Mrs. (Robinson) Brown:

846- <u>George H. Brown</u>, (Wadleigh: Levi[7], Levi[6], Abraham[5], Mary[4], Robert[3], Robert[2], John[1]), d. 1899. Occ. Stone Mason. Res. Exeter, N.H. (Ref. 30)

847- <u>Alice Brown</u>, (Wadleigh: Levi[7], Levi[6], Abraham[5], Mary[4], Robert[3], Robert[2], John[1]). no data. Occ. author of several books, assoc. with "Youth's Companion" in Boston. Res. Boston, Mass. (Ref. 30)

Issue of 565- Sewell Brown and Mrs. (Robinson) Brown:

848- <u>son Brown</u>, (Wadleigh: Levi[6], Abraham[5], Mary[4], Robert[3], Robert[2], John[1]). no data. Occ. ship carpenters. Res. Newburyport, Mass. (Ref. 30)

849- <u>son Brown</u>, (Wadleigh: Levi[6], Abraham[5], Mary[4], Robert[3], Robert[2], John[1]). no data. Occ. ship carpenters. Res. Newburyport, Mass. (Ref. 30)

850- <u>Mary E. Brown</u>, (Wadleigh: Levi[6], Abraham[5], Mary[4], Robert[3], Robert[2], John[1]), d. alive in 1900. Res. Levi Brown homestead in Hampton Falls, N.H. (Ref. 30)

851- <u>Martha Brown</u>, (Wadleigh: Levi[6], Abraham[5], Mary[4], Robert[3], Robert[2], John[1]). no data. (Ref. 30)

Issue of 566- Samuel[4] Melcher and Elizabeth (Hilliard) Melcher:

852- <u>Joseph</u>[5] <u>Melcher</u>, (Wadleigh: Samuel[7], Samuel[6], Elizabeth[5], Benjamin[4], Mary[3], Robert[2], John[1]; Melcher: Samuel[4], Samuel[3], Samuel[2], (?)[1]), b. ca. 1769, d. 1858.   m. Polly Rowell. no additional data. Res. Melcher Homestead in Hampton, N.H., Occ. Cattle dealer. (Ref. 30)

1100 - Joseph H.	1104 - Betsey
1101 - Samuel	1105 - Hannah
1102 - Almira	1106 - Sally
1103 - Polly	

853- <u>Levi</u>[5] <u>Melcher</u>, (Wadleigh: Samuel[7], Samuel[6], Elizabeth[5], Benjamin[4], Mary[3], Robert[2], John[1]; Melcher: Samuel[4], Samuel[3], Samuel[2], (?)[1]), b. ca 1776, d. 1847.   m. Hannah Tilton, d. of Caleb Tilton. no additional data. Res. Boston, Mass. Occ. Merchant. (Ref. 30)

854- <u>Hannah</u>[5] <u>Melcher</u>, (Wadleigh: Samuel[7], Samuel[6], Elizabeth[5], Benjamin[4], Mary[3], Robert[2], John[1]; Melcher: Samuel[4], Samuel[3], Samuel[2], (?)[1]).   m. Thomas Leavitt of Hampton Falls, N.H. no additional data. (Ref. 30)

Issue of 570- John[7] Wadleigh and Mary (Call) Wadleigh:

855- <u>Mark John</u>[8] <u>Wadleigh</u>, (John[7], Joseph[6], Joseph[5], Joseph[4], Henry[3], Robert[2], John[1]), b. in (presum.) Exeter, N.H., d. March 13, 1887 in Kensington, N.H. killed by a falling tree in the same way and the same place as his father. m. Livinia Bowley of Exeter. no additional data. (Ref. 3)

1107 - Mary Ann	1111 - son
1108 - George Augustus Plummer	
1109 - William Frank	1112 - Cora E.
1110 - Ida E.	1113 - Ruth Call

Issue of 571- Betsey[7] Wadleigh:

856- Martha F. Shaw, (Wadleigh: Joseph[6], Joseph[5], Joseph[4], Henry[3], Robert[2], John[1]), b. April 12, 1806 in (presum.) Kensington, N.H. (Ref. 3)

Issue of Levi Tilton and 571- Betsey (Wadleigh) Tilton:

857- Nathan Tilton, (Wadleigh: Betsey[7], Joseph[6], Joseph[5], Joseph[4], Henry[3], Robert[2], John[1]), b. July 12, 1818 in East Kingston, N.H., d. August 28, 1897. m. Mary P. Brown. no additional data. (Ref. 3)

1114 - Levi Benson	1116 - Herbert Abel
1115 - Joseph A.	1117 - Frank Blake

Issue of 572- Joseph Dearborn[7] Wadleigh and Sarah (Patten) Wadleigh:

858- Nancy[8] Wadleigh, (Joseph Dearborn[7], Joseph[6], Joseph[5], Joseph[4], Henry[3], Robert[2], John[1]), b. May 12, 1808 in Kensington, N.H., d. October 25, 1831. (Ref. 3)

859- James[8] Wadleigh, (Joseph Dearborn[7], Joseph[6], Joseph[5], Joseph[4], Henry[3], Robert[2], John[1]), b. March 12, 1812 in Kensington, N.H., d. August 27, 1814. died in childhood. (Ref. 3)

860- Sally[8] Wadleigh, (Joseph Dearborn[7], Joseph[6], Joseph[5], Joseph[4], Henry[3], Robert[2], John[1]), b. May 5, 1814 in Kensington, N.H., d. May 5, 1844. (Ref. 3)

861- Mary[8] Wadleigh, (Joseph Dearborn[7], Joseph[6], Joseph[5], Joseph[4], Henry[3], Robert[2], John[1]), b. November 17, 1816 in Kensington, N.H., d. March 5, 1842. (Ref. 3)

862- Jonathan B.[8] Wadleigh, (Joseph Dearborn[7], Joseph[6], Joseph[5], Joseph[4], Henry[3], Robert[2], John[1]), b. November 17, 1822 in Kensington, N.H. Occ. Railroad passenger Conductor. (Ref. 3)

863- Joseph Plummer[8] Wadleigh, (Joseph Dearborn[7], Joseph[6], Joseph[5], Joseph[4], Henry[3], Robert[2], John[1]), b. June 14, 1826 in Kensington, N.H., d. August 5, 1855 near Lawrence, Mass. in a Railroad accident. Occ. locomotive engineer. (Ref. 3)

Issue of 574- Jeremiah[7] Wadleigh and Elizabeth B. (Blake) Wadleigh:

864- son[8] Wadleigh, (Jeremiah[7], Joseph[6], Joseph[5], Joseph[4], Henry[3], Robert[2], John[1]), b. 1844 in Kensington, N.H. died in infancy. (Ref. 3)

865- George[8] Wadleigh, (Jeremiah[7], Joseph[6], Joseph[5], Joseph[4], Henry[3], Robert[2], John[1]), b. 1845 in Kensington, N.H., d. (presum.) 1908 in Missouri. (Ref. 3)

866- Ellery Channing[8] Wadleigh, (Jeremiah[7], Joseph[6], Joseph[5], Joseph[4], Henry[3], Robert[2], John[1]), b. October 12, 1846 in Kensington, N.H. m. Sarah J. Lafavor of South Weare, N.H. no additional data. Charter member Lincoln Council No. 21, Junior Order United American Mechanics, org. March 10, 1897 in Kensington. (Ref. 3, 21)

867- son[8] Wadleigh, (Jeremiah[7], Joseph[6], Joseph[5], Joseph[4], Henry[3], Robert[2], John[1]), b. 1844 in Kensington, N.H. died young. (Ref. 3)

868- <u>Ann Eliza</u>[8] Wadleigh, (Jeremiah[7], Joseph[6], Joseph[5], Joseph[4], Henry[3], Robert[2], John[1]), b. August 1, 1849 in Kensington, N.H., d. June 26, 1872 in Kensington. (Ref. 3)

Issue of 575- Mark[7] Wadleigh and Sarah (Bullock) Wadleigh:

869- <u>Mark</u>[8] Wadleigh, (Mark[7], Joseph[6], Joseph[5], Joseph[4], Henry[3], Robert[2], John[1]), b. July 14, 1821 in Kensington, N.H., d. September 7, 1887. m. Harriett Simpson of Stratham, N.H. no additional data. Occ. farmer. (Ref. 3)
      1118 - Howard   1120 - Frank Otis
      1119 - Hortence Mills

870- <u>Alwin C.</u>[8] Wadleigh, (Mark[7], Joseph[6], Joseph[5], Joseph[4], Henry[3], Robert[2], John[1]), b. September 13, 1824 in Kensington, N.H., d. July 17, 1833. died in adolescence. (Ref. 3)

871- <u>Sarah E.</u>[8] Wadleigh, (Mark[7], Joseph[6], Joseph[5], Joseph[4], Henry[3], Robert[2], John[1]), b. November 18, 1827 in Kensington, N.H., d. December 4, 1865 in East Kingston, N.H. m. Eliphalet C. Greeley of Gilmanton, N.H., b. June 3, 1817 in Gilmanton, d. July 1905 in East Kingston. Res. East Kingston, N.H. (Ref. 3)
      1121 - Emily E.   1123 - Josiah Bartlett
      1122 - Alwin W.   1124 - George E.

872- <u>George J.</u>[8] Wadleigh, (Mark[7], Joseph[6], Joseph[5], Joseph[4], Henry[3], Robert[2], John[1]), b. January 8, 1830 in Kensington, N.H., d. August 16, 1832. died in childhood. (Ref. 3)

873- <u>Ruth Ann</u>[8] Wadleigh, (Mark[7], Joseph[6], Joseph[5], Joseph[4], Henry[3], Robert[2], John[1]), b. June 12, 1832 in Kensington, N.H., d. June 16, 1856. unmarried. (Ref. 3)

874- <u>Sarah Coffin</u>[8] Wadleigh, (Mark[7], Joseph[6], Joseph[5], Joseph[4], Henry[3], Robert[2], John[1]), b. October 25, 1836 in Kensington, N.H., d. March 29, 1837. died in childhood. (Ref. 3)

Issue of 576- Sewall[7] Wadleigh and Susan (Sanborn) Wadleigh:

875- <u>Harriett</u>[8] Wadleigh, (Sewall[7], Joseph[6], Joseph[5], Joseph[4], Henry[3], Robert[2], John[1]), b. June 30, 1821 in Kensington, N.H. m. George W. Morrill. no additional data. (Ref. 3)
```
            1125 - Henry Sewell    1128 - Alice
            1126 - Zora            1129 - Hattie
            1127 - Stephen Benson
```

876- <u>Sewall</u>[8] Wadleigh, (Sewall[7], Joseph[6], Joseph[5], Joseph[4], Henry[3], Robert[2], John[1]), b. July 26, 1823 in Kensington, N.H., d. September 10, 1825. died in childhood. (Ref. 3)

877- <u>Cyrus Dearborn</u>[8] Wadleigh, (Sewall[7], Joseph[6], Joseph[5], Joseph[4], Henry[3], Robert[2], John[1]), b. May 1, 1826 in Kensington, N.H.   m. December 7, 1848 at Hampton Falls, N.H. Rhoda Elizabeth Sanborn of Hampton Falls, d. of John Prescott and Sally (Cram) Sanborn of Hampton Falls, b. December 14, 1826 in Hampton Falls. Occ. (in 1856) Liquor Agent. (Ref. 3)
```
            1130 - Edith          1133 - Helen Sinclar
            1131 - Ida Frances    1134 - Melvin Clarence
            1132 - Isabel Cram    1135 - John Sewell
```

878- <u>Susan W.</u>[8] Wadleigh, (Sewall[7], Joseph[6], Joseph[5], Joseph[4], Henry[3], Robert[2], John[1]), b. February 2, 1829 in Kensington, N.H., d. July 4, 1904 in Kensington, N.H. m. April 5, 1854 George Albert Chase of Hampton Falls, N.H., d. December 20, 1863 in Kensington. (Ref. 3)
```
            1136 - Marianna Barker 1138 - Sarah Susan
            1137 - Abbie Florence  1139 - Kate Melissa
```

Issue of 583- William Henry[7] Wadleigh and
Mehitable (Masters) (Mellon) Wadleigh:

879- Lucy Jane[8] Wadleigh, (William
Henry[7],William Henry[6], Joseph[5], Joseph[4],
Henry[3], Robert[2], John[1]), b. July 31, 1844 in
Kensington, N.H. m. Warren Lamprey of
Kensington. no additional data. (Ref. 2, 3)
        1140 - Anna Marshall   1142 - John William
        1141 - Howard Lovell

880- Frank Lawrence[8] Wadleigh, (William Henry[7],
William Henry[6], Joseph[5], Joseph[4], Henry[3],
Robert[2], John[1]), b. July 25, 1846 in
Kensington, N.H., d. December 30, 1932 in
Hampton Falls. N.H. m. Sarah A. Evans of
Kensington, d. of Charles A. Evans of
Kensington, d. May 30, 1891 in Kensington.
(Ref. 2, 3)
        1143 - Arthur Garfield   1144 - Ray Emery

881- Ellen Foster[8] Wadleigh, (William Henry[7],
William Henry[6], Joseph[5], Joseph[4], Henry[3],
Robert[2], John[1]), b. November 4, 1848 in
Kensington, N.H. m. 1st Charles W. Green of
Hampton Falls, N.H. m. 2nd Frank H. Lord of
Salem Mass., and Hampton Falls, no additional
data. Charter member, Sons of Temperance.
(Ref. 2, 3, 21)
        1145 - Herbert W.   1146 - Henry

882- Anna Marshall[8] Wadleigh, (William Henry[7],
William Henry[6], Joseph[5], Joseph[4], Henry[3],
Robert[2], John[1]), b. December 7, 1850 in
Kensington, N.H., d. November 3, 1868 in
Kensington. died in adolescence. (Ref. 2, 3)

883- Charles Fremont[8] Wadleigh, (William
Henry[7], William Henry[6], Joseph[5], Joseph[4],
Henry[3], Robert[2], John[1]), b. July 2, 1856 in
Kensington, N.H., d. November 25, 1896. m.
June 6, 1877 Annie S. Lane of Hampton Falls,

N.H., d. of Levi E. Lane of Hampton Falls, b.
November 20, 1855 in Hampton Falls. d.
September 28, 1932. (Ref. 3)

  1147 - Mabelle Lane 1150 - Laurence E.
  1148 - Frances M. 1151 - Helen
  1149 - Alice H.

**Issue of 584- Daniel Foster[7] Wadleigh and
Lucinda (Libby) Wadleigh:**

884- <u>Charles Edwin</u>[8] Wadleigh, (Daniel Foster[7],
William Henry[6], Joseph[5], Joseph[4], Henry[3],
Robert[2], John[1]), b. October 3, 1843 in
Kensington, N.H., d. December 26 (or 6), 1913
in Green Ridge, Pettis Co., Mo. m. May 29,
1871 in Gardner, Grundy Co., Ill. Hannah Mary[9]
Brewster, (Edwin Flavel[8], Silas[7], Jacob[6],
Peter[5], William[4], Benjamin[3], Jonathan[2],
William[1] Brewster), b. December 3, 1851 in
Gardner, Grundy Co., Ill., d. April 26, 1936 in
Green Ridge, Pettis Co., Mo. Res. Kensington &
Epsom N.H., Rutland, Ill. & Green Ridge, Mo.
(Ref. 1, 2, 3)

  1152 - Daniel Edward 1157 - Helen Mary
  1153 - Walter Emory 1158 - Robert Leroy
  1154 - Nettie Florence 1159 - Clarence Levi
  1155 - James Augustus 1160 - Leslie Earl
  1156 - Fannie Lorena

885- <u>Helen Maria</u>[8] Wadleigh, (Daniel Foster[7],
William Henry[6], Joseph[5], Joseph[4], Henry[3],
Robert[2], John[1]), b. July 11, 1845 in Epsom,
N.H., d. June 14, 1909 in Decatur, Ill. m.
October 9, 1846 in Green Ridge, Mo. J. Vincent
Willis of Springfield, Ill., b. October 9 1846
near (presum.) Springfield, Ill., d. May 16,
1930 in Oswego, Ill., Occ. Congregational
minister, teacher (5 years) (Ref. 2, 3)

  1161 - Elmer Pierre 1164 - Clara Martha
  1162 - Estella Pearl 1165 - Fred
  1163 - Jesse Irene 1166 - Claire W.

886- <u>Maaura</u>[8] <u>Wadleigh</u>, (Daniel Foster[7], William Henry[6], Joseph[5], Joseph[4], Henry[3], Robert[2], John[1]), b. July 4 1847 at Epsom, N.H., d. November 23, 1911 at Green Ridge, Mo., m. March 6, 1867 James B. McCampbell, s. of Andrew, and Elizabeth (Kessling) McCampbell of Preble Co. Oh., b. November 11, 1843 in Preble Co., d. 1921 in (presum.) Green Ridge, Mo. Res. Epsom, N.H., Rutland, Ill., & Green Ridge, Mo. (Ref. 2, 3)

1167 - Henry Harrison	1170 - Daniel Roy
1168 - Emory	1171 - Dency Lucinda
1169 - James Randolph	

887- <u>Abbie Jane</u>[8] <u>Wadleigh</u>, (Daniel Foster[7], William Henry[6], Joseph[5], Joseph[4], Henry[3], Robert[2], John[1]), b. February 7, 1850 in Epsom, N.H., d. October 27, 1861 in Rutland, Ill. died in childhood. (Ref. 2, 3)

888- <u>Everett</u>[8] <u>Wadleigh</u>, (Daniel Foster[7], William Henry[6], Joseph[5], Joseph[4], Henry[3], Robert[2], John[1]), b. May 19, 1852 in Epsom, N.H., d. February 22, 1924 in Green Ridge, Mo., m. May 25, 1876 in Green Ridge, Mo. Martha Isabelle[2] Anderson, (George[1] Anderson), d. of George[1] Anderson of Lincolnshire, England and Mary (Robinson) Anderson of Hamilton Co. Oh., b. March 24, 1859 in Chenoa, Ill., d. May 2, 1901 in Green Ridge, Mo., Res. Epsom, N.H., Rutland, Ill., & Green Ridge, Mo. (Ref. 2, 3)

1172 - Bertha May	1178 - Hazel Carrie
1173 - Lucinda Mary	1179 - Florence Emma
1174 - Hattie Belle	1180 - Anna
1175 - Louis Henry	1181 - Leo Earl
1176 - Alma Edna	1182 - Cleo Pearl
1177 - Jennie Opal	

889- <u>Clara Eugenia</u>[8] <u>Wadleigh</u>, (Daniel Foster[7], William Henry[6], Joseph[5], Joseph[4], Henry[3], Robert[2], John[1]), b. June 28, 1854 in Epsom, N.H., d. January 2, 1862 in Rutland, Ill. died in childhood. (Ref. 2, 3)

890- <u>Henry Libby</u>[8] <u>Wadleigh</u>, (Daniel Foster[7], William Henry[6], Joseph[5], Joseph[4], Henry[3], Robert[2], John[1]), b. December 11, 1857 in Rutland, Ill., d. May 29, 1931 in Cheraw, Colo., m. 1st January 29, 1883 Mary E. Fowler, d. of Elmer F. and Sarah (Donaldson) Fowler of Green Ridge, Mo., b. August 4, 1857, d. October 15, 1886 in Green Ridge, Pettis Co., Mo. m. 2nd December 15, 1887 Rosetta Adelaide[9] (Brewster) Williams, (Brewster: Edwin Flavel[8], Silas[7], Jacob[6], Peter[5], William[4], Benjamin[3], Jonathan[2], William[1] Brewster), d. of Edwin Flavel[8] and Ruth (Gleason) Brewster, wid. of Joseph Lewis Williams of Providence, Providence Co., R.I. (who was s. of Joseph Lewis of Providence), b. August 25, 1856, d. January 19, 1934. Res. Rutland, Ill., Green Ridge, Mo., Sugar City, Crowley Co. Colo. (February 21, 1902 and following) & Cheraw, Otero Co., Colo. (Ref. 1, 2, 3) 1183 - 1184 by 1st wife, 1185 - 1191 by 2nd wife.

1183	- Fred Elmer	1188	- Harold Brewster
1184	- Arthur Gilbert	1189	- Eugene Henry
1185	- Ralph Libby	1190	- Edna Rose
1186	- Joseph Everett	1191	- Mary Emma
1187	- Herbert Calvin		

Issue of John Frances Gove and 585- Sarah Jane (Wadleigh) Gove:

891- <u>Aaron Gove</u>, (Wadleigh: Sarah Jane[7], William Henry[6], Joseph[5], Joseph[4], Henry[3], Robert[2], John[1]). no data. (Ref. 2)

892- <u>Frank Gove</u>, (Wadleigh: Sarah Jane[7], William Henry[6], Joseph[5], Joseph[4], Henry[3], Robert[2], John[1]). no data. (Ref. 2)

893- <u>Francis Gove</u>, (Wadleigh: Sarah Jane[7], William Henry[6], Joseph[5], Joseph[4], Henry[3], Robert[2], John[1]), m. Eugene Baldwin. no additional data. (Ref. 2)

Issue of 586- Joseph Dearborn[7] Wadleigh and Frances Esther (Prescott) Wadleigh:

894- Joseph Brazure[8] Wadleigh, (Joseph Dearborn[7], William Henry[6], Joseph[5], Joseph[4], Henry[3], Robert[2], John[1]), b. 1844 Exeter, N.H., d. 1864 in Point Burnside, Ky. (Battle of Antietam) (Ref. 2, 3)

895- George Henry[8] Wadleigh, (Joseph Dearborn[7], William Henry[6], Joseph[5], Joseph[4], Henry[3], Robert[2], John[1]), b. May 3, 1848 in Exeter, N.H. (Ref. 3 states Kensington, N.H.), d. September 9, 1906 in Green Ridge, Mo. m. May 9, 1868 in Exeter, N.H. Mary Kendrick Goodwin of Deerfield, Mass., d. of John D. and Maria Shores (Kendrick) Goodwin of Exeter, N.H., b. July 17, 1848 in Deerfield, Mass. (Ref. 3 states Amesbury, Mass.), d. August 18, 1916 in Green Ridge, Mo. Occ. Farmer. (Ref. 2, 3)
    1192 - Carrie Russell
    1193 - Myrtle May Williams

896- Caroline (or Carrie) Russell[8] Wadleigh, (Joseph Dearborn[7], William Henry[6], Joseph[5], Joseph[4], Henry[3], Robert[2], John[1]), b. May 19, 1850 in Exeter N.H., d. August 13, 1866 in Exeter. died in adolescence. (Ref. 2, 3)

897- Jennie Russell[8] Wadleigh, (Joseph Dearborn[7], William Henry[6], Joseph[5], Joseph[4], Henry[3], Robert[2], John[1]), b. January 16, 1862 in (presum.) Exeter, N.H., orphaned dau. of a Union Soldier, and adopted., d. August 20, 1945 in Green Ridge, Mo., m. December 22, 1879 in Green Ridge, Mo. Nathan Brockway Reed, s. of Hial Reed of N.Y., b. January 19, 1856, d. November 11, 1949. (Ref. 2, 3)

1194 - Ethel Grace	1199 - Charlie Voss
1195 - Joe Brockway	1200 - Florence Esther
1196 - Bessie Helen	1201 - Mildred Fayolla
1197 - Ida Mae	1202 - Donald
1198 - George Beaman	

Issue of 589- John H.[7] Wadleigh and Pauline
P. (Kimball) Wadleigh:

898- Inez Menerva[8] Wadleigh, (John H.[7], William
Henry[6], Joseph[5], Joseph[4], Henry[3], Robert[2],
John[1]), b. November 8, 1853 in Kensington,
N.H., d. January 12, 1919 in Rutland, Ill.
(Ref. 2, 3)

899- Mary A.[8] Wadleigh, (John H.[7], William
Henry[6], Joseph[5], Joseph[4], Henry[3], Robert[2],
John[1]), b. 1859 in Rutland, Ill., d. 1937 in
Rutland, Ill.,   m. Sheldon Scofield Winans, b.
1856, d. 1931. (Ref. 2)

900- Laura D.[8] Wadleigh, (John H.[7], William
Henry[6], Joseph[5], Joseph[4], Henry[3], Robert[2],
John[1]), b. 1861 in (presum.) Rutland, Ill., d.
1923 in Rutland, Ill., m. Rowland Mullin, b.
1858, d. 1934. (Ref. 2)
       1203 - Earl

901- William H.[8] Wadleigh, (John H.[7], William
Henry[6], Joseph[5], Joseph[4], Henry[3], Robert[2],
John[1]), b. 1864 in (presum.) Rutland, Ill., d.
July 19, 1931 in Rutland, Ill.,   m. Jennie Dye,
b. 1870, d. December 17, 1919 in Rutland, Ill.
(Ref. 2)
       1204 - Reed

Issue of 591- John[7] Wadleigh and Betsy (Cole)
Wadleigh:

902- John[8] Wadleigh, (John[7], Simon Dearborn[6],
Benjamin[5], Joseph[4], Henry[3], Robert[2], John[1]), b.
December 28, 1804 in Hill, N.H., d. March 15,
1883 in East Andover, N.H. m. 1st August 28,
1832 Dolly Bailey of Andover, N.H., d. of John,
and Mary (Currier) Bailey of Andover, b. May 8
1809 in Andover, d. October 21, 1870 in East
Andover.   m. 2nd January 13, 1874 Mary (Cloud)

Pettigrew, wid. of Mr. Pettigrew. no
additional data. Res. Hill, Andover, and East
Andover, N.H., and in Vermont. (Ref. 3)   1205 -
1208 by 1st wife.
> 1205 - John Buren   1207 - Annie W.
> 1206 - Mary Love   1208 - George Andrew

903- Achsah[8] Wadleigh, (John[7], Simon Dearborn[6],
Benjamin[5], Joseph[4], Henry[3], Robert[2], John[1]), b.
August 6, 1806 in Hill, N.H. m. (presum.)
Thomas Favor of Hill, -or- Mr. Hersey. no
additional data. (Ref. 3)

904- Mary[8] Wadleigh, (John[7], Simon Dearborn[6],
Benjamin[5], Joseph[4], Henry[3], Robert[2], John[1]), b.
July 29, 1809 in Hill, N.H. (Ref. 3)

905- Joseph[8] Wadleigh, (John[7], Simon Dearborn[6],
Benjamin[5], Joseph[4], Henry[3], Robert[2], John[1]), b.
in Hill, N.H. (Ref. 3)

906- Levi C.[8] Wadleigh, (John[7], Simon
Dearborn[6], Benjamin[5], Joseph[4], Henry[3], Robert[2],
John[1]), m. 1st Mary McCrilliss of Amesbury,
Mass. m. 2nd Elizabeth Hall of Exeter, N.H.
m. 3rd Amanda Bonney of Me. no additional
data. (Ref. 3) 1209 - 1212 by 1st wife.
> 1209 - Susan Elizabeth   1211 - Fannie
> 1210 - George Clinton   1212 - Levi C.

Issue of 592- Newell[7] Wadleigh and Filey (Chatterton) Wadleigh:

907- Permelia[8] Wadleigh, (Newell[7], Simon
Dearborn[6], Benjamin[5], Joseph[4], Henry[3], Robert[2],
John[1]), b. June 1808 in Bolton, Quebec, Canada,
d. December 18, 1844 in (presum.) Waterville,
Canada, bur. Waterville, Canada. m. Horace
Hovey of Hatley, Quebec, Canada. no additional
data. (Ref. 3)

908- <u>Hiram Gilmore</u>[8] <u>Wadleigh</u>, (Newell[7], Simon
Dearborn[6], Benjamin[5], Joseph[4], Henry[3], Robert[2],
John[1]), b. March 12, 1810 in Bolton, Quebec,
Canada, d. December 26, 1852 in Boston, Mass.
m. July 26, 1839 in Boston Philitia Goodnow, b.
July 3, 1811 in Grafton, Vt., d. April 27, 1876
in Boston. (Ref. 3)
  1213 - Harriet Louisa   1215 - Frank H. Newell
  1214 - Charles Edwin

909- <u>Frank H. Newell</u>[8] <u>Wadleigh</u>, (Newell[7], Simon
Dearborn[6], Benjamin[5], Joseph[4], Henry[3], Robert[2],
John[1]), b. September 15, 1852 in Boston, Mass.,
d. March 11, 1853 in Boston, Mass. died in
infancy. (Ref. 3)

Issue of 600- James[7] Wadleigh and Eunice (Farnham) Wadleigh:

910- <u>Hannah Piper</u>[8] <u>Wadleigh</u>, (James[7], James[6],
James[5], Joseph[4], Henry[3], Robert[2], John[1]), b.
December 12, 1803 in Sanbornton, N.H. m.
February 28, 1860 Calvin Pollard of Hudson,
N.H., d. April 24, 1871. Res. Hudson, and
Sanbornton, N.H. (Ref. 3)

911- <u>James C.</u>[8] <u>Wadleigh</u>, (James[7], James[6],
James[5], Joseph[4], Henry[3], Robert[2], John[1]), b.
November 16, 1805 in Sanbornton, N.H., d.
January 17, 1870 of Bright's disease. m.
November 24, 1831 Hannah P. Pearson, d. of
Jethro Pearson of Meredith Ridge, N.H. no
additional data. Occ. Mason, and Farmer. Res.
Sanbornton, and Meredith Ridge, N.H. (Ref. 3)
  1216 - John Burley 1217 - Luther Jethro

912- <u>Esther</u>[8] <u>Wadleigh</u>, (James[7], James[6], James[5],
Joseph[4], Henry[3], Robert[2], John[1]), b. December
17, 1807 in Sanbornton, N.H. m. June 12, 1828
John S. Burley. no additional data. (Ref. 3)

WADLEIGH GENEALOGY   EIGHTH GENERATION

913- <u>Nathaniel Farnham</u>[8] <u>Wadleigh</u>, (James[7],
James[6], James[5], Joseph[4], Henry[3], Robert[2],
John[1]), b. August 12, 1816 in Sanbornton, N.H.,
d. September 8, 1879 of dropsy. m. February
27, 1845 Sally Merrill Plumer, d. of Stephen
Plumer. no additional data. (Ref. 3)
     1218 - Cynthia Ann

**Issue of 601- Joseph[7] Wadleigh and Phebe
(Dustin) Wadleigh:**

914- <u>Lydia Dustin</u>[8] <u>Wadleigh</u>, (Joseph[7], James[6],
James[5], Joseph[4], Henry[3], Robert[2], John[1]), b.
October 12, 1804 in Sanbornton, N.H. m.
November 5, 1828 Asa[3] Swain. no additional
data. (Ref. 3)

915- <u>Warren</u>[8] <u>Wadleigh</u>, (Joseph[7], James[6],
James[5], Joseph[4], Henry[3], Robert[2], John[1]), b.
December 29, 1807 in Sanbornton, N.H. m. April
27, 1835 Harriett O. Thomas, b. August 14, 1807
in Sanbornton, N.H. (Ref. 3)
   1219 - Kendall   1221 - Washington Irving
   1220 - Annie Fogg   1222 - Horace Wayland

916- <u>Shadrach</u>[8] <u>Wadleigh</u>, (Joseph[7], James[6],
James[5], Joseph[4], Henry[3], Robert[2], John[1]), b.
November 9, 1810 in Sanbornton, N.H. m.
January 22, 1836 Huldah S. Hunt, d. of Abraham
P. Hunt of Sanbornton, N.H. no additional
data. (Ref. 3)
     1223 - Phebe Ann

917- <u>Benjamin Mason</u>[8] <u>Wadleigh</u>, (Joseph[7],
James[6], James[5], Joseph[4], Henry[3], Robert[2],
John[1]), b. December 21, 1817 in Sanbornton,
N.H., d. October 8, 1878 in Sanbornton of
consumption. m. in Freedom, N.H. October 2,
1851 Mary J. Foss of Freedom, d. of Peletiah
and Jane (Harmon) Foss (Peletiah is s. of Loren
Foss), b. February 5, 1823 in Freedom. (Ref. 3)

WADLEIGH - 163

918- Joseph Dustin[8] Wadleigh, (Joseph[7], James[6], James[5], Joseph[4], Henry[3], Robert[2], John[1]), b. May 11, 1823 in Sanbornton, N.H. m. May 28, 1848 Sarah S. Hunt, d. of Abraham P. Hunt. no additional data. (Ref. 3)
   1224 - George Hunt   1225 - Clairber Ann

Issue of 604- John[7] Wadleigh and Sarah (Taylor) Wadleigh:

919- Molly Blake[8] Wadleigh, (John[7], James[6], James[5], Joseph[4], Henry[3], Robert[2], John[1]), b. August 20, 1815 in Sanbornton, N.H., d. March 25, 1817. died in childhood. (Ref. 3)

920- Molly Blake[8] Wadleigh, (John[7], James[6], James[5], Joseph[4], Henry[3], Robert[2], John[1]), b. May 25, 1817 in Sanbornton, N.H., d. July 29, 1818. died in childhood. (Ref. 3)

921- Jonathan Taylor[8] Wadleigh, (John[7], James[6], James[5], Joseph[4], Henry[3], Robert[2], John[1]), b. May 14, 1819 in Sanbornton, N.H., d. April 18, 1874. m. January 1, 1843 Betsey Thomas, d. of Joseph Thomas. no additional data. Occ. farmer. Res. Sanbornton, Franklin and Hill, N.H. (Ref. 3)
   1226 - Josephine Louise 1228 - Walter Kendall
   1227 - Charlotte Fogg

922- Sarah Ann Bartlett[8] Wadleigh, (John[7], James[6], James[5], Joseph[4], Henry[3], Robert[2], John[1]), b. August 21, 1821 in Sanbornton, N.H. m. March 24, 1844 Charles B. Perley. no additional data. (Ref. 3)

923- Elizabeth Malcher[8] Wadleigh, (John[7], James[6], James[5], Joseph[4], Henry[3], Robert[2], John[1]), b. November 2, 1825 in Sanbornton, N.H. Res. Boston, Mass. (Ref. 3)

924- John Blake[8] Wadleigh, (John[7], James[6], James[5], Joseph[4], Henry[3], Robert[2], John[1]), b. April 25, 1829 in Sanbornton, N.H. m. 1st December 27, 1860 Helen May Parker, d. of I. T. Parker, b. November 30, 1838, d. October 9, 1862. m. 2nd November 9, 1864 Abby Ruthena Tilton of Deerfield, N.H., d. of Jeremiah D. and Abigail F. Tilton, b. ca. 1842. (Ref. 3) no issue by 1st wife, 1229 - 1232 by 2nd wife.

  1229 - Oscar Stearns   1231 - Fred Tilton
  1230 - John Parker   1232 - Helen Abbie

925- Daniel Taylor[8] Wadleigh, (John[7], James[6], James[5], Joseph[4], Henry[3], Robert[2], John[1]), b. March 2, 1835 in Sanbornton, N.H. m. April 1861 Hannah P. Burley, d. of John S. Burley. no additional data. Res. farmer on the old Wadleigh homestead. (Ref. 3)

  1233 - Fred Burley   1235 - Sarah Esther
  1234 - William Augustus 1236 - Mary Percy

Issue of 607- Asa[7] Wadleigh and Lucy (Woodman) Wadleigh:

926- James Monroe[8] Wadleigh, (Asa[7], James[6], James[5], Joseph[4], Henry[3], Robert[2], John[1]), b. 1827 in Sanbornton, N.H. m. January 4, 1859 Caroline Stall of Boston, Mass. no additional data. (Ref. 3)

927- Jacob Woodman[8] Wadleigh, (Asa[7], James[6], James[5], Joseph[4], Henry[3], Robert[2], John[1]), b. April 25, 1829 in Sanbornton, N.H., d. August 2, 1836 in Laconia, N.H. m. April 26, 1853 Eliza A. Sanborn, d. of Daniel Sanborn. no additional data. (Ref. 3)

928- Mary Mason[8] Wadleigh, (Asa[7], James[6], James[5], Joseph[4], Henry[3], Robert[2], John[1]), b. May 1, 1840 in Sanbornton, N.H., d. November 25, 1866 in Roxbury, Mass. (Ref. 3)

Issue of 608- Dearborn[7] Wadleigh and Polly (Hayes) Wadleigh:

929- John[8] Wadleigh, (Dearborn[7], John[6], James[5], Joseph[4], Henry[3], Robert[2], John[1]), b. 1806 in Meredith, N.H., d. 1873. m. Ann Hanaford, b. 1810, d. 1866. (Ref. 3)

    1237 - LeRoi B.   1139 - John Dearborn
    1238 - Martha Abby   1140 - Mary Ann

Issue of 618- James Dearborn[7] Wadleigh and Phebe (Chase) Wadleigh:

930- Polly[8] Wadleigh, (James Dearborn[7], Joseph[6], James[5], Joseph[4], Henry[3], Robert[2], John[1]), b. June 14, 1817 in Sanbornton, N.H., d. October 11, 1821 in Sanbornton, N.H. died in childhood. (Ref. 3)

931- Charles Joseph[8] Wadleigh, (James Dearborn[7], Joseph[6], James[5], Joseph[4], Henry[3], Robert[2], John[1]), b. February 8, 1824 in Sanbornton, N.H., d. November 21, 1874 in Mannerville, Dodge Co., Minn. m. April 14, 1846 Ann Maria Gage, d. of David R. Gage. no additional data. Occ. Farmer in Mannerville, Minn. (Ref. 3)

    1241 - Martha O.   1243 - Charles J.
    1242 - Eve J.

932- Maranda[8] Wadleigh, (James Dearborn[7], Joseph[6], James[5], Joseph[4], Henry[3], Robert[2], John[1]), b. July 26, 1829 in Sanbornton, N.H. m. Shadrach T. Smith. no additional data. (Ref. 3)

Issue of 620- Newell[7] Wadleigh and Mrs. Wadleigh:

933- <u>daughter</u>[8] <u>Wadleigh</u>, (Newell[7], Joseph[6], James[5], Joseph[4], Henry[3], Robert[2], John[1]). no additional data. (Ref. 3)

934- <u>Joseph</u>[8] <u>Wadleigh</u>, (Newell[7], Joseph[6], James[5], Joseph[4], Henry[3], Robert[2], John[1]), b. June 17, 1835 in Sanbornton, N.H. m. February 5, 1856 Julia A. Henry, b. July 18, 1835. (Ref. 3)
        1244 - Josephine Mary   1247 - Olivia
        1245 - Juann   1248 - Henry Albert
        1246 - Jude C.

Issue of 621- Joseph[7] Wadleigh and Sally (Quimby) Wadleigh:

935- <u>Nathaniel Read</u>[8] <u>Wadleigh</u>, (Joseph[7], Joseph[6], James[5], Joseph[4], Henry[3], Robert[2], John[1]), b. May 11, 1826 in Sanbornton, N.H in (presum.) Kensington, N.H. (Ref. 3)

936- <u>Harper Quimby</u>[8] <u>Wadleigh</u>, (Joseph[7], Joseph[6], James[5], Joseph[4], Henry[3], Robert[2], John[1]), b. April 26, 1828 in Sanbornton, N.H. Changed name to Harper Wadleigh Quimby. Last res. (presum.) Herrin, Illinois. (Ref. 3)

937- <u>Nancy Morrill</u>[8] <u>Wadleigh</u>, (Joseph[7], Joseph[6], James[5], Joseph[4], Henry[3], Robert[2], John[1]), no data. (Ref. 3)

938- <u>G rish</u>[8] <u>Wadleigh</u>, (Joseph[7], Joseph[6], James[5], Joseph[4], Henry[3], Robert[2], John[1]), b. January 25, 1832 in Sanbornton, N.H., d. in Morley, St. Lawrence Co, N.Y. m. Hattie Lawrence of Manchester, N.H. no additional data. (Ref. 3)

WADLEIGH GENEALOGY   EIGHTH GENERATION

939- Hiram Porter[8] Wadleigh, (Joseph[7], Joseph[6],
James[5], Joseph[4], Henry[3], Robert[2], John[1]), b.
August 2, 1835 in Sanbornton, N.H., m. January
8, 1860 Mary W. Morrison, d. of Thomas
Morrison. no additional data. (Ref. 3)
        1249 - Elmer Albert

940- Gustave Bartlett[8] Wadleigh, (Joseph[7],
Joseph[6], James[5], Joseph[4], Henry[3], Robert[2],
John[1]), b. July 7, 1838 in Sanbornton, N.H. m.
June 23, 1855 Abbie Eaton of Bristol, N.H., b.
May 13, 1840. Occ. carpenter. (Ref. 3)
        1250 - Ida Belle   1251 - Albert Prescot

941- Fannie[8] Wadleigh, (Joseph[7], Joseph[6],
James[5], Joseph[4], Henry[3], Robert[2], John[1]), b.
August 10, 1839 in Sanbornton, N.H. m. Issac
B. Vergin. no additional data. (Ref. 3)

942- Sarah[8] Wadleigh, (Joseph[7], Joseph[6],
James[5], Joseph[4], Henry[3], Robert[2], John[1]), b.
March 3, 1842 in Sanbornton, N.H., d. in
(presum.) Boston, Mass. Occ. dressmaker. Res.
Sanbornton, N.H. and Boston, Mass. (Ref. 3)

943- Albert Prescott[8] Wadleigh, (Joseph[7],
Joseph[6], James[5], Joseph[4], Henry[3], Robert[2],
John[1]), b. February 23, 1844 in Sanbornton,
N.H., d. January 20, 1863 of measles in
Falmouth, Va. as a soldier in the 12th N.H.
Regiment during the Civil War. (Ref. 3)

944- Martha Ellen[8] Wadleigh, (Joseph[7], Joseph[6],
James[5], Joseph[4], Henry[3], Robert[2], John[1]), b.
June 15, 1846 in Sanbornton, N.H. m. October
9, 1864 James R. Philbrick of Kittery, Me. no
additional data. (Ref. 3)
        1252 - Cora Belle

WADLEIGH - 168

945- <u>Clarissa Weeks</u>[8] Wadleigh, (Joseph[7], Joseph[6], James[5], Joseph[4], Henry[3], Robert[2], John[1]), b. August 27, 1849 in Sanbornton, N.H. m. 1870 Belder W. Morgan. no additional data. (Ref. 3)

    1253 - Zelle Belle

946- <u>George Eli</u>[8] Wadleigh, (Joseph[7], Joseph[6], James[5], Joseph[4], Henry[3], Robert[2], John[1]), b. August 5, 1851 in Sanbornton, N.H. m. Alzina Bradley of Andover, Mass. no additional data. Occ. carpenter. Res. Sanbornton and Manchester, N.H. (Ref. 3)

947- <u>Lucy</u>[8] Wadleigh, (Joseph[7], Joseph[6], James[5], Joseph[4], Henry[3], Robert[2], John[1]), b. July 1856 in Sanbornton, N.H. m. May 14, 1874 Frank L. Prescott as his second wife. no data. (Ref. 3)

Issue of 623- Chase Weeks[7] Wadleigh and Marcia M. (Whitcher) Wadleigh:

948- <u>Alonzo</u>[8] Wadleigh, (Chase Weeks[7], Joseph[6], James[5], Joseph[4], Henry[3], Robert[2], John[1]), b. January 14, 1833 in Sanbornton, N.H. m. January 12, 1859 Nancy[3] Chute, d. of Noah[2] Chute, b. March 29, 1831 Occ. farmer, and sawmill operator. (Ref. 3)

949- <u>Melissa</u>[8] Wadleigh, (Chase Weeks[7], Joseph[6], James[5], Joseph[4], Henry[3], Robert[2], John[1]), b. November 1833 in Sanbornton, N.H., d. February 12, 1835 in Sanbornton. died in childhood. (Ref. 3)

950- <u>Melissa Colby</u>[8] Wadleigh, (Chase Weeks[7], Joseph[6], James[5], Joseph[4], Henry[3], Robert[2], John[1]), b. October 25, 1845 in Sanbornton, N.H. m. March 6, 1869 Charles Calley, b. March 12, 1818. (Ref. 3)

Issue of 624- Simon Hayes[7] Wadleigh and Jane B. (Sleeper) Wadleigh:

951- George Weston[8] Wadleigh, (Simon Hayes[7], Joseph[6], James[5], Joseph[4], Henry[3], Robert[2], John[1]), b. 1835 in Bristol, N.H. Res. (last known) Concord, Mass. (Ref. 3)

952- John Hayes[8] Wadleigh, (Simon Hayes[7], Joseph[6], James[5], Joseph[4], Henry[3], Robert[2], John[1]), b. January 24, 1837 in Bristol, N.H. m. June 17, 1858 Mary Lela Stiles, d. of Orrin A. Stiles of Moretown, Vt. Res. Braintree, and Randolph, Vt. (Ref. 3)
    1254 - Frank Weston   1256 - Mabel Ellen
    1255 - John Bartlett

953- Mary Ellen[8] Wadleigh, (Simon Hayes[7], Joseph[6], James[5], Joseph[4], Henry[3], Robert[2], John[1]), b. April 9, 1830 in Bristol, N.H. m. May 13, 1859 Henry K. W. Currier. no additional data. Res. Woburn, Mass. (Ref. 3)
    1257 - Nathaniel

954- Anna T.[8] Wadleigh, (Simon Hayes[7], Joseph[6], James[5], Joseph[4], Henry[3], Robert[2], John[1]), b. in Bristol, N.H., d. September 3, 1844. died in childhood. (Ref. 3)

Issue of 625- William P.[7] Wadleigh and Lydia (Neal) Wadleigh:

955- Joseph[8] Wadleigh, (William P.[7], Simeon[6], James[5], Joseph[4], Henry[3], Robert[2], John[1]), b. in Meredith, N.H. m. Lydia Moore. no additional data. (Ref. 3)
    1258 - Julia   1259 - Mary Etta

956- Simeon F.[8] Wadleigh, (William P.[7], Simeon[6], James[5], Joseph[4], Henry[3], Robert[2],

John[1]), b. October 25, 1815 in Meredith, N.H.,
d. April 1, 1895. m. Emily Cox, b. June 12,
1808, d. February 8, 1895. (Ref. 3)

957- William S.[8] Wadleigh, (William P.[7],
Simeon[6], James[5], Joseph[4], Henry[3], Robert[2],
John[1]), b. November 21, 1817 in Meredith, N.H,
d. June 19, 1819. died in childhood. (Ref. 3)

958- William H.[8] Wadleigh, (William P.[7],
Simeon[6], James[5], Joseph[4], Henry[3], Robert[2],
John[1]), b. January 10, 1821 in Meredith, N.H.,
d. January 13, 1902. m. Rebecca Wood, b. April
1825, d. May 20, 1911. (Ref. 3)

959- Nancy[8] Wadleigh, (William P.[7], Simeon[6],
James[5], Joseph[4], Henry[3], Robert[2], John[1]), b.
1824 in Meredith, N.H., d. 1887. m. 961-
Charles[8] Wadleigh, (Stephen G.[7], Simeon[6],
James[5], Joseph[4], Henry[3], Robert[2], John[1]), b.
1821, d. 1888. (Ref. 3) For issue SEE: 961-
Charles [8] Wadleigh.

960- Mary Jane[8] Wadleigh, (William P.[7],
Simeon[6], James[5], Joseph[4], Henry[3], Robert[2],
John[1]), b. 1828 in Meredith, N.H. m. Newell J.
Tilton. no additional data. (Ref. 3)

Issue of 627- Stephen G.[7] Wadleigh and Polly
(Neal) Wadleigh:

961- Charles[8] Wadleigh, (Stephen G.[7], Simeon[6],
James[5], Joseph[4], Henry[3], Robert[2], John[1]), b. in
Meredith, N.H. m. 959- Nancy[8] Wadleigh,
(William P.[7], Simeon[6], James[5], Joseph[4], Henry[3],
Robert[2], John[1]). no additional data. (Ref. 3)

962- Abigail[8] Wadleigh, (Stephen G.[7], Simeon[6],
James[5], Joseph[4], Henry[3], Robert[2], John[1]), b. in

Meredith, N.H. m. Benjamin Wiggin. no
additional data. (Ref. 3)

963- Edward F.[8] Wadleigh, (Stephen G.[7],
Simeon[6], James[5], Joseph[4], Henry[3], Robert[2],
John[1]), b. in Meredith, N.H. m. Carrie Canney.
no additional data. (Ref. 3)

**Issue of 627- Stephen G.[7] Wadleigh and Olive
(Neal) Wadleigh:**

964- Polly[8] Wadleigh, (Stephen G.[7], Simeon[6],
James[5], Joseph[4], Henry[3], Robert[2], John[1]), b. in
Meredith, N.H. m. Charles Weeks. no
additional data. (Ref. 3)

965- Jane[8] Wadleigh, (Stephen G.[7], Simeon[6],
James[5], Joseph[4], Henry[3], Robert[2], John[1]), b. in
Meredith, N.H. m. John Mead Neal. no
additional data. (Ref. 3)

966- Olive[8] Wadleigh, (Stephen G.[7], Simeon[6],
James[5], Joseph[4], Henry[3], Robert[2], John[1]), b. in
Meredith, N.H. did not marry. (Ref. 3)

**Issue of 628- William[7] Wadleigh and Emily A.
(Dearborn) Wadleigh:**

967- George W.[8] Wadleigh, (William[7], Enoch[6],
James[5], Joseph[4], Henry[3], Robert[2], John[1]), b.
January 12, 1845 in Exeter, N.H., d. March 13,
1927 in Exeter. did not marry. (Ref. 3)

968- John M.[8] Wadleigh, (William[7], Enoch[6],
James[5], Joseph[4], Henry[3], Robert[2], John[1]), b.
July 6, 1846 in Exeter, N.H., d. March 25, 1927
(Ref. 27: March 26, 1925)in Exeter. did not
marry. Occ. Hotel keeper, land developer and
lumbering business. Res. Exeter. (Ref. 3)

969- Emma Josephine[8] Wadleigh, (William[7], Enoch[6], James[5], Joseph[4], Henry[3], Robert[2], John[1]), b. December 15, 1848 in Exeter, N.H., d. January 6, 1914. m. Harry Raybold. no additional data. (Ref. 3)

970- Ada Margaret[8] Wadleigh, (William[7], Enoch[6], James[5], Joseph[4], Henry[3], Robert[2], John[1]), b. September 15, 1851 in Exeter, N.H., d. August 11, 1910. did not marry. (Ref. 3)

971- Frank H.[8] Wadleigh, (William[7], Enoch[6], James[5], Joseph[4], Henry[3], Robert[2], John[1]), b. July 2, 1855 in Exeter, N.H., d. December 14, 1939 in Exeter. Occ. Farmer, Dir. of Jady Hill Land Co. Res. Exeter on family farm on Linden St. (Ref. 3, 27)

972- Minnie Cora[8] Wadleigh, (William[7], Enoch[6], James[5], Joseph[4], Henry[3], Robert[2], John[1]), b. March 6, 1860 in Exeter, N.H., d. July 5, 1922. m. October 29, 1885 George Winkley Pollard of South Newmarket, N.H. no additional data. (Ref. 3)

Issue of Nathaniel Maloon and 633- Betsey (Wadleigh) Maloon:

973- Sophia Maloon, (Wadleigh: Betsey[7], Joseph/Josiah[6], James[5], Joseph[4], Henry[3], Robert[2], John[1]), b. in Meredith, N.H. m. Llewelyn Ballard, b. in Belfast, Me. (Ref. 3)

Issue of 634- Dexter[7] Wadleigh and Mrs. Wadleigh:

974- Dexter E.[8] Wadleigh, (Dexter[7], Joseph/Josiah[6], James[5], Joseph[4], Henry[3], Robert[2], John[1]). no additional data. (Ref. 3)

Issue of Alfred Love Stokes and 636- Frances Wentworth (Wadleigh) Stokes:

975- <u>Mary Wadleigh</u> Stokes, (Wadleigh: Frances Wentworth[7], Albra[6], Ebenezer[5], John[4], Daniel[3], John[2], John[1]). no additional data. (Ref. 3)

Issue of 640- John[7] Wadleigh and Melessa Wadleigh:

976- daughter[8] Wadleigh, (John[7], John[6], Elisha[5], John[4], Daniel[3], John[2], John[1]), b. February 17 1857 in Manchester, N.H. (Ref. 3)

Issue of 644- George W.[7] Wadleigh and Abigail (Edgecomb) Wadleigh:

977- <u>Clarence</u>[8] Wadleigh, (George W.[7], James[6], Elisha[5], John[4], Daniel[3], John[2], John[1]), b. in Kezar Falls, Me. (Ref. 3)

978- <u>George W.</u>[8] Wadleigh, (George W.[7], James[6], Elisha[5], John[4], Daniel[3], John[2], John[1]). no data. (Ref. 3)

979- <u>Ernest W.</u>[8] Wadleigh, (George W.[7], James[6], Elisha[5], John[4], Daniel[3], John[2], John[1]), b. in either Kezar Falls, Me. or Buxton, Me. m. Lizzie H. Kezar of Parsonfield, Me. no additional data. Occ. h. Carpenter, w. teacher. Res. Freedom, N.H. and Parsonfield. Me. (Ref. 3)

980- <u>Fred</u>[8] Wadleigh, (George W.[7], James[6], Elisha[5], John[4], Daniel[3], John[2], John[1]). no data. (Ref. 3)

Issue of Ebenezer Swain and 662- Abigail
(Wadleigh) Swain:

981- H. A. Swain, (Wadleigh: Abigail,
Nathaniel), b. 1821. m. 1st 1846 Lydia Thorne.
m. 2nd 1893 Hattie A. Easter of Center Harbor,
N.H. no additional data. (Ref. 3)

Issue of 671- Rufus Wadleigh, and Mary Cram:

982- Olive Wadleigh, (Wadleigh: Rufus), b.
August 1829 in Bolton, Quebec, Canada. m.
Mansell Blake of Weare, N.H. no additional
data. (Ref. 3)

983- John Wadleigh, (Wadleigh: Rufus), b.
October 22, 1830 in Bolton, Quebec, Canada. m.
January 15, 18(55?) Melissa Barrett of
Manchester, N.H. no additional data. (Ref. 3)

984- Electa Wadleigh, (Wadleigh: Rufus), b.
September 21, 1832 in Bolton, Quebec, Canada.
m. 1st Sumner Beard. m. 2nd. Cyrus W.
Flanders. no additional data. (Ref. 3)

985- Hannah K. Wadleigh, (Wadleigh: Rufus), b.
September 21, 1834 in Bolton, Quebec, Canada.
m. Alfred Fales of Lyme, N.H. no additional
data. (Ref. 3)

986- Moses Wadleigh, (Wadleigh: Rufus), b. ca.
1836, died in childhood. (Ref. 3)

987- James Wadleigh, (Wadleigh: Rufus), b. ca.
1838, died in childhood. (Ref. 3)

988- <u>Cynthia</u> <u>Wadleigh</u>, (Wadleigh: Rufus), b.
October 30, 1840 in Weare, N.H.   m. Lucian B.
Richards.   no additional data.   (Ref. 3)

989- <u>Moses</u> <u>C.</u> <u>Wadleigh</u>, (Wadleigh: Rufus), b.
August 10, 1843 in Weare, N.H.   m. Delia (or
Celite) Hall of Rumney, N.H.   no additional
data.   (Ref. 3)

990- <u>Emma</u> <u>R.</u> <u>Wadleigh</u>, (Wadleigh: Rufus), b.
August 22, 1850 in Weare, N.H.   m. Lucian
Durrell.   no additional data.   (Ref. 3)

Issue of 672- Henry M.[6] Smith and Hannah (Hurd) Smith:

991- Isaiah Waldron[7] Smith, (Wadleigh: Henry M.[8], Sally[7], Richard[6], Mary[5], Elizabeth[4], Jonathan[3], Joanna[2], John[1]; Gilman: Henry M.[8], Sally[7], Richard[6], Mary[5], Elizabeth[4], Mary[3], John[2], Edward[1]; Smith: Henry M.[8], Waldron[5], John W.[4], Jonathan[3], Jonathan[2], Robert[1]), m. Rhoda Wills. no additional data. (Ref. 49)
     1260 - Fred Linwood

Issue of 681- Rev. John[8] Graves and Merial (Mason) Graves:

992- David Haslem[9] Graves, (Wadleigh: John[8], James[7], Ruth[6], Dean[5], John[4], John[3], Robert[2], John[1]; Graves: John[8], James[7], David[6], James[5], Samuel[4], Abraham[3], Mark[2], Samuel[1]), b. September 25, 1840, d. June 16, 1917. m. Theresa Louisa Cooke, d. of Benajah and Nancy Page (Morse) Cooke. no additional data. Res. Selma, N.C. (Ref. 12)
     1261 - Leonie   1264 - Victor Morse
     1262 - Clarence D.   1265 - Bertie M.
     1263 - John Ernest

Issue of 683- Ira Wadleigh Boyce and Mrs. Boyce:

993- Jesse Wadleigh Boyce, (Wadleigh: Ira Wadleigh[8], Polly[7], Benjamin[6], Dean[5], John[4], John[3], Robert[2], John[1]), b. in Sioux Falls, So. Dak. no additional data. (Ref. 3)

Issue of 688- Frank Wadleigh Sargent and Mrs.
Sargent:

994- <u>Paul E. Sargent</u>, (Wadleigh: Frank
Wadleigh[8], Ruth[7], Benjamin[6], Dean[5], John[4],
John[3], Robert[2], John[1]), b. in Candia, N.H. no
additional data. (Ref. 3)

Issue of 694- Benjamin Dean[8] Wadleigh and
Sarah (Goodrich) Wadleigh:

995- <u>John[9] Wadleigh</u>, (Benjamin Dean[8], Benjamin
Dean[7], Dean[6], Dean[5], John[4], John[3], Robert[2],
John[1]), b. 1844 in Salisbury, Mass. m. Sarah
Ford. no additional data. (Ref. 3)
        1266 - Benjamin

996- <u>Nellie[9] Wadleigh</u>, (Benjamin Dean[8],
Benjamin Dean[7], Dean[6], Dean[5], John[4], John[3],
Robert[2], John[1]), b. in Salisbury, Mass. no
additional data. (Ref. 3)

997- <u>Jane[9] Wadleigh</u>, (Benjamin Dean[8], Benjamin
Dean[7], Dean[6], Dean[5], John[4], John[3], Robert[2],
John[1]), b. in Salisbury, Mass. no additional
data. (Ref. 3)

Issue of 697- David E.[8] Wadleigh and
Mehitable (Currier) Wadleigh:

998- <u>David[9] Wadleigh</u>, (David E.[8], Benjamin
Dean[7], Dean[6], Dean[5], John[4], John[3], Robert[2],
John[1]), no data. (Ref. 3)

999- <u>Porter[9] Wadleigh</u>, (David E.[8], Benjamin
Dean[7], Dean[6], Dean[5], John[4], John[3], Robert[2],
John[1]), b. in Salisbury, Mass. m. Cora Godsoe,
b. in Salisbury, Mass. (Ref. 3)
        1267 - daughter   1268 - Albert P.

Issue of 711- Samuel[8] Wadleigh and Mary A. (Morrill) Wadleigh:

1000- <u>Orrin</u>[9] <u>Wadleigh</u>, (Samuel[8], Samuel[7], Philip[6], Moses[5], Ephriam[4], John[3], Robert[2], John[1]), b. October 14, 1850 in Salisbury, Mass. d. April 17, 1896. Occ. operated fruit store in Amesbury, Mass. (Ref. 3)

Issue of 722- Frederick A.[8] Wadleigh and Mrs. Wadleigh: NOTE: Possibly two marriages.

1001- <u>Abby Elizabeth</u>[9] <u>Wadleigh</u>, (Frederick A.[8], John[7], Philip[6], Moses[5], Ephriam[4], John[3], Robert[2], John[1]), b. January 16, 1845 in Guilford, Vt. (Ref. 3)

1002- <u>John Frederick</u>[9] <u>Wadleigh</u>, (Frederick A.[8], John[7], Philip[6], Moses[5], Ephriam[4], John[3], Robert[2], John[1]), b. January 23, 1850 in Arlington, Vt., d. 1861. died in childhood. (Ref. 3)

1003- <u>George Hutchinson</u>[9] <u>Wadleigh</u>, (Frederick A.[8], John[7], Philip[6], Moses[5], Ephriam[4], John[3], Robert[2], John[1]), b. August 5, 1852 in Arlington, Vt. (Ref. 3)

1004- <u>Mary Louisa</u>[9] <u>Wadleigh</u>, (Frederick A.[8], John[7], Philip[6], Moses[5], Ephriam[4], John[3], Robert[2], John[1]), b. August 2, 1862 in Arlington, Vt., d. 1881. died in adolescence. (Ref. 3)

1005- <u>Bertha Katherine</u>[9] <u>Wadleigh</u>, (Frederick A.[8], John[7], Philip[6], Moses[5], Ephriam[4], John[3], Robert[2], John[1]), b. January 11, 1868 in East Berkshire, Vt., d. December 28, 1870. died in childhood. (Ref. 3)

1006- <u>Katherine Grace</u>[9] Wadleigh, (Frederick A.[8], John[7], Philip[6], Moses[5], Ephriam[4], John[3], Robert[2], John[1]), b. December 28, 1870 in East Berkshire, Vt. (Ref. 3)

1007- <u>Edna Blanche</u>[9] Wadleigh, (Frederick A.[8], John[7], Philip[6], Moses[5], Ephriam[4], John[3], Robert[2], John[1]), b. May 8, 1873 in East Berkshire, Vt. (Ref. 3)

1008- <u>Frederick Paul</u>[9] Wadleigh, (Frederick A.[8], John[7], Philip[6], Moses[5], Ephriam[4], John[3], Robert[2], John[1]), b. November 17, 1877 in East Berkshire, Vt. (Ref. 3)

Issue of George Carlton and 724- Hannah Maria (Wadleigh) Carlton:

1009- <u>Ida Maria</u> Carlton, (Wadleigh: Hannah Maria[8], John[7], Philip[6], Moses[5], Ephriam[4], John[3], Robert[2], John[1]), b. August 10, 1847 in Bradford, N.H. (Ref. 3)

1010- <u>Anna</u> Carlton, (Wadleigh: Hannah Maria[8], John[7], Philip[6], Moses[5], Ephriam[4], John[3], Robert[2], John[1]), b. April 12, 1849 in Bradford, N.H. (Ref. 3)

1011- <u>Henrietta</u> Carlton, (Wadleigh: Hannah Maria[8], John[7], Philip[6], Moses[5], Ephriam[4], John[3], Robert[2], John[1]), b. May 23, 1852 in Bradford, N.H., d. October 3. 1852. died in childhood. (Ref. 3)

1012- <u>John Herbert</u> Carlton, (Wadleigh: Hannah Maria[8], John[7], Philip[6], Moses[5], Ephriam[4], John[3], Robert[2], John[1]), b. December 25, 1853 in Bradford, N.H. (Ref. 3)

Issue of 736- Ephriam[8] Wadleigh and Abbie
(Eaton) Wadleigh:

1013- <u>Mae Warren</u>[9] <u>Wadleigh</u>, (Ephriam[8],
Eliphalet[7], Ephriam[6], Moses[5], Ephriam[4], John[3],
Robert[2], John[1]), b. in Salisbury, Mass. m. Mr.
Currier. no additional data. (Ref. 3)
        1269 - George

Issue of Eben P. Fowler and 746- Polly
(Wadleigh) Fowler:

1014- <u>Lizzie A. Fowler</u>, (Wadleigh: Polly[8],
Ezekiel[7], Ephriam[6], Moses[5], Ephriam[4], John[3],
Robert[2], John[1]), b. in Salisbury, Mass. d. May
25, 1865 in Salisbury. died in childhood.
(Ref. 3)

Issue of 747- Charles T. P.[8] Wadleigh and
Hannah P. (Corliss) Wadleigh:

1015- <u>Jonathan C.</u>[9] <u>Wadleigh</u>, (Charles T. P.[8],
Ezekiel[7], Ephriam[6], Moses[5], Ephriam[4], John[3],
Robert[2], John[1]), b. November 17, 1853 in
Salisbury, Mass. m. November 16, 1879 Abbie A.
Smith of Salisbury. d. December 20, 1924 at 71
Market St. in Salisbury (now Amesbury). Res.
Amesbury, Mass. (Ref. 3)
        1270 - Eliza B.   1272 - Hannah
        1271 - Jonathan C.   1273 - Abbie Smith

Issue of 748- Eben Pearson[8] Wadleigh and Jane
(Kendrick) Wadleigh:

1016- <u>Cyrus Pearson</u>[9] <u>Wadleigh</u>, (Eben Pearson[8],
Ezekiel[7], Ephriam[6], Moses[5], Ephriam[4], John[3],
Robert[2], John[1]), b. April 4, 1852 in Amesbury,
Mass., d. January 5, 1902 in Amesbury. m.
Elizabeth Ann Hoyt of Amesbury. d. of Hosea,
and Judith Hoyt, no additional data. (w. m.

2nd John West). Res. Main St., Amesbury, Mass.
(Ref. 3)

    1274 - Susie W.   1277 - C. Edward
    1275 - Frank A.   1278 - Florence
    1276 - Bertha E.

1017- <u>Sarah Jane</u>[9] <u>Wadleigh</u>, (Eben Pearson[8], Ezekiel[7], Ephriam[6], Moses[5], Ephriam[4], John[3], Robert[2], John[1]), b. 1857 in Amesbury, Mass., d. August 31, 1936. m. in Newburyport, Mass. January 1, 1881 Edwin Lundberg. no additional data. (Ref. 3)

    1279 - Josie   1281 - Maude
    1280 - Edith

1018- <u>Willie</u>[9] <u>Wadleigh</u>, (Eben Pearson[8], Ezekiel[7], Ephriam[6], Moses[5], Ephriam[4], John[3], Robert[2], John[1]). died in childhood. no data. (Ref. 3)

1019- <u>Charles William</u>[9] <u>Wadleigh</u>, (Eben Pearson[8], Ezekiel[7], Ephriam[6], Moses[5], Ephriam[4], John[3], Robert[2], John[1]), b. August 21, 1861 in Amesbury, Mass. m. March 26, 1883 Anna Josephine Sargent. no additional data. Res. Amesbury, Mass. (Ref. 3)

    1282 - Laura Jane

Issue of George T. Williams and 749- Hannah (Wadleigh) Williams:

1020- <u>George T. Williams</u>, (Wadleigh: Hannah[8], Ezekiel[7], Ephriam[6], Moses[5], Ephriam[4], John[3], Robert[2], John[1]), b. 1857 in Salisbury, Mass., d. 1928 in Amesbury, Mass. m. Etta L. Davis, b. 1863, d. 1935 in Amesbury. (Ref. 3)

Issue of 755- Amasa[8] Wadleigh and Zelphia P. (Jones) Wadleigh:

1021- <u>Viola</u>[9] Wadleigh, (Amasa[8], John[7], Benjamin[6], Thomas[5], Benjamin[4], Robert[3], Robert[2], John[1]), b. December 31, 1838 in Hatley, Quebec, Canada. m. Bradley Jones. no additional data. (Ref. 3)

1022- <u>John R.</u>[9] Wadleigh, (Amasa[8], John[7], Benjamin[6], Thomas[5], Benjamin[4], Robert[3], Robert[2], John[1]), b. April 26, 1841 in Hatley, Quebec, Canada, d. June 23, 1864 in Brattleboro, Vt. enlisted in U.S. Army, and died of battle wounds. (Ref. 3)

Issue of 758- Eliphalet[8] Wadleigh and Ruth M. (Pressey) Wadleigh:

1023- <u>Alonzo</u>[9] Wadleigh, (Eliphalet[8], Benjamin[7], Benjamin[6], Thomas[5], Benjamin[4], Robert[3], Robert[2], John[1]), b. ca. 1827. m. a woman. no additional data. Res. Chicago, Ill. (Ref. 25-969)

1024- <u>Benjamin F.</u>[9] Wadleigh, (Eliphalet[8], Benjamin[7], Benjamin[6], Thomas[5], Benjamin[4], Robert[3], Robert[2], John[1]), b. December 23, 1829. m. February 6, 1859 Caroline E. Chase, b. February 16, 1839. (Ref. 25-970)
     1283 - Frank Eugene   1285 - Marion Inez
     1284 - Elmer Ernest

1025- <u>Mary Mianda</u>[9] Wadleigh, (Eliphalet[8], Benjamin[7], Benjamin[6], Thomas[5], Benjamin[4], Robert[3], Robert[2], John[1]), b. April 22, 1833 in Kirby, Vt. m. 1855 Leonard George, s. of Daniel George of Manchester, N.H. and Betsey F. (Stevens) George of Goffstown, N.H., d. November 27, 1887. Res. Winona, Winona Co. Minn., Yankton, Yankton Co. S.D. and Mt.

Vernon, Davison Co. S.D.   (Ref. 25-970)
        1286 - son   1288 - daughter
        1287 - son

1026- <u>Corliss</u>[9] <u>Wadleigh</u>, (Eliphalet[8],
Benjamin[7], Benjamin[6], Thomas[5], Benjamin[4],
Robert[3], Robert[2], John[1]), b. September 23, 1835
in Kirby, Vt. m. in Boston, Mass. February 25,
1874 Elmina S. K. Brigham, d. of Edward and
Frances Brigham of Boston. no additional data.
Res. Boston and Medford Mass. Occ. sale of
flour. (Ref. 25-970)
        1289 - Mina Beulah   1290 - Corliss

**Issue of 759- Luther[8] Wadleigh and Eliza
(Little) Wadleigh:**

1027- <u>Benjamin F.</u>[9] <u>Wadleigh</u>, (Luther[8],
Benjamin[7], Benjamin[6], Thomas[5], Benjamin[4],
Robert[3], Robert[2], John[1]), b. July 13, 1832.
(Ref. 25-970)

1028- <u>Alonzo K.</u>[9] <u>Wadleigh</u>, (Luther[8], Benjamin[7],
Benjamin[6], Thomas[5], Benjamin[4], Robert[3],
Robert[2], John[1]), b. February 28, 1834. (Ref.
25-970)

1029- <u>Carlos B.</u>[9] <u>Wadleigh</u>, (Luther[8], Benjamin[7],
Benjamin[6], Thomas[5], Benjamin[4], Robert[3],
Robert[2], John[1]), b. January 23, 1836. (Ref.
25-970)

1030- <u>Mary N.</u>[9] <u>Wadleigh</u>, (Luther[8], Benjamin[7],
Benjamin[6], Thomas[5], Benjamin[4], Robert[3],
Robert[2], John[1]), b. April 9, 1838. (Ref. 25-
970)

1031- <u>George B.</u>[9] <u>Wadleigh</u>, (Luther[8], Benjamin[7],
Benjamin[6], Thomas[5], Benjamin[4], Robert[3],

Robert[2], John[1]), b. November 12, 1840. (Ref. 25-970)

1032- <u>Eliza A.</u>[9] <u>Wadleigh</u>, (Luther[8], Benjamin[7], Benjamin[6], Thomas[5], Benjamin[4], Robert[3], Robert[2], John[1]), b. December 25, 1842. (Ref. 25-970)

1033- <u>Maria</u>[9] <u>Wadleigh</u>, (Luther[8], Benjamin[7], Benjamin[6], Thomas[5], Benjamin[4], Robert[3], Robert[2], John[1]), b. August 21, 1851. m. October 26, 1873 Abram Dunning of Charleston, Me. no additional data. (Ref. 25-970)

1034- <u>Addie</u>[9] <u>Wadleigh</u>, (Luther[8], Benjamin[7], Benjamin[6], Thomas[5], Benjamin[4], Robert[3], Robert[2], John[1]). no additional data. (Ref. 25-970)

Issue of 760- Erastus[8] Wadleigh and Elvina (Chellis) Wadleigh:

1035- <u>Milton B.</u>[9] <u>Wadleigh</u>, (Erastus[8], Benjamin[7], Benjamin[6], Thomas[5], Benjamin[4], Robert[3], Robert[2], John[1]), b. December 4, 1839. (Ref. 25)

1036- <u>B. Frank</u>[9] <u>Wadleigh</u>, (Erastus[8], Benjamin[7], Benjamin[6], Thomas[5], Benjamin[4], Robert[3], Robert[2], John[1]), b. July 13, 1841, d. November 14, 1841. died in infancy. (Ref. 25)

1037- <u>Mary Elvira</u>[9] <u>Wadleigh</u>, (Erastus[8], Benjamin[7], Benjamin[6], Thomas[5], Benjamin[4], Robert[3], Robert[2], John[1]), b. 1847, d. April 20, 1880, (adopted, Father John Ellis, Mother Dolly (Chellis) Ellis), m. May 9, 1878, Charles C. Holmes of Salisbury, Mass. no additional data. (Ref. 25)

Issue of 765- Benjamin[8] Wadleigh and Hannah P. (Young) Wadleigh:

1038- Arthur Edison[9] Wadleigh, (Benjamin[8], Benjamin[7], Benjamin[6], Thomas[5], Benjamin[4], Robert[3], Robert[2], John[1]), b. July 2, 1852 in Sunapee, N.H.   Occ. Wholesale Grocer in Boston, Mass.   (Ref. 3, 25-976)

1039- William Young[9] Wadleigh, (Benjamin[8], Benjamin[7], Benjamin[6], Thomas[5], Benjamin[4], Robert[3], Robert[2], John[1]), b. November 10, 1854 in Sunapee, N.H.   m. December 25, 1877 Fanny Boynton of Milford, N.H.   no additional data. Occ. Wholesale Grocer in Boston.   (Ref. 3, 25-976)

1040- Benjamin F.[9] Wadleigh, (Benjamin[8], Benjamin[7], Benjamin[6], Thomas[5], Benjamin[4], Robert[3], Robert[2], John[1]), b. May 25, 1865 in Sunapee, N.H., d. October 15, 1868.   died in childhood.   (Ref. 3, 25-976)

1041- Gilbert H.[9] Wadleigh, (Benjamin[8], Benjamin[7], Benjamin[6], Thomas[5], Benjamin[4], Robert[3], Robert[2], John[1]), b. May 10, 1867, d. August 28, 1869.   died in childhood.   (Ref. 25-976)

1042- May Helene[9] Wadleigh, (Benjamin[8], Benjamin[7], Benjamin[6], Thomas[5], Benjamin[4], Robert[3], Robert[2], John[1]), b. January 23, 1869, d. September 24, 1871.   died in childhood. (Ref. 25-976)

Issue of 768- George Alfred[7] Pillsbury and Margaret Sprague (Carleton) Pillsbury:

1043- Charles Alfred[8] Pillsbury, (Wadleigh: George Alfred[8], Susanna[7], Benjamin[6], Thomas[5],

Benjamin[4], Robert[3], Robert[2], John[1]; Pillsbury:
George Alfred[7], John[6], Micajah[5], Caleb[4],
Caleb[3], Moses[2], William[1]), b. December 3, 1842
in Warner, N.H., d. September 17, 1899 in
Minneapolis, Minn. m. in Dunbarton, N.H.
September 12, 1866 Mary Ann Stinson of
Dunbarton, d. of Charles and Mary Ann (Poor)
Stinson, b. August 1, 1841 in Dunbarton, d.
September 26, 1902 in Minneapolis. Ed. Academy
at New London, Conn. and Dartmouth Univ.
Clerked and gained interest in merchant firm in
Montreal Quebec, Canada before moving to
Minneapolis and joining 770- John Sargent[7]
Pillsbury in a flour milling business. This
business grew as C. A. Pillsbury & Co. and was
joined by father and brother 1045- Fred
Carleton[8] Pillsbury. Was a student of improved
milling processes and incorporated all
improvements which was the secret of the
business's growth and he adopted a plan of
profit-sharing which enabled the firm to remain
solvent in tough times. (Ref. 50-28)
   1291 - George Alfred   1294 - John Sargent
   1292 - Margaret Carleton
   1293 - Charles Stinson

1044- Mary A.[8] Pillsbury, (Wadleigh: George
Alfred[8], Susanna[7], Benjamin[6], Thomas[5],
Benjamin[4], Robert[3], Robert[2], John[1]; Pillsbury:
George Alfred[7], John[6], Micajah[5], Caleb[4],
Caleb[3], Moses[2], William[1]), b. April 25, 1849 in
Warner, N.H., d. May 11, 1849 in Warner. died
in infancy. (Ref. 50-25)

1045- Fred Carleton[8] Pillsbury, (Wadleigh:
George Alfred[8], Susanna[7], Benjamin[6], Thomas[5],
Benjamin[4], Robert[3], Robert[2], John[1]; Pillsbury:
George Alfred[7], John[6], Micajah[5], Caleb[4],
Caleb[3], Moses[2], William[1]), b. July 29, 1827 in
Concord, N.H., d. October 18, 1901 in
Minneapolis, Minn., m. in Minneapolis October
19, 1876 Alice Thayer Cook, d. of Samuel B. and
Harriot Topliff (Perry) Cook, b. October 7,
1857 in Quincy, Mass., d. after 1937. Worked

as clerk in hardware business of 770- John
Sargent[7] Pillsbury in St. Anthony Falls, Minn.
Later a partner in C.A. Pillsbury & Co. After
the sale to an English syndicate, formed
Northwest Consolidated Milling Co. remaining a
director until his death. Also was director of
First National Bank and Swedish-American Bank
of Minneapolis. Served as president of the
State Agricultural Society in charge of
improving the Minnesota State Fair and
establishing the Pillsbury Model Farm in
Wayzata, Minn. Was active in Masons and the
Shrine and in the Baptist Church. (Ref. 50-29)

1295 - George Alfred	1298 - Marian
1296 - Harriot Topliff	1299 - Helen Margaret
1297 - Carleton Cook	1300 - Alice

Issue of Enoch P. Cummings and 769- Dolly Wadleigh[7] (Pillsbury) Cummings:

1046- Alfred Pillsbury Cummings, (Wadleigh:
Dolly Wadleigh[8], Susanna[7], Benjamin[6], Thomas[5],
Benjamin[4], Robert[3], Robert[2], John[1]; Pillsbury:
Dolly Wadleigh[8], John[6], Micajah[5], Caleb[4],
Caleb[3], Moses[2], William[1]), b. September 23,
1838 in Sutton, N.H. (Ref. 50-23)

1047- Charles E. Cummings, (Wadleigh: Dolly
Wadleigh[8], Susanna[7], Benjamin[6], Thomas[5],
Benjamin[4], Robert[3], Robert[2], John[1]; Pillsbury:
Dolly Wadleigh[8], John[6], Micajah[5], Caleb[4],
Caleb[3], Moses[2], William[1]), b. August 5, 1843 in
Sutton, N.H. (Ref. 50-23)

Issue of 770- John Sargent[7] Pillsbury and Mahala (Fisk) Pillsbury:

1048- Addie Eva[8] Pillsbury, (Wadleigh: John
Sargent[8], Susanna[7], Benjamin[6], Thomas[5],
Benjamin[4], Robert[3], Robert[2], John[1]; Pillsbury:
John Sargent[7], John[6], Micajah[5], Caleb[4], Caleb[3],

Moses[2], William[1]), adopted, b. 1860, d. 1884.
m. 1882 Charles M. Webster of Minneapolis,
Minn. no additional data. (Ref. 50-27)

1049- <u>Susan M.</u>[8] <u>Pillsbury</u>, (Wadleigh: John
Sargent[8], Susanna[7], Benjamin[6], Thomas[5],
Benjamin[4], Robert[3], Robert[2], John[1]; Pillsbury;
John Sargent[7], John[6], Micajah[5], Caleb[4], Caleb[3],
Moses[2], William[1]), b. June 23 1863 in
Minneapolis, Minn., d. Sept 3, 1891 in
Minneapolis, m. November 23, 1885 Fred B.
Snyder of Minneapolis. no additional data.
(Ref. 50-27)
        1301 - John Pillsbury

1050- <u>Sarah Belle</u>[8] <u>Pillsbury</u>, (Wadleigh: John
Sargent[8], Susanna[7], Benjamin[6], Thomas[5],
Benjamin[4], Robert[3], Robert[2], John[1]; Pillsbury;
John Sargent[7], John[6], Micajah[5], Caleb[4], Caleb[3],
Moses[2], William[1]), b. June 30, 1866 in
Minneapolis, Minn. m. June 28, 1892 Edward
Cheney Gale of Minneapolis. no additional
data. (Ref. 50-27)
        1302 - Richard Pillsbury

1051- <u>Alfred Fisk</u>[8] <u>Pillsbury</u>, (Wadleigh: John
Sargent[8], Susanna[7], Benjamin[6], Thomas[5],
Benjamin[4], Robert[3], Robert[2], John[1]; Pillsbury;
John Sargent[7], John[6], Micajah[5], Caleb[4], Caleb[3],
Moses[2], William[1]), b. October 20, 1869 in
Minneapolis, Minn. m. in Boston, Mass. May 15,
1899 Eleanor Louise Field, d. of Chief Justice
(of Massachusetts) Walbridge Abner and Eliza
Ellen (McCloon) Field. no additional data.
Ed. Univ. of Minn. and Univ. of Minnesota Law
School. Was treasurer of Pillsbury Flour Mills
Co., became president of Minneapolis Art
Institute, director of First National Bank and
Trust, the Twin City Rapid Transit Co. and
Minneapolis Symphony Orchestra. Was a member
of Minneapolis Park Board and trustee of
Farmers-Mechanics Savings Bank. (Ref. 50-27)

Issue of 772- Horace^8 Wadleigh and Sally
(Wright) Wadleigh:

no issue

Issue of 778- Ephriam^8 Wadleigh and Mary
Elizabeth (Smith) Wadleigh:

1052- Oliva Alice^9 Wadleigh, (Ephriam^8, Peter^7,
Jonathan^6, Thomas^5, Benjamin^4, Robert^3,
Robert^2, John^1), b. May 24, 1848 in Northfield,
N.H. m. January 1, 1885 Peter K. Gile of
Northfield. no additional data. Occ. farmer.
Res. Franklin and Northfield, N.H. (Ref. 3)

1053- Adelaide Phillips^9 Wadleigh, (Ephriam^8,
Peter^7, Jonathan^6, Thomas^5, Benjamin^4, Robert^3,
Robert^2, John^1), b. December 14, 1855 in
Northfield, N.H. unmarried. (Ref. 3)

1054- Smith Glidden^9 Wadleigh, (Ephriam^8,
Peter^7, Jonathan^6, Thomas^5, Benjamin^4, Robert^3,
Robert^2, John^1), b. 1857 in Northfield, N.H.
m. 1883 Flora Getchell of Washington, Vt. no
additional data. Occ. night watchman. (Ref. 3)

Issue of 781- Ebenezer Eastman^8 Wadleigh and
Mrs. (Elkins) Wadleigh:

1055- Elkins^9 Wadleigh, (Ebenezer Eastman^8,
Ebenezer^7, Jonathan^6, Thomas^5, Benjamin^4,
Robert^3, Robert^2, John^1), no additional data.
Res. Salem, Mass. (Ref. 3)

Issue of Timothy H. Loverin and 785- Juliana[8] (Wadleigh) Loverin:

1056- Adeline Loverin, (Wadleigh: Juliana[8], Daniel[7], Thomas[6], Thomas[5], Benjamin[4], Robert[3], Robert[2], John[1]), m. 1st December 23, 1836, Lysander H. Carroll. m. 2nd John L. Taggart of Contoocookville, N.H. no additional data. Res. Contoocookville. (Ref. 25-980) 1303 - 1304 by 1st h.
    1303 - Ella B.   1304 - Jennie B.

1057- Charles Loverin, (Wadleigh: Juliana[8], Daniel[7], Thomas[6], Thomas[5], Benjamin[4], Robert[3], Robert[2], John[1]). m. Lois Farmer. no additional data. Res. Iona, Mich. (Ref. 25-980)
    1305 - Lois   1306 - Edward H.

1058- Julia Loverin, (Wadleigh: Juliana[8], Daniel[7], Thomas[6], Thomas[5], Benjamin[4], Robert[3], Robert[2], John[1]). m. James McWayne of Iona, Mich. no additional data. Res. Grand Rapids, Mich. (Ref. 25-980)

Issue of 786- Philip S. Harvey[8] Wadleigh and Rhoda W. (Kendrick) Wadleigh:

1059- Julia A.[9] Wadleigh, (Philip S. Harvey[8], Daniel[7], Thomas[6], Thomas[5], Benjamin[4], Robert[3], Robert[2], John[1]), b. March 25, 1845, alive in 1902. m. Benjamin F. Heath of Warner, N.H. no additional data. (Ref. 25-980)

Issue of Charles Bean and 788- Augusta (Wadleigh) Bean:

no issue

Issue of 792- Edward W. Dodge and Eliza N. (Jones) Dodge:

1060- <u>Susan Maria Dodge</u>, (Wadleigh: Edward W.[8], Polly[7], Thomas[6], Thomas[5], Benjamin[4], Robert[3], Robert[2], John[1]). no data. (Ref. 25-981)

1061- <u>Jennie Greeley Dodge</u>, (Wadleigh: Edward W.[8], Polly[7], Thomas[6], Thomas[5], Benjamin[4], Robert[3], Robert[2], John[1]). no data. (Ref. 25-981)

Issue of 794- Nathaniel Cheney and Rebecca (Goodrich) Cheney:

1062- <u>Emma Cheney</u>, (Wadleigh: Nathaniel[8], Mehitibel[7], Thomas[6], Thomas[5], Benjamin[4], Robert[3], Robert[2], John[1]). no data. (Ref. 25-981)

1063- <u>Flora Cheney</u>, (Wadleigh: Nathaniel[8], Mehitibel[7], Thomas[6], Thomas[5], Benjamin[4], Robert[3], Robert[2], John[1]). no data. (Ref. 25-981)

Issue of Jabez Townsend and 796- Sally (Wadleigh) Townsend:

1064- <u>Sarah Townsend</u>, (Wadleigh: Sally[8], Thomas[7], Thomas[6], Thomas[5], Benjamin[4], Robert[3], Robert[2], John[1]). no data. (Ref. 25-981)

Issue of 797- Thomas[8] Wadleigh and Abbie (Prescott) Wadleigh:

1065- <u>Prescott T.[9] Wadleigh</u>, (Thomas[8], Thomas[7], Thomas[6], Thomas[5], Benjamin[4], Robert[3], Robert[2],

John^1). m. Kate Jones. no additional data.
(Ref. 25-981)
   1307 - Miriam

1066- <u>Sarah</u>^{9} <u>Wadleigh</u>, (Thomas^8, Thomas^7,
Thomas^6, Thomas^5, Benjamin^4, Robert^3, Robert^2,
John^1). no data. (Ref. 25-981)

**Issue of 800- James M. Burnham and Emma F.
(Marston) Burnham:**

1067- <u>Walter M. Burnham</u>, (Wadleigh: James M.^{8},
Susanna^7, Thomas^6, Thomas^5, Benjamin^4, Robert^3,
Robert^2, John^1). no data. (Ref. 25-981)

1068- <u>John C. Burnham</u>, (Wadleigh: James M.^{8},
Susanna^7, Thomas^6, Thomas^5, Benjamin^4, Robert^3,
Robert^2, John^1). no data. (Ref. 25-981)

**Issue of 801- John F. Burnham and Satrica W.
(Peabody) Burnham:**

1069- <u>Herbert B. Burnham</u>, (Wadleigh: John F.^{8},
Susanna^7, Thomas^6, Thomas^5, Benjamin^4, Robert^3,
Robert^2, John^1). no data. (Ref. 25-982)

1070- <u>Susan W. Burnham</u>, (Wadleigh: John F. ^{8},
Susanna^7, Thomas^6, Thomas^5, Benjamin^4, Robert^3,
Robert^2, John^1). no data. (Ref. 25-982)

1071- <u>Addie L. Burnham</u>, (Wadleigh: John F.^{8},
Susanna^7, Thomas^6, Thomas^5, Benjamin^4, Robert^3,
Robert^2, John^1). no data. (Ref. 25-982)

1072- <u>Mary E. Burnham</u>, (Wadleigh: John F.^{8},
Susanna^7, Thomas^6, Thomas^5, Benjamin^4, Robert^3,
Robert^2, John^1). no data. (Ref. 25-982)

Issue of 801- John F. Burnham and Frances E. (Richmond) Burnham:

1073- <u>Clara B. Burnham</u>, (Wadleigh: John F.[8], Susanna[7], Thomas[6], Thomas[5], Benjamin[4], Robert[3], Robert[2], John[1]). no data. (Ref. 25-982)

Issue of 802- Edward D. Burnham and Georgie B. (Davis) Burnham:

1074- <u>Nathan D. Burnham</u>, (Wadleigh: Edward D.[8], Susanna[7], Thomas[6], Thomas[5], Benjamin[4], Robert[3], Robert[2], John[1]). no data. (Ref. 25-982)

1075- <u>Grace L. Burnham</u>, (Wadleigh: Edward D.[8], Susanna[7], Thomas[6], Thomas[5], Benjamin[4], Robert[3], Robert[2], John[1]). no data. (Ref. 25-982)

1076- <u>Fred T. Burnham</u>, (Wadleigh: Edward D.[8], Susanna[7], Thomas[6], Thomas[5], Benjamin[4], Robert[3], Robert[2], John[1]). no data. (Ref. 25-982)

1077- <u>Frank P. Burnham</u>, (Wadleigh: Edward D.[8], Susanna[7], Thomas[6], Thomas[5], Benjamin[4], Robert[3], Robert[2], John[1]). no data. (Ref. 25-982)

1078- <u>Charles D. Burnham</u>, (Wadleigh: Edward D.[8], Susanna[7], Thomas[6], Thomas[5], Benjamin[4], Robert[3], Robert[2], John[1]). no data. (Ref. 25-982)

Issue of 809- Bainbridge[8] Wadleigh and Ann Marie (Putnam) Wadleigh:

1079- <u>Caroline[9] Wadleigh</u>, (Bainbridge[8], John Dow[7], Moses[6], Thomas[5], Benjamin[4], Robert[3], Robert[2], John[1]), b. in Milford, N.H. m.

Washington B. Thomas.   no additional data.
(Ref. 3)

1080- (unnamed)^9 Wadleigh, (Bainbridge^8, John
Dow^7, Moses^6, Thomas^5, Benjamin^4, Robert^3,
Robert^2, John^1), b. February 17, 1857 in
Manchester, N.H. (Ref. 3)

1081- Helen Putnam^9 Wadleigh, (Bainbridge^8,
John Dow^7, Moses^6, Thomas^5, Benjamin^4, Robert^3,
Robert^2, John^1), b. May 5, 1859 in Manchester,
N.H., d. November 99, 1931 in Boston, Mass.   m.
Samuel Hoar.   (Ref. 3)

**Issue of 818- Charles Colby and H. (Clement)
Colby:**

1082- Sarah Colby, (Wadleigh: Charles^8,
Lucinda^7, Susanna^6, Thomas^5, Benjamin^4,
Robert^3, Robert^2, John^1), m. Mr. Trumbull.   no
additional data.   (Ref. 25-979)

1083- Nathan Colby, (Wadleigh: Charles^8,
Lucinda^7, Susanna^6, Thomas^5, Benjamin^4,
Robert^3, Robert^2, John^1).   m. Eunice.   no
additional data.   (Ref. 25-979)

1084- Fred Colby, (Wadleigh: Charles^8,
Lucinda^7, Susanna^6, Thomas^5, Benjamin^4,
Robert^3, Robert^2, John^1), m. Eva Patten.   no
additional data.   (Ref. 25-979)

**Issue of John Putney and 822- Lucinda
(Robertson) Putney:**

1085- Susie Putney, (Wadleigh: Lucinda^8,
Sarah^7, Susanna^6, Thomas^5, Benjamin^4, Robert^3,
Robert^2, John^1),   m. E. Herman Carroll, of

Warner, N.H. no additional data. (Ref. 25-979)

      1308 - Lee

Issue of 824- John Robertson and Mattie (Page) Robertson:

1086- Sarah Robertson, (Wadleigh: John[8], Sarah[7], Susanna[6], Thomas[5], Benjamin[4], Robert[3], Robert[2], John[1]), no data. (Ref. 25-979)

1087- Carl Robertson, (Wadleigh: John[8], Sarah[7], Susanna[6], Thomas[5], Benjamin[4], Robert[3], Robert[2], John[1]), no data. (Ref. 25-979)

1088- Sadie Robertson, (Wadleigh: John[8], Sarah[7], Susanna[6], Thomas[5], Benjamin[4], Robert[3], Robert[2], John[1]), no data. (Ref. 25-979)

Issue of 825- Benjamin E. Badger and Rachel (Eastman) Badger:

1089- Gertrude Badger, (Wadleigh: Benjamin E.[8], Sophronia[7], Susanna[6], Thomas[5], Benjamin[4], Robert[3], Robert[2], John[1]), m. Will Stone. no additional data. (Ref. 25-979)

1090- William Badger, (Wadleigh: Benjamin E.[8], Sophronia[7], Susanna[6], Thomas[5], Benjamin[4], Robert[3], Robert[2], John[1]), no data. (Ref. 25-979)

1091- Estella Badger, (Wadleigh: Benjamin E.[8], Sophronia[7], Susanna[6], Thomas[5], Benjamin[4], Robert[3], Robert[2], John[1]), no data. (Ref. 25-979)

WADLEIGH GENEALOGY   NINTH GENERATION

Issue of 826- William Badger and Fannie
Badger:

1092- <u>Walter Badger</u>, (Wadleigh: William[8],
Sophronia[7], Susanna[6], Thomas[5], Benjamin[4],
Robert[3], Robert[2], John[1]), no data. (Ref. 25-
979)

1093- <u>Sadie Badger</u>, (Wadleigh: William[8],
Sophronia[7], Susanna[6], Thomas[5], Benjamin[4],
Robert[3], Robert[2], John[1]), no data. (Ref. 25-
979)

Issue of 833- Joseph Bartlett[8] Wadleigh and
Edith E. (Geneney) Wadleigh:

1094- <u>Joseph Bartlett[9] Wadleigh</u>, (Joseph
Bartlett[8], Daniel[7], Daniel[6], John[5], Benjamin[4],
Robert[3], Robert[2], John[1]), b. August 23, 1888.
(Ref. 3)

1095- <u>Clarence B.[9] Wadleigh</u>, (Joseph Bartlett[8],
Daniel[7], Daniel[6], John[5], Benjamin[4], Robert[3],
Robert[2], John[1]), b. August 19, 1895. m. 1922
Cornelia Elizabeth French, b. 1895. (Ref. 3)

Issue of 835- Elwell[8] Wadleigh and Ella F.
Wadleigh:

1096- <u>Percy[9] Wadleigh</u>, (Elwell[8], Oliver[7],
Jose[6], Joseph[5], Joseph[4], Robert[3], Robert[2],
John[1]), b. in Brentwood, N.H. Occ. lumber
dealer. (Ref. 3)

1097- <u>a daughter[9] Wadleigh</u>, (Elwell[8], Oliver[7],
Jose[6], Joseph[5], Joseph[4], Robert[3], Robert[2],
John[1]), m. Frank H. Fernald of Nottingham,
N.H. no additional data. (Ref. 3)

WADLEIGH - 197

Issue of Edward E. Capehart and 844- Sara
Pierce[8] (Wadley) Capehart:

1098- Wadleigh Pierce Capehart, (Wadleigh:
Sara Pierce[8], Dole[7], Enos Dole[6], Joseph[5],
Joseph[4], Robert[3], Robert[2], John[1]), no data.
(Ref. 3)

1099- Everett Dole Capehart, (Wadleigh: Sara
Pierce[8], Dole[7], Enos Dole[6], Joseph[5], Joseph[4],
Robert[3], Robert[2], John[1]), b. June 26, 1890 in
Portsmouth, N.H. (Ref. 3)

Issue of 852- Joseph[5] Melcher and Polly
(Rowell) Melcher:

1100- Joseph H.[9] Melcher, (Wadleigh: Joseph[8],
Samuel[7], Samuel[6], Elizabeth[5], Benjamin[4], Mary[3],
Robert[2], John[1]; Melcher: Joseph[5], Samuel[4],
Samuel[3], Samuel[2], (?)[1]), no data. Res.
Stoughton, Mass. (Ref. 30)

1101- Samuel[9] Melcher, (Wadleigh: Joseph[8],
Samuel[7], Samuel[6], Elizabeth[5], Benjamin[4], Mary[3],
Robert[2], John[1]; Melcher: Joseph[5], Samuel[4],
Samuel[3], Samuel[2], (?)[1]), b. ca. 1806. Res.
Melcher Homestead in Hampton Falls, N.H. did
not marry. (Ref. 30)

1102- Almira[9] Melcher, (Wadleigh: Joseph[8],
Samuel[7], Samuel[6], Elizabeth[5], Benjamin[4], Mary[3],
Robert[2], John[1]; Melcher: Joseph[5], Samuel[4],
Samuel[3], Samuel[2], (?)[1]), m. Robert S. Prescott
of Hampton Falls, N.H. no additional data.
(Ref. 30)

1103- Polly[9] Melcher, (Wadleigh: Joseph[8],
Samuel[7], Samuel[6], Elizabeth[5], Benjamin[4], Mary[3],
Robert[2], John[1]; Melcher: Joseph[5], Samuel[4],
Samuel[3], Samuel[2], (?)[1]), m. Caleb Sanborn of

Kensington, N.H. no data. (Ref. 30)
     1309 - daughter

1104- Betsey^9 Melcher, (Wadleigh: Joseph^8,
Samuel^7, Samuel^6, Elizabeth^5, Benjamin^4, Mary^3,
Robert^2, John^1; Melcher: Joseph^5, Samuel^4,
Samuel^3, Samuel^2, (?)^1), m. Jewett Sanborn Jr.
of Kensington, N.H. no data. (Ref. 30)

1105- Hannah^9 Melcher, (Wadleigh: Joseph^8,
Samuel^7, Samuel^6, Elizabeth^5, Benjamin^4, Mary^3,
Robert^2, John^1; Melcher: Joseph^5, Samuel^4,
Samuel^3, Samuel^2, (?)^1), m. Thomas Capen of
Stoughton, Mass. no additional data. (Ref. 30)

1106- Sally^9 Melcher, (Wadleigh: Joseph^8,
Samuel^7, Samuel^6, Elizabeth^5, Benjamin^4, Mary^3,
Robert^2, John^1; Melcher: Joseph^5, Samuel^4,
Samuel^3, Samuel^2, (?)^1), m. James Sanborn of
Seabrook, N.H. no additional data. (Ref. 30)

**Issue of 855- Mark John^8 Wadleigh and Livinia
(Bowley) Wadleigh:**

1107- Mary Ann^9 Wadleigh, (Mark John^8, John^7,
Joseph^6, Joseph^5, Joseph^4, Henry^3, Robert^2,
John^1), b. February 17, 1841 in Kensington,
N.H. m. 1st Joseph Flood. m. 2nd Elder
Graves. m. 3rd Mr. MaCoy. no additional data.
(Ref. 3)

1108- George Augustus Plummer^9 Wadleigh, (Mark
John^8, John^7, Joseph^6, Joseph^5, Joseph^4,
Henry^3, Robert^2, John^1), b. 1844 in Kensington,
N.H., d. September 8, 1913 in Haverhill, Mass.,
struck by trolley. unmarried. Civil War
veteran. (Ref. 3)

1109– <u>William Frank</u>^{9} <u>Wadleigh</u>, (Mark John^8, John^7, Joseph^6, Joseph^5, Joseph^4, Henry^3, Robert^2, John^1), b. March 10, 1845 in Kensington, N.H., d. 1864. NOTE: Ref. 21 cites Frank H. Wadleigh killed in Civil War action August 17, 1864, age 19. (Ref. 3, 21)

1110– <u>Ida E.</u>^{9} <u>Wadleigh</u>, (Mark John^8, John^7, Joseph^6, Joseph^5, Joseph^4, Henry^3, Robert^2, John^1), b. February 8, 1852 in Kensington, N.H. (Ref. 3)

1111– <u>son</u>^{9} <u>Wadleigh</u>, (Mark John^8, John^7, Joseph^6, Joseph^5, Joseph^4, Henry^3, Robert^2, John^1), died in infancy. no additional data. (Ref. 3)

1112– <u>Cora E.</u>^{9} <u>Wadleigh</u>, (Mark John^8, John^7, Joseph^6, Joseph^5, Joseph^4, Henry^3, Robert^2, John^1), b. April 27, 1859 in Kensington, N.H. (Ref. 3)

1113– <u>Ruth Call</u>^{9} <u>Wadleigh</u>, (Mark John^8, John^7, Joseph^6, Joseph^5, Joseph^4, Henry^3, Robert^2, John^1), b. July 26, 1862 in Kensington, N.H., d. March 17, 1890 in Kensington. m. 1118– Howard^9 Wadleigh, (Mark^8, Mark^7, Joseph^6, Joseph^5, Joseph^4, Henry^3, Robert^2, John^1), b. in Kensington. (Ref. 3) For issue see 1118– Howard^9 Wadleigh

Issue of 857– Nathan Tilton and Mary P. (Brown) Tilton:

1114– <u>Levi Benson</u> <u>Tilton</u>, (Wadleigh: Nathan Tilton^8, Betsey^7, Joseph^6, Joseph^5, Joseph^4, Henry^3, Robert^2, John^1), b. October 5, 1846 in East Kingston, N.H., d. January 28, 1923 in Exeter, N.H., m. Sarah Frances Tilton of Fremont, N.H., d. 1935/6 in Exeter, N.H. Res.

Middle Road, site 50 (M 50) in Kensington 1876-
1884. (Ref. 3, 21)
        1310 - Henry   1311 - Emma

1115- Joseph A. Tilton, (Wadleigh: Nathan
Tilton[8], Betsey[7], Joseph[6], Joseph[5], Joseph[4],
Henry[3], Robert[2], John[1]), b. December 19, 1851
in East Kingston, N.H., d. December 24, 1924 in
East Kingston. m. Mary Olive Forsyth of South
Hampton, N.H., d. in East Kingston. (Ref. 3)
        1312 - Ella   1313 - Forrest

1116- Herbert Abel Tilton, (Wadleigh: Nathan
Tilton[8], Betsey[7], Joseph[6], Joseph[5], Joseph[4],
Henry[3], Robert[2], John[1]), b. August 18, 1855 in
East Kingston, N.H., m. 1st Ada Blake of
Kensington, N.H. m. 2nd Mary F. Andrews. no
additional data. (Ref. 3)

1117- Frank Blake Tilton, (Wadleigh: Nathan
Tilton[8], Betsey[7], Joseph[6], Joseph[5], Joseph[4],
Henry[3], Robert[2], John[1]), b. June 25, 1860 in
East Kingston, N.H., d. December 17, 1922 in
East Kingston. m. February 24, 1892 1129-
Kate Melissa Chase, (Wadleigh: Susan[8],
Sewall[7], Joseph[6], Joseph[5], Joseph[4], Henry[3],
Robert[2], John[1]), of Kensington, N.H. no
additional data. (Ref. 3)
   1314 - Philip Nathan   1316 - Lewis Blake
   1315 - Albert Chase

**Issue of 869- Mark[8] Wadleigh and Harriett
(Simpson) Wadleigh:**

1118- Howard[9] Wadleigh, (Mark[8], Mark[7], Joseph[6],
Joseph[5], Joseph[4], Henry[3], Robert[2], John[1]), b.
in Kensington, N.H. m. 1st 1113- Ruth Call[9]
Wadleigh, (Mark John[8], John[7], Joseph[6], Joseph[5],
Joseph[4], Henry[3], Robert[2], John[1]), b. July 26,
1862 in Kensington, N.H., d. March 17, 1890 in
Kensington. m. 2nd Nellie Flood. no

additional data. (Ref. 3)   1317 - 1318 by 1st
wife, 1319 - 1320 by 2nd wife.
    1317 - Harriett   1319 - son
    1318 - Walter L.   1320 - Mark W.

1119- Hortence Mills[9] Wadleigh, (Mark[8], Mark[7],
Joseph[6], Joseph[5], Joseph[4], Henry[3], Robert[2],
John[1]), b. October 24, 1861 in Kensington,
N.H., d. April 28, 1889 in Salem, Mass.
unmarried. (Ref. 3)

1120- Frank Otis[9] Wadleigh, (Mark[8], Mark[7],
Joseph[6], Joseph[5], Joseph[4], Henry[3], Robert[2],
John[1]), b. January 6, 1868 in Kensington, N.H.,
d. in Exeter, N.H. (Ref. 3)

**Issue of Eliphalet Greeley and 871- Sarah E.
(Wadleigh) Greeley:**

1121- Emily E. Greeley, (Wadleigh: Sarah E.[8],
Mark[7], Joseph[6], Joseph[5], Joseph[4], Henry[3],
Robert[2], John[1]), b. January 19, 1857 in East
Kingston, N.H., d. in "the West" (at daughter's
home - named Rastman). m. Charles, d. January
1936 (by B & M Railroad train). Res. Exeter,
N.H. (Ref. 3)

1122- Alwin W. Greeley, (Wadleigh: Sarah E.[8],
Mark[7], Joseph[6], Joseph[5], Joseph[4], Henry[3],
Robert[2], John[1]), b. July 14, 1859 in East
Kingston, N.H. m. Sarah A. C. Austin, no
additional data. (Ref. 3)

1123- Josiah Bartlett Greeley, (Wadleigh:
Sarah E.[8], Mark[7], Joseph[6], Joseph[5], Joseph[4],
Henry[3], Robert[2], John[1]), b. January 1, 1862 in
East Kingston, N.H., d. September 25, 1936 in
East Kingston. m. Fannie A. Dow, no additional
data. (Ref. 3)

1124- George E. Greeley, (Wadleigh: Sarah E.[8], Mark[7], Joseph[6], Joseph[5], Joseph[4], Henry[3], Robert[2], John[1]), b. November 27, 1865 in East Kingston, N.H. m. Mary S. Osbourne, no additional data. (Ref. 3)

Issue of George W. Morrill and 875- Harriett (Wadleigh) Morrill:

1125- Henry Sewall Morrill, (Wadleigh: Harriett[8], Sewall[7], Joseph[6], Joseph[5], Joseph[4], Henry[3], Robert[2], John[1]), no data. (Ref. 3)

1126- Zora Morrill, (Wadleigh: Harriett[8], Sewall[7], Joseph[6], Joseph[5], Joseph[4], Henry[3], Robert[2], John[1]), no data. (Ref. 3)

1127- Stephen Benson Morrill, (Wadleigh: Harriett[8], Sewall[7], Joseph[6], Joseph[5], Joseph[4], Henry[3], Robert[2], John[1]), no data. (Ref. 3)

1128- Alice Morrill-Wiggin, (Wadleigh: Harriett[8], Sewall[7], Joseph[6], Joseph[5], Joseph[4], Henry[3], Robert[2], John[1]), b.   adpt. by Mr. and Mrs. Wiggin of South Hampton, N.H. m. 1st a man in Amesbury, Mass. m. 2nd in South Hampton Albert W. Paige of South Hampton, d. in Amesbury, Mass. no additional data. Res. Kansas where 1st husband and one child died, and Amesbury, Mass. (Ref. 3)

1129- Hattie Morrill, (Wadleigh: Harriett[8], Sewall[7], Joseph[6], Joseph[5], Joseph[4], Henry[3], Robert[2], John[1]), no data. (Ref. 3)

Issue of 877- Cyrus Dearborn[8] Wadleigh and
Rhoda Elizabeth (Sanborn) Wadleigh:

1130- Edith[9] Wadleigh, (Cyrus Dearborn[8],
Sewall[7], Joseph[6], Joseph[5], Joseph[4], Henry[3],
Robert[2], John[1]), b. December 30, 1850 in
Kensington, N.H., d. December 30, 1850 in
Kensington. died in infancy. (Ref. 3)

1131- Ida Frances[9] Wadleigh, (Cyrus Dearborn[8],
Sewall[7], Joseph[6], Joseph[5], Joseph[4], Henry[3],
Robert[2], John[1]), b. March 5, 1852 in
Kensington, N.H., d. November 6, 1855 in
Kensington. died in childhood. (Ref. 3)

1132- Isabel Cram[9] Wadleigh, (Cyrus Dearborn[8],
Sewall[7], Joseph[6], Joseph[5], Joseph[4], Henry[3],
Robert[2], John[1]), b. August 20, 1854 in
Kensington, N.H., d. November 6, 1925 in
Exeter, N.H. m. 1st December 2, 1877 Charles
W. Giles of East Kingston, N.H., b. in Lee
N.H., d. February 28, 1900 at "Moulton's
Ridge". m. 2nd December 3, 1907 Benjamin
George Moulton of Kensington, d. April 8, 1911
in Kensington. Res. Kensington and Exeter,
N.H. (Ref. 3)

1133- Helen Sinclar[9] Wadleigh, (Cyrus
Dearborn[8], Sewall[7], Joseph[6], Joseph[5], Joseph[4],
Henry[3], Robert[2], John[1]), b. March 9, 1857 in
Kensington, N.H., d. July 5, 1906 in
Newburyport, Mass. m. September 21, of some
year James P. Chase of Stratham, N.H., no
additional data. (Ref. 3)

1134- Melvin Clarence[9] Wadleigh, (Cyrus
Dearborn[8], Sewall[7], Joseph[6], Joseph[5], Joseph[4],
Henry[3], Robert[2], John[1]), b. May 10, 1859 in
Kensington, N.H. (Ref. 3)

1135- John Sewall[9] Wadleigh, (Cyrus Dearborn[8], Sewall[7], Joseph[6], Joseph[5], Joseph[4], Henry[3], Robert[2], John[1]), b. January 30, 1866 in Kensington, N.H. m. May 18, 1892 Lottie May Prescott of Hampton Falls, N.H., d. of Alva D. Prescott of Hampton Falls, and Menerva (Chase) Prescott of Stratham, N.H., d. December 19, 1893 in Amesbury, Mass. following childbirth. Res. 2 Cushing St., Amesbury, Mass. (Ref. 3)
        1321 - Lottie Edna

Issue of George Albert Chase and 878- Susan W. (Wadleigh) Chase:

1136- Marianna Barker Chase, (Wadleigh: Susan W.[8], Sewall[7], Joseph[6], Joseph[5], Joseph[4], Henry[3], Robert[2], John[1]), b. February 21, 1855 in Kensington, N.H., d. March 6, 1935 in Exeter, N.H. m. October 4, 1888 Willis J. Comings of Lee, N.H., d. in Exeter. (Ref. 3)
        1322 - Joseph T.   1323 - Bertha

1137- Abbie Florence Chase, (Wadleigh: Susan W.[8], Sewall[7], Joseph[6], Joseph[5], Joseph[4], Henry[3], Robert[2], John[1]), b. February 24, 1857 in Kensington, N.H., d. October 12, 1912 in North Hampton, N.H. m. December 23, 1882 John P. Taylor of North Hampton, b. January 28, 1853, d. May 25, 1908 in North Hampton. (Ref. 3)
    1324 - Walter E.   1326 - Anna
    1325 - Blanche   1327 - Frank

1138- Sarah Susan Chase, (Wadleigh: Susan W.[8], Sewall[7], Joseph[6], Joseph[5], Joseph[4], Henry[3], Robert[2], John[1]), b. March 9, 1859 in Kensington, N.H., d. October 16, 1919 in East Kingston, N.H. unmarried. Occ. schoolteacher in East Kingston, N.H. (Ref. 3)

1139- <u>Kate Melissa Chase</u>, (Wadleigh: Susan
W.[8], Sewall[7], Joseph[6], Joseph[5], Joseph[4],
Henry[3], Robert[2], John[1]), b. November 19, 1863
in Kensington, N.H. m. February 24, 1892
1117- Frank Blake Tilton, (Wadleigh: Nathan
Tilton[8], Betsey[7], Joseph[6], Joseph[5], Joseph[4],
Henry[3], Robert[2], John[1]) of East Kingston, N.H.,
b. June 25, 1860 in East Kingston, d. December
17, 1922 in East Kingston. (Ref. 3) For
issue, see 1117- Frank Blake Tilton.

**Issue of Warren Lamprey and 879- Lucy Jane
(Wadleigh) Lamprey:**

1140- <u>Anna Marshal Lamprey</u>, (Wadleigh: Lucy
Jane[8], William Henry[7], William Henry[6], Joseph[5],
Joseph[4], Henry[3], Robert[2], John[1]), b. in
Kensington, N.H. m. October 20, 1898 Rev.
David[1] Fraser, b. in Scotland. (Ref. 3)

1141- <u>Howard Lovell Lamprey</u>, (Wadleigh: Lucy
Jane[8], William Henry[7], William Henry[6], Joseph[5],
Joseph[4], Henry[3], Robert[2], John[1]), b. in
Kensington, N.H. m. September 1, 1897 Abbie J.
Corson, d. of Plummer J. and Sarah H. (Cram)
Corson of Raymond, N.H., no additional data.
Res. Manchester, N.H. (Ref. 3)

1142- <u>John William Lamprey</u>, (Wadleigh: Lucy
Jane[8], William Henry[7], William Henry[6], Joseph[5],
Joseph[4], Henry[3], Robert[2], John[1]), b. in
Kensington, N.H. m. Ethel Blake of Kensington,
d. of Thomas H. and Cynthia (Batchelder) Blake
of Kensington. no additional data. (Ref. 3)

**Issue of 880- Frank Lawrence[8] Wadleigh and
Sarah A. (Evans) Wadleigh:**

1143- <u>Arthur Garfield[9] Wadleigh</u>, (Frank
Lawrence[8], William Henry[7], William Henry[6],
Joseph[5], Joseph[4], Henry[3], Robert[2], John[1]), b.

December 1, 1881 in Kensington, N.H., d. June
4, 1930 at Mass. General Hosp. in Boston,
Mass., bur. Kensington, N.H. m. October 20,
1915 Flora A. Ronzano of Boston, Mass., no
additional data. (Ref. 2, 3)
>   1328 - Frances Mason   1330 - Robert Evans
>   1329 - William Henry

1144- Ray Emery[9] Wadleigh, (Frank Lawrence[8],
William Henry[7], William Henry[6], Joseph[5],
Joseph[4], Henry[3], Robert[2], John[1]), b. November
30, 1887 in Kensington, N.H. m. Alice Kimball
of Salt Lake City, Ut. no additional data.
(Ref. 2, 3)
>   1331 - Sarah L.   1332 - Frank Leland

**Issue of Charles W. Green and 881- Ellen
Foster (Wadleigh) Green:**

1145- Herbert W. Green, (Wadleigh: Ellen
Foster[8], William Henry[7], William Henry[6],
Joseph[5], Joseph[4], Henry[3], Robert[2], John[1]), b.
in Hampton Falls, N.H. Res. Brentwood, N.H.
(Ref. 3)

1146- Henry Green, (Wadleigh: Ellen Foster[8],
William Henry[7], William Henry[6], Joseph[5],
Joseph[4], Henry[3], Robert[2], John[1]), b. in Hampton
Falls, N.H. Res. Boston, Mass. (Ref. 3)

**Issue of 883- Charles Fremont[8] Wadleigh and
Annie S. (Lane) Wadleigh:**

1147- Mabelle Lane[9] Wadleigh, (Charles
Fremont[8], William Henry[7], William Henry[6],
Joseph[5], Joseph[4], Henry[3], Robert[2], John[1]), b.
August 13, 1877 in Hampton Falls, N.H. m. July
12, 1906 William H. McDavitt, b. July 7, 1871,
d. September 3, 1932 in Glendale, Cal. (Ref. 3)
>   1333 - Helen M.

1148- <u>Frances M.</u>[9] <u>Wadleigh</u>, (Charles Fremont[8], William Henry[7], William Henry[6], Joseph[5], Joseph[4], Henry[3], Robert[2], John[1]), b. February 12, 1881 in Hampton Falls. N.H. m. October 12, 1906 Arthur W. Brown of Hampton Falls, b. July 20, 1873 in Hampton Falls. Res. Hampton Falls, N.H. (Ref. 3)

1334	- Charles W.	1337	- Elinoir
1335	- Lois W.	1338	- Ernest H.
1336	- Harold A.	1339	- Winthrop M.

1149- <u>Alice H.</u>[9] <u>Wadleigh</u>, (Charles Fremont[8], William Henry[7], William Henry[6], Joseph[5], Joseph[4], Henry[3], Robert[2], John[1]), b. April 19, 1884 in Hampton Falls, N.H., d. November 12, 1887 in Kensington, N.H. died in childhood. (Ref. 3)

1150- <u>Laurence E.</u>[9] <u>Wadleigh</u>, (Charles Fremont[8], William Henry[7], William Henry[6], Joseph[5], Joseph[4], Henry[3], Robert[2], John[1]), b. November 3, 1886 in Hampton Falls, N.H. m. September 3, 1919 Laura E. Goodwin of Exeter, N.H., no additional data. Res. Lane Farm in Hampton Falls, N.H. (Ref. 3)

1151- <u>Helen</u>[9] <u>Wadleigh</u>, (Charles Fremont[8], William Henry[7], William Henry[6], Joseph[5], Joseph[4], Henry[3], Robert[2], John[1]), b. July 28, 1896 in Hampton Falls, N.H. m. June 10, 1919 Frank C. Keegan, no additional data. (Ref. 3)

1340	- Frank C.	1342	- James Y.
1341	- Howard W.		

Issue of 884- Charles Edwin[8] Wadleigh and Hannah Mary (Brewster) Wadleigh:

1152- <u>Daniel Edward</u>[9] <u>Wadleigh</u>, (Charles Edwin[8], Daniel Foster[7], William Henry[6], Joseph[5], Joseph[4], Henry[3], Robert[2], John[1]), b. April 4, 1872 in Green Ridge, Pettis Co. Mo., d.

February 14, 1946 in Ukiah, Cal., bur.
Brownsville, Neb., m. March 21, 1903 Ida[3]
Scott, (Harry[2], Thomas[1]) of Raymond, Clark Co.,
S.D., d. of Harry[2] Scott and Mary Ellen[3]
(Payne) Scott, (Payne: Thomas[2], John[1]) of
Racine Co. Wis., b. August 27, 1884 in
(presum.) Raymond, d. October 1, 1950 in
Watertown, S.D. Occ. farmer, vintner. Res.
Crocker, S.D. and Brownsville, Neb. (Ref. 1,
2, 9)

1343 - Charles Harry	1348 - Fredrick Lee
1344 - Erwin Walter	1349 - Ada Margaret
1345 - Elmer Edward	1350 - Alta Beatrice
1346 - Erline Myrtle	1351 - Ida Ilene
1347 - Robert David	

1153- Walter Emory[9] Wadleigh, (Charles Edwin[8],
Daniel Foster[7], William Henry[6], Joseph[5],
Joseph[4], Henry[3], Robert[2], John[1]), b. November
23, 1874 in Green Ridge, Pettis Co., Mo., d.
September 16, 1948 in Sedalia, Mo., bur.
Sedalia. m. in Kansas City, Mo. February 3,
1909 Viola Oxendine of Knoxville, Knox Co.
Tenn., no additional data. Occ. carpenter. no
children. (Ref. 1, 2)

1154- Nettie Florence[9] Wadleigh, (Charles
Edwin[8], Daniel Foster[7], William Henry[6],
Joseph[5], Joseph[4], Henry[3], Robert[2], John[1]), b.
February 7, 1877 in Green Ridge, Pettis Co.,
Mo. d. January 23, 1960 in Green Ridge, Pettis
Co., Mo. bur. at Windsor, Mo. m. in Green
Ridge, January 8, 1902 William S. Bell, d.
January 8, 1962. Occ. w. schoolteacher in Mo.
and S.D., (Ref. 1, 2)

1352 - Bernice Nelva	1354 - Hazel Caroline
1353 - Mary Lorene	1355 - Howard Charles

1155- James Augustus[9] Wadleigh, (Charles
Edwin[8], Daniel Foster[7], William Henry[6],
Joseph[5], Joseph[4], Henry[3], Robert[2], John[1]), b.
August 26, 1879 in Green Ridge, Mo., d. July
10, 1961 in Sedalia, Mo., bur. Green Ridge. m.

January 6, 1910 Minnie W. Wharton, b. January
15, 1888, d. October 8, 1951. Served in
Spanish-American War. Occ. ranch hand and
railroad worker. Res. Montana and Sedalia, Mo.
(Ref. 1, 2)
           1356 - Paul Edward   1357 - Omer Basil

1156- Fannie Lorena[9] Wadleigh, (Charles Edwin[8],
Daniel Foster[7], William Henry[6], Joseph[5],
Joseph[4], Henry[3], Robert[2], John[1]), b. December
9, 1881 in Green Ridge, Pettis Co., Mo., d.
November 2, 1969 in Boise, Ida. m. December
23, 1903 William[2] Lunstrum (Peter[1]), s. of
Peter[1] Lunstrum and Caroline[1] Lunstrum,
immigrants from Sweden, b. May 11, 1880, d.
August 15, 1967. (Ref. 1, 2)
   1358 - Mervyn Wayne   1361 - Inez Lorraine
   1359 - Fordyce Wilbur 1362 - Richard Maurice
   1360 - Carl Kenneth

1157- Helen Mary[9] Wadleigh, (Charles Edwin[8],
Daniel Foster[7], William Henry[6], Joseph[5],
Joseph[4], Henry[3], Robert[2], John[1]), b. January
15, 1886 in Green Ridge, Pettis Co. Mo., d.
October 25, 1969. m. May 9, 1909 Charles Arvid
Johnson, b. February 3, 1881, d. January 5,
1954. (Ref. 1, 2)
           1363 - Lois   1364 - Carl Arvid

1158- Robert Leroy[9] Wadleigh, (Charles Edwin[8],
Daniel Foster[7], William Henry[6], Joseph[5],
Joseph[4], Henry[3], Robert[2], John[1]), b. August 22,
1888 in Green Ridge, Mo., d. November 10, 1954
in Sedalia, Mo. m. June 26, 1912 Amy L. White,
d. of Samuel and Elvira (Crawford) White, b.
July 5, 1888. (Ref. 1, 2)
           1365 - Harold W.   1367 - Ella Dorothy
           1366 - Glen C.

1159- Clarence Levi[9] Wadleigh, (Charles Edwin[8],
Daniel Foster[7], William Henry[6], Joseph[5],
Joseph[4], Henry[3], Robert[2], John[1]), b. December

11, 1891 in Green Ridge, Mo., d. November 27, 1963 in Sedalia, Mo. m. April 10, 1918 Nadyne Elizabeth Smith, b. December 27, 1896. (Ref. 1, 2)

    1368 - Hallie Jane   1369 - Josephine

1160- **Leslie Earl**[9] Wadleigh, (Charles Edwin[8], Daniel Foster[7], William Henry[6], Joseph[5], Joseph[4], Henry[3], Robert[2], John[1]), b. May 18, 1895 in Green Ridge, Mo., d. March 14, 1965 in Sedalia, Mo. m. 1st Sidney Brown Leffler. m. 2nd June 6, 1959 Lillian Marie (Wear) Swerngin, d. of George W. and Sarah (Taylor) Wear, wid. of James F. Swerngin (had m. 1946), b. December 18, 1902 in Pettis Co. Mo., d. January 16, 1978 in Sedalia, Mo. Served in France in World War I. no children. (Ref. 1, 2)

Issue of J. Vincent Willis and 885- Helen Maria (Wadleigh) Willis:

1161- **Elmer Pierre Willis**, (twin), (Wadleigh: Helen Maria[8], Daniel Foster[7], William Henry[6], Joseph[5], Joseph[4], Henry[3], Robert[2], John[1]), b. May 15, 1876, d. November 26, 1879 in (presum.) Green Ridge, Mo. died in childhood. (Ref. 2)

1162- **Estella Pearl Willis**, (twin), (Wadleigh: Helen Maria[8], Daniel Foster[7], William Henry[6], Joseph[5], Joseph[4], Henry[3], Robert[2], John[1]), b. May 15, 1876, d. July 17, 1920 in (presum.) Green Ridge, Mo. m. Lon Baldwin, no additional data. (Ref. 2)

    1370 - Bill   1371 - Clifford

1163- **Jessie Irene Willis**, (Wadleigh: Helen Maria[8], Daniel Foster[7], William Henry[6], Joseph[5], Joseph[4], Henry[3], Robert[2], John[1]), b. April 7, 1881 in Beardstown, Ill., d. March 2, 1960 in Aurora, Ill., bur. Oswego, Ill. unmarried (Ref. 2)

1164- Clara Martha Willis, (Wadleigh: Helen
Maria[8], Daniel Foster[7], William Henry[6],
Joseph[5], Joseph[4], Henry[3], Robert[2], John[1]), b.
June 1, 1883 in Meadville, Mo., d. January 6,
1973 in (presum.) Oswego, Ill. unmarried
(Ref. 2)

1165- Fred Willis, (Wadleigh: Helen Maria[8],
Daniel Foster[7], William Henry[6], Joseph[5],
Joseph[4], Henry[3], Robert[2], John[1]), b. 1884/5, d.
February 3, 1959 in Oswego, Ill. m. December
22, 1908 Lettie, no additional data. (Ref. 2)

1166- Claire W. Willis, (Wadleigh: Helen
Maria[8], Daniel Foster[7], William Henry[6],
Joseph[5], Joseph[4], Henry[3], Robert[2], John[1]), b.
October 26, 1892 in Custer City, S.D., d. May
28, 1920 in Oswego, Ill. m. "a piano teacher",
no additional data. (Ref. 2)

**Issue of James B. McCampbell and 886- Maaura
(Wadleigh) McCampbell:**

1167- Henry Harrison McCampbell, (Wadleigh:
Maaura[8], Daniel Foster[7], William Henry[6],
Joseph[5], Joseph[4], Henry[3], Robert[2], John[1]), b.
March 7, 1868 in Ill., d. December 8, 1947 in
(presum.) Green Ridge, Mo., bur. Green Ridge.
m. December 19, 1894 Cora Elvis Wilkerson, b.
December 4, 1868, d. November 14, 1916. (Ref.
2)
         1372 - Bruce

1168- Emory McCampbell, (Wadleigh: Maaura[8],
Daniel Foster[7], William Henry[6], Joseph[5],
Joseph[4], Henry[3], Robert[2], John[1]), b. February
18. died in childhood. (Ref. 2)

1169- James Randolph McCampbell, (Wadleigh:
Maaura[8], Daniel Foster[7], William Henry[6],

Joseph[5], Joseph[4], Henry[3], Robert[2], John[1]), b. October 10, 1878 in Green Ridge Mo., d. January 30, 1947 in Windsor, Mo., bur. Green Ridge. m. April 17, 1901 in Green Ridge 1184- Ethel Grace Reed, (Wadleigh: Jennie Russell[8], Joseph Dearborn[7], William Henry[6], Joseph[5], Joseph[4], Henry[3], Robert[2], John[1]), b. May 31, 1881, d. April 19, 1948. (Ref. 2)

   1373 - James H.   1374 - Glenda

1170- <u>Daniel Roy McCampbell</u>, (Wadleigh: Maaura[8], Daniel Foster[7], William Henry[6], Joseph[5], Joseph[4], Henry[3], Robert[2], John[1]), b. September 12, 1880 in Green Ridge, Mo., d. December 13, 1920 in Green Ridge. m. June 23, 1909 in Green Ridge Phyllis Georgia Pfaff, b. September 2, 1884, d. October 30, 1955. (Ref. 2)

1375 - Mary	1378 - Dency
1376 - Maybelle	1379 - Anne Hite
1377 - Myrtle	1380 - Daniel

1171- <u>Dency Lucinda McCampbell</u>, (Wadleigh: Maaura[8], Daniel Foster[7], William Henry[6], Joseph[5], Joseph[4], Henry[3], Robert[2], John[1]), b. November 26, 1883 in Green Ridge, Mo., d. August 9, 1959 in Windsor, Mo. m. January 24, 1906 or July 24, 1906 in Green Ridge Everett Ernest Brown, no additional data. (Ref. 2)

1381 - Lloyd	1385 - Emory
1382 - Earl	1386 - James Newton
1383 - Eldon	1387 - Kenneth Eugene
1384 - Roy	

Issue of 888- Everett[8] Wadleigh and Martha Isabelle (Anderson) Wadleigh:

1172- <u>Bertha May[9] Wadleigh</u>, (Everett[8], Daniel Foster[7], William Henry[6], Joseph[5], Joseph[4], Henry[3], Robert[2], John[1]), b. December 31, 1877 in Green Ridge, Mo., d. January 13, 1910 in Davenport, Ia., bur. Green Ridge. m. in Green

Ridge October 5, 1897 Robert Culbert Kyd, s. of
John and Annie Culbert Kyd, b. June 20, 1874 in
Green Ridge, d. November 18, 1953 in Des
Moines, Ia. bur. at Green Ridge Cemetary.
(Ref. 2)
        1388 - Beatrice Pearl   1391 - Mary Louise
        1389 - Walter Burns   1392 - Alma Emma
        1390 - Annabel

1173- Lucinda Mary[9] Wadleigh, (Everett[8], Daniel
Foster[7], William Henry[6], Joseph[5], Joseph[4],
Henry[3], Robert[2], John[1]), b. August 5, 1879 in
Green Ridge, Mo., d. January 29, 1966 in
Sedalia, Mo., bur. Green Ridge. m. March 8,
1908 in Green Ridge Charles Kyd Proctor, s of
William and Isabelle (Kyd) Proctor, b. November
10, 1873 in Green Ridge, d. April 26, 1941 in
Green Ridge. Occ. farmer. (Ref. 2)

1174- Hattie Belle[9] Wadleigh, (Everett[8], Daniel
Foster[7], William Henry[6], Joseph[5], Joseph[4],
Henry[3], Robert[2], John[1]), b. September 24, 1881
in Green Ridge, Mo., d. March 12, 1919 in
Sedalia, Mo., bur. in Green Ridge. m. February
5, 1905 in Green Ridge, Mo. George Washington
Paige, s. of Martin Van Buren Paige and
Maryette Permelia (Austin) Paige, b. February
28, 1883 in Green Ridge, d. October 25, 1948 in
Sedalia. (Ref. 2)
        1393 - Audrey Belle   1396 - Gladys Lorene
        1394 - Louis Leroy   1397 - Charles Earl
        1395 - Forest Martin

1175- Louis Henry[9] Wadleigh, (Everett[8], Daniel
Foster[7], William Henry[6], Joseph[5], Joseph[4],
Henry[3], Robert[2], John[1]), b. December 11, 1886
in Green Ridge, Mo., d. February 26, 1963 in
Windsor, Mo., bur. Green Ridge. m. December 2,
1914 in Green Ridge Ona Pearl Upton, d. of
Joseph and Louisa Jane (Stetzel) Upton, b. June
28, 1891 in Green Ridge, d. October 10, 1977 in
Windsor, bur. Green Ridge Cemetery. Occ.
Farmer and Storekeeper. Res. Brandon and Green

Ridge, Mo.   (Ref. 2)
  1398 - Elmer Wright   1401 - Iva Lou
  1399 - Cleo Louise   1402 - Harvery Everett
  1400 - Mabel Lucille

1176- Alma Edna[9] Wadleigh, (Everett[8], Daniel
Foster[7], William Henry[6], Joseph[5], Joseph[4],
Henry[3], Robert[2], John[1]), b. May 25, 1889 in
Green Ridge, Mo., d. January 15, 1983 in
Sedalia, Mo. m. June 22, 1913 in Green Ridge
Oxel Leonard Johnson, s. of Frank A. and
Wilheminia (Erickson) Johnson, b. October 9
1885 in Sedalia, d. January 20, 1960 in
Sedalia, bur. Memorial Park Cemetery.   Occ. h.
bakery w. M.K.T. RR mechanic.   (Ref, 2)
        1403 - Lillian Frances

1177- Jennie Opal[9] Wadleigh, (Everett[8], Daniel
Foster[7], William Henry[6], Joseph[5], Joseph[4],
Henry[3], Robert[2], John[1]), b. August 12, 1891 in
Green Ridge, Mo., d. December 26, 1972 in
Sedalia, Mo. bur. Memorial Park Cemetery.   m.
June 30, 1926 in Green Ridge John Ferdinand
Goering, s. of Charles and Louisa Goering, b.
March 30, 1876 in Ames, Kan.,   d. June 22, 1947
in Sedalia. Occ. farmer. Res. Columbia and
Sedalia, Mo. (Ref. 2)

1178- Hazel Carrie[9] Wadleigh, (Everett[8], Daniel
Foster[7], William Henry[6], Joseph[5], Joseph[4],
Henry[3], Robert[2], John[1]), b. August 13, 1892 in
Green Ridge, Mo., d. February 24, 1961 in
Sedalia, Mo., bur. Mount Vernon Cemetery, Pilot
Grove, Mo. m. August 13, 1918 in Sedalia
Neville Benton Licklider, s. of Thomas M. and
Barbara J. (Hill) Licklider, b. October 12,
1884 in Pleasant Green, Mo., d. March 25, 1942
in Sedalia, bur. Mount Vernon Cemetery. Occ.
Painter. Res. Green Ridge and Sedalia, Mo.
(Ref. 2)
        1404 - Norwood

1179- <u>Florence Emma</u>[9] <u>Wadleigh</u>, (Everett[8],
Daniel Foster[7], William Henry[6], Joseph[5],
Joseph[4], Henry[3], Robert[2], John[1]), b. November
22, 1894 in Green Ridge, Mo., d. February 10,
1980 in Windsor, Mo., m. March 7, 1923 Walter
Burton Walkup, s. of John J. and Elizabeth H.
(Bland) Walkup, b. April 4, 1880 in Pettis Co.
Mo., d. December 4, 1952 in Sedalia, Mo., bur.
Laurel Oak Cemetery in Windsor. Occ. farmer
and realtor. Res. Green Ridge, Brandon and
Sedalia, Mo. and Fullerton, Cal. (Ref. 2)
        1405 - Thelma May

1180- <u>Anna</u>[9] <u>Wadleigh</u>, (Everett[8], Daniel
Foster[7], William Henry[6], Joseph[5], Joseph[4],
Henry[3], Robert[2], John[1]), b. January 5, 1896 in
Green Ridge, Mo., d. July 25, 1896 in Green
Ridge. died in childhood. (Ref. 2)

1181- <u>Leo Earl</u>[9] <u>Wadleigh</u>, (Everett[8], Daniel
Foster[7], William Henry[6], Joseph[5], Joseph[4],
Henry[3], Robert[2], John[1]), (twin) b. July 15,
1898 in Green Ridge, Mo., d. June 14, 1903 in
Green Ridge, Mo.   died in childhood. (Ref. 2)

1182- <u>Cleo Pearl</u>[9] <u>Wadleigh</u>, (Everett[8], Daniel
Foster[7], William Henry[6], Joseph[5], Joseph[4],
Henry[3], Robert[2], John[1]), (twin) b. July 15,
1898 in Green Ridge, Mo., d. March 25, 1900 in
Green Ridge. died in childhood. (Ref. 2)

**Issue of 890- Henry Libby[8] Wadleigh and Mary
E. (Fowler) Wadleigh:**

1183- <u>Fred Elmer</u>[9] <u>Wadleigh</u>, (Henry Libby[8],
Daniel Foster[7], William Henry[6], Joseph[5],
Joseph[4], Henry[3], Robert[2], John[1]), b. July 20,
1884 in Green Ridge, Mo., d. March 26, 1940.
m. 1st February 6, 1910 Mabel Edith Lenocker,
b. October 10, 1889, d. June 13, 1930, m. 2nd
June 11, 1936 Lucy Martin, b. November 7, 1895,

d. March 6, 1964.   (Ref. 1, 2)   1406 - 1409 by
1st wife.
    1406 - Irene   1408 - Edith Marie
    1407 - Walter Raymond 1409 - Myrtle Evelyn

1184- <u>Arthur Gilbert</u>[9] <u>Wadleigh</u>, (Henry[5] Libby[8],
Daniel Foster[7], William Henry[6], Joseph[5],
Joseph[4], Henry[3], Robert[2], John[1]), b. February
21, 1886 in Green Ridge, Mo. m. April 22, 1914
Elizabeth Guis, b. March 2, 1888, d. July 24,
1971. (Ref. 1, 2)
    1410 - Arthur Milton   1412 - Ronald Gale
    1411 - Kenneth Herbert

**Issue of 890- Henry Libby[8] Wadleigh and
Rosetta Adelaide (Brewster) (Williams)
Wadleigh:**

1185- <u>Ralph Libby</u>[9] <u>Wadleigh</u>, (Henry Libby[8],
Daniel Foster[7], William Henry[6], Joseph[5],
Joseph[4], Henry[3], Robert[2], John[1]), b. March 21,
1889 in Green Ridge, Mo., d. November 12, 1971,
m. 1st April 27, 1912 Mamie Francis Uhls, b.
April 22, 1893, d. December 7, 1918.   m. 2nd
January 8, 1931 Susan Cobb, b. June 24, 1899.
m. 3rd June 27, 1963 Jemima Lucy Walter, b.
December 27, 1892, d. July 7, 1966. (Ref. 1,
2)   1413 - 1417 by 1st wife, 1418 - 1422 by
2nd wife.
    1413 - Woodrow Wilson   1418 - Ralph Norman
    1414 - Pearl Marie   1419 - Alma Darlene
    1415 - Charles Elmer   1420 - Leland Arthur
    1416 - Twyla Mae   1421 - Lloyd Dale
    1417 - Helen Alice   1422 - Ronald Dale

1186- <u>Joseph Everett</u>[9] <u>Wadleigh</u>, (Henry[5] Libby[8],
Daniel Foster[7], William Henry[6], Joseph[5],
Joseph[4], Henry[3], Robert[2], John[1]), b. December
14, 1890 in Green Ridge, Mo., d. August 18,
1975 in LaJunta, Otero Co., Colo. m. June 3,
1917 Irene Irwin, b. June 10, 1893 at Emporia,
Lyon Co., Kan., d. July 21, 1973 at LaJunta.

(Ref. 1, 2)
1423 - Esther Irene   1425 - Roger Alan
1424 - Vere louise   1426 - John Richard

1187- Herbert Calvin[9] Wadleigh, (Henry Libby[8], Daniel Foster[7], William Henry[6], Joseph[5], Joseph[4], Henry[3], Robert[2], John[1]), (twin) b. July 10, 1893 in Green Ridge, Mo. m. March 24, 1921 Ellen Wilson, b. November 27, 1897. (Ref. 1, 2)
1427 - Eileen Marie   1428 - Robert Wilson

1188- Harold Brewster[9] Wadleigh, (Henry Libby[8], Daniel Foster[7], William Henry[6], Joseph[5], Joseph[4], Henry[3], Robert[2], John[1]), (twin) b. July 10, 1893 in Green Ridge, Mo., d. March 23, 1978 in Vale Ore. m. February 23, 1919, Olive Joyce Basinger, b. May 25, 1899. (Ref. 1, 2)
1429 - Elva Aldina   1432 - Calvin Herbert
1430 - Joyce Ellen   1433 - Oleda Kay
1431 - Dean Alvin

1189- Eugene Henry[9] Wadleigh, (Henry Libby[8], Daniel Foster[7], William Henry[6], Joseph[5], Joseph[4], Henry[3], Robert[2], John[1]), b. June 29, 1895 in Green Ridge, Mo., d. June 30, 1973 in Tucson, Ariz., bur. Nomte Vista, Rio Grande Co., Colo. m. October 10, 1922 Ruth Lorina Talkelm, b. October 7, 1894. (Ref. 1, 2)
1434 - Donald Lee   1436 - Glen Eugene
1435 - Robert Henry

1190- Edna Rose[9] Wadleigh, (Henry Libby[8], Daniel Foster[7], William Henry[6], Joseph[5], Joseph[4], Henry[3], Robert[2], John[1]), b. May 15, 1897 in Green Ridge, Mo., d. November 4, 1934. m. August 26, 1915 Reno Ray Nice, b. April 28, 1895. (Ref. 1, 2)
1437 - Mable Leota   1441 - Ruth Ellen
1438 - Harry Alfred   1442 - Dorothy Mae
1439 - Ida Rose   1443 - Gwendolyn Alt
1440 - Howard Fred   1444 - Robert Louis

1191- <u>Mary Emma</u>[9] <u>Wadleigh</u>, (Henry Libby[8],
Daniel Foster[7], William Henry[6], Joseph[5],
Joseph[4], Henry[3], Robert[2], John[1]), b. May 29,
1900 in Green Ridge, Mo. d. January 30, 1975
in Medford, Jackson Co., Ore., m. July 3, 1921
in Cheraw, Colo. Orland Bazil Rector, b.
October 9, 1890 at Fall Branch, Green Co.,
Tenn., d. February 15, 1948 in Titusville, Fla.
(Ref. 1, 2)

1445 - Leona Evalyn	1447 - Velma JoAnn
1446 - John Orland	1448 - Mary Carol

**Issue of 895- George Henry[8] Wadleigh and Mary
Kendrick (Goodwin) Wadleigh:**

1192- <u>Carrie Russell</u>[9] <u>Wadleigh</u>, (George Henry[8],
Joseph Dearborn[7], William Henry[6], Joseph[5],
Joseph[4], Henry[3], Robert[2], John[1]), b. January 6,
1870 in Green Ridge, Mo., d. July 10, 1871 in
Green Ridge. died in childhood. (Ref. 2)

1193- <u>Myrtle May Williams</u>[9] <u>Wadleigh</u>, (George
Henry[8], Joseph Dearborn[7], William Henry[6],
Joseph[5], Joseph[4], Henry[3], Robert[2], John[1]), b.
February 23, 1877 in Dwight, Ill., d. August
22, 1968 in Green Ridge, Mo. m. May 29, 1904
in Green Ridge Armsteat Harland Morris, b.
March 17, 1878, d. March 31, 1937. (Ref. 2)

**Issue of Nathan Brockway Reed and 897- Jennie
Russell (Wadleigh) Reed:**

1194- <u>Ethel Grace</u> <u>Reed</u>, (Wadleigh: Jennie
Russell[8], Joseph Dearborn[7], William Henry[6],
Joseph[5], Joseph[4], Henry[3], Robert[2], John[1]), b.
May 31, 1881, d. April 19, 1948. m. 1169-
James Randolph McCampbell, (Wadleigh: Maaura[8],
Daniel Foster[7], William Henry[6], Joseph[5],
Joseph[4], Henry[3], Robert[2], John[1]), s. of James
B. and Maaura (Wadleigh) McCampbell, b. October
10, 1878 in Green Ridge, Mo., d. January 30,

1947 in Windsor, Mo. (Ref. 2, 3) For issue
see 1169- James Randolph McCampbell

1195- <u>Joe</u> <u>Brockway</u> <u>Reed</u>, (Wadleigh: Jennie
Russell[8], Joseph Dearborn[7], William Henry[6],
Joseph[5], Joseph[4], Henry[3], Robert[2], John[1]), no
data. (Ref. 2, 3)

1196- <u>Bessie</u> <u>Helen</u> <u>Reed</u>, (Wadleigh: Jennie
Russell[8], Joseph Dearborn[7], William Henry[6],
Joseph[5], Joseph[4], Henry[3], Robert[2], John[1]), m.
Frank Wilson. no additional data. (Ref. 2, 3)

1197- <u>Ida</u> <u>Mae</u> <u>Reed</u>, (Wadleigh: Jennie
Russell[8], Joseph Dearborn[7], William Henry[6],
Joseph[5], Joseph[4], Henry[3], Robert[2], John[1]), m.
Mr. Strickrod. no additional data. (Ref. 2, 3)

1198- <u>George</u> <u>Beaman</u> <u>Reed</u>, (Wadleigh: Jennie
Russell[8], Joseph Dearborn[7], William Henry[6],
Joseph[5], Joseph[4], Henry[3], Robert[2], John[1]), no
data. (Ref. 2, 3)

1199- <u>Charlie</u> <u>Voss</u> <u>Reed</u>, (Wadleigh: Jennie
Russell[8], Joseph Dearborn[7], William Henry[6],
Joseph[5], Joseph[4], Henry[3], Robert[2], John[1]), no
data. (Ref. 2)

1200- <u>Florence</u> <u>Esther</u> <u>Reed</u>, (Wadleigh: Jennie
Russell[8], Joseph Dearborn[7], William Henry[6],
Joseph[5], Joseph[4], Henry[3], Robert[2], John[1]), no
data. (Ref. 2)

1201- <u>Mildred</u> <u>Fayolla</u> <u>Reed</u>, (Wadleigh: Jennie
Russell[8], Joseph Dearborn[7], William Henry[6],
Joseph[5], Joseph[4], Henry[3], Robert[2], John[1]), no
data. (Ref. 2)

WADLEIGH GENEALOGY   NINTH GENERATION

1202- <u>Donald Reed</u>, (Wadleigh: Jennie Russell[8], Joseph Dearborn[7], William Henry[6], Joseph[5], Joseph[4], Henry[3], Robert[2], John[1]), no data. (Ref. 2)

Issue of Rowland Mullin and 900- Laura D. (Wadleigh) Mullin:

1203- <u>Earl Mullin</u>, (Wadleigh: Laura D.[8], John H.[7], William Henry[6], Joseph[5], Joseph[4], Henry[3], Robert[2], John[1]), b. 1885, d. 1947. m. Mabel Boyd, b. 1888, d. 1974. (Ref. 2)

Issue of 901- William H.[8] Wadleigh and Jennie (Dye) Wadleigh:

1204- <u>Reed[9] Wadleigh</u>, (William H.[8], John H.[7], William Henry[6], Joseph[5], Joseph[4], Henry[3], Robert[2], John[1]), no data. (Ref. 2)

Issue of 902- John[8] Wadleigh and Dolly (Bailey) Wadleigh:

1205- <u>John Buren[9] Wadleigh</u>, (John[8], John[7], Simon Dearborn[6], Benjamin[5], Joseph[4], Henry[3], Robert[2], John[1]), b. September 6, 1833 in Hill, N.H. m. 1st October 22, 1858 Jane Harriett Brown, d. of Joseph and Hannah (Greeley) Brown of Andover, N.H., b. April 10, 1837, d. July 10, 1864. m. 2nd Viola Lydia Brown, d. of Joseph and Hannah (Greeley) Brown of Andover, s. of Jane Harriett (Brown) Wadleigh. no additional data. (Ref. 3) 1449 - 1451 by 1st wife. 1452 - 1455 by 2nd wife.

1449 - Frank Eugene	1453 - Maurice Colman
1450 - _____ Sidney	1454 - Jennie May
1451 - Fred Joseph	1455 - John
1452 - Robert Lee	

1206- <u>Mary Love</u>[9] Wadleigh, (John[8], John[7], Simon Dearborn[6], Benjamin[5], Joseph[4], Henry[3], Robert[2], John[1]), b. September 19, 1839 in Hill, N.H., d. January 22, 1873. (Ref. 3)

1207- <u>Annie W.</u>[9] Wadleigh, (John[8], John[7], Simon Dearborn[6], Benjamin[5], Joseph[4], Henry[3], Robert[2], John[1]), b. June 17, 1846 in Hill, N.H., m. July 7, 1874 Cyrus Webster Bartlett. no additional data. (Ref. 3)

1208- <u>George Andrew</u>[9] Wadleigh, (John[8], John[7], Simon Dearborn[6], Benjamin[5], Joseph[4], Henry[3], Robert[2], John[1]), b. March 28, 1850 in Hill, N.H., d. August 20, 1852. died in childhood. (Ref. 3)

Issue of 906- Levi C.[8] Wadleigh and Mary Susan (McCrilliss) Wadleigh:

1209- <u>Susan Elizabeth</u>[9] Wadleigh, (Levi[8], John[7], Simon Dearborn[6], Benjamin[5], Joseph[4], Henry[3], Robert[2], John[1]), b. in Haverhill, Mass. (Ref. 3)

1210- <u>George Clinton</u>[9] Wadleigh, (Levi[8], John[7], Simon Dearborn[6], Benjamin[5], Joseph[4], Henry[3], Robert[2], John[1]), b. December 1, 1846 in Haverhill, Mass., d. December 9, 1922 in Haverhill. m. 1889 Alma Laura Hodgedon, d. of Reuben S. Hodgedon and Abbie A. (McClinch) Hodgedon of Maine, no additional data. (Ref. 3)

1211- <u>Fannie</u>[9] Wadleigh, (Levi[8], John[7], Simon Dearborn[6], Benjamin[5], Joseph[4], Henry[3], Robert[2], John[1]), b. in Haverhill, Mass. m. Lewis C. Merrill of Manchester, N.H., no additional data. (Ref. 3)
    1456 - Henry Wadleigh

1212- <u>Levi C.</u>^{9} <u>Wadleigh</u>, (Levi^8, John^7, Simon
Dearborn^6, Benjamin^5, Joseph^4, Henry^3, Robert^2,
John^1), b. in Haverhill, N.H. m. Gertrude
Bridgeman, no additional data. (Ref. 3)
      1457 - Clinton Bridgeman
      1458 - Everlyn Bridgeman

**Issue of 908- Hiram Gilmore^8 Wadleigh and
Philitia (Goodnow) Wadleigh:**

1213- <u>Harriet Louisa</u>^{9} <u>Wadleigh</u>, (Hiram
Gilmore^8, Newell^7, Simon Dearborn^6, Benjamin^5,
Joseph^4, Henry^3, Robert^2, John^1). b. April 18,
1840 in Boston, Mass. m. in Boston, John N.
Dearborn, d. April 1, 1924 in Bridgeport, Conn.
(Ref. 3)
   1459 - Arthur Burton   1460 - Ada Estelle

1214- <u>Charles Edwin</u>^{9} <u>Wadleigh</u>, (Hiram Gilmore^8,
Newell^7, Simon Dearborn^6, Benjamin^5, Joseph^4,
Henry^3, Robert^2, John^1). b. March 29, 1844 in
Boston, Mass., d. January 1931 in Boston.
reference to 2 marriages. (Ref. 3)
   1461 - Bertha Goodnow   1462 - Charles A.

1215- <u>Frank H. Newell</u>^{9} <u>Wadleigh</u>, (Hiram
Gilmore^8, Newell^7, Simon Dearborn^6, Benjamin^5,
Joseph^4, Henry^3, Robert^2, John^1). b. September
15, 1852 in Boston, Mass., d. March 11, 1853 in
Boston. died in childhood. (Ref. 3)

**Issue of 911- James C.^{8} Wadleigh and Hannah
P. (Pearson) Wadleigh:**

1216- <u>John Burley</u>^{9} <u>Wadleigh</u>, (James C.^{8},
James^7, James^6, James^5, Joseph^4, Henry^3,
Robert^2, John^1), b. December 3, 1833 in
Meredith Ridge, N.H., d. September 3, 1836.
died in childhood. (Ref. 3)

1217- Luther Jethro[9] Wadleigh, (James C.[8],
James[7], James[6], James[5], Joseph[4], Henry[3],
Robert[2], John[1]), b. October 3, 1835 in Meredith
Ridge, N.H. m. January 26, 1860 Abbie Johnson
of Orange, N.H., d. of David and Catherine
Johnson of Orange, b. February 20, 1840 in
Salisbury, N.H. Res. Orange and North
Sanbornton, N.H. Occ. owner of Piper Saw Mill
and a mason in Bristol and Upper Bartlett, N.H.
(Ref. 3)

1463 - Horace David	1466 - Fred James
1464 - James	1467 - Arthur Albert
1465 - Walter Luther	1468 - John Burden

**Issue of 913- Nathaniel Farnham[8] Wadleigh and
Sally Merrill (Plumer) Wadleigh:**

1218- Cynthia Ann[9] Wadleigh, (Nathaniel
Farnham[8], James[7], James[6], James[5], Joseph[4],
Henry[3], Robert[2], John[1]), b. December 28, 1850
in Sanbornton, N.H. (Ref. 3)

**Issue of 915- Warren[8] Wadleigh and Harriett
O. (Thomas) Wadleigh:**

1219- Kendall[9] Wadleigh, (Warren[8], Joseph[7],
James[6], James[5], Joseph[4], Henry[3], Robert[2],
John[1]), b. February 27, 1839 in Sanbornton,
N.H., d. July 3, 1865 in Lake Village,
N.H. (Ref. 3)

1220- Annie Fogg[9] Wadleigh, (Warren[8], Joseph[7],
James[6], James[5], Joseph[4], Henry[3], Robert[2],
John[1]), b. June 16, 1842 in Sanbornton, N.H.
m. February 22, 1876 Elias F. Smith of
Rochester, N.H. (or N.Y.) (or of Lebanon, Ref.
3 cites both), no additional data. Served in
Civil War. (Ref. 3)

1221- <u>Washington Irving</u>^{9} <u>Wadleigh</u>, (Warren^8, Joseph^7, James^6, James^5, Joseph^4, Henry^3, Robert^2, John^1), b. November 21, 1845 in Sanbornton, N.H. m. January 21, 1874 in Astoria, Ore. Florence L. Van Dusen, no additional data. Res. Seattle, Wash. (Ref. 3)

1222- <u>Horace Wayland</u>^{9} <u>Wadleigh</u>, (Warren^8, Joseph^7, James^6, James^5, Joseph^4, Henry^3, Robert^2, John^1), b. May 18, 1848 in Sanbornton, N.H. (Ref. 3)

Issue of 916- Shadrach^8 Wadleigh and Huldah S. (Hunt) Wadleigh:

1223- <u>Phebe Ann</u>^{9} <u>Wadleigh</u>, (Shadrach^8, Joseph^7, James^6, James^5, Joseph^4, Henry^3, Robert^2, John^1), b. November 22, 1836 in Sanbornton, N.H. m. Aaron Woodman, no additional data. (Ref. 3)

Issue of 918- Joseph Dustin^8 Wadleigh and Sarah S. (Hunt) Wadleigh:

1224- <u>George Hunt</u>^{9} <u>Wadleigh</u>, (Joseph Dustin^8, Joseph^7, James^6, James^5, Joseph^4, Henry^3, Robert^2, John^1), b. November 17, 1850 in Sanbornton, N.H. (Ref. 3)

1225- <u>Clariber Ann</u>^{9} <u>Wadleigh</u>, (Joseph Dustin^8, Joseph^7, James^6, James^5, Joseph^4, Henry^3, Robert^2, John^1), b. January 19, 1853 in Sanbornton, N.H. (Ref. 3)

Issue of 921- Jonathan Taylor[8] Wadleigh and Betsey (Thomas) Wadleigh:

1226- Josephine Louise[9] Wadleigh, (Jonathan Taylor[8], John[7], James[6], James[5], Joseph[4], Henry[3], Robert[2], John[1]), b. July 24, 1844 in Sanbornton, N.H. m. August 2, 1869 Clinton Blake, b. August 2, 1839. (Ref. 3)

1227- Charlotte Fogg[9] Wadleigh, (Jonathan Taylor[8], John[7], James[6], James[5], Joseph[4], Henry[3], Robert[2], John[1]), b. May 26, 1852 in Franklin, N.H. m. May 26, 1875 Phineas A. Nourse of Franklin Falls, N.H., no additional data. (Ref. 3)

1228- Walter Kendall[9] Wadleigh, (Jonathan Taylor[8], John[7], James[6], James[5], Joseph[4], Henry[3], Robert[2], John[1]), b. April 7, 1864 in Franklin, N.H. (Ref. 3)

Issue of 924- John Blake[8] Wadleigh and Abby Ruthena (Tilton) Wadleigh:

1229- Oscar Stearns[9] Wadleigh, (John Blake[8], John[7], James[6], James[5], Joseph[4], Henry[3], Robert[2], John[1]), b. July 24, 1865 in Sanbornton, N.H. (Ref. 3)

1230- John Parker[9] Wadleigh, (John Blake[8], John[7], James[6], James[5], Joseph[4], Henry[3], Robert[2], John[1]), b. January 21, 1869 in Sanbornton, N.H. (Ref. 3)

1231- Fred Tilton[9] Wadleigh, (John Blake[8], John[7], James[6], James[5], Joseph[4], Henry[3], Robert[2], John[1]), b. November 2, 1870 in Sanbornton, N.H. (Ref. 3)

1232- Helen Abbie[9] Wadleigh, (John Blake[8],
John[7], James[6], James[5], Joseph[4], Henry[3],
Robert[2], John[1]), b. April 26, 1872 in
Sanbornton, N.H. (Ref. 3)

**Issue of 925- Daniel Taylor[8] Wadleigh and
Hannah P. (Burley) Wadleigh:**

1233- Fred Burley[9] Wadleigh, (Daniel Taylor[8],
John[7], James[6], James[5], Joseph[4], Henry[3],
Robert[2], John[1]), b. May 15, 1862 in Sanbornton,
N.H., d. April 8, 1865 in Sanbornton. died in
childhood from diptheria. (Ref. 3)

1234- William Augustus[9] Wadleigh, (Daniel
Taylor[8], John[7], James[6], James[5], Joseph[4],
Henry[3], Robert[2], John[1]), b. July 1863 in
Sanbornton, N.H., d. March 27, 1865 in
Sanbornton. died in childhood from diptheria.
(Ref. 3)

1235- Sarah Esther[9] Wadleigh, (Daniel Taylor[8],
John[7], James[6], James[5], Joseph[4], Henry[3],
Robert[2], John[1]), b. July 29, 1865 in
Sanbornton, N.H. (Ref. 3)

1236- Mary Percy[9] Wadleigh, (Daniel Taylor[8],
John[7], James[6], James[5], Joseph[4], Henry[3],
Robert[2], John[1]), b. January 16, 1867 in
Sanbornton, N.H. (Ref. 3)

**Issue of 929- John[8] Wadleigh and Mary Ann
(Hanaford) Wadleigh:**

1237- Le Roi B.[9] Wadleigh, (John[8], Dearborn[7],
John[6], James[5], Joseph[4], Henry[3], Robert[2],
John[1]), b. 1833 in Meredith N.H., d. 1918. m.
Catherine Polluck, no additional data. (Ref. 3)

1238- Martha Abby[9] Wadleigh, (John[8], Dearborn[7], John[6], James[5], Joseph[4], Henry[3], Robert[2], John[1]), b. 1838 in Meredith, N.H., d. 1864. m. G. P. Bricket, no additional data. (Ref. 3)

1239- John Dearborn[9] Wadleigh, (John[8], Dearborn[7], John[6], James[5], Joseph[4], Henry[3], Robert[2], John[1]), b. 1849 in Meredith, N.H., d. November 10, 1872. m. Emma A., b. ca. 1850, d. July 20, 1883. (Ref. 3)

1240- Mary Ann[9] Wadleigh, (John[8], Dearborn[7], John[6], James[5], Joseph[4], Henry[3], Robert[2], John[1]), b. 1852 in Meredith, N.H. m. Frank P. Loffingwell, no additional data. (Ref. 3)

Issue of 931- Charles Joseph[8] Wadleigh and Ann Maria (Gage) Wadleigh:

1241- Martha O.[9] Wadleigh, (Charles Joseph[8], James Dearborn[7], Joseph[6], James[5], Joseph[4], Henry[3], Robert[2], John[1]), b. June 21, 1860. (Ref. 3)

1242- Eve J.[9] Wadleigh, (Charles Joseph[8], James Dearborn[7], Joseph[6], James[5], Joseph[4], Henry[3], Robert[2], John[1]), b. January 5, 1865. (Ref. 3)

1243- Charles J.[9] Wadleigh, (Charles Joseph[8], James Dearborn[7], Joseph[6], James[5], Joseph[4], Henry[3], Robert[2], John[1]), b. April 4, 1867, d. May 3, 1867. died in infancy. (Ref. 3)

Issue of 934- Joseph[8] Wadleigh and Julia A. (Henry) Wadleigh:

1244- Josephine Mary[9] Wadleigh, (Joseph[8], Newell[7], Joseph[6], James[5], Joseph[4], Henry[3],

WADLEIGH GENEALOGY   NINTH GENERATION

Robert[2], John[1]), b. March 7, 1857 in Lowell,
Mass. m. January 16, 1879 Charles A. Snow of
Montpellier, Vt., no other data. (Ref. 3)

1245- Juann[9] Wadleigh, (Joseph[8], Newell[7],
Joseph[6], James[5], Joseph[4], Henry[3], Robert[2],
John[1]), b. September 5, 1858 in Lowell, Mass.
(Ref. 3)

1246- Jude C.[9] Wadleigh, (Joseph[8], Newell[7],
Joseph[6], James[5], Joseph[4], Henry[3], Robert[2],
John[1]), b. July 11, 1860 in Lowell, Mass.
(Ref. 3)

1247- Olivia[9] Wadleigh, (Joseph[8], Newell[7],
Joseph[6], James[5], Joseph[4], Henry[3], Robert[2],
John[1]), b. March 11, 1863 in Lowell, Mass.
(Ref. 3)

1248- Henry Albert[9] Wadleigh, (Joseph[8],
Newell[7], Joseph[6], James[5], Joseph[4], Henry[3],
Robert[2], John[1]), b. October 1, 1866 in Lowell,
Mass., d. July 8, 1867. died in infancy.
(Ref. 3)

Issue of 939- Hiram Porter[8] Wadleigh and Mary
W. (Morrison) Wadleigh:

1249- Elmer Albert[9] Wadleigh, (Hiram Porter[8],
Joseph[7], Joseph[6], James[5], Joseph[4], Henry[3],
Robert[2], John[1]), b. August 10, 1862 in
Sanbornton, N.H. (Ref. 3)

Issue of 940- Gustave Bartlett[8] Wadleigh and
Abbie (Eaton) Wadleigh:

1250- Ida Belle[9] Wadleigh, (Gustave Bartlett[8],
Joseph[7], Joseph[6], James[5], Joseph[4], Henry[3],

Robert[2], John[1]), b. August 23, 1839 in Hill, N.H. (Ref. 3)

1251- Albert Prescott[9] Wadleigh, (Gustave Bartlett[8], Joseph[7], Joseph[6], James[5], Joseph[4], Henry[3], Robert[2], John[1]), b. August 11, 1865 in Hill, N.H. (Ref. 3)

Issue of James R. Philbrick and 944- Martha Ellen[8] (Wadleigh) Philbrick:

1252- Cora Belle Philbrick, (Wadleigh: Martha Ellen[8], Joseph[7], Joseph[6], James[5], Joseph[4], Henry[3], Robert[2], John[1]), b. June 3, 1866. (Ref. 3)

Issue of Belder W. Morgan and 945- Clarissa Weeks[8] (Wadleigh) Morgan:

1253- Zelle Belle Morgan, (Wadleigh: Clarissa Weeks[8], Joseph[7], Joseph[6], James[5], Joseph[4], Henry[3], Robert[2], John[1]), b. October 27, 1874 in Franklin, N.H. (Ref. 3)

Issue of 952- John Hayes[8] Wadleigh and Mary Lela (Stiles) Wadleigh:

1254- Frank Weston[9] Wadleigh, (John Hayes[8], Simon Hayes[7], Joseph[6], James[5], Joseph[4], Henry[3], Robert[2], John[1]), b. February 2, 1869 in Braintree, Vt. m. January 23, 1892 Winnie A. Riford, no additional data. (Ref. 3)
        1469 - Carroll Riford

1255- John Bartlett[9] Wadleigh, (John Hayes[8], Simon Hayes[7], Joseph[6], James[5], Joseph[4], Henry[3], Robert[2], John[1]), b. February 17, 1874 in Braintree, Vt. (Ref. 3)

1256- <u>Mabel Ellen</u>[9] <u>Wadleigh</u>, (John Hayes[8], Simon Hayes[7], Joseph[6], James[5], Joseph[4], Henry[3], Robert[2], John[1]), b. March 1, 1876 in Randolph, Vt. (Ref. 3)

Issue of Henry K. W. Currier and 953- Mary Ellen[8] (Wadleigh) Currier:

1257- <u>Nathaniel Currier</u>, (Wadleigh: Mary Ellen[8], Simon Hayes[7], Joseph[6], James[5], Joseph[4], Henry[3], Robert[2], John[1]), b. June 9, 1863 in Canaan, N.H. (Ref. 3)

Issue of 955- Joseph[8] Wadleigh and Lydia (Moore) Wadleigh:

1258- <u>Julia</u>[9] <u>Wadleigh</u>, (Joseph[8], William P.[7], Simeon[6], James[5], Joseph[4], Henry[3], Robert[2], John[1]), b. in Meredith, N.H., d. in Sanbornton, N.H., bur. in Swampscott, Mass. m. William Cole of Meredith. no additional data. Res. Swampscott, Mass. (Ref. 3)

1259- <u>Mary Etta</u>[9] <u>Wadleigh</u>, (Joseph[8], William P.[7], Simeon[6], James[5], Joseph[4], Henry[3], Robert[2], John[1]), b. in Meredith, N.H. m. William Severence, no additional data. (Ref. 3)

Issue of 991- Isaiah Waldron[7] Smith and Rhoda (Wills) Smith:

1260- <u>Fred Linwood</u>[8] Smith, (Wadleigh: Isaiah Waldron[9], Henry M.[8], Sally[7], Richard[6], Mary[5], Elizabeth[4], Jonathan[3], Joanna[2], John[1]; Gilman: Isaiah Waldron[9], Henry M.[8], Sally[7], Richard[6], Mary[5], Elizabeth[4], Mary[3], John[2], Edward[1]; Smith: Isaiah Waldron[7], Henry M.[6], Waldron[5], John W.[4], Jonathan[3], Jonathan[2], Robert[1]), m. Lillian Toothaker, no additional data. (Ref. 49)

    1470 - Richard C.

Issue of 992- David Haslem[9] Graves and Theresa Louisa (Cooke) Graves:

1261- <u>Leonie</u>[10] <u>Graves</u>, (Wadleigh: David Haslem[9], John[8], James[7], Ruth[6], Dean[5], John[4], John[3], Robert[2], John[1]; Graves: David Haslem[9], John[8], James[7], David[6], James[5], Samuel[4], Abraham[3], Mark[2], Samuel[1]), b. February 18, 1970. m. September 6, 1893 John E. Vann of Winton, N.C., no additional data. (Ref. 12)

1262- <u>Clarence D.</u>[10] <u>Graves</u>, (Wadleigh: David Haslem[9], John[8], James[7], Ruth[6], Dean[5], John[4], John[3], Robert[2], John[1]; Graves: David Haslem[9], John[8], James[7], David[6], James[5], Samuel[4], Abraham[3], Mark[2], Samuel[1]), b. February 9, 1872. m. November 1, 1900 Octavia Bate of Louisville, Ky. Occ. Minister. Res. Dublin, Ga. (Ref. 12)

1263- <u>John Ernest</u>[10] <u>Graves</u>, (Wadleigh: David Haslem[9], John[8], James[7], Ruth[6], Dean[5], John[4], John[3], Robert[2], John[1]; Graves: David Haslem[9],

John[8], James[7], David[6], James[5], Samuel[4],
Abraham[3], Mark[2], Samuel[1]), b. February 3, 1874.
m. October 10, 1906 Mary B. Parlin, d. of
Charles H. Parlin of Carrabelle, Fla., Res.
Gainesville, Fla. (Ref. 12)

1264- <u>Victor Morse</u>[10] <u>Graves</u>, (Wadleigh: David
Haslem[9], John[8], James[7], Ruth[6], Dean[5], John[4],
John[3], Robert[2], John[1]; Graves: David Haslem[9],
John[8], James[7], David[6], James[5], Samuel[4],
Abraham[3], Mark[2], Samuel[1]), b. February 25,
1876. m. November 19, 1907 Emily Louise Holt,
d. of Linn Banks and Mary (Mebane) Holt, Res.
New York, N.Y., Ed. Univ. of North Carolina.
(Ref. 12)
    1471 - Mary Louise Holt

1265- <u>Bertie M.</u>[10] <u>Graves</u>, (Wadleigh: David
Haslem[9], John[8], James[7], Ruth[6], Dean[5], John[4],
John[3], Robert[2], John[1]; Graves: David Haslem[9],
John[8], James[7], David[6], James[5], Samuel[4],
Abraham[3], Mark[2], Samuel[1]), b. December 3, 1879,
d. February 9, 1935. (Ref. 12)

**Issue of 995- John[9] Wadleigh and Sarah (Ford)
Wadleigh:**

1266- <u>Benjamin</u>[10] <u>Wadleigh</u>, (John[9], Benjamin
Dean[8], Benjamin Dean[7], Dean[6], Dean[5], John[4],
John[3], Robert[2], John[1]), b. in Salisbury, Mass.,
d. February 19, 1937 in Amesbury, Mass. did
not marry. (Ref. 3)

**Issue of 999- Porter[9] Wadleigh and Cora
(Godsoe) Wadleigh:**

1267- <u>daughter</u>[10] <u>Wadleigh</u>, (Porter[9], David E.[8],
Benjamin Dean[7], Dean[6], Dean[5], John[4], John[3],
Robert[2], John[1]), no additional data. (Ref. 3)

WADLEIGH GENEALOGY   TENTH GENERATION

1268- <u>Albert P.</u>[10] <u>Wadleigh</u>, (Porter[9], David
E.[8], Benjamin Dean[7], Dean[6], Dean[5], John[4],
John[3], Robert[2], John[1]), Res. Merrimac, Mass.
(Ref. 3)

**Issue of Mr. Currier and 1013- Mae Warren
(Wadleigh) Currier:**

1269- <u>George Currier</u>, (Wadleigh: Mae Warren[9],
Ephriam[8], Eliphalet[7], Ephriam[6], Moses[5],
Ephriam[4], John[3], Robert[2], John[1]), m. Gertrude
Hollander of Amesbury, Mass., no additional
data. (Ref. 3)

**Issue of 1015- Jonathan C.[9] Wadleigh and
Abbie A. (Smith) Wadleigh:**

1270- <u>Eliza B.</u>[10] <u>Wadleigh</u>, (Jonathan C.[9],
Charles T. P.[8], Ezekiel[7], Ephriam[6], Moses[5],
Ephriam[4], John[3], Robert[2], John[1]), b. January 3,
1882 in Salisbury, Mass., d. January 8, 1882 in
Salisbury, Mass. died in infancy. (Ref. 3)

1271- <u>Jonathan C.</u>[10] <u>Wadleigh</u>, (Jonathan C.[9],
Charles T. P.[8], Ezekiel[7], Ephriam[6], Moses[5],
Ephriam[4], John[3], Robert[2], John[1]), b. October
31, 1883 in Salisbury, Mass. m. April 25,
1906, Alice J. Whittemore of Chester, N.H., no
additional data. (Ref. 3)
        1472 - Doris W.

1272- <u>Hannah</u>[10] <u>Wadleigh</u>, (Jonathan C.[9], Charles
T. P.[8], Ezekiel[7], Ephriam[6], Moses[5], Ephriam[4],
John[3], Robert[2], John[1]), b. January 29, 1886 in
Amesbury, Mass. m. June 18, 1911, Harry F.
Merrow, Res. in Haverhill, Mass. (Ref. 3)

1273- <u>Abbie Smith</u>[10] <u>Wadleigh</u>, (Jonathan C.[9],
Charles T. P.[8], Ezekiel[7], Ephriam[6], Moses[5],

Ephriam[4], John[3], Robert[2], John[1]), b. March 15, 1890 in Amesbury, Mass., d. March 17, 1890 in Amesbury. died in infancy. (Ref. 3)

Issue of 1016- Cyrus Pearson[9] Wadleigh and Elizabeth Ann (Hoyt) Wadleigh:

1274- <u>Susie W.</u>[10] Wadleigh, (Cyrus Pearson[9], Eben Pearson[8], Ezekiel[7], Ephriam[6], Moses[5], Ephriam[4], John[3], Robert[2], John[1]), b. December 8, 1876 in Amesbury, Mass. m. July 5, 1910 Fred N. Colby, no additional data. (Ref. 3)

1275- <u>Frank A.</u>[10] Wadleigh, (Cyrus Pearson[9], Eben Pearson[8], Ezekiel[7], Ephriam[6], Moses[5], Ephriam[4], John[3], Robert[2], John[1]), b. November 29, 1880 in Amesbury, Mass. m. September 24, 1909 Emma Sutherland of Amesbury. no additional data. (Ref. 3)
    1473 - Elsa M.   1474 - Mildred E.

1276- <u>Bertha E.</u>[10] Wadleigh, (Cyrus Pearson[9], Eben Pearson[8], Ezekiel[7], Ephriam[6], Moses[5], Ephriam[4], John[3], Robert[2], John[1]), b. April 17, 1885 in Amesbury, Mass. m. September 25, 1911 Charles R. Hodgkins, Jr., d. 1937. (Ref. 3)

1277- <u>C. Edward</u>[10] Wadleigh, (Cyrus Pearson[9], Eben Pearson[8], Ezekiel[7], Ephriam[6], Moses[5], Ephriam[4], John[3], Robert[2], John[1]), b. November 13, 1886 in Amesbury, Mass., d. October 23, 1894. died in childhood. (Ref. 3)

1278- <u>Florence A.</u>[10] Wadleigh, (Cyrus Pearson[9], Eben Pearson[8], Ezekiel[7], Ephriam[6], Moses[5], Ephriam[4], John[3], Robert[2], John[1]), b. June 19, 1892 in Amesbury, Mass., d. March 13, 1915 in South Hampton, N.H. m. January 10, 1909 Hulbert R. Jennings, no additional data. (Ref. 3)
    1475 - Hulbert Randall 1476 - Charles L.

Issue of Edwin Lundberg and 1017- Sarah Jane (Wadleigh) Lundberg:

1279- <u>Josie Lundberg</u>, (Wadleigh: Sarah Jane[9], Eben Pearson[8], Ezekiel[7], Ephriam[6], Moses[5], Ephriam[4], John[3], Robert[2], John[1]), b. ca. 1882 in Amesbury, Mass. m. Charles Evans, no additional data. (Ref. 3)

1280- <u>Edith Lundberg</u>, (Wadleigh: Sarah Jane[9], Eben Pearson[8], Ezekiel[7], Ephriam[6], Moses[5], Ephriam[4], John[3], Robert[2], John[1]), b. ca. 1885 in Amesbury, Mass. m. Perley Leck, no additional data. (Ref. 3)

1281- <u>Maude Lundberg</u>, (Wadleigh: Sarah Jane[9], Eben Pearson[8], Ezekiel[7], Ephriam[6], Moses[5], Ephriam[4], John[3], Robert[2], John[1]), b. ca. 1887 in Amesbury, Mass. m. Walter Hudson, no additional data. (Ref. 3)

Issue of 1019- Charles William[9] Wadleigh and Anna Josephine (Sargent) Wadleigh:

1282- <u>Laura Jane[10]</u> Wadleigh, (Charles William[9], Eben Pearson[8], Ezekiel[7], Ephriam[6], Moses[5], Ephriam[4], John[3], Robert[2], John[1]), b. ca. 1889 in Amesbury, Mass., (alive in 1937 in Portland, Me.). m. 1st William Quimby, m. 2nd Mr. Connor, no additional data. (Ref. 3) 1477 by 1st h., 1478 by 2nd h.
    1477 - Raymond   1478 - daughter

Issue of 1024- Benjamin F.[9] Wadleigh and Caroline E. (Chase) Wadleigh:

1283- <u>Frank Eugene[10]</u> Wadleigh, (Benjamin F.[9], Eliphalet[8], Benjamin[7], Benjamin[6], Thomas[5], Benjamin[4], Robert[3], Robert[2], John[1]), b. December 26, 1865. (Ref. 25-970)

1284- <u>Elmer Ernest</u>[10] <u>Wadleigh</u>, (Benjamin F.[9], Eliphalet[8], Benjamin[7], Benjamin[6], Thomas[5], Benjamin[4], Robert[3], Robert[2], John[1]), b. May 16, 1874. (Ref. 25-970)

1285- <u>Marion Inez</u>[10] <u>Wadleigh</u>, (Benjamin F.[9], Eliphalet[8], Benjamin[7], Benjamin[6], Thomas[5], Benjamin[4], Robert[3], Robert[2], John[1]), b. February 17, 1881. (Ref. 25-970)

Issue of Leonard George and 1025- Mary Mianda (Wadleigh) George:

1286- <u>son</u> George, (Wadleigh: Mary Mianda[9], Eliphalet[8], Benjamin[7], Benjamin[6], Thomas[5], Benjamin[4], Robert[3], Robert[2], John[1]), b. in Minnesota. (Ref. 25-970)

1287- <u>son</u> George, (Wadleigh: Mary Mianda[9], Eliphalet[8], Benjamin[7], Benjamin[6], Thomas[5], Benjamin[4], Robert[3], Robert[2], John[1]), b. in Minnesota, d. after 1902. (Ref. 25-970)

1288- <u>daughter</u> <u>George</u>, (Wadleigh: Mary Mianda[9], Eliphalet[8], Benjamin[7], Benjamin[6], Thomas[5], Benjamin[4], Robert[3], Robert[2], John[1]), b. in Minnesota, d. after 1902. (Ref. 25-970)

Issue of 1026- Corliss[9] Wadleigh and Elmina S. K. (Brigham) Wadleigh:

1289- <u>Mina Beulah</u>[10] <u>Wadleigh</u>, (Corliss[9], Eliphalet[8], Benjamin[7], Benjamin[6], Thomas[5], Benjamin[4], Robert[3], Robert[2], John[1]), b. March 19, 1875. (Ref. 25-970)

1290- <u>Corliss</u>[10] <u>Wadleigh, Jr.</u>, (Corliss[9], Eliphalet[8], Benjamin[7], Benjamin[6], Thomas[5],

Benjamin[4], Robert[3], Robert[2], John[1]), b. August 19, 1880. (Ref. 25-970)

Issue of 1043- Charles Alfred[8] Pillsbury and Mary Ann (Stinson) Pillsbury:

1291- <u>George Alfred[9] Pillsbury</u>, (Wadleigh: Charles Alfred[9], George Alfred[8], Susanna[7], Benjamin[6], Thomas[5], Benjamin[4], Robert[3], Robert[2], John[1]; Pillsbury: Charles Alfred[8], George Alfred[7], John[6], Micajah[5], Caleb[4], Caleb[3], Moses[2], William[1]), b. October 4, 1871 in Minneapolis, Minn., d. December 22, 1872. died in childhood. (Ref. 50-29)

1292- <u>Margaret Carleton[9] Pillsbury</u>, (Wadleigh: Charles Alfred[9], George Alfred[8], Susanna[7], Benjamin[6], Thomas[5], Benjamin[4], Robert[3], Robert[2], John[1]; Pillsbury: Charles Alfred[8], George Alfred[7], John[6], Micajah[5], Caleb[4], Caleb[3], Moses[2], William[1]), b. July 18, 1876 in Minneapolis, Minn., d. April 26, 1881. died in childhood. (Ref. 50-29)

1293- <u>Charles Stinson[9] Pillsbury</u>, (Wadleigh: Charles Alfred[9], George Alfred[8], Susanna[7], Benjamin[6], Thomas[5], Benjamin[4], Robert[3], Robert[2], John[1]; Pillsbury: Charles Alfred[8], George Alfred[7], John[6], Micajah[5], Caleb[4], Caleb[3], Moses[2], William[1]), b. December 6, 1878 in Minneapolis, Minn. (twin). m. in Minneapolis December 7, 1901 Helen Pendleton Winston, d. of Philip Bickerton and Katharine Deborah (Stevens) Winston, b. October 16, 1878 in Minneapolis. Ed. Univ. of Minnesota 1900. Vice-Pres. of Pillsbury Flour Mills Co., director of First National Bank, First Minneapolis Trust Co. and Minneapolis, St. Paul and Sault Ste. Marie Railroad (the Soo Line). (Ref. 50-30)
 1479 - Philip Winston 1481 - Katharine Stevens
 1480 - Mary Stinson   1482 - Helen Winston

1294- <u>John Sargent</u>[9] Pillsbury, (Wadleigh:
Charles Alfred[9], George Alfred[8], Susanna[7],
Benjamin[6], Thomas[5], Benjamin[4], Robert[3],
Robert[2], John[1]; Pillsbury: Charles Alfred[8],
George Alfred[7], John[6], Micajah[5], Caleb[4],
Caleb[3], Moses[2], William[1]), b. December 6, 1878
in Minneapolis, Minn. (twin). m. in
Minneapolis December 5, 1911 Eleanor Jerusha
Lawler of Mitchell, S.D., d. of John Dinan and
Ella (Sturgis) Lawler, b. August 31, 1887 in
Mitchell. Ed. Univ. of Minnesota 1900. Vice
President and Chairman of the Board of
Pillsbury Flour Mills Co., director of
Wisconsin Central Railroad, Northwestern
National Bank and Atlantic Elevator Co. Res.
Wayzata, Minn. (Ref. 50-32)
    1483 - John Sargent   1487 - Jane Lawler
    1484 - Edmund Pennington
    1485 - Ella Sturgis   1488 - George Sturgis
    1486 - Charles Alfred

**Issue of 1045- Fred Carleton[8] Pillsbury and
Alice Thayer (Cook) Pillsbury:**

1295- <u>George Alfred</u>[9] Pillsbury, (Wadleigh:
Fred Carleton[9], George Alfred[8], Susanna[7],
Benjamin[6], Thomas[5], Benjamin[4], Robert[3],
Robert[2], John[1]; Pillsbury: Fred Carleton[8],
George Alfred[7], John[6], Micajah[5], Caleb[4],
Caleb[3], Moses[2], William[1]), b. December 12, 1877
in Minneapolis, Minn., d. November 24, 1881.
died in childhood. (Ref. 50-30)

1296- <u>Harriot Topliff</u>[9] Pillsbury, (Wadleigh:
Fred Carleton[9], George Alfred[8], Susanna[7],
Benjamin[6], Thomas[5], Benjamin[4], Robert[3],
Robert[2], John[1]; Pillsbury: Fred Carleton[8],
George Alfred[7], John[6], Micajah[5], Caleb[4],
Caleb[3], Moses[2], William[1]), b. December 9, 1879
in Minneapolis, Minn., d. June 29, 1925 in
Pasadena, Cal. m. in Minneapolis April 23,
1902 Harold Osgood Ayer, b. July 9, 1877 in
Buenos Aires, Argentina, S.A., d. July 15, 1925
in Pasadena. (Ref. 50-30)
    1489 - Alice Pillsbury   1490 - Ann Dana

1297- <u>Carleton Cook</u>[9] <u>Pillsbury</u>, (Wadleigh:
Fred Carleton[9], George Alfred[8], Susanna[7],
Benjamin[6], Thomas[5], Benjamin[4], Robert[3],
Robert[2], John[1]; Pillsbury: Fred Carleton[8],
George Alfred[7], John[6], Micajah[5], Caleb[4],
Caleb[3], Moses[2], William[1]), b. May 13, 1882 in
Minneapolis, Minn., d. July 1910. (Ref. 50-30)

1298- <u>Marian</u>[9] <u>Pillsbury</u>, (Wadleigh: Fred
Carleton[9], George Alfred[8], Susanna[7], Benjamin[6],
Thomas[5], Benjamin[4], Robert[3], Robert[2], John[1];
Pillsbury: Fred Carleton[8], George Alfred[7],
John[6], Micajah[5], Caleb[4], Caleb[3], Moses[2],
William[1]), b. June 7, 1884 in Minneapolis,
Minn., d. January 17, 1887. died in childhood.
(Ref. 50-30)

1299- <u>Helen Margaret</u>[9] <u>Pillsbury</u>, (Wadleigh:
Fred Carleton[9], George Alfred[8], Susanna[7],
Benjamin[6], Thomas[5], Benjamin[4], Robert[3],
Robert[2], John[1]; Pillsbury: Fred Carleton[8],
George Alfred[7], John[6], Micajah[5], Caleb[4],
Caleb[3], Moses[2], William[1]), b. August 27, 1886
in Minneapolis, Minn. m. in Minneapolis March
26, 1908 Robert Daniels Bardwell, Jr., b. June
4, 1884 in Pittsfield, Mass. (Ref. 50-30)
         1491 - Beatrice Pillsbury
         1492 - Robert Daniels

1300- <u>Alice</u>[9] <u>Pillsbury</u>, (Wadleigh: Fred
Carleton[9], George Alfred[8], Susanna[7], Benjamin[6],
Thomas[5], Benjamin[4], Robert[3], Robert[2], John[1];
Pillsbury: Fred Carleton[8], George Alfred[7],
John[6], Micajah[5], Caleb[4], Caleb[3], Moses[2],
William[1]), b. April 22, 1889 in Minneapolis,
Minn. m. in Pasadena, Cal. Stanton W. Forsman,
no additional data. (Ref. 50-30)
   1493 - Stanton W.   1495 - Harriot Pillsbury
   1494 - Anne Nichols   1496 - Fred Carleton

Issue of Fred B. Snyder and 1049- Susan M. (Pillsbury) Snyder:

1301- <u>John Pillsbury Snyder</u>, (Wadleigh: Susan M.[9], John Sargent[8], Susanna[7], Benjamin[6], Thomas[5], Benjamin[4], Robert[3], Robert[2], John[1]; Pillsbury: Susan M.[8], John Sargent[7], John[6], Micajah[5], Caleb[4], Caleb[3], Moses[2], William[1]), b. January 8, 1888. m. Nelle Stevenson, no additional data. (Ref. 50-27)
       1497 - John Pillsbury
       1498 - Thomas Stevenson
       1499 - Susan Pillsbury

Issue of Edward Cheney Gale and 1050- Sarah Belle (Pillsbury) Gale:

1302- <u>Richard Pillsbury Gale</u>, (Wadleigh: Sarah Belle[9], John Sargent[8], Susanna[7], Benjamin[6], Thomas[5], Benjamin[4], Robert[3], Robert[2], John[1]; Pillsbury: Sarah Belle[8], John Sargent[7], John[6], Micajah[5], Caleb[4], Caleb[3], Moses[2], William[1]), b. October 30, 1900. m. Isobel Rising, d. of Benjamin A. Rising of St. Paul, Minn., no additional data. (Ref. 50-27)
       1500 - Richard Pillsbury   1501 - Alfred

Issue of Lysander H. Carroll and 1056- Adeline (Loverin) Carroll:

1303- <u>Ella B. Carroll</u>, (Wadleigh: Adeline[9], Juliana[8], Daniel[7], Thomas[6], Thomas[5], Benjamin[4], Robert[3], Robert[2], John[1]), b. December 1856. m. Mr. Nason of Concord, N.H. no additional data. (Ref. 25-980)

1304- <u>Jennie B. Carroll</u>, (Wadleigh: Adeline[9], Juliana[8], Daniel[7], Thomas[6], Thomas[5], Benjamin[4], Robert[3], Robert[2], John[1]), b. June 1863. m. Mr. Davis of Contoocookville, no additional data. (Ref. 25-980)

Issue of 1057- Charles Loverin and Lois (Farmer) Loverin:

1305- Lois Loverin, (Wadleigh: Charles[9], Juliana[8], Daniel[7], Thomas[6], Thomas[5], Benjamin[4], Robert[3], Robert[2], John[1]), m. Mr. Tiffany, no additional data. (Ref. 25-980)

1306- Edward H. Loverin, (Wadleigh: Charles[9], Juliana[8], Daniel[7], Thomas[6], Thomas[5], Benjamin[4], Robert[3], Robert[2], John[1]), no data. (Ref. 25-980)

Issue of 1065- Prescott T.[9] Wadleigh and Kate (Jones) Wadleigh:

1307- Miriam[10] Wadleigh, (Prescott T.[9], Thomas[8], Thomas[7], Thomas[6], Thomas[5], Benjamin[4], Robert[3], Robert[2], John[1]), no additional data. (Ref. 25-981)

Issue of E. Herman Carroll and 1085- Susie (Putney) Carroll:

1308- Lee Carroll, (Wadleigh: Susie[9], Lucinda[8], Sarah[7], Susanna[6], Thomas[5], Benjamin[4], Robert[3], Robert[2], John[1]), no data. (Ref. 25-979)

Issue of Caleb Sanborn and 1103- Polly (Melcher) Sanborn:

1309- daughter Sanborn, (Wadleigh: Polly[9], Joseph[8], Samuel[7], Samuel[6], Elizabeth[5], Benjamin[4], Mary[3], Robert[2], John[1]; Melcher: Polly[6], Joseph[5], Samuel[4], Samuel[3], Samuel[2], (?)[1]), m. David C. Hawes of New Bedford, Mass., no additional data. (Ref. 30)

Issue of 1114- Levi Benson Tilton and Sarah Frances Tilton:

1310- Henry Tilton, (Wadleigh: Levi Benson[9], Nathan[8], Betsey[7], Joseph[6], Joseph[5], Joseph[4], Henry[3], Robert[2], John[1]), b. in East Kingston, N.H. m. Grace G. York of Kensington, N.H., d. of John W. and Marcia (Godfrey) York, (NOTE: John W. York is s. of Daniel G. and Betsy (Nudd) York of Kensington. John s. is Archie and grs. is John W. York who lived on the John Nudd Farm of Kensington.), no additional data. (Ref. 3, 21)

1311- Emma Tilton, (Wadleigh: Levi Benson[9], Nathan[8], Betsey[7], Joseph[6], Joseph[5], Joseph[4], Henry[3], Robert[2], John[1]), m. Mr. Hayes, no additional data. (Ref. 3)

Issue of 1115- Joseph A. Tilton and Mary Olive (Forsyth) Tilton:

1312- Ella Tilton, (Wadleigh: Joseph A.[9], Nathan[8], Betsey[7], Joseph[6], Joseph[5], Joseph[4], Henry[3], Robert[2], John[1]), b. in East Kingston, N.H. (Ref. 3)

1313- Forrest Tilton, (Wadleigh: Joseph A.[9], Nathan[8], Betsey[7], Joseph[6], Joseph[5], Joseph[4], Henry[3], Robert[2], John[1]), b. in East Kingston, N.H. (Ref. 3)

Issue of 1117- Frank Blake Tilton and 1139- Kate Melissa (Chase) Tilton:

1314- Philip Nathan Tilton, (Wadleigh: Frank Blake[9], Nathan[8], Betsey[7], Joseph[6], Joseph[5], Joseph[4], Henry[3], Robert[2], John[1]), b. May 9, 1895 in E. Kingston, N.H. (Ref. 3)

1315- Albert Chase Tilton, (Wadleigh: Frank
Blake^9, Nathan^8, Betsey^7, Joseph^6, Joseph^5,
Joseph^4, Henry^3, Robert^2, John^1), b. July 6,
1896 in E. Kingston, N.H. m. Hilda Meadow, no
additional data. (Ref. 3)

1316- Lewis Blake Tilton, (Wadleigh: Frank
Blake^9, Nathan^8, Betsey^7, Joseph^6, Joseph^5,
Joseph^4, Henry^3, Robert^2, John^1), b. March 1898
in E. Kingston, N.H. m. Margaret M. Corbett of
Boston, Mass., no additional data. (Ref. 3)
        1502 - Jean Louise

**Issue of 1118- Howard^9 Wadleigh and 1113-
Ruth Call^9 (Wadleigh) Wadleigh:**

1317- Harriett^{10} Wadleigh, (Howard^9, Mark^8,
Mark^7, Joseph^6, Joseph^5, Joseph^4, Henry^3,
Robert^2, John^1), b. Kensington, N.H. (Ref. 3)

1318- Walter L.^{10} Wadleigh, (Howard^9, Mark^8,
Mark^7, Joseph^6, Joseph^5, Joseph^4, Henry^3,
Robert^2, John^1), b. October 21, 1888 in
Kensington, N.H., d. December 18, 1888 in
Kensington. died in infancy. (Ref. 3)

**Issue of 1118- Howard^9 Wadleigh and Nellie
(Flood) Wadleigh:**

1319- son Wadleigh, (Howard^9, Mark^8, Mark^7,
Joseph^6, Joseph^5, Joseph^4, Henry^3, Robert^2,
John^1), b. September 14, 1891 in Kensington,
N.H. died young (Ref. 3)

1320- Mark W.^{10} Wadleigh, (Howard^9, Mark^8,
Mark^7, Joseph^6, Joseph^5, Joseph^4, Henry^3,
Robert^2, John^1), b. April 1895 in Kensington,
N.H., d. May 20, 1895 in Kensington. died in
infancy. (Ref. 3)

Issue of 1135- John Sewall[9] Wadleigh and Lottie May (Prescott) Wadleigh:

1321- Lottie Edna[10] Wadleigh, (John Sewall[9], Cyrus Dearborn[8], Sewall[7], Joseph[6], Joseph[5], Joseph[4], Henry[3], Robert[2], John[1]), b. December 11, 1893 in Amesbury, Mass. Res. Amesbury, Mass. (Ref. 3)

Issue of Willis J. Comings and 1136- Marianna Barker (Chase) Comings:

1322- Joseph T. Comings, (Wadleigh: Marianna Barker[9], Susan W.[8], Sewall[7], Joseph[6], Joseph[5], Joseph[4], Henry[3], Robert[2], John[1]), b. January 1, 1890 in Kensington, N.H., d. ca. 1950. m. Esther Sweeney of Kensington, no additional data. Served in WWI. First Cmdr. Amer. Legion Post. Occ. Tax Collector. Res. Exeter, N.H. (Ref. 3, 27)

1323- Bertha Comings, (Wadleigh: Marianna Barker[9], Susan W.[8], Sewall[7], Joseph[6], Joseph[5], Joseph[4], Henry[3], Robert[2], John[1]), b. in Kensington, N.H. Res. Exeter, N.H.   (Ref. 3)

Issue of John P. Taylor and 1137- Abbie Florence (Chase) Taylor:

1324- Walter E. Taylor, (Wadleigh: Abbie Florence[9], Susan W.[8], Sewall[7], Joseph[6], Joseph[5], Joseph[4], Henry[3], Robert[2], John[1]), b. April 23, 1883 in North Hampton, N.H., d. January 13, 1919 in North Hampton. (Ref. 3)

1325- Blanche Taylor, (Wadleigh: Abbie Florence[9], Susan W.[8], Sewall[7], Joseph[6], Joseph[5], Joseph[4], Henry[3], Robert[2], John[1]), b. in North Hampton, N.H. m. Paul Batchelder of Hampton Falls, N.H., no other data.   (Ref. 3)

1326- <u>Anna Taylor</u>, (Wadleigh: Abbie Florence[9], Susan W.[8], Sewall[7], Joseph[6], Joseph[5], Joseph[4], Henry[3], Robert[2], John[1]), b. September 1885 in North Hampton, N.H. m. Percy Jewell of Stratham, N.H., no additional data. (Ref. 3)

1327- <u>Frank Taylor</u>, (Wadleigh: Abbie Florence[9], Susan W.[8], Sewall[7], Joseph[6], Joseph[5], Joseph[4], Henry[3], Robert[2], John[1]), b. August 14, 1888 in North Hampton, N.H. (Ref. 3)

Issue of 1143- Arthur Garfield[9] Wadleigh and Flora A. (Ronzano) Wadleigh:

1328- <u>Frances Mason</u>[10] <u>Wadleigh</u>, (Arthur Garfield[9], Frank Lawrence[8], William Henry[7], William Henry[6], Joseph[5], Joseph[4], Henry[3], Robert[2], John[1]), b. January 22, 1919 in Exeter, N.H., d. June 26, 1938 in Kensington, N.H. (Ref. 2, 3)

1329- <u>William Henry</u>[10] <u>Wadleigh</u>, (Arthur Garfield[9], Frank Lawrence[8], William Henry[7], William Henry[6], Joseph[5], Joseph[4], Henry[3], Robert[2], John[1]), b. December 21, 1923 in Exeter, N.H. m. May 16, 1948 in South Hampton, N.H. Virginia Marie Hellen of Amesbury, Mass., d. of James Abe Hellen and Nettie May (McKinley) Hellen, b. July 14, 1928 in Amesbury, Mass. Res. Kensington, N.H.,   Occ. Machinist at G.E. Plant in Lynn, Mass. (Ref. 2, 3)
   1503 - Virginia Francis   1505 - Pamela Lynne
   1504 - Constance Jean

1330- <u>Robert Evans</u>[10] <u>Wadleigh</u>, (Arthur Garfield[9], Frank Lawrence[8], William Henry[7], William Henry[6], Joseph[5], Joseph[4], Henry[3], Robert[2], John[1]), b. June 12, 1926 in Exeter, N.H. m. November 16, 1947 Ellen Elizaabeth Eastman of Kensington, N.H., d. of Howard

Charles Eastman and Amy Janvin Eastman, b. May 31, 1928 in Seabrook, N.H. Occ. Salesman and tool manufacturing. Res. Kensington, N.H. (Ref. 2, 3)
    1506 - Howard Garfield   1508 - William Otis
    1507 - Robert Arthur

Issue of 1144- Ray Emery[9] Wadleigh and Alice (Kimball) Wadleigh:

1331- <u>Sarah L.</u>[10] Wadleigh, (Ray Emery[9], Frank Lawrence[8], William Henry[7], William Henry[6], Joseph[5], Joseph[4], Henry[3], Robert[2], John[1]), b. September 1920. (Ref. 2, 3)

1332- <u>Frank Leland</u>[10] Wadleigh, (Ray Emery[9], Frank Lawrence[8], William Henry[7], William Henry[6], Joseph[5], Joseph[4], Henry[3], Robert[2], John[1]), b. October 1924. (Ref. 2, 3)

Issue of William H. McDavitt and 1147- Mabelle Lane[9] (Wadleigh) McDavitt:

1333- <u>Helen M.</u> McDavitt, (Wadleigh: Mabelle Lane[9], Charles Fremont[8], William Henry[7], William Henry[6], Joseph[5], Joseph[4], Henry[3], Robert[2], John[1]), b. December 4, 1905 in Hampton Falls, N.H. m. June 17, 1929 Raymond H. Perry of Hampton Falls. no additional data. (Ref. 3)

Issue of Arthur W. Brown and 1148- Frances M.[9] (Wadleigh) Brown:

1334- <u>Charles W. Brown</u>, (Wadleigh: Frances M.[9], Charles Fremont[8], William Henry[7], William Henry[6], Joseph[5], Joseph[4], Henry[3], Robert[2], John[1]), b. July 16, 1909 in Hampton Falls, N.H. m. June 25, 1934 Sylina M. Kimball of Atkinson, N.H., no additional data. (Ref. 3)

1335- Lois W. Brown, (Wadleigh: Frances M.[9], Charles Fremont[8], William Henry[7], William Henry[6], Joseph[5], Joseph[4], Henry[3], Robert[2], John[1]), b. May 2, 1911 in Hampton Falls, N.H. (Ref. 3)

1336- Harold A. Brown, (Wadleigh: Frances M.[9], Charles Fremont[8], William Henry[7], William Henry[6], Joseph[5], Joseph[4], Henry[3], Robert[2], John[1]), b. July 21, 1913 in Hampton Falls, N.H. (Ref. 3)

1337- Elinor F. Brown, (Wadleigh: Frances M.[9], Charles Fremont[8], William Henry[7], William Henry[6], Joseph[5], Joseph[4], Henry[3], Robert[2], John[1]), b. December 12, 1915 in Hampton Falls, N.H. (Ref. 3)

1338- Ernest H. Brown, (Wadleigh: Frances M.[9], Charles Fremont[8], William Henry[7], William Henry[6], Joseph[5], Joseph[4], Henry[3], Robert[2], John[1]), b. January 13, 1918 in Hampton Falls, N.H. (Ref. 3)

1339- Winthrop M. Brown, (Wadleigh: Frances M.[9], Charles Fremont[8], William Henry[7], William Henry[6], Joseph[5], Joseph[4], Henry[3], Robert[2], John[1]), b. February 3, 1921 in Hampton Falls, N.H. (Ref. 3)

Issue of Frank C. Keegan and 1151- Helen[9] (Wadleigh) Keegan:

1340- Frank C. Keegan, (Wadleigh: Helen[9], Charles Fremont[8], William Henry[7], William Henry[6], Joseph[5], Joseph[4], Henry[3], Robert[2], John[1]), b. October 20, 1921 in Greenfield, Mass. (Ref. 3)

1341- <u>Howard W. Keegan</u>, (Wadleigh: Helen[9], Charles Fremont[8], William Henry[7], William Henry[6], Joseph[5], Joseph[4], Henry[3], Robert[2], John[1]), b. November 17, 1923 in Greenfield, Mass. (Ref. 3)

1342- <u>James Y. Keegan</u>, (Wadleigh: Helen[9], Charles Fremont[8], William Henry[7], William Henry[6], Joseph[5], Joseph[4], Henry[3], Robert[2], John[1]), b. November 17, 1923 in Greenfield, Mass. (Ref. 3)

Issue of 1152- Daniel Edward[9] Wadleigh and Ida[3] (Scott) Wadleigh:

1343- <u>Charles Harry[10] Wadleigh</u>, (Daniel Edward[9], Charles Edwin[8], Daniel Foster[7], William Henry[6], Joseph[5], Joseph[4], Henry[3], Robert[2], John[1]), b. November 11, 1903 in Clark Co. S.D., d. November 8, 1987 in Lennox, S.D. m. in Lennox June 8, 1938 Alma Christina[4] Plucker, (John Poppen[3], Menne Albert[2], Wessel[1]), d. of John Poppen and Christina (Witte) Plucker of Lennox, b. October 6, 1910 in Lennox. Res. Albuquerque, N.M., Volin, Alpena, Mt. Vernon and Lennox, S.D., and Jasper, Minn. Occ. h.s. teacher and missionary, w. nurse, teacher and missionary. (Ref. 1, 9, 32)
   1509 - Donald Elvin   1511 - Ruth Ann Eleanor
   1510 - Steven Erwin

1344- <u>Erwin Walter[10] Wadleigh</u>, (Daniel Edward[9], Charles Edwin[8], Daniel Foster[7], William Henry[6], Joseph[5], Joseph[4], Henry[3], Robert[2], John[1]), b. March 13, 1906 in Clark Co. S.D. did not marry. Res. El Centro, Cal. Occ. truck farmer. (Ref. 1, 9)

1345- <u>Elmer Edward[10] Wadleigh</u>, (Daniel Edward[9], Charles Edwin[8], Daniel Foster[7], William Henry[6],

Joseph[5], Joseph[4], Henry[3], Robert[2], John[1]), b.
April 27, 1909 in Clark Co. S.D. m. in Clark,
Clark Co. S.D. February 4, 1935 Mabel Seip, b.
January 19, 1912. Res. Mt. Vernon, S.D. Occ.
Farmer. (Ref. 1, 9)

  1512 - David Elmer   1515 - Jerry Keith
  1513 - Dale LeRoy   1516 - Eugene Edward
  1514 - Richard Lee

1346- Erline Myrtle[10] Wadleigh, (Daniel
Edward[9], Charles Edwin[8], Daniel Foster[7],
William Henry[6], Joseph[5], Joseph[4], Henry[3],
Robert[2], John[1]), b. April 22, 1910 in Clark Co.
S.D. m. June 22, 1933 Erwin Fredrick Schimmel,
b. October 8, 1904, d. July 12, 1971. Res.
Butler, Clark Co. S.D., Occ. Farmer. (Ref. 1,
9)

        1517 - Lester Edward

1347- Robert David[10] Wadleigh, (Daniel Edward[9],
Charles Edwin[8], Daniel Foster[7], William Henry[6],
Joseph[5], Joseph[4], Henry[3], Robert[2], John[1]), b.
June 26, 1912 in Clark Co. S.D., d. in Hot
Springs, S.D. m. July 3, 1941 Dorothy
Elizabeth Seip, b. April 22, 1920. Served in
WWII as Medical Corpsman on the Normandy
Beachhead. Res. Hot Springs, S.D. Occ.
Medical Practitioner with Veteran's Admin.
(Ref. 1, 9)

  1518 - Robert Daniel   1520 - Susan Kay
  1519 - Bruce Edward

1348- Fredrick Lee[10] Wadleigh, (Daniel Edward[9],
Charles Edwin[8], Daniel Foster[7], William Henry[6],
Joseph[5], Joseph[4], Henry[3], Robert[2], John[1]), b.
September 16, 1914 in Clark Co. S.D. m.
January 1, 1940 Mildred Ethel Newman of
Marshall, Minn., no additional data. Res. Long
Beach, Cal. Occ. Navy Officer, Corporate
executive and investment analyst. no children.
(Ref. 1, 9)

1349- <u>Ada Margaret</u>[10] Wadleigh, (Daniel Edward[9], Charles Edwin[8], Daniel Foster[7], William Henry[6], Joseph[5], Joseph[4], Henry[3], Robert[2], John[1]), b. October 18, 1916 in Clark Co. S.D. m. January 29, 1937 Otis Cogdill, b. March 4, 1909. Res. Brownsville, Neb. and Runningwater, S.D. Occ. River Boat Pilot. (Ref. 1, 9)

      1521 - Sally Ann   1524 - Anita Louise
      1522 - Peggy Lou   1525 - Gifford Lane
      1523 - Connie Kay

1350- <u>Alta Beatrice</u>[10] Wadleigh, (Daniel Edward[9], Charles Edwin[8], Daniel Foster[7], William Henry[6], Joseph[5], Joseph[4], Henry[3], Robert[2], John[1]), b. February 8, 1919 in Clark Co, S.D. m. November 28, 1941 Edson Taylor, b. November 28, 1917. Res. Independence, Mo. (Ref. 1, 9)

      1526 - Ronald Lee   1528 - Elizabeth Ann
      1527 - Larry Eugene

1351- <u>Ida Ilene</u>[10] Wadleigh, (Daniel Edward[9], Charles Edwin[8], Daniel Foster[7], William Henry[6], Joseph[5], Joseph[4], Henry[3], Robert[2], John[1]), b. April 26, 1926 in Clark Co., S.D. m. June 17, 1946 Edward Charles Gusso, b. March 3, 1918. Res. Watertown, S.D. Occ. h. Trucker, w. Dietitian. (Ref. 1)

      1529 - Roxe Lea   1531 - Rochelle Ilene
      1530 - Rodney Brock   1532 - Renea Pauline

Issue of 1153- Walter Emory[9] Wadleigh and Viola (Oxendine) Wadleigh:

no issue

Issue of William S. Bell and 1154- Nettie Florence[9] (Wadleigh) Bell:

1352- <u>Bernice Nelva Bell</u>, (Wadleigh: Nettie Florence[9], Charles Edwin[8], Daniel Foster[7], William Henry[6], Joseph[5], Joseph[4], Henry[3], Robert[2], John[1]), b. July 1, 1903. m. April 1922 Guy Pfetcher, s. of Wesley Edwin and Lula Adlaide Pfetcher, b. October 5, 1890. Res. Windsor, Henry Co., Mo.   (Ref. 1, 2)

1353- <u>Mary Lorene Bell</u>, (Wadleigh: Nettie Florence[9], Charles Edwin[8], Daniel Foster[7], William Henry[6], Joseph[5], Joseph[4], Henry[3], Robert[2], John[1]), b. July 24, 1905. m. February 17, 1934 George Dewey Paul, s. of Robert Ele and Matilda (Williams) Paul, b. April 29, 1905 in Sedalia, Pettis Co. Mo. (Ref. 1, 2)
    1533 - William Greg

1354- <u>Hazel Caroline Bell</u>, (Wadleigh: Nettie Florence[9], Charles Edwin[8], Daniel Foster[7], William Henry[6], Joseph[5], Joseph[4], Henry[3], Robert[2], John[1]), b. February 8, 1909. m. in Green Ridge Mo. December 25, 1929 George Thomas Johnson, s. of George Vest and Mary Leigh (Colbert) Johnson, b. July 19, 1910, div. August 1946. (Ref. 1)
    1534 - George Colbert   1536 - Sandra Sue
    1535 - Caroline Kay

1355- <u>Howard Charles Bell</u>, (Wadleigh: Nettie Florence[9], Charles Edwin[8], Daniel Foster[7], William Henry[6], Joseph[5], Joseph[4], Henry[3], Robert[2], John[1]), b. September 9, 1911, d. March 31, 1967, m. June 2, 1934 Hattie Pearl Lane, d. of George Lane, b. March 3, 1915. (Ref. 1)
    1537 - Stanley Ray   1538 - Daniel Robert

Issue of 1155- James Augustus[9] Wadleigh and Minnie W. (Wharton) Wadleigh:

1356- <u>Paul Edward</u>[10] Wadleigh, (James Augustus[9], Charles Edwin[8], Daniel Foster[7], William Henry[6], Joseph[5], Joseph[4], Henry[3], Robert[2], John[1]), b. May 16, 1914. m. 1st Edith Harlan, div. m. 2nd Rose E. Knaver, d. November 30, 1972 in Kansas City, Jackson Co. Mo. (Ref. 1) 1539 - 1540 by 1st w.
  1539 - Arvilla D.   1540 - Karen Jean

1357- <u>Omer Basil</u>[10] Wadleigh, (James Augustus[9], Charles Edwin[8], Daniel Foster[7], William Henry[6], Joseph[5], Joseph[4], Henry[3], Robert[2], John[1]), b. February 12, 1920. m. September 15, 1940 Iva Anna Hall, d. of Ralph Winfield and Iva Partheua (Thomas) Hall, b. January 26, 1920. (Ref. 1)
  1541 - Charles Edward   1543 - Twyla Ann
  1542 - Roger Basil

Issue of William[2] Lunstrum and 1156- Fannie Lorena (Wadleigh) Lunstrum:

1358- <u>Mervyn Wayne</u>[3] Lunstrum, (Wadleigh: Fannie Lorena[9], Charles Edwin[8], Daniel Foster[7], William Henry[6], Joseph[5], Joseph[4], Henry[3], Robert[2], John[1]; Lunstrum: William[2], Peter[1]), b. January 9, 1906 in Green Ridge, Pettis Co. Mo. m. in Payette, Payette Co. Ida. October 5, 1930 Margaret Ruth Shamberger, d. of William Shamberger and Maude Shamberger, b. September 27, 1901 in Silver King, Ida. Occ. official for Idaho Power Co. (Ref. 1)
  1544 - William Bruce   1546 - Ralph David
  1545 - Carolyn Beth   1547 - Margaret Paige

1359- <u>Fordyce Wilbur</u>[3] Lunstrum, (Wadleigh: Fannie Lorena[9], Charles Edwin[8], Daniel Foster[7], William Henry[6], Joseph[5], Joseph[4], Henry[3], Robert[2], John[1]; Lunstrum: William[2], Peter[1]),

b. October 18, 1908 in Green Ridge, Pettis Co.
Mo. m. in Mountain Home, Elmore Co. Ida.
October 4, 1936 Virginia Marie Stoner, b. June
15, 1912 in Nampa, Canyon Co. Ida. (Ref. 1)
        1548 - Susan Beth

1360- <u>Carl Kenneth</u>[3] Lunstrum, (Wadleigh:
Fannie Lorena[9], Charles Edwin[8], Daniel Foster[7],
William Henry[6], Joseph[5], Joseph[4], Henry[3],
Robert[2], John[1]; Lunstrum: William[2], Peter[1]),
b. March 5, 1912 in Boise, Ada Co. Ida. m. in
Chicago, Cook Co. Ill. December 31, 1943 Mary
Foster, d. of John Foster and Mary K. Foster,
b. March 16, 1923 in Chicago, Cook Co. Ill.
Ed. B.S. in Dairying and Bacteriology from
Univ. of Idaho/Moscow and M.S. from Iowa State
Univ. (Ref. 1)

1549 - Carl Kenneth	1556 - Mark Joseph
1550 - James Peter	1557 - Kristen Miriam
1551 - Melissa Ann	1558 - Theresa Frances
1552 - Thomas Michael	1559 - Janel Anne
1553 - William John	1560 - Joel Anthony
1554 - Mary Trivette	1561 - Erin Carla
1555 - Karen Elizabeth	

1361- <u>Inez Lorraine</u>[3] Lunstrum, (Wadleigh:
Fannie Lorena[9], Charles Edwin[8], Daniel Foster[7],
William Henry[6], Joseph[5], Joseph[4], Henry[3],
Robert[2], John[1]; Lunstrum: William[2], Peter[1]),
b. July 5, 1916 in Boise, Canyon Co. Ida. m.
in Boise, Ida. August 9, 1941 John Philip
McKibbin, s. of Samuel and Katherine McKibbin,
b. June 11, 1914 in Boise, Ida. (Ref. 1)

1562 - John Edward	1564 - Steven James
1563 - Philip David	1565 - Ann Elizabeth

1362- <u>Richard Maurice</u>[3] Lunstrum, (Wadleigh:
Fannie Lorena[9], Charles Edwin[8], Daniel Foster[7],
William Henry[6], Joseph[5], Joseph[4], Henry[3],
Robert[2], John[1]; Lunstrum: William[2], Peter[1]),
b. February 28, 1923 in Boise, Canyon Co. Ida.
m. in Seattle, King Co. Wash. May 3, 1946 Sally
Louise Greenrod, b. January 23, 1923 in

Diagonal, Ringgold Co. Ia.   Stationed on
Johnson Island when attacked by Japanese and
was stationed in England as AAF pilot in WW II.
(Ref. 1)
        1566 - Gregory Paul   1568 - Eric Richard
        1567 - Kirk William

**Issue of Charles Arvid Johnson and 1157-
Helen Mary (Wadleigh) Johnson:**

1363- <u>Lois Johnson</u>, (Wadleigh; Helen Mary[9],
Charles Edwin[8], Daniel Foster[7], William Henry[6],
Joseph[5], Joseph[4], Henry[3], Robert[2], John[1]), b.
July 1, 1911. m. September 21, 1935 Glen
Mahlon Rhodes, b. April 12, 1904. (Ref. 1, 2)
   1569 - Glenda Joyce   1571 - Anita Carol
   1570 - Arvid Elmer   1572 - Connie Fay

1364- <u>Carl Arvid Johnson</u>, (Wadleigh: Helen
Mary[9], Charles Edwin[8], Daniel Foster[7], William
Henry[6], Joseph[5], Joseph[4], Henry[3], Robert[2],
John[1]), no data. (Ref. 1, 2)

**Issue of 1158- Robert Leroy[9] Wadleigh and Amy
L. (White) Wadleigh:**

1365- <u>Harold W.</u>[10] Wadleigh, (Robert Leroy[9],
Charles Edwin[8], Daniel Foster[7], William Henry[6],
Joseph[5], Joseph[4], Henry[3], Robert[2], John[1]), b.
May 31, 1913, d. March 25, 1962. (Ref. 1)

1366- <u>Glen C.</u>[10] Wadleigh, (Robert Leroy[9],
Charles Edwin[8], Daniel Foster[7], William Henry[6],
Joseph[5], Joseph[4], Henry[3], Robert[2], John[1]), b.
November 22, 1917, d. November 22, 1922. died
in childhood. (Ref. 1, 2)

1367- <u>Ella Dorothy</u>[10] Wadleigh, (Robert Leroy[9],
Charles Edwin[8], Daniel Foster[7], William Henry[6],

Joseph[5], Joseph[4], Henry[3], Robert[2], John[1]), b.
October 26, 1924. m. November 18, 1942 Roy
Chester Wissman, s. of Jacob J. and Maude
Florence (Davis) Wissman, b. October 1, 1923.
(Ref. 1, 2)
    1573 - Richard Leroy   1575 - Sharon Anne
    1574 - James Joseph

**Issue of 1159- Clarence Levi[9] Wadleigh and
Nadyne Elizabeth (Smith) Wadleigh:**

1368- Hallie Jane[10] Wadleigh, (Clarence Levi[9],
Charles Edwin[8], Daniel Foster[7], William Henry[6],
Joseph[5], Joseph[4], Henry[3], Robert[2], John[1]), b.
August 17, 1927. m. October 17, 1959 Herman M.
Meisenheimer, s. of Peter M. and Katherine
(Friess) Meisenheimer, b. April 17, 1920 in
Pilot Grove, Cooper Co. Mo. (Ref. 1, 2)
    1576 - Calvin Levi   1577 - Bonnie Elizabeth

1369- Josephine[10] Wadleigh, (Clarence Levi[9],
Charles Edwin[8], Daniel Foster[7], William Henry[6],
Joseph[5], Joseph[4], Henry[3], Robert[2], John[1]), b.
July 2, 1929. m. December 10, 1950 Terry
Benson, b. March 27, 1926. (Ref. 1, 2)
    1578 - Deborah Jane   1579 - Paul David

**Issue of 1160- Leslie Earl[9] Wadleigh and
Sidney Brown (Leffler) Wadleigh:**

no issue

**Issue of 1160- Leslie Earl[9] Wadleigh and
Lillian Marie (Wear) (Swerngin) Wadleigh:**

no issue

Issue of Lon Baldwin and 1162- Estella Pearl Willis:

1370- <u>Bill Baldwin</u>, (Wadleigh: Estella Pearl[9], Helen Maria[8], Daniel Foster[7], William Henry[6], Joseph[5], Joseph[4], Henry[3], Robert[2], John[1]), no data. Res. Pittsburgh, Kan. (Ref. 2)

1371- <u>Clifford Baldwin</u>, (Wadleigh: Estella Pearl[9], Helen Maria[8], Daniel Foster[7], William Henry[6], Joseph[5], Joseph[4], Henry[3], Robert[2], John[1]), no data. Res. Ft. Scott, Kan. (Ref. 2)

Issue of 1167- Henry Harrison McCampbell and Cora Elvis (Wilkerson) McCampbell:

1372- <u>Bruce McCampbell</u>, (Wadleigh: Henry Harrison[9], Maaura[8], Daniel Foster[7], William Henry[6], Joseph[5], Joseph[4], Henry[3], Robert[2], John[1]), no data. (Ref. 2)

Issue of 1169- James Randolph McCampbell and 1194- Ethel Grace (Reed) McCampbell:

1373- <u>James H. McCampbell</u>, (Wadleigh: James Randolph[9], Maaura[8], Daniel Foster[7], William Henry[6], Joseph[5], Joseph[4], Henry[3], Robert[2], John[1]), no data. (Ref. 2)

1374- <u>Glenda McCampbell</u>, (Wadleigh: James Randolph[9], Maaura[8], Daniel Foster[7], William Henry[6], Joseph[5], Joseph[4], Henry[3], Robert[2], John[1]), no data. (Ref. 2)

Issue of 1170- Daniel Roy McCampbell and Phyllis Georgia (Pfaff) McCampbell:

1375- <u>Mary McCampbell</u>, (Wadleigh: Daniel Roy[9], Maaura[8], Daniel Foster[7], William Henry[6], Joseph[5], Joseph[4], Henry[3], Robert[2], John[1]), no data. (Ref. 2)

1376- <u>Maybelle McCampbell</u>, (Wadleigh: Daniel Roy[9], Maaura[8], Daniel Foster[7], William Henry[6], Joseph[5], Joseph[4], Henry[3], Robert[2], John[1]), no data. (Ref. 2)

1377- <u>Myrtle McCampbell</u>, (Wadleigh: Daniel Roy[9], Maaura[8], Daniel Foster[7], William Henry[6], Joseph[5], Joseph[4], Henry[3], Robert[2], John[1]), no data. (Ref. 2)

1378- <u>Dency McCampbell</u>, (Wadleigh: Daniel Roy[9], Maaura[8], Daniel Foster[7], William Henry[6], Joseph[5], Joseph[4], Henry[3], Robert[2], John[1]), no data. (Ref. 2)

1379- <u>Anna Hite McCampbell</u>, (Wadleigh: Daniel Roy[9], Maaura[8], Daniel Foster[7], William Henry[6], Joseph[5], Joseph[4], Henry[3], Robert[2], John[1]), no data. (Ref. 2)

1380- <u>Daniel McCampbell</u>, (Wadleigh: Daniel Roy[9], Maaura[8], Daniel Foster[7], William Henry[6], Joseph[5], Joseph[4], Henry[3], Robert[2], John[1]), no data. (Ref. 2)

Issue of Everett Ernest Brown and 1171- Dency Lucinda (McCampbell) Brown:

1381- <u>Lloyd Brown</u>, (Wadleigh: Dency Lucinda[9], Maaura[8], Daniel Foster[7], William Henry[6], Joseph[5], Joseph[4], Henry[3], Robert[2], John[1]), no data. (Ref. 2)

1382- <u>Earl</u> <u>Brown</u>, (Wadleigh: Dency Lucinda[9], Maaura[8], Daniel Foster[7], William Henry[6], Joseph[5], Joseph[4], Henry[3], Robert[2], John[1]), no data. (Ref. 2)

1383- <u>Eldon</u> <u>Brown</u>, (Wadleigh: Dency Lucinda[9], Maaura[8], Daniel Foster[7], William Henry[6], Joseph[5], Joseph[4], Henry[3], Robert[2], John[1]), no data. (Ref. 2)

1384- <u>Roy</u> <u>Brown</u>, (Wadleigh: Dency Lucinda[9], Maaura[8], Daniel Foster[7], William Henry[6], Joseph[5], Joseph[4], Henry[3], Robert[2], John[1]), no data. (Ref. 2)

1385- <u>Emory</u> <u>E.</u> <u>Brown</u>, (Wadleigh: Dency Lucinda[9], Maaura[8], Daniel Foster[7], William Henry[6], Joseph[5], Joseph[4], Henry[3], Robert[2], John[1]), no data. (Ref. 2)

1386- <u>James</u> <u>Newton</u> <u>Brown</u>, (Wadleigh: Dency Lucinda[9], Maaura[8], Daniel Foster[7], William Henry[6], Joseph[5], Joseph[4], Henry[3], Robert[2], John[1]), no data. (Ref. 2)

1387- <u>Kenneth</u> <u>Eugene</u> <u>Brown</u>, (Wadleigh: Dency Lucinda[9], Maaura[8], Daniel Foster[7], William Henry[6], Joseph[5], Joseph[4], Henry[3], Robert[2], John[1]), no data. (Ref. 2)

Issue of Robert Culbert Kyd and 1172- Bertha May (Wadleigh) Kyd:

1388- <u>Beatrice</u> <u>Pearl</u> <u>Kyd</u>, (Wadleigh: Bertha May[9], Everett[8], Daniel Foster[7], William Henry[6], Joseph[5], Joseph[4], Henry[3], Robert[2], John[1]), b. August 5, 1899 in Green Ridge Mo., d. January 21, 1900. died in infancy. (Ref. 2)

1389- <u>Walter Burns Kyd</u>, (Wadleigh: Bertha May^9, Everett^8, Daniel Foster^7, William Henry^6, Joseph^5, Joseph^4, Henry^3, Robert^2, John^1), b. December 28, 1900 in Grundy Center, Ia., d. March 31, 1985 in Des Moines, Ia., bur. Masonic Cemetery, Des Moines, m. in Des Moines September 1, 1923 Linnea Blanche Lind, b. November 4, 1899 in Des Moines, d. December 12, 1981 in Des Moines. (Ref 2)
    1580 - John Robert

1390- <u>Annabel Kyd</u>, (Wadleigh: Bertha May^9, Everett^8, Daniel Foster^7, William Henry^6, Joseph^5, Joseph^4, Henry^3, Robert^2, John^1), b. February 18, 1903 in Grundy Center, Ia. m. in Des Moines, Ia. June 3, 1924 Carroll Riley, s. of John Albert Riley of Cleveland, Ill. (b. November 20, 1874 in Cleveland,-d. January 8, 1953 in Des Moines) and Jeanette Jones Riley of Newton, Ia. (b. January 9, 1872 in Newton,- d. June 5, 1959 in Des Moines), b. July 11, 1897 in Colfax, Ia., d. November 17, 1977 in Veteran's Hospital, Des Moines. Occ. h. Rate clerk for Great Western RR, w. lunch room manager. (Ref. 2)
    1581 - Don Albert

1391- <u>Mary Louise Kyd</u>, (Wadleigh: Bertha May^9, Everett^8, Daniel Foster^7, William Henry^6, Joseph^5, Joseph^4, Henry^3, Robert^2, John^1), b. March 24, 1906 in Grundy Center, Ia. m. in Brooklyn, New York 1930 Harold E. Lang, d. June 30, 1971. Res. Suffern, New York. (Ref. 2)

1392- <u>Alma Emma Kyd</u>, (Wadleigh: Bertha May^9, Everett^8, Daniel Foster^7, William Henry^6, Joseph^5, Joseph^4, Henry^3, Robert^2, John^1), b. March 5, 1909 in Jackson Co. Minn. m. in Eldora, Ia. May 3, 1929 Clifford Minnie Hogan, s. of James Francis and Martha Julia (Myers) Hogan, b. March 25, 1900 in Iowa Falls, Ia., d. December 18, 1974 in Iowa Falls. bur. at Friends Cemetery, Iowa Falls. Occ.

Construction worker. (Ref. 2)

1582	- Ramona Elizabeth	1587	- Keith Allen
1583	- Robert Clifford	1588	- Alma Margaret
1584	- James Colbert	1589	- June Louise
1585	- Francis Walter	1590	- Donald Dean
1586	- Gerald Thomas	1591	- Robert Allen

Issue of George Washington Paige and 1174-Hattie Belle (Wadleigh) Paige:

1393- Audrey Belle Paige, (Wadleigh: Hattie Belle[9], Everett[8], Daniel Foster[7], William Henry[6], Joseph[5], Joseph[4], Henry[3], Robert[2], John[1]), b. October 24, 1906 in Green Ridge, Mo. m. December 14, 1927 in Green Ridge Albert Edward Upton, s. of Joseph and Louisa Jane (Stetzel) Upton, b. January 14, 1904 in New Mexico Terr., d. July 23, 1984 in Green Ridge, bur. at Green Ridge Cemetery. Occ. Poultry farmer and businessman. (Ref. 2)

1592	- Joseph Edward	1594	- Clyde Mervin
1593	- George LeRoy	1595	- Alice Louise

1394- Louis Leroy Paige, (Wadleigh: Hattie Belle[9], Everett[8], Daniel Foster[7], William Henry[6], Joseph[5], Joseph[4], Henry[3], Robert[2], John[1]), b. October 14, 1908 in Green Ridge Mo., d. March 17, 1978 in Dallas, Texas, bur. at Green Ridge Cemetery. m. June 11, 1934 in Sedalia, Mo. Mary Helen Staats, d. of Ross Barckalow and Opal Leona (Lounsbury) Staats, b. July 11, 1911 in Montrose, Colo. Occ. Carpenter. Res. Beaumont and Dallas Tex. (Ref. 2)

1596	- Marilee	1597	- Robert Leross

1395- Forest Martin Paige, (Wadleigh: Hattie Belle[9], Everett[8], Daniel Foster[7], William Henry[6], Joseph[5], Joseph[4], Henry[3], Robert[2], John[1]), b. January 2, 1912 in Sedalia, Mo., d. October 28, 1975 in Dallas, Tex., bur. Laurel Oak Cemetery, Windsor, Mo.   m. March 19, 1938

in Osceola, Ia. Ruth Loretta Howard, d. of
Clarence Fred and Isabelle (Jones) Howard, b.
December 23, 1914 in Windsor, d. September 26,
1966 in Dallas, bur. Laurel Oak Cemetery,
Windsor, Occ. Carpenter. Res. Beaumont and
Dallas, Tex. (Ref. 2)

      1598 - Mary Etta   1600 - Howard Lee
      1599 - Janet Sue   1601 - David Martin

1396- Gladys Lorene Paige, (Wadleigh: Hattie
Belle[9], Everett[8], Daniel Foster[7], William
Henry[6], Joseph[5], Joseph[4], Henry[3], Robert[2],
John[1]), b. April 22, 1913 in Sedalia, Mo. m.
August 24, 1933 in Green Ridge, Mo. Hoyt Seldon
Holley, s. of George Seldon and Lucy Mabel
(Gentry) Holley, b. June 22, 1908 in Avery,
Mo., d. February 14, 1979 in Warsaw, Mo., bur.
Shawnee Cemetery. Occ Farmer. Res. Warsaw,
Mo. (Ref. 2)

    1602 - Gerald Robert   1605 - Kenneth Carl
    1603 - Shirley Jean   1606 - Betty Ann
    1604 - Hoyt Allen   1607 - Ruby Belle

1397- Charles Earl Paige, (Wadleigh: Hattie
Belle[9], Everett[8], Daniel Foster[7], William
Henry[6], Joseph[5], Joseph[4], Henry[3], Robert[2],
John[1]), b. February 27, 1919 in Sedalia, Mo.
m. December 26, 1942 in Atlanta, Ga. Stella
Rosenmae Edmundson, d. of Robert Leonard and
Mariah Elizabeth (Stevens) Edmundson, b.
December 10, 1922 in Green Ridge, Mo. Occ. h.
Soil Conservationist w. Library Clerk. Res.
Lebanon, Mo. (Ref. 2)

    1608 - Charles Earl   1610 - Patricia Ann
    1609 - George Leonard

**Issue of 1175- Louis Henry[9] Wadleigh and Ona
Pearl (Upton) Wadleigh:**

1398- Elmer Wright[10] Wadleigh, (Louis Henry[9],
Everett[8], Daniel Foster[7], William Henry[6],
Joseph[5], Joseph[4], Henry[3], Robert[2], John[1]), b.

June 2, 1916 in Green Ridge, Mo. m. 1st
March 8, 1941 in Beaumont, Tex. Ida Mae
Robinson, d. of Robert Vebois and Alma Ethel
(Lloyd) Robinson, b. May 20, 1919 in Beaumont,
d. May 11, 1983 in Beaumont. m. 2nd August 5,
1984 in Beaumont Christine Ann (Prater) Nobles,
d. of E. M. and Ethel Prater, b. of Donald
Combs Prater, wid. of W. O. Nobles, b. July 30,
1923 in Atlanta Ga. Occ. h. Carpenter, 2nd w.
Real Estate Sales and Management. Res.
Beaumont, Tex. (Ref. 2)   1611 - 1613 by 1st
wife.
>   1611 - Carol Lee   1613 - Lucinda Rae
>   1612 - Myrna Kay

1399- Cleo Louise[10] Wadleigh, (Louis Henry[9],
Everett[8], Daniel Foster[7], William Henry[6],
Joseph[5], Joseph[4], Henry[3], Robert[2], John[1]), b.
November 14, 1917 in Green Ridge, Mo., d.
December 10, 1979 in Harlingen, Tex., bur.
Green Ridge Cemetery. m. March 9, 1937 in
Sedalia, Mo. Loy Harris Smith, s. of Ovid
Harris and Ruth Annie (Egbert) Smith, b.
November 7, 1913 in Johnson Co., Mo. Occ.
Farmer. Res. Green Ridge, Mo.   (Ref. 2)
>   1614 - Juan Loy   1615 - Errol Louis

1400- Mabel Lucille[10] Wadleigh, (Louis Henry[9],
Everett[8], Daniel Foster[7], William Henry[6],
Joseph[5], Joseph[4], Henry[3], Robert[2], John[1]), b.
April 1, 1922 in Brandon, Mo. m. October 26,
1941 in Green Ridge, Mo. Lee Ezra Templeton, s.
of Curby T. and Myrtle B. (Groshong) Templeton,
b. May 2, 1921 in Green Ridge. Occ. h.-w.
Templeton Realty Co. Res. Kansas City and
Raytown, Mo. (Ref. 2)
>   1616 - Sherry Sue   1618 - Oneta Jan
>   1617 - April Lyn   1619 - Lisa Michele

1401- Iva Lou[10] Wadleigh, (Louis Henry[9],
Everett[8], Daniel Foster[7], William Henry[6],
Joseph[5], Joseph[4], Henry[3], Robert[2], John[1]), b.

March 25, 1924 in Brandon, Mo. m. September
27, 1942 in Green Ridge, Mo. James Wesley
Bullard III, s. of James Wesley Bullard, Jr.
and Edna Pearl (Case) Bullard,   b. April 12,
1921 in Smithton, Mo. Occ. h. teacher
and Presbyterian Minister. Res. Kansas City,
Green Ridge, Warrensburg, Rolla, Pacific,
Holden, Springfield, and Urich, Mo. and in
Cal., N.M., La., So. Car. and Colo. (Ref. 2)
    1620 - James Wesley   1622 - Loring Louis
    1621 - Rebecca Cheryl   1623 - Deborah Carol

1402- Harvey Everett[10] Wadleigh, (Louis Henry[9],
Everett[8], Daniel Foster[7], William Henry[6],
Joseph[5], Joseph[4], Henry[3], Robert[2], John[1]), b.
January 17, 1930 in Windsor, Mo. m. June 19,
1955 in Green Ridge, Mo. Shirley Jean Williams,
d. of Harley M. and Imogene (Thompson)
Williams, b. January 10, 1935 in Sedalia, Mo.
Occ. h. teacher and school administrator w.
teaching assistant. Res. Warrensburg, Leeton,
Green Ridge, and Raytown, Mo.   Ed. B.S. in
Physical Education and M.S. in Education from
Univ. of Missouri/Warrensburg. (Ref. 2)
    1624 - Gregory Scott   1626 - Douglas Louis
    1625 - Lori Dawn

Issue of Oxel Leonard Johnson and 1176- Alma Edna (Wadleigh) Johnson:

1403- Lillian Frances Johnson, (Wadleigh: Alma
Edna[9], Everett[8], Daniel Foster[7], William
Henry[6], Joseph[5], Joseph[4], Henry[3], Robert[2],
John[1]), b. August 28, 1920 in Sedalia, Mo., d.
August 28, 1920 in Sedalia, Mo. died in
infancy. (Ref. 2)

Issue of John Ferdinand Goering and 1177- Jennie Opal (Wadleigh) Goering:

no issue

Issue of Neville Benton Licklider and 1178- Hazel Carrie (Wadleigh) Licklider:

1404- Norwood Licklider, (Wadleigh: Hazel Carrie[9], Everett[8], Daniel Foster[7], William Henry[6], Joseph[5], Joseph[4], Henry[3], Robert[2], John[1]), b. October 29, 1924 in Sedalia, Mo. m. November 25, 1948 in Kansas City, Mo. Charlotte Lynn Hastings, d. of Albert Ensign and Rosella Grace (Wade) Hastings, b. January 18, 1925 in Coffeyville, Kan. Served in Europe in WW II. Occ. Sales and Marketing for Missouri Pacific RR. Res. Joplin and Kansas City, Mo., Wichita, Kan., Denver, Colo., Seattle, Wash., and Medford, Ore. (Ref. 2)

    1627 - Alan Benton   1628 - Jane Carrie

Issue of Walter Burton Walkup and 1179- Florence Emma (Wadleigh) Walkup:

1405- Thelma May Walkup, (Wadleigh: Florence Emma[9], Everett[8], Daniel Foster[7], William Henry[6], Joseph[5], Joseph[4], Henry[3], Robert[2], John[1]), b. November 19, 1926 in Sedalia, Mo., d. January, 4, 1927 in Sedalia. died in infancy. (Ref. 2)

Issue of 1183- Fred Elmer[9] Wadleigh and Mabel Edith (Lenocker) Wadleigh:

1406- Irene[10] Wadleigh, (Fred Elmer[9], Henry Libby[8], Daniel Foster[7], William Henry[6], Joseph[5], Joseph[4], Henry[3], Robert[2], John[1]), b. December 7, 1911. m. May 3, 1934 John Martin, b. November 11, 1909. (Ref. 2)

    1629 - Leota Faye   1630 - Lois Irene

1407- Walter Raymond[10] Wadleigh, (Fred Elmer[9], Henry Libby[8], Daniel Foster[7], William Henry[6], Joseph[5], Joseph[4], Henry[3], Robert[2], John[1]), b. December 16, 1918, d. July 29, 1950. (Ref. 2)

1408- Edith Marie[10] Wadleigh, (Fred Elmer[9], Henry Libby[8], Daniel Foster[7], William Henry[6], Joseph[5], Joseph[4], Henry[3], Robert[2], John[1]), b. November 14, 1924. m. 1st May 19, 1951 Theodore French, b. May 22, 1927. m. 2nd September 5, 1964 Douglas Hill, b. November 21, 1951. (Ref. 2)

1409- Myrtle Evelyn[10] Wadleigh, (Fred Elmer[9], Henry Libby[8], Daniel Foster[7], William Henry[6], Joseph[5], Joseph[4], Henry[3], Robert[2], John[1]), b. October 4, 1928. m. April 26, 1951 Ralph Daehn, b. June 28, 1929. (Ref. 2)
      1631 - Debra Lynn 1632 - Charles William

Issue of 1184- Arthur Gilbert[9] Wadleigh and Elizabeth (Guis) Wadleigh:

1410- Arthur Milton[10] Wadleigh, (Arthur Gilbert[9], Henry Libby[8], Daniel Foster[7], William Henry[6], Joseph[5], Joseph[4], Henry[3], Robert[2], John[1]), b. July 5, 1917. (Ref. 1, 2)

1411- Kenneth Herbert[10] Wadleigh, (Arthur Gilbert[9], Henry Libby[8], Daniel Foster[7], William Henry[6], Joseph[5], Joseph[4], Henry[3], Robert[2], John[1]), b. June 9, 1919. m. Bea Peters, no additional data. (Ref. 1, 2)
      1633 - Deborah Susan 1634 - Patrice Marie

1412- Ronald Gale[10] Wadleigh, (Arthur Gilbert[9], Henry Libby[8], Daniel Foster[7], William Henry[6], Joseph[5], Joseph[4], Henry[3], Robert[2], John[1]), b. September 24, 1926. m. July 8, 1955 Phyllis Harriman, no additional data. (Ref. 1, 2)
      1635 - Janet Susan   1637 - Alan Arthur
      1636 - Ronald Gale   1638 - Lois Ann

Issue of 1185- Ralph Libby[9] Wadleigh and
Mamie Francis (Uhls) Wadleigh:

1413- <u>Woodrow Wilson</u>[10] <u>Wadleigh</u>, (Ralph Libby[9],
Henry Libby[8], Daniel Foster[7], William Henry[6],
Joseph[5], Joseph[4], Henry[3], Robert[2], John[1]), b.
March 7, 1913 in Cheraw, Otero Co. Colo., d.
December 8, 19__. m. February 17, 1939 Ruby
Irene Davis, no additional data. (Ref. 1, 2)
       1639 - Nelda Juline 1640 - John Curtis

1414- <u>Pearl Marie</u>[10] <u>Wadleigh</u>, (Ralph Libby[9],
Henry Libby[8], Daniel Foster[7], William Henry[6],
Joseph[5], Joseph[4], Henry[3], Robert[2], John[1]), b.
April 1914, d. June 1914. died in infancy.
(Ref. 1, 2)

1415- <u>Charles Elmer</u>[10] <u>Wadleigh</u>, (Ralph Libby[9],
Henry Libby[8], Daniel Foster[7], William Henry[6],
Joseph[5], Joseph[4], Henry[3], Robert[2], John[1]), b.
March 31, 1915. m. August 31, 19__ Clo Reed,
no additional data. (Ref. 1, 2)
       1641 - Frances Marie 1642 - Charles Vernon

1416- <u>Twyla Mae</u>[10] <u>Wadleigh</u>, (Ralph Libby[9],
Henry Libby[8], Daniel Foster[7], William Henry[6],
Joseph[5], Joseph[4], Henry[3], Robert[2], John[1]), b.
October 13, 1916. m. April 11, 1937 Jennings
Sayre, b. October 19, 1912, d. June 9, 1974.
(Ref. 1, 2)
          1643 - William Jennings   1645 - Marilyn
          1644 - Louanna

1417- <u>Helen Alice</u>[10] <u>Wadleigh</u>, (Ralph Libby[9],
Henry Libby[8], Daniel Foster[7], William Henry[6],
Joseph[5], Joseph[4], Henry[3], Robert[2], John[1]), b.
March 27, 1918. m. July 17, 1938 Marion
Barklow, b. June 28, 1910. (Ref. 1, 2)
          1646 - Virginia Sue 1647 - Kenneth Rowan

Issue of 1185- Ralph Libby[9] Wadleigh and Susan (Cobb) Wadleigh:

1418- <u>Ralph Norman</u>[10] Wadleigh, (Ralph Libby[9], Henry Libby[8], Daniel Foster[7], William Henry[6], Joseph[5], Joseph[4], Henry[3], Robert[2], John[1]), b. June 14, 1932. m. July 23, 1960 Susanne Schmidt, b. August 11, 1929. (Ref. 1, 2)
    1648 - Michael Norman   1649 - Leslie Herbert

1419- <u>Alma Darlene</u>[10] Wadleigh, (Ralph Libby[9], Henry Libby[8], Daniel Foster[7], William Henry[6], Joseph[5], Joseph[4], Henry[3], Robert[2], John[1]), b. September 22, 1933. m. August 3, 1952 Royce B. Clark, Jr., b. August 5, 1933. (Ref. 1, 2)
    1650 - Michael Royce   1652 - Larry Brian
    1651 - Steven Douglas 1653 - Diane Lynette

1420- <u>Leland Arthur</u>[10] Wadleigh, (Ralph Libby[9], Henry Libby[8], Daniel Foster[7], William Henry[6], Joseph[5], Joseph[4], Henry[3], Robert[2], John[1]), b. August 21, 1935. m. September 27, 1958 Dorothy Andronaco, b. June 20, 1936. (Ref. 1, 2)
    1654 - Laura Joanne   1655 - Linda

1421- <u>Lloyd Dale</u>[10] Wadleigh, (Ralph Libby[9], Henry Libby[8], Daniel Foster[7], William Henry[6], Joseph[5], Joseph[4], Henry[3], Robert[2], John[1]), b. January 10, 1938. m. September 1, 1969 Linda Hildebrandt, no additional data. (Ref. 1, 2)
    1656 - Rachel

1422- <u>Ronald Dean</u>[10] Wadleigh, (Ralph Libby[9], Henry Libby[8], Daniel Foster[7], William Henry[6], Joseph[5], Joseph[4], Henry[3], Robert[2], John[1]), b. June 29, 1942. m. July 19, 1972 Shirley Hill, b. July 3, 1933. (Ref. 1, 2)

Issue of 1185- Ralph Libby[9] Wadleigh and
Jemima Lucy (Walter) Wadleigh:

no issue

Issue of 1185- Joseph Everett[9] Wadleigh and
Irene (Irwin) Wadleigh:

1423- Esther Irene[10] Wadleigh, (Joseph
Everett[9], Henry Libby[8], Daniel Foster[7], William
Henry[6], Joseph[5], Joseph[4], Henry[3], Robert[2],
John[1]), b. April 15, 1918. m. January 30, 1942
Robert Lee Roy Ross, Jr., b. July 16, 1916.
(Ref. 1, 2)
    1657 - Irene Marie   1660 - Robert Lee Roy
    1658 - Kerry Lee   1661 - Richard Edward
    1659 - Roberta Lynne   1662 - Craig William

1424- Vere Louise[10] Wadleigh, (Joseph Everett[9],
Henry Libby[8], Daniel Foster[7], William Henry[6],
Joseph[5], Joseph[4], Henry[3], Robert[2], John[1]), b.
March 18, 1922. m. January 27, 1942 Emmett L.
Lane, b. March 27, 1917. (Ref. 1, 2)
    1663 - Allen Ross   1667 - Murray Wadleigh
    1664 - Caren Margaret   1668 - Holly Diane
    1665 - Christine Louise
    1666 - Forrest Emmett

1425- Roger Alan[10] Wadleigh, (Joseph Everett[9],
Henry Libby[8], Daniel Foster[7], William Henry[6],
Joseph[5], Joseph[4], Henry[3], Robert[2], John[1]), b.
June 8, 1929. m. April 11, 1953 Montine
Pruitt, b. November 19, 1929. (Ref. 1, 2)
    1669 - Alan Michael

1426- John Richard[10] Wadleigh, (Joseph
Everett[9], Henry Libby[8], Daniel Foster[7], William
Henry[6], Joseph[5], Joseph[4], Henry[3], Robert[2],
John[1]), b. April 10, 1934. m. June 6, 1958
Lyndall Brown, b. June 30, 1937. (Ref. 1, 2)
    1670 - Linda Louise   1672 - John Joseph
    1671 - Sharon Kaye   1673 - Kenneth Lee

Issue of 1187- Herbert Calvin[9] Wadleigh and Ellen (Wilson) Wadleigh:

1427- Eileen Marie[10] Wadleigh, (Herbert Calvin[9], Henry Libby[8], Daniel Foster[7], William Henry[6], Joseph[5], Joseph[4], Henry[3], Robert[2], John[1]), b. August 14, 1926. m. May 30, 1948 Charles Gimer, no additional data. (Ref. 1, 2)
    1674 - Peggy Eileen 1676 - Robert Charles
    1675 - Mary Ellen   1677 - Kathleen Louise

1428- Robert Wilson[10] Wadleigh, (Herbert Calvin[9], Henry Libby[8], Daniel Foster[7], William Henry[6], Joseph[5], Joseph[4], Henry[3], Robert[2], John[1]), b. April 28, 1929. m. June 29, 1957 Mary Ann Fletcher, b. September 13, 1932. (Ref. 1, 2)
    1678 - Patti Ann 1679 - Robert Mark

Issue of 1188- Harold Brewster[9] Wadleigh and Olive Joyce (Basinger) Wadleigh:

1429- Elva Aldina[10] Wadleigh, (Harold Brewster[9], Henry Libby[8], Daniel Foster[7], William Henry[6], Joseph[5], Joseph[4], Henry[3], Robert[2], John[1]), b. November 29, 1919. m. 1st May 17, 1940 Ernest Klein, b. October 18, 1917, div. m. 2nd November 10, 1976 Wilbur Lewis Springer, b. January 2, 1906. (Ref. 1, 2) 1680 - 1682 by 1st wife.
    1680 - Elva Myreen 1682 - Norvyn Bruce
    1681 - Ernestine Gay

1430- Joyce Ellen[10] Wadleigh, (Harold Brewster[9], Henry Libby[8], Daniel Foster[7], William Henry[6], Joseph[5], Joseph[4], Henry[3], Robert[2], John[1]), b. February 20, 1924. m. February 7, 1943 Kenneth Dayton, b. June 17, 1923. (Ref. 1, 2)
    1683 - Cheryle Ann 1685 - Katherine Jeanne
    1684 - Judith Lynne

1431- Dean Alvin[10] Wadleigh, (Harold Brewster[9],
Henry Libby[8], Daniel Foster[7], William Henry[6],
Joseph[5], Joseph[4], Henry[3], Robert[2], John[1]), b.
October 28, 1929, d. February 13, 1930. died
in infancy. (Ref. 1, 2)

1432- Calvin Herbert[10] Wadleigh, (Harold
Brewster[9], Henry Libby[8], Daniel Foster[7],
William Henry[6], Joseph[5], Joseph[4], Henry[3],
Robert[2], John[1]), b. March 27, 1933. m. May 10,
1958 Phyllis (LaRoe) LeKar, d. of Harold Erwin
and Dorothy May (Young) LaRoe, b. March 3,
1936. (Ref. 1, 2)
  1686 - Linda Diane   1688 - Janet Sue
  1687 - Steven Calvin 1689 - Michelle Roe Ann

1433- Oleda Kay[10] Wadleigh, (Harold Brewster[9],
Henry Libby[8], Daniel Foster[7], William Henry[6],
Joseph[5], Joseph[4], Henry[3], Robert[2], John[1]), b.
February 1, 1938. (Ref. 1, 2)

**Issue of 1189- Eugene Henry[9] Wadleigh and
Ruth Lorina (Talkelm) Wadleigh:**

1434- Donald Lee[10] Wadleigh, (Eugene Henry[9],
Henry Libby[8], Daniel Foster[7], William Henry[6],
Joseph[5], Joseph[4], Henry[3], Robert[2], John[1]), b.
December 22, 1923. m. May 19, 1956 Mary Jane
Trueba, b. February 20, 1929. (Ref. 1, 2)
      1690 - Michael John 1692 - Monica Jill
      1691 - Mark James

1435- Robert Henry[10] Wadleigh, (Eugene Henry[9],
Henry Libby[8], Daniel Foster[7], William Henry[6],
Joseph[5], Joseph[4], Henry[3], Robert[2], John[1]), b.
April 17, 1926. m. June 19, 1950 Ruth Hatton,
b. September 15, 1931. (Ref. 1, 2)
      1693 - Dale Eugene 1696 - Robert Allen
      1694 - Donna Lee   1697 - Nancy Ellen
      1695 - Barbara Sue

1436- <u>Glen Eugene</u>[10] Wadleigh, (Eugene Henry[9], Henry Libby[8], Daniel Foster[7], William Henry[6], Joseph[5], Joseph[4], Henry[3], Robert[2], John[1]), b. January 12, 1929. m. October 1, 1950 Frances McIntosh, b. March 28, 1931. (Ref. 1, 2)
        1698 - Karen Sue   1700 - Debra Frances
        1699 - Michele Allyn 1701 - Marianne

Issue of Reno Ray Nice and 1190- Edna Rose[9] (Wadleigh) Nice:

1437- <u>Mabel Leota Nice</u>, (Wadleigh: Edna Rose[9], Henry Libby[8], Daniel Foster[7], William Henry[6], Joseph[5], Joseph[4], Henry[3], Robert[2], John[1]), b. Maryc 22, 1916. m. March 25, 1934 Karl Enns, b. August 1, 1924 (maybe 1914). (Ref. 1, 2)
        1702 - Bernice Leota 1705 - Kenneth Eugene
        1703 - Vernon Royse 1706 - Karen Faye
        1704 - Ronald Karl   1707 - Carolyn Rose

1438- <u>Harry Alfred Nice</u>, (Wadleigh: Edna Rose[9], Henry Libby[8], Daniel Foster[7], William Henry[6], Joseph[5], Joseph[4], Henry[3], Robert[2], John[1]), b. April 12, 1918. m. December 9, 194_ Magdalena Edelman, b. July 5, 1921. (Ref. 1, 2)
        1708 - Stanley Ray   1712 - James Clifford
        1709 - Mary Joyce   1713 - Esther Rose
        1710 - Lester Wayne 1714 - Edward Eugene
        1711 - Eldon Lee

1439- <u>Ida Rose Nice</u>, (Wadleigh: Edna Rose[9], Henry Libby[8], Daniel Foster[7], William Henry[6], Joseph[5], Joseph[4], Henry[3], Robert[2], John[1]), b. January 13, 1920. m. July 18, 1937 Clayton Wolfer, b. January 11, 1915. (Ref. 1, 2)
        1715 - Doris LaVerne 1718 - Miriam Jean
        1716 - Dianne Joyce 1719 - Marvin Doyle
        1717 - Alta Rose

1440- <u>Howard Fred Nice</u>, (Wadleigh: Edna Rose[9], Henry Libby[8], Daniel Foster[7], William Henry[6],

Joseph[5], Joseph[4], Henry[3], Robert[2], John[1]), b.
September 9, 1922. m. March 1, 194_ Leulla
Wolfer, b. October 24, 1921. (Ref. 1, 2)
    1720 - Marlene Yvonne 1723 - Gary Duane
    1721 - Judith Ann   1724 - Dennis Leone
    1722 - Loren Howard   1725 - Douglas Dean

1441- Ruth Ellen Nice, (Wadleigh: Edna Rose[9],
Henry Libby[8], Daniel Foster[7], William Henry[6],
Joseph[5], Joseph[4], Henry[3], Robert[2], John[1]), b.
April 22, 1925. m. June 30, 1943 Robert
Coblentz, b. April 12, 1927. (Ref. 1, 2)
  1726 - Freddie LaVerne 1729 - Thomas Robert
  1727 - Daniel Keith   1730 - Gaylord Ralph
  1728 - Patricia Ellen   1731 - Debra Diane

1442- Dorothy Mae Nice, (Wadleigh: Edna Rose[9],
Henry Libby[8], Daniel Foster[7], William Henry[6],
Joseph[5], Joseph[4], Henry[3], Robert[2], John[1]), July
10, 1927. m. November 10, 194_ Lynn Wolfer, b.
January 9, 1926. (Ref. 1, 2)
    1732 - Lynn Eileen   1735 - Beverly Ann
    1733 - Kathryn Faye   1736 - Byron Duane
    1734 - Ronald Reno

1443- Gwendolyn Alta Nice, (Wadleigh: Edna
Rose[9], Henry Libby[8], Daniel Foster[7], William
Henry[6], Joseph[5], Joseph[4], Henry[3], Robert[2],
John[1]), b. January 11, 1932. m. January 19,
1949 Theron Edward Killian, b. January 30,
1927. (Ref. 1, 2)
    1737 - Barbara Sue   1739 - James Edward
    1738 - Reno Richard   1740 - Sandra Marie

1444- Robert Louis Nice, (Wadleigh: Edna Rose[9],
Henry Libby[8], Daniel Foster[7], William Henry[6],
Joseph[5], Joseph[4], Henry[3], Robert[2], John[1]), b.
October 30, 1934. m. December 19, 1953 Fern
Amy Roth, b. January 17, 1935. (Ref. 1, 2)
    1741 - Linda Luanna 1743 - Julia Rene
    1742 - Carmen Marie 1744 - Kendra Lynette

Issue of Orland Bazil Rector and 1191- Mary
Emma (Wadleigh) Rector:

1445- Leona Evalyn Rector, (Wadleigh: Mary
Emma[9], Henry Libby[8], Daniel Foster[7], William
Henry[6], Joseph[5], Joseph[4], Henry[3], Robert[2],
John[1]), b. June 13, 1923 at Galeton, Weld Co.,
Colo. m. November 25, 1945 at Medford, Jackson
Co., Ore. Harrison Gray Otis Meyer of New York
City, b. May 9, 1919 in Manhattan, New York,
N.Y. (Ref. 1, 2)
     1745 - Laurence Gray   1748 - Jeffrey Wayne
     1746 - Charles Edwin
     1747 - Elizabeth Annette

1446- John Orland Rector, (Wadleigh: Mary
Emma[9], Henry Libby[8], Daniel Foster[7], William
Henry[6], Joseph[5], Joseph[4], Henry[3], Robert[2],
John[1]), b. November 3, 1925 at Galeton, Weld
Co., Colo. m. January 2, 1948 Netta Rose
(Brown) Lowney, b. August 5, 1918 at Gifford,
Champaign Co., Ill. (Ref. 1, 2)

1447- Velma JoAnn Rector, (Wadleigh: Mary
Emma[9], Henry Libby[8], Daniel Foster[7], William
Henry[6], Joseph[5], Joseph[4], Henry[3], Robert[2],
John[1]), b. January 1, 1934 at Glendale,
Maricopa Co., Ariz., d. December 19, 1966 in
Portland, Ore. m. August 10, 195_ in Portland,
Washington Co., Ore. James Henry Heffler, Jr.,
b. May 155, 1931 in Portland, Washington Co.,
Ore. (Ref. 1, 2)
     1749 - Charlene Marie   1751 - Rachel Ann
     1750 - James Henry

1448- Mary Carol Rector, (Wadleigh: Mary Emma[9],
Henry Libby[8], Daniel Foster[7], William Henry[6],
Joseph[5], Joseph[4], Henry[3], Robert[2], John[1]), b.
December 29, 1936 at Cliff, Grant Co., N.M. m.
March 11, 1960 William Ray Arnold, b. March 12,
1930 in Medford, Ore. (Ref. 1, 2)
     1752 - Scott William

Issue of 1205- John Buren[9] Wadleigh and Jane Harriet (Buren):

1449- Frank Eugene[10] Wadleigh, (John Buren[9], John[8], John[7], Simon Dearborn[6], Benjamin[5], Joseph[4], Henry[3], Robert[2], John[1]), b. May 10, 1860 at Haverhill, N.H., d. March 29, 1881 at East Andover, N.H.   (Ref. 3)

1450- Sidney[10] Wadleigh, (John Buren[9], John[8], John[7], Simon Dearborn[6], Benjamin[5], Joseph[4], Henry[3], Robert[2], John[1]), b. April 15, 1862 in Andover, N.H. m. March 12, 1890 Hattie E. Henderson, no additional data. Res. Lakeport, N.H.   (Ref. 3)

1451- Fred Joseph[10] Wadleigh, (John Buren[9], John[8], John[7], Simon Dearborn[6], Benjamin[5], Joseph[4], Henry[3], Robert[2], John[1]), b. June 18, 1863 at Haverhill, N.H., d. September 1, 1863 at Haverhill. died in infancy. (Ref. 3)

Issue of 1205- John Buren[9] Wadleigh and Viola Lydia (Brown) Wadleigh:

1452- Robert Lee[10] Wadleigh, (John Buren[9], John[8], John[7], Simon Dearborn[6], Benjamin[5], Joseph[4], Henry[3], Robert[2], John[1]), b. October 23, 1865 at Andover, N.H. m. January 1, 1889 Anastasia Bretton, no additional data. Res. Lakeport, N.H.   (Ref. 3)

1453- Maurice Colman[10] Wadleigh, (John Buren[9], John[8], John[7], Simon Dearborn[6], Benjamin[5], Joseph[4], Henry[3], Robert[2], John[1]), b. March 1, 1868 at Andover, N.H. m. October 29, 1890 Belle M. Valie, no additional data. Res. Concord, N.H.   (Ref. 3)

1454- Jennie May[10] Wadleigh, (John Buren[9], John[8], John[7], Simon Dearborn[6], Benjamin[5], Joseph[4], Henry[3], Robert[2], John[1]), b. September 29, 1870 in Andover, N.H. m. December 21, 1891 Frank P. W. Dickenson, no additional data. Res. Franklin, N.H.   (Ref. 3)

1455- John[10] Wadleigh, (John Buren[9], John[8], John[7], Simon Dearborn[6], Benjamin[5], Joseph[4], Henry[3], Robert[2], John[1]), b. November 3, 1878 in Andover, N.H. m. December 25, 190_ Katherine Morrison of East Andover, N.H., no additional data. (Ref. 3)

Issue of Lewis C. Merrill and 1211- Fannie (Wadleigh) Merrill:

1456- Henry Wadleigh Merrill, (Wadleigh: Fannie[9], Levi[8], John[7], Simon Dearborn[6], Benjamin[5], Joseph[4], Henry[3], Robert[2], John[1]), no data. (Ref. 3)

Issue of 1212- Levi C.[9] Wadleigh and Gertude (Bridgeman) Wadleigh:

1457- Clinton Bridgeman[10] Wadleigh, (Levi C.[9], Levi[8], John[7], Simon Dearborn[6], Benjamin[5], Joseph[4], Henry[3], Robert[2], John[1]), no data. (Ref. 3)

1458- Everlyn Bridgeman[10] Wadleigh, (Levi C.[9], Levi[8], John[7], Simon Dearborn[6], Benjamin[5], Joseph[4], Henry[3], Robert[2], John[1]), no data. (Ref. 3)

Issue of John N. Dearborn and 1213- Harriet Louisa (Wadleigh) Dearborn:

1459- <u>Arthur Burton</u> <u>Dearborn</u>, (Wadleigh: Harriet Louisa^9, Hiram Gilmore^8, Newell^7, Simon Dearborn^6, Benjamin^5, Joseph^4, Henry^3, Robert^2, John^1), no data. (Ref. 3)

1460- <u>Ada Estelle</u> <u>Dearborn</u>, (Wadleigh: Harriet Louisa^9, Hiram Gilmore^8, Newell^7, Simon Dearborn^6, Benjamin^5, Joseph^4, Henry^3, Robert^2, John^1), m. Horace Winfield Smith, of Bridgeport, Conn., no additional data. (Ref. 3)

Issue of 1214- Charles Edwin^9 Wadleigh

1461- <u>Bertha Goodnow</u>^{10} <u>Wadleigh</u>, (Charles Edwin^9, Hiram Gilmore^8, Newell^7, Simon Dearborn^6, Benjamin^5, Joseph^4, Henry^3, Robert^2, John^1), b. in Boston, Mass. m. 1898 Fred Webber, Res. Astoria, Ore. (Ref. 3)

1462- <u>Charles A.</u>^{10} <u>Wadleigh</u>, (Charles Edwin^9, Hiram Gilmore^8, Newell^7, Simon Dearborn^6, Benjamin^5, Joseph^4, Henry^3, Robert^2, John^1), b. in Boston, Mass. no additional data. (Ref. 3)

Issue of 1217- Luther Jethro^9 Wadleigh and Abbie (Johnson) Wadleigh:

1463- <u>Horace David</u>^{10} <u>Wadleigh</u>, (Luther Jethro^9, James C.^{8}, James^7, James^6, James^5, Joseph^4, Henry^3, Robert^2, John^1), b. April 26, 1861 in Sanbornton, N.H., d. February 3, 1865 in Sanbornton. died in childhood. (Ref. 3)

1464- <u>James</u>^{10} <u>Wadleigh</u>, (Luther Jethro^9, James C.^{8}, James^7, James^6, James^5, Joseph^4, Henry^3, Robert^2, John^1), b. January 31, 1865 in

Sanbornton, N.H., d. February 20, 1865 in
Sanbornton. died in infancy. (Ref. 3)

1465- Walter Luther[10] Wadleigh, (Luther
Jethro[9], James C.[8], James[7], James[6], James[5],
Joseph[4], Henry[3], Robert[2], John[1]), b. April 25,
1866. no additional data. (Ref. 3)

1466- Fred James[10] Wadleigh, (Luther Jethro[9],
James C.[8], James[7], James[6], James[5], Joseph[4],
Henry[3], Robert[2], John[1]), b. September 13, 1869.
(Ref. 3)

1467- Arthur Albert[10] Wadleigh, (Luther
Jethro[9], James C.[8], James[7], James[6], James[5],
Joseph[4], Henry[3], Robert[2], John[1]), b. May 5,
1871 in Bristol, N.H., d. February 4, 1878 in
Bristol. died in childhood. (Ref. 3)

1468- John Burden[10] Wadleigh, (Luther Jethro[9],
James C.[8], James[7], James[6], James[5], Joseph[4],
Henry[3], Robert[2], John[1]), b. March 13, 1873 in
Bristol, N.H. (Ref. 3)

**Issue of 1254- Frank Weston[9] Wadleigh and
Winnie A. (Riford) Wadleigh:**

1469- Carroll Riford[10] Wadleigh, (Frank
Weston[9], John Hayes[8], Simon Hayes[7], Joseph[6],
James[5], Joseph[4], Henry[3], Robert[2], John[1]), b.
April 20, 1892 in Braintree, Vt. (Ref. 3)

Issue of 1260- Fred Linwood[8] Smith and Lillian (Toothaker) Smith:

1470- <u>Richard C.</u>[9] Smith, (Wadleigh: Fred
Linwood[10], Isaiah Waldron[9], Henry M.[8], Sally[7],
Richard[6], Mary[5], Elizabeth[4], Jonathan[3],
Joanna[2], John[1]; Smith: Fred Linwood[8], Isaiah
Waldron[7], Henry M.[6], Waldron[5], John W.[4],
Jonathan[3], Jonathan[2], Robert[1]), m. Fay E.
Jacques, no additional data. (Ref. 49)
    1753 - Danny D.

Issue of 1264- Victor Morse[10] Graves and Emily Louise (Holt) Graves:

1471- <u>Mary Louise Holt</u>[11] Graves, (Wadleigh:
Victor Morse[10], David Haslem[9], John[8], James[7],
Ruth[6], Dean[5], John[4], John[3], Robert[2], John[1];
Graves: Victor Morse[10], David Haslem[9], John[8],
James[7], David[6], James[5], Samuel[4], Abraham[3],
Mark[2], Samuel[1]), b. July 18, 1915. (Ref. 12)

Issue of 1271- Jonathan C.[10] Wadleigh and Alice J. (Whittemore) Wadleigh:

1472- <u>Doris W.</u>[11] Wadleigh, (Jonathan C.[10],
Jonathan C.[9], Charles T. P.[8], Ezekiel[7],
Ephraim[6], Moses[5], Ephraim[4], John[3], Robert[2],
John[1]), b. March 21, 1912 in Amesbury, Mass.
(Ref. 3)

Issue of 1275- Frank A.[10] Wadleigh and Emma (Sutherland) Wadleigh:

1473- <u>Elsa M.</u>[11] Wadleigh, (Frank A.[10], Cyrus
Pearson[9], Eben Pearson[8], Ezekiel[7], Ephraim[6],
Moses[5], Ephraim[4], John[3], Robert[2], John[1]), b.

July 29, 1911 in Amesbury, Mass. m. May 13,
1934 Lawrence Kerwin, no data. (Ref. 3)

1474- <u>Mildred</u> E.[11] <u>Wadleigh</u>, (Frank A.[10], Cyrus
Pearson[9], Eben Pearson[8], Ezekiel[7], Ephraim[6],
Moses[5], Ephraim[4], John[3], Robert[2], John[1]), b.
June 19, 1913 in Amesbury, Mass. m. November
21, 1931 George Price, no data. (Ref. 3)

**Issue of Hulbert R. Jennings and 1278-
Florence A. (Wadleigh) Jennings:**

1475- <u>Hulbert</u> <u>Randall</u> <u>Jennings</u>, (Wadleigh:
Florence A.[10], Cyrus Pearson[9], Eben Pearson[8],
Ezekiel[7], Ephraim[6], Moses[5], Ephraim[4], John[3],
Robert[2], John[1]), b. August 23, 1910 in
Amesbury, Mass. (Ref. 3)

1476- <u>Charles</u> L. <u>Jennings</u>, (Wadleigh: Florence
A.[10], Cyrus Pearson[9], Eben Pearson[8], Ezekiel[7],
Ephraim[6], Moses[5], Ephraim[4], John[3], Robert[2],
John[1]), b. June 8, 1913 in South Hampton, N.H.,
d. June 10, 1913 in South Hampton. died in
infancy. (Ref. 3)

**Issue of William Quimby and 1282- Laura Jane
(Wadleigh) Quimby:**

1477- <u>Raymond</u> <u>Quimby</u>, (Wadleigh: Laura Jane[10],
Charles William[9], Eben Pearson[8], Ezekiel[7],
Ephriam[6], Moses[5], Ephriam[4], John[3], Robert[2],
John[1]), b. ca. 1911 in Amesbury, Mass. (Ref. 3)

**Issue of Mr. Connor and 1282- Laura Jane
(Wadleigh) (Quimby) Connor:**

1478- <u>(daughter)</u> <u>Connor</u>, (Wadleigh: Laura
Jane[10], Charles William[9], Eben Pearson[8],

Ezekiel[7], Ephriam[6], Moses[5], Ephriam[4], John[3], Robert[2], John[1]), b. ca. 1918. Res. Portland, Me. (Ref. 3)

Issue of 1293- Charles Stinson[9] Pillsbury and Helen Pendleton (Winston) Pillsbury:

1479- <u>Philip Winston[10]</u> Pillsbury, (Wadleigh: Charles Stinson[10], Charles Alfred[9], George Alfred[8], Susanna[7], Benjamin[6], Thomas[5], Benjamin[4], Robert[3], Robert[2], John[1]; Pillsbury: Charles Stinson[9], Charles Alfred[8], George Alfred[7], John[6], Micajah[5], Caleb[4], Caleb[3], Moses[2], William[1]), b. April 10, 1903 in Minneapolis, Minn. m. in Minneapolis July 5, 1934 Eleanor Bellows, d. of Henry Adams and Mary (Sanger) Bellows, b. January 16, 1913 in Minneapolis. Ed. h. Yale 1924, w. Smith College. director Pillsbury Flour Mills. (Ref. 50-33)
    1754 - Philip Winston   1755 - Henry Adams

1480- <u>Mary Stinson[10]</u> Pillsbury, (Wadleigh: Charles Stinson[10], Charles Alfred[9], George Alfred[8], Susanna[7], Benjamin[6], Thomas[5], Benjamin[4], Robert[3], Robert[2], John[1]; Pillsbury: Charles Stinson[9], Charles Alfred[8], George Alfred[7], John[6], Micajah[5], Caleb[4], Caleb[3], Moses[2], William[1]), b. November 14, 1904 in Minneapolis, Minn. m. in Minneapolis December 7, 1929 Oswald Bates Lord, s. of Charles Edwin and Lucie Taylor (Weart) Lord, b. March 15, 1903 in Tarrytown, N.Y. Ed. h. Yale 1926, w. Smith College 1927. Res. New York, N.Y. (Ref. 50-31)
    1756 - Charles Pillsbury   1758 - Richard
    1757 - Winston

1481- <u>Katharine Stevens[10]</u> Pillsbury, (Wadleigh: Charles Stinson[9], Charles Alfred[9], George Alfred[8], Susanna[7], Benjamin[6], Thomas[5], Benjamin[4], Robert[3], Robert[2], John[1]; Pillsbury:

Charles Stinson[9], Charles Alfred[8], George Alfred[7], John[6], Micajah[5], Caleb[4], Caleb[3], Moses[2], William[1]), b. December 11, 1905 in Minneapolis, Minn. m. in Paris, France Elliott Bates McKee, s. of McKee Dunn and Henrietta (Bates) McKee, b. November 26, 1904 in Washington, D.C. Ed. h. Yale 1926, w. Smith College 1927. Occ. Banker. Res. Mt. Kisco, N.Y. (Ref. 50-31)
    1759 - Philip Winston   1760 - Elliott Bates

1482- Helen Winston[10] Pillsbury, (Wadleigh: Charles Stinson[10], Charles Alfred[9], George Alfred[8], Susanna[7], Benjamin[6], Thomas[5], Benjamin[4], Robert[3], Robert[2], John[1]; Pillsbury: Charles Stinson[9], Charles Alfred[8], George Alfred[7], John[6], Micajah[5], Caleb[4], Caleb[3], Moses[2], William[1]), b. November 18, 1907 in Minneapolis, Minn. m. in Minneapolis John Austin Becker, Jr., s. of John Austin and Minne Belle (Skinner) Becker, b. January 2, 1906 in Albany, N.Y. Ed. h. Princeton Univ., w. Smith College 1928. Occ. Banker. Res. Castleton-on-Hudson, N.Y. (Ref. 50-31)
    1761 - Katharine Winston   1762 - Elizabeth

Issue of 1483- John Sargent[9] Pillsbury and Eleanor Jerusha (Lawler) Pillsbury:

1483- John Sargent[10] Pillsbury, Jr., (Wadleigh: John Sargent[10], Charles Alfred[9], George Alfred[8], Susanna[7], Benjamin[6], Thomas[5], Benjamin[4], Robert[3], Robert[2], John[1]; Pillsbury: John Sargent[9], Charles Alfred[8], George Alfred[7], John[6], Micajah[5], Caleb[4], Caleb[3], Moses[2], William[1]), b. October 28, 1912 in Minneapolis, Minn. m. in New York, N.Y. Katharine Harrison Clark, d. of Donaldson and Katharine (Harrison) Clark of Guilford, Conn. and New York, N.Y., b. May 23, 1916 in New Haven, Conn. Ed. Yale 1935 and Univ. of Minnesota Law School. (Ref. 50-32)

1484- <u>Edmund Pennington</u>[10] Pillsbury, (Wadleigh:
John Sargent[10], Charles Alfred[9], George
Alfred[8], Susanna[7], Benjamin[6], Thomas[5],
Benjamin[4], Robert[3], Robert[2], John[1]; Pillsbury:
John Sargent[9], Charles Alfred[8], George Alfred[7],
John[6], Micajah[5], Caleb[4], Caleb[3], Moses[2],
William[1]), b. December 22, 1913 in Minneapolis,
Minn. Ed. Yale 1936. (Ref. 50-33)

1485- <u>Ella Sturgis</u>[10] Pillsbury, (Wadleigh:
John Sargent[10], Charles Alfred[9], George
Alfred[8], Susanna[7], Benjamin[6], Thomas[5],
Benjamin[4], Robert[3], Robert[2], John[1]; Pillsbury:
John Sargent[9], Charles Alfred[8], George Alfred[7],
John[6], Micajah[5], Caleb[4], Caleb[3], Moses[2],
William[1]), b. October 11, 1915 in Minneapolis,
Minn. m. in Minneapolis Thomas Manville
Crosby, s. of Franklin Mussey and Harriet
(McKnight) Crosby of Minneapolis and Wayzata,
Minn. no additional data. Ed. w. Vassar
College. (Ref. 50-33)

1486- <u>Charles Alfred</u>[10] Pillsbury, (Wadleigh:
John Sargent[10], Charles Alfred[9], George
Alfred[8], Susanna[7], Benjamin[6], Thomas[5],
Benjamin[4], Robert[3], Robert[2], John[1]; Pillsbury:
John Sargent[9], Charles Alfred[8], George Alfred[7],
John[6], Micajah[5], Caleb[4], Caleb[3], Moses[2],
William[1]), b. April 4, 1917 in Minneapolis,
Minn. Ed. Yale. (Ref. 50-33)

1487- <u>Jane Lawler</u>[10] Pillsbury, (Wadleigh: John
Sargent[10], Charles Alfred[9], George Alfred[8],
Susanna[7], Benjamin[6], Thomas[5], Benjamin[4],
Robert[3], Robert[2], John[1]; Pillsbury: John
Sargent[9], Charles Alfred[8], George Alfred[7],
John[6], Micajah[5], Caleb[4], Caleb[3], Moses[2],
William[1]), b. February 13, 1920 in Minneapolis,
Minn. (Ref. 50-33)

1488- <u>George Sturgis</u>[10] Pillsbury, (Wadleigh:
John Sargent[10], Charles Alfred[9], George

Alfred[8], Susanna[7], Benjamin[6], Thomas[5], Benjamin[4], Robert[3], Robert[2], John[1]; Pillsbury: John Sargent[9], Charles Alfred[8], George Alfred[7], John[6], Micajah[5], Caleb[4], Caleb[3], Moses[2], William[1]), b. July 17, 1921 in Minneapolis, Minn. (Ref. 50-33)

Issue of Harold Osgood Ayer and 1296- Harriot Topliff (Pillsbury) Ayer:

1489- <u>Alice</u> <u>Pillsbury</u> <u>Ayer</u>, (Wadleigh: Harriot Topliff[10], Fred Carleton[9], George Alfred[8], Susanna[7], Benjamin[6], Thomas[5], Benjamin[4], Robert[3], Robert[2], John[1]; Pillsbury: Harriot Topliff[9], Fred Carleton[8], George Alfred[7], John[6], Micajah[5], Caleb[4], Caleb[3], Moses[2], William[1]), b. August 8, 1903 in Savannah, Ga. (twin). m. in Pasadena, Cal. Charles Edward Veltman of Amsterdam, Holland. Res. Amsterdam, Holland. (Ref. 50-30)
   1763 - Harold Charles 1764 - Harriot Pillsbury

1490- <u>Ann</u> <u>Dana</u> <u>Ayer</u>, (Wadleigh: Harriot Topliff[10], Fred Carleton[9], George Alfred[8], Susanna[7], Benjamin[6], Thomas[5], Benjamin[4], Robert[3], Robert[2], John[1]; Pillsbury: Harriot Topliff[9], Fred Carleton[8], George Alfred[7], John[6], Micajah[5], Caleb[4], Caleb[3], Moses[2], William[1]), b. August 8, 1903 in Savannah, Ga. (twin). m. 1st in Pasadena, Cal. William Rathbun Hees, Jr., m. 2nd Arthur Weston Hickson Brown, no additional data. (Ref. 50-30) 1765 - by 1st h.
      1765 - William Rathbun

Issue of Robert Daniels Bardwell, Jr. and 1299- Helen Margaret (Pillsbury) Bardwell:

1491- <u>Beatrice</u> <u>Pillsbury</u> <u>Bardwell</u>, (Wadleigh: Helen Margaret[10], Fred Carleton[9], George Alfred[8], Susanna[7], Benjamin[6], Thomas[5],

Benjamin[4], Robert[3], Robert[2], John[1]; Pillsbury:
Helen Margaret[9], Fred Carleton[8], George
Alfred[7], John[6], Micajah[5], Caleb[4], Caleb[3],
Moses[2], William[1]), b. January 17, 1909 in
Minneapolis, Minn. m. in Pittsfield, Mass.
June 8, 1935 Ernst Karl von Mertens, no
additional data. (Ref. 50-30)

1492- <u>Robert Daniels Bardwell, III</u>, (Wadleigh:
Helen Margaret[10], Fred Carleton[9], George
Alfred[8], Susanna[7], Benjamin[6], Thomas[5],
Benjamin[4], Robert[3], Robert[2], John[1]; Pillsbury:
Helen Margaret[9], Fred Carleton[8], George
Alfred[7], John[6], Micajah[5], Caleb[4], Caleb[3],
Moses[2], William[1]), b. November 28, 1920. (Ref.
50-30)

**Issue of Stanton W. Forsman and 1300- Alice
(Pillsbury) Forsman:**

1493- <u>Stanton W. Forsman, Jr.</u>, (Wadleigh: Fred
Carleton[9], George Alfred[8], Susanna[7], Benjamin[6],
Thomas[5], Benjamin[4], Robert[3], Robert[2], John[1];
Pillsbury: Fred Carleton[8], George Alfred[7],
John[6], Micajah[5], Caleb[4], Caleb[3], Moses[2],
William[1]), b. December 13, 1914 in Pasadena,
Cal. (Ref. 50-30)

1494- <u>Anne Nichols Forsman</u>, (Wadleigh: Fred
Carleton[9], George Alfred[8], Susanna[7], Benjamin[6],
Thomas[5], Benjamin[4], Robert[3], Robert[2], John[1];
Pillsbury: Fred Carleton[8], George Alfred[7],
John[6], Micajah[5], Caleb[4], Caleb[3], Moses[2],
William[1]), b. June 23, 1916 in Pasadena, Cal.
(Ref. 50-30)

1495- <u>Harriot Pillsbury Forsman</u>, (Wadleigh:
Fred Carleton[9], George Alfred[8], Susanna[7],
Benjamin[6], Thomas[5], Benjamin[4], Robert[3],
Robert[2], John[1]; Pillsbury: Fred Carleton[8],
George Alfred[7], John[6], Micajah[5], Caleb[4],

Caleb[3], Moses[2], William[1]), b. December 31, 1917 in Pasadena, Cal. (Ref. 50-30)

1496- <u>Fred Carleton Forsman</u>, (Wadleigh: Fred Carleton[9], George Alfred[8], Susanna[7], Benjamin[6], Thomas[5], Benjamin[4], Robert[3], Robert[2], John[1]; Pillsbury: Fred Carleton[8], George Alfred[7], John[6], Micajah[5], Caleb[4], Caleb[3], Moses[2], William[1]), b. November 14, 1922 in Pasadena, Cal. (Ref. 50-30)

Issue of 1301- John Pillsbury Snyder and Nelle (Stevenson) Pillsbury:

1497- <u>John Pillsbury Snyder</u>, (Wadleigh: John Pillsbury[10], Susan M.[9], John Sargent[8], Susanna[7], Benjamin[6], Thomas[5], Benjamin[4], Robert[3], Robert[2], John[1]; Pillsbury: John Pillsbury[9], Susan M.[8], John Sargent[7], John[6], Micajah[5], Caleb[4], Caleb[3], Moses[2], William[1]), b. July 10, 1913. m. June 23, 1936 Anne Morrison, no additional data. (Ref. 50-27)

1498- <u>Thomas Stevenson Snyder</u>, (Wadleigh: John Pillsbury[10], Susan M.[9], John Sargent[8], Susanna[7], Benjamin[6], Thomas[5], Benjamin[4], Robert[3], Robert[2], John[1]; Pillsbury: John Pillsbury[9], Susan M.[8], John Sargent[7], John[6], Micajah[5], Caleb[4], Caleb[3], Moses[2], William[1]), b. March 12, 1915. (Ref. 50-30)

1499- <u>Susan Pillsbury Snyder</u>, (Wadleigh: John Pillsbury[10], Susan M.[9], John Sargent[8], Susanna[7], Benjamin[6], Thomas[5], Benjamin[4], Robert[3], Robert[2], John[1]; Pillsbury: John Pillsbury[9], Susan M.[8], John Sargent[7], John[6], Micajah[5], Caleb[4], Caleb[3], Moses[2], William[1]), b. February 25, 1918. (Ref. 50-30)

Issue of 1302- Richard Pillsbury Gale and Isobel (Rising) Gale:

1500- <u>Richard Pillsbury Gale</u>, (Wadleigh: Richard Pillsbury[10], Sarah Belle[9], John Sargent[8], Susanna[7], Benjamin[6], Thomas[5], Benjamin[4], Robert[3], Robert[2], John[1]; Pillsbury: Richard Pillsbury[9], Sarah Belle[8], John Sargent[7], John[6], Micajah[5], Caleb[4], Caleb[3], Moses[2], William[1]), b. November 26, 1924. (Ref. 50-27)

1501- <u>Alfred Gale</u>, (Wadleigh: Richard Pillsbury[10], Sarah Belle[9], John Sargent[8], Susanna[7], Benjamin[6], Thomas[5], Benjamin[4], Robert[3], Robert[2], John[1]; Pillsbury: Richard Pillsbury[9], Sarah Belle[8], John Sargent[7], John[6], Micajah[5], Caleb[4], Caleb[3], Moses[2], William[1]), b. February 14, 1927. (Ref. 50-30)

Issue of 1316- Lewis Blake Tilton and Margaret M. (Corbett) Tilton:

1502- <u>Jean Louise Tilton</u>, (Wadleigh: Lewis Blake[10], Frank Blake[9], Nathan[8], Betsey[7], Joseph[6], Joseph[5], Joseph[4], Henry[3], Robert[2], John[1]), b. November 9, 1928 in East Kingston, N.H. (Ref. 3)

Issue of 1329- William Henry[10] Wadleigh and Virginia Marie (Hellen) Wadleigh:

1503- <u>Virginia Francis[11] Wadleigh</u>, (William Henry[10], Arthur Garfield[9], Frank Lawrence[8], William Henry[7], William Henry[6], Joseph[5], Joseph[4], Henry[3], Robert[2], John[1]), b. February 27, 1949 in Exeter, N.H. m. August 15, 1970 Steven Robert Tessier of Stratham, N.H. no additional data. Res. Yukon, Okla. (Ref. 2)

1504- <u>Constance Jean</u>[11] <u>Wadleigh</u>, (William Henry[10], Arthur Garfield[9], Frank Lawrence[8], William Henry[7], William Henry[6], Joseph[5], Joseph[4], Henry[3], Robert[2], John[1]), b. July 14, 1952 in Exeter, N.H. m. September 15, 1973 in Kensington, N.H. Frederick William Durham of Webster, N.Y., no additional data. Res. Newton, Me., Occ. Art, Farmer. (Ref. 2)

   1766 - Alison April   1768 - Michael Wadleigh
   1767 - Naomi Elizabeth

1505- <u>Pamela Lynne</u>[11] <u>Wadleigh</u>, (William Henry[10], Arthur Garfield[9], Frank Lawrence[8], William Henry[7], William Henry[6], Joseph[5], Joseph[4], Henry[3], Robert[2], John[1]), b. June 6, 1955 in Exeter, N.H., d. March 19, 1982 at Dana Farber Cancer Institute, Boston, Mass. died of cancer (Ref. 2)

Issue of 1330- Robert Evans[10] Wadleigh and Ellen Elizabeth (Eastman) Wadleigh:

1506- <u>Howard Garfield</u>[11] <u>Wadleigh</u>, (Robert Evans[10], Arthur Garfield[9], Frank Lawrence[8], William Henry[7], William Henry[6], Joseph[5], Joseph[4], Henry[3], Robert[2], John[1]), b. February, 7, 1953 in Amesbury, Mass. (Ref. 2)

1507- <u>Robert Arthur</u>[11] <u>Wadleigh</u>, (Robert Evans[10], Arthur Garfield[9], Frank Lawrence[8], William Henry[7], William Henry[6], Joseph[5], Joseph[4], Henry[3], Robert[2], John[1]), b. June 7, 1955 in Amesbury, Mass. (Ref. 2)

1508- <u>William Otis</u>[11] <u>Wadleigh</u>, (Robert Evans[10], Arthur Garfield[9], Frank Lawrence[8], William Henry[7], William Henry[6], Joseph[5], Joseph[4], Henry[3], Robert[2], John[1]), b. November 14, 1959 in Amesbury, Mass. (Ref. 2)

Issue of 1343- Charles Harry[10] Wadleigh and Alma Christina (Plucker) Wadleigh:

1509- Donald Elvin[11] Wadleigh, (Charles Harry[10], Daniel Edward[9], Charles Edwin[8], Daniel Foster[7], William Henry[6], Joseph[5], Joseph[4], Henry[3], Robert[2], John[1]), b. March 5, 1945 in Albuquerque, N.M. m. June 29, 1970 in Lennox, S.D. Cheryl Ann (Roddy) Palmer of Bloomington, Minn., d. of Galen Roddy of Duluth, Minn. and Nona Joyce (Hart) Roddy of Minneapolis, Minn., div. of Arthur Gideon Palmer of Minneapolis and Jacksonville, Fla. b. February 1, 1947 in Minneapolis. Ed. Civil Engineering, S.D. School of Mines and Technology, Res. Rapid City, S.D., Richfield, Apple Valley and Red Wing, Minn., Alexandria, Va., and Elmhurst, Crete, and Park Forest, Ill. Occ. h. Civil Engineer, Chief of Operations U.S. Army Corps of Engineers-Chicago District, w. novelist. (Ref. 1, 9) 1769 - 1770 by 1st h., adopted
     1769 - Tiffany Ann   1770 - Shawn Paul

1510- Steven Erwin[11] Wadleigh, (Charles Harry[10], Daniel Edward[9], Charles Edwin[8], Daniel Foster[7], William Henry[6], Joseph[5], Joseph[4], Henry[3], Robert[2], John[1]), b. January 17, 1947 in Albuquerque, N.M., d. January 18, 1947. died in infancy. (Ref. 1, 9)

1511- Ruth Ann Eleanor[11] Wadleigh, (Charles Harry[10], Daniel Edward[9], Charles Edwin[8], Daniel Foster[7], William Henry[6], Joseph[5], Joseph[4], Henry[3], Robert[2], John[1]), b. August 9, 1950 in Albuquerque, N.M., adpt. August 17, 1950, did not marry. Res. Redfield, S.D. (Ref. 1, 9)

Issue of 1345- Elmer Edward[10] Wadleigh and Mabel (Seip) Wadleigh:

1512- David Elmer[11] Wadleigh, (Elmer Edward[10], Daniel Edward[9], Charles Edwin[8], Daniel Foster[7],

William Henry[6], Joseph[5], Joseph[4], Henry[3], Robert[2], John[1]), b. March 21, 1936 in Mitchell, S.D. m. June 10, 1971 in Mitchell Rosalyn Johnson, b. October 31, 1944. Occ. Farmer, Welder. Res. Mt. Vernon, S.D. (Ref. 1, 9)
    1771 - Amber Rose

1513- <u>Dale LeRoy</u>[11] Wadleigh, (Elmer Edward[10], Daniel Edward[9], Charles Edwin[8], Daniel Foster[7], William Henry[6], Joseph[5], Joseph[4], Henry[3], Robert[2], John[1]), b. May 15, 1939 in Mitchell, S.D. m. December 29, 1965 in Keystone, S.D. Bess Kingsbury of Keystone, b. February 24, 1943 in Keystone, div. 1987. Ed. h. BS in Mining Engineering S.D. School of Mines and Technology, w. BA Univ. of Colorado/Boulder, Occ. Mining Engineer w/ Amoco Oil and Bureau of Land Management. Res. Mt. Vernon and Rapid City, S.D., Ketchikan and Tok Junction Alas., Denver Colo. and Cheyenne, Wyo. Served in USAF. (Ref. 1, 9) 1772 - 1774 by 1st w.
   1772 - Cindy Leigh   1774 - Jeanette
   1773 - Theressa Ann

1514- <u>Richard Lee</u>[11] Wadleigh, (Elmer Edward[10], Daniel Edward[9], Charles Edwin[8], Daniel Foster[7], William Henry[6], Joseph[5], Joseph[4], Henry[3], Robert[2], John[1]), b. October 24, 1943 in Mitchell, S.D. m. August 9, 1969 in Mt. Vernon, S.D. Karen Hille, b. March 11, 1941. Ed. BS in Geology, S.D. School of Mines and Technology, Occ. Farmer and Geologist w/ Amoco Oil and USAF, Res. Rapid City and Mt. Vernon, S.D., Omaha, Neb. and Denver, Colo. (Ref. 1, 9)
     1775 - Shawn Lee   1776 - Sarah Louise

1515- <u>Jerry Keith</u>[11] Wadleigh, (Elmer Edward[10], Daniel Edward[9], Charles Edwin[8], Daniel Foster[7], William Henry[6], Joseph[5], Joseph[4], Henry[3], Robert[2], John[1]), b. October 21, 1945 in Mitchell, S.D. m. August 29, 1965 in Mt. Vernon, S.D. Darlene Stickley, b. March 11,

1947. Ed. BA in Education Dakota Wesleyan Univ., Occ. Farmer and H.S. administrator in Columbus, Neb. and Mt. Vernon, S.D. Res. Rapid City and Mt. Vernon, S.D., Valentine and Columbus, Neb. (Ref. 1, 9)
        1777 - Eric Keith 1779 - Dena May
        1778 - Bryan Keith

1516- Eugene Edward[11] Wadleigh, (Elmer Edward[10], Daniel Edward[9], Charles Edwin[8], Daniel Foster[7], William Henry[6], Joseph[5], Joseph[4], Henry[3], Robert[2], John[1]), b. October 25, 1951 in Mitchell, S.D. m. June 3, 1972 in Mt. Vernon, S.D. Cindy Jacobson, b. August 29, 1950. Ed. BS in Geological Engineering at S.D. School of Mines and Technology, Occ. Engineer w/ Amoco Oil in Denver, Colo. and Farmer. Res. Rapid City and Mt. Vernon, S.D., Denver, Colo. (Ref. 1, 9)
        1780 - Peggy Lynn 1781 - Glen Martin

Issue of Erwin Fredrick Schimmel and 1346- Erline Myrtle (Wadleigh) Schimmel:

1517- Lester Edward Schimmel, (Wadleigh: Erline Myrtle[10], Daniel Edward[9], Charles Edwin[8], Daniel Foster[7], William Henry[6], Joseph[5], Joseph[4], Henry[3], Robert[2], John[1]), b. January 26, 1935, near Butler in Day Co. S.D. m. October 24, 1956 at American Lutheran Church in Webster, S.D. Violetta Rose McCrea of Twin Brooks, S.D., d. of Kenneth D. and Margaret H. (Schwandt) McCrea of Kilborn Township, Grant Co., S.D., b. February 17, 1938 in Kilborn Township, Grant Co. S.D. Served in U.S. Army 1957-59. Occ. Farmer and Carpenter, Res. Webster, Butler and Twin Brooks, S.D. (Ref. 1, 9)
     1782 - Karla Kay   1783 - Kevin Lester

Issue of 1347- Robert David[10] Wadleigh and
Dorothy Elizabeth (Seip) Wadleigh:

1518- Robert Daniel[11] Wadleigh, (Robert
David[10], Daniel Edward[9], Charles Edwin[8], Daniel
Foster[7], William Henry[6], Joseph[5], Joseph[4],
Henry[3], Robert[2], John[1]), b. July 15, 1943 in
Hot Springs, S.D. m. May 7, 1968 in Hot
Springs Sandra Kay Bruer, d. of Homer Bruer and
Mrs. (Larsen) Bruer, b. December 25, 1950. Ed.
h. & w. BA from Black Hills State College,
Occ. Retailer and USDA in Brownsville, Tex.,
Res. Spearfish, S.D. Newcastle, Warland and
Sheridan, Wyo., and Brownsville. (Ref. 1, 9)
    1784 - Daniel Edward   1785 - Dana

1519- Bruce Edward[11] Wadleigh, (Robert David[10],
Daniel Edward[9], Charles Edwin[8], Daniel Foster[7],
William Henry[6], Joseph[5], Joseph[4], Henry[3],
Robert[2], John[1]), b. September 25, 1946 in Hot
Springs, S.D. m. August 28, 1971 at American
Embassy, Saigon, Vietnam Nguyen Thi Mai Law, b.
April 23, 1951, d. of Nuyegn Law. div. Nov.
1986. Ed. BS in Bus. Adm. from Huron College,
Occ. U.S.A.F. Career. Res. Seoul Korea,
London England. (Ref. 1, 9)
    1786 - Robert Bruce   1787 - Mai Lai

1520- Susan Kay[11] Wadleigh, (Robert David[10],
Daniel Edward[9], Charles Edwin[8], Daniel Foster[7],
William Henry[6], Joseph[5], Joseph[4], Henry[3],
Robert[2], John[1]), b. May 30, 1954 in Hot
Springs, S.D. m. March 20, 1977 in Hot
Springs Richard Alan McMichael, b. March 12,
1956 in Hot Springs, s. of James and Verle
(Rust) McMichael. Ed. w. R.N. Mt. Marty
College, Yankton, S.D., Occ. w. Registered
Nurse w/ USAF, h. U.S.A.F. Career Off.,   Res.
Texas, New Mexico, Holland, and Ogden, Utah and
Omaha, Nebr. (Ref. 1, 9)
    1788 - Jason Bradley 1790 - Jessica Marie
    1789 - Robert James

WADLEIGH GENEALOGY   ELEVENTH GENERATION

Issue of 1348- Fredrick Lee[10] Wadleigh and
Mildred Ethel (Newman) Wadleigh:

no issue

Issue of Otis Cogdill and 1349- Ada Margaret
(Wadleigh) Cogdill:

1521- Sally Ann Cogdill, (Wadleigh: Ada
Margaret[10], Daniel Edward[9], Charles Edwin[8],
Daniel Foster[7], William Henry[6], Joseph[5],
Joseph[4], Henry[3], Robert[2], John[1]), b. November
12, 1937 at Auburn, Neb. m. May 27, 1956 Paul
Hendrickson, s. of Forest Ernest and Mary
Izetta (Turner) Hendrickson of Brownsville,
Neb., b. March 27, 1935. Occ. River Boat
Pilot, Res. Brownsville and Dakota City, Neb.,
Runningwater and Springfield, S.D. and
Columbus, Ky. (Ref. 1, 9)
        1791 - Guy Lee   1793 - Paula Ann
        1792 - Troy Ernest

1522- Peggy Lou Cogdill, (Wadleigh: Ada
Margaret[10], Daniel Edward[9], Charles Edwin[8],
Daniel Foster[7], William Henry[6], Joseph[5],
Joseph[4], Henry[3], Robert[2], John[1]), b. August 1,
1939 in Auburn, Neb. m. 1959 in Las Vegas,
Nev. Al Lopez, no additional data. Occ.
U.S.A.F. Career (ret.), Airline Mechanic. Res.
Brownsville, Neb. and Riverside, Cal. (Ref. 1,
9)
        1794 - David Dean   1796 - Alan Roman
        1795 - Alisa Lynn

1523- Connie Kay Cogdill, (Wadleigh: Ada
Margaret[10], Daniel Edward[9], Charles Edwin[8],
Daniel Foster[7], William Henry[6], Joseph[5],
Joseph[4], Henry[3], Robert[2], John[1]), b. October
25, 1945 in Brownsville, Neb. m. June 16, 1969
Jerome Staples, s. of John and Florence
(Primus) Staples, b. July 13, 1943 at Butte,
Neb. Occ. Electronic Repair Business. Res.

Jamestown, N.D., Sioux City, Ia., Neligh and
Ponca, Neb. and Gregory and Springfield, S.D.
(Ref. 1, 9)
   1797 - Jay Dean   1799 - Jody Lee
   1798 - Jeffery Dean   1800 - Jonathan Jerome

1524- <u>Anita</u> <u>Louise</u> <u>Cogdill</u>, (Wadleigh: Ada
Margaret[10], Daniel Edward[9], Charles Edwin[8],
Daniel Foster[7], William Henry[6], Joseph[5],
Joseph[4], Henry[3], Robert[2], John[1]), b. September
9, 1950 at Auburn, Neb. m. September 23, 1972
Rocco Minino, Jr., s. of Rocco Minino, Sr. and
Francis (Shott) Minino, b. December 21, 1950 at
Omaha, Neb. Occ. U.S. Navy Career, Res. Omaha
and Bellevue, Neb., Mitchell and Springfield,
S.D., Sunnyvale, Cal., and Kingsville, Tex.
(Ref. 1, 9)
     1801 - Amy Louise   1803 - Rocco III
     1802 - Lori Lynne

1525- <u>Gifford</u> <u>Lane</u> <u>Cogdill</u>, (Wadleigh: Ada
Margaret[10], Daniel Edward[9], Charles Edwin[8],
Daniel Foster[7], William Henry[6], Joseph[5],
Joseph[4], Henry[3], Robert[2], John[1]), b. January
27, 1959 at Sioux City, Ia. m. August 8, 1981
Amy Benson, b. February 2, 1960. Ed. h. Univ.
of Nebr. at Omaha and Grace College, w. R.N.
Occ. Administrator St. Joseph Hospital, Omaha.
Res. Omaha, Neb. (Ref. 1, 9)
     1804 - Christopher 1805 - Chris Joy

**Issue of Edson Taylor and 1350- Alta Beatrice
(Wadleigh) Taylor:**

1526- <u>Ronald</u> <u>Lee</u> <u>Taylor</u>, (Wadleigh: Alta
Beatrice[10], Daniel Edward[9], Charles Edwin[8],
Daniel Foster[7], William Henry[6], Joseph[5],
Joseph[4], Henry[3], Robert[2], John[1]), b. March 18,
1942 at Auburn, Neb. m. 1st June 8, 1963
Gloria Jean Sousley, b. June 9, 1944, div.
1969. m. 2nd Carol Jean Myers, b. January 1,
in Rayville, Mo., d. of Floyd Rash and Mae Dean

Rash, sibl. Wayne Myers, Ron Rash, and David
Rash. Ed. Pilot and Fire Academy,   Occ.
Carpenter and Fire Fighter. Res. Sibly, Mo.
(Ref. 1, 9). 1806 by 1st wife, 1807 - 1809 by
2nd wife.
    1806 - Michael Sc   - Mihal Myers
    1807 - Mark Myers   1809 - Marty Myers

1527- <u>Larry</u> <u>Eugene</u> <u>Taylor</u>, (Wadleigh: Alta
Beatrice[10], Daniel Edward[9], Charles Edwin[8],
Daniel Foster[7], William Henry[6], Joseph[5],
Joseph[4], Henry[3], Robert[2], John[1]), b. July 28,
1943 in Independence Mo. m. November 14, 1970,
Stephanie Dethlought, b. November 22, 1951.
Occ. h. self-employed painter, w. V.P. of Bank
in Independence, Mo., Res. Independence, Mo.
(Ref. 1, 9)
    1810 - Megan Ashley

1528- <u>Elizabeth</u> <u>Ann</u> <u>Taylor</u>, (Wadleigh: Alta
Beatrice[10], Daniel Edward[9], Charles Edwin[8],
Daniel Foster[7], William Henry[6], Joseph[5],
Joseph[4], Henry[3], Robert[2], John[1]), b. December
23, 1951 in Independence, Mo. m. Raymond
Dowell, b. May 27, 1950. Occ. h. Specialty
Mechanic, Res. Kansas City, Mo. (Ref. 1, 9)
  1811 - Jason Alexander 1812 - Adam Edward

**Issue of Edward Charles Gusso and 1351- Ida
Ilene (Wadleigh) Gusso:**

1529- <u>Roxe</u> <u>Lea</u> <u>Gusso</u>, (Wadleigh: Ida Ilene[10],
Daniel Edward[9], Charles Edwin[8], Daniel Foster[7],
William Henry[6], Joseph[5], Joseph[4], Henry[3],
Robert[2], John[1]), b. February 7, 1947 in
Watertown, S.D. m. August 14, 1966 Allen
Peterson, b. October 23, 1945. Occ. Voc.
Teacher w/ Minn. State Prison System. Res.
Roseville and Moose Lake Minn. (Ref. 1, 9)
    1813 - Troy Allen 1815 - Tiffany Lynn
    1814 - Tonya Lee

1530- Rodney Brock Gusso, (Wadleigh: Ida
Ilene[10], Daniel Edward[9], Charles Edwin[8], Daniel
Foster[7], William Henry[6], Joseph[5], Joseph[4],
Henry[3], Robert[2], John[1]), b. April 14, 1949 in
Watertown, S.D. m. June 6, 1970 Carol
Lindner, b. March 3, 1950. Occ. h.
Manufacturing w. Recr. Dir of Retirement Home.
Res. Watertown, S.D. (Ref. 1, 9)
    1816 - Gregory Edward 1818 - Susan
    1817 - Robert Charles

1531- Rochelle Ilene Gusso, (Wadleigh: Ida
Ilene[10], Daniel Edward[9], Charles Edwin[8], Daniel
Foster[7], William Henry[6], Joseph[5], Joseph[4],
Henry[3], Robert[2], John[1]), b. January 4, 1952 in
Watertown, S.D. m. July 1, 1972 Arlyn
Wadsworth, b. June 8, 1950. Occ. w/ 3M Co.,
Res. Brookings, S.D. (Ref. 1, 9)
    1819 - Craig Arnold 1820 - Chris Arlyn

1532- Renea Pauline Gusso, (Wadleigh: Ida
Ilene[10], Daniel Edward[9], Charles Edwin[8], Daniel
Foster[7], William Henry[6], Joseph[5], Joseph[4],
Henry[3], Robert[2], John[1]), b. December 30, 1953
in Watertown, S.D. m. June 29, 1974 Phillip
Brooks, b. November 9, 1949. Occ. w. Pulmonary
Treatment Technician, h. Security Guard. Res.
Rucksbay, Wis. (Ref. 1, 9)
    1821 - Eric Steven   1823 - Johanna
    1822 - Kelly Ilene

**Issue of Guy Pfetcher and 1352- Bernice Nelva
(Bell) Pfetcher:**

no issue

Issue of George Dewey Paul and 1353- Mary Lorene (Bell) Paul:

1533- <u>William</u> <u>Greg</u> <u>Paul</u>, (Wadleigh: Mary Lorene^{10}, Nettie Florence^9, Charles Edwin^8, Daniel Foster^7, William Henry^6, Joseph^5, Joseph^4, Henry^3, Robert^2, John^1), b. September 30, 1942. m. 1st August 21, 1966 Mary Kathryn McKamie, b. December 26, 1948. div. m. 2nd August 13, 1977 Beverly Porter, no additional data. Occ. Regent of Mid-Western Texas Univ. at Wichita Falls. Res. Henrietta, Tex. (Ref. 1) 1824 by 1st wife.
    1824 - Michele Renee

Issue of George Thomas Johnson and 1354- Hazel Caroline (Bell) Johnson:

1534- <u>George</u> <u>Colbert</u> <u>Johnson</u>, (Wadleigh: Hazel Caroline^{10}, Nettie Florence^9, Charles Edwin^8, Daniel Foster^7, William Henry^6, Joseph^5, Joseph^4, Henry^3, Robert^2, John^1), b. October 23, 1933 in Kansas City, Jackson Co., Mo. m. 1st August 20, 1959 Jacque Chambers, d. of James and Dorothy (Keys) Chambers of Barrington, Ill, b. March 1938. div. m. 2nd March 1, 1968 in Houston, Harris Co. Tex. Hilda Franceska^1 Kolbusz, d. of Miklos and Franceska (Meininger) Kolbusz, b. January 10, 1934 in Gyoma, Hungary. (Ref. 1) 1825 by 1st wife.
    1825 - James Richard Colbert

1535- <u>Caroline</u> <u>Kay</u> <u>Johnson</u>, (Wadleigh: Hazel Caroline^{10}, Nettie Florence^9, Charles Edwin^8, Daniel Foster^7, William Henry^6, Joseph^5, Joseph^4, Henry^3, Robert^2, John^1), b. January 29, 1940. m. June 22, 1958 Gary Louis Turner, s. of Lewis Carlyle and Laden (Miles) Turner, b. August 29, 1938. (Ref. 1)
    1826 - Chera Leigh   1828 - Gregory Alan
    1827 - Jona Lynn

1536- <u>Sandra</u> <u>Sue</u> <u>Johnson</u>, (Wadleigh: Hazel
Caroline[10], Nettie Florence[9], Charles Edwin[8],
Daniel Foster[7], William Henry[6], Joseph[5],
Joseph[4], Henry[3], Robert[2], John[1]), b. January
31, 1943. did not marry. Res. Sedalia, Mo.
(Ref. 1)

**Issue of 1355- Howard Charles Bell and Hattie
Pearl (Lane) Bell:**

1537- <u>Stanley</u> <u>Ray</u> <u>Bell</u>, (Wadleigh: Howard
Charles[10], Nettie Florence[9], Charles Edwin[8],
Daniel Foster[7], William Henry[6], Joseph[5],
Joseph[4], Henry[3], Robert[2], John[1]), b. November
24, 1946. m. March 1, 1969 Ann Thompson, no
additional data. (Ref. 1)
        1829 - Karen Alice

1538- <u>Daniel</u> <u>Robert</u> <u>Bell</u>, (Wadleigh: Howard
Charles[10], Nettie Florence[9], Charles Edwin[8],
Daniel Foster[7], William Henry[6], Joseph[5],
Joseph[4], Henry[3], Robert[2], John[1]), b. December
5, 1947. m. June 26, 1971 Susan Lee Guthrie,
no additional data. (Ref. 1)
        1830 - Erin Lee

**Issue of 1356- Paul Edward[10] Wadleigh and
Edith (Harlan) Wadleigh:**

1539- <u>Arvilla</u> <u>D.</u>[11] Wadleigh, (Paul Edward[10],
James Augustus[9], Charles Edwin[8], Daniel
Foster[7], William Henry[6], Joseph[5], Joseph[4],
Henry[3], Robert[2], John[1]), b. September 18, 1938.
m. 1st May 23, 1958 James Daugherty, div. m.
2nd Duke Collins, d. 1975. no additional data.
(Ref. 1)   1831 - 1832 by 1st husb., 1833 - 1834
by 2nd husb.
    1831 - James Paul   1833 - Susan Elaine
    1832 - Christopher Lee   1834 - Sandra Jean

1540- <u>Karen Jean</u>[11] Wadleigh, (Paul Edward[10], James Augustus[9], Charles Edwin[8], Daniel Foster[7], William Henry[6], Joseph[5], Joseph[4], Henry[3], Robert[2], John[1]), b. July 11, 1941. m. November 18, 1961 John Holmberg, b. May 5, 1941. (Ref. 1)

   1835 - John Scott   1837 - Jeanette Rene
   1836 - Jeannie Marie 1838 - Jennifer Lynn

Issue of 1357- Omer Basil[10] Wadleigh and Iva Anna (Hall) Wadleigh:

1541- <u>Charles Edward</u>[11] Wadleigh, (Omer Basil[10], James Augustus[9], Charles Edwin[8], Daniel Foster[7], William Henry[6], Joseph[5], Joseph[4], Henry[3], Robert[2], John[1]), b. October 22, 1942. m. June 1, 1963 Judith Kay Gardner, d. of Alva and Mary (Ures) Gardner, b. March 9, 1942. (Ref. 1)

    1839 - Michael Edward 1840 - Michelle Rene

1542- <u>Roger Basil</u>[11] Wadleigh, (Omer Basil[10], James Augustus[9], Charles Edwin[8], Daniel Foster[7], William Henry[6], Joseph[5], Joseph[4], Henry[3], Robert[2], John[1]), b. June 4, 1947. m. March 8 1969 Minnie Bell Gardner, b. August 5, 1947. (Ref. 1)

   1841 - Tara Leanne 1842 - Susann Augusta

1543- <u>Twyla Ann</u>[11] Wadleigh, (Omer Basil[10], James Augustus[9], Charles Edwin[8], Daniel Foster[7], William Henry[6], Joseph[5], Joseph[4], Henry[3], Robert[2], John[1]), b. October 15, 1949. m. June 7, 1969 William Wayne Campbell, b. December 28, 1949. (Ref. 1)

   1843 - Kelly Wayne

Issue of 1358- Mervyn Wayne[3] Lunstrum and
Margaret Ruth (Shamberger) Lunstrum:

1544- <u>William Bruce</u>[4] <u>Lunstrum</u>, (Wadleigh:
Fannie Lorena[9], Charles Edwin[8], Daniel Foster[7],
William Henry[6], Joseph[5], Joseph[4], Henry[3],
Robert[2], John[1]; Lunstrum: Mervyn Wayne[3],
William[2], Peter[1]), b. January 5, 1935 in
Payette, Payette Co. Ida. m. June 20, 1959 in
Laurel, Prince Georges Co., Md., Valerie
Josephine Kroll, d. of Alvin and Josephine
(Ross) Kroll, b. October 16, 1936 in Kellog,
Shoshone Co. Ida. Ed. Univ. of Idaho at
Moscow. (Ref. 1)
    1844 - Bryan Ross   1845 - Megan Beth

1545- <u>Carolyn Beth</u>[4] <u>Lunstrum</u>, (Wadleigh:
Fannie Lorena[9], Charles Edwin[8], Daniel Foster[7],
William Henry[6], Joseph[5], Joseph[4], Henry[3],
Robert[2], John[1]; Lunstrum: Mervyn Wayne[3],
William[2], Peter[1]), b. September 15, 1937 in
Payette, Payette Co., Ida. Ed. Univ. of
Idaho/Moscow. (Ref. 1)

1546- <u>Ralph David</u>[4] <u>Lunstrum</u>, (Wadleigh: Fannie
Lorena[9], Charles Edwin[8], Daniel Foster[7],
William Henry[6], Joseph[5], Joseph[4], Henry[3],
Robert[2], John[1]; Lunstrum: Mervyn Wayne[3],
William[2], Peter[1]), b. (twin) September 25, 1942
in Payette, Payette Co. Ida. m. 1965 Kandy
Robb Cameron, b. July 21, 1947 in Orange Co.,
Cal. div. 1970. (Ref. 1)
        1846 - Lorena Sue

1547- <u>Margaret Paige</u>[4] <u>Lunstrum</u>, (Wadleigh:
Fannie Lorena[9], Charles Edwin[8], Daniel Foster[7],
William Henry[6], Joseph[5], Joseph[4], Henry[3],
Robert[2], John[1]; Lunstrum: Mervyn Wayne[3],
William[2], Peter[1]), b. (twin) September 25, 1942
in Payette, Payette Co. Ida., m. October 2,
1962 in Pocatello, Bannock Co., Ida. Alan James
Skille, s. of Elmer J. and Ellen Hendrickson
(Skille) Grotting, b. December 3, 1941 in

Astoria, Clatsop Co. Ore. (Ref. 1)
   1847 - Keith Alan   1848 - Margit Christine

**Issue of 1359- Fordyce Wilbur[3] Lunstrum, and
Virginia Marie (Stoner) Lunstrum:**

1548- Susan Beth[4] Lunstrum, (Wadleigh: Fordyce
Wilbur[10], Fannie Lorena[9], Charles Edwin[8],
Daniel Foster[7], William Henry[6], Joseph[5],
Joseph[4], Henry[3], Robert[2], John[1]; Lunstrum:
Fordyce Wilbur[3], William[2], Peter[1]), b. June 2,
1948. m. James Petty, b. Meridian, Ada Co.,
Ida. (Ref. 1)
   1849 - Valarie Jo 1850 - Dana Joanne

**Issue of 1360- Carl Kenneth[3] Lunstrum, and
Mary (Foster) Lunstrum:**

1549- Carl Kenneth[4] Lunstrum, (Wadleigh: Carl
Kenneth[10], Fannie Lorena[9], Charles Edwin[8],
Daniel Foster[7], William Henry[6], Joseph[5],
Joseph[4], Henry[3], Robert[2], John[1]; Lunstrum:
Carl Kenneth[3], William[2], Peter[1]), b. November
21, 1944 in Fredrick, Fredrick Co. Md., m.
November 7, 1967 in Spokane, Spokane Co. Wash.
Madeline Elizabeth Kane, b. September 17, 1945
in Butte, Silver Bow Co., Mont. (Ref. 1)
   1851 - Sarah Kristine 1853 - Casey Matthew
   1852 - Amy Kathleen   1854 - Kristen Patrick

1550- James Peter[4] Lunstrum, (Wadleigh: Carl
Kenneth[10], Fannie Lorena[9], Charles Edwin[8],
Daniel Foster[7], William Henry[6], Joseph[5],
Joseph[4], Henry[3], Robert[2], John[1]; Lunstrum:
Carl Kenneth[3], William[2], Peter[1]), b. February
2, 1946 in Nampa, Canyon Co. Ida., m. June 2,
1972 in Payette, Ida. Patricia Jane Godschalx,
b. March 21, 1951 in Payette. (Ref. 1)
   1855 - Eric Godschalx   1856 - Elizabeth Mary

1551- <u>Melissa Ann</u>[4] Lunstrum, (Wadleigh: Carl
Kenneth[10], Fannie Lorena[9], Charles Edwin[8],
Daniel Foster[7], William Henry[6], Joseph[5],
Joseph[4], Henry[3], Robert[2], John[1]; Lunstrum:
Carl Kenneth[3], William[2], Peter[1]), b. November
22, 1948 in Nampa, Ida. no other data. (Ref. 1)

1552- <u>Thomas Michael</u>[4] Lunstrum, (Wadleigh:
Carl Kenneth[10], Fannie Lorena[9], Charles Edwin[8],
Daniel Foster[7], William Henry[6], Joseph[5],
Joseph[4], Henry[3], Robert[2], John[1]; Lunstrum:
Carl Kenneth[3], William[2], Peter[1]), b. December
23, 1950 in Nampa, Ida., d. January 13, 1971.
(Ref. 1)

1553- <u>William John</u>[4] Lunstrum, (Wadleigh: Carl
Kenneth[10], Fannie Lorena[9], Charles Edwin[8],
Daniel Foster[7], William Henry[6], Joseph[5],
Joseph[4], Henry[3], Robert[2], John[1]; Lunstrum:
Carl Kenneth[3], William[2], Peter[1]), b. December
1, 1952 in Nampa, Ida. (Ref. 1)

1554- <u>Mary Trivette</u>[4] Lunstrum, (Wadleigh: Carl
Kenneth[10], Fannie Lorena[9], Charles Edwin[8],
Daniel Foster[7], William Henry[6], Joseph[5],
Joseph[4], Henry[3], Robert[2], John[1]; Lunstrum:
Carl Kenneth[3], William[2], Peter[1]), b. October
31, 1954 in Nampa, Ida., m. September 17, 1977
in Nampa, Ida. Fredrick James Gosten, b.
October 27, 1953, (Ref. 1)

1555- <u>Karen Elizabeth</u>[4] Lunstrum, (Wadleigh:
Carl Kenneth[10], Fannie Lorena[9], Charles Edwin[8],
Daniel Foster[7], William Henry[6], Joseph[5],
Joseph[4], Henry[3], Robert[2], John[1]; Lunstrum:
Carl Kenneth[3], William[2], Peter[1]), b. July 10,
1956 in Nampa, Ida. (Ref. 1)

1556- <u>Mark Joseph</u>[4] Lunstrum, (Wadleigh: Carl
Kenneth[10], Fannie Lorena[9], Charles Edwin[8],
Daniel Foster[7], William Henry[6], Joseph[5],

Joseph[4], Henry[3], Robert[2], John[1]; Lunstrum:
Carl Kenneth[3], William[2], Peter[1]), b. January
22, 1958. (Ref. 1)

1557- <u>Kristen Miriam</u>[4] <u>Lunstrum</u>, (Wadleigh:
Carl Kenneth[10], Fannie Lorena[9], Charles Edwin[8],
Daniel Foster[7], William Henry[6], Joseph[5],
Joseph[4], Henry[3], Robert[2], John[1]; Lunstrum:
Carl Kenneth[3], William[2], Peter[1]), b. April 30,
1959. (Ref. 1)

1558- <u>Theresa Frances</u>[4] <u>Lunstrum</u>, (Wadleigh:
Carl Kenneth[10], Fannie Lorena[9], Charles Edwin[8],
Daniel Foster[7], William Henry[6], Joseph[5],
Joseph[4], Henry[3], Robert[2], John[1]; Lunstrum:
Carl Kenneth[3], William[2], Peter[1]), b. November
14, 1960. (Ref. 1)

1559- <u>Janel Anne</u>[4] <u>Lunstrum</u>, (Wadleigh: Carl
Kenneth[10], Fannie Lorena[9], Charles Edwin[8],
Daniel Foster[7], William Henry[6], Joseph[5],
Joseph[4], Henry[3], Robert[2], John[1]; Lunstrum:
Carl Kenneth[3], William[2], Peter[1]), b. (twin)
January 17, 1963. (Ref. 1)

1560- <u>Joel Anthony</u>[4] <u>Lunstrum</u>, (Wadleigh: Carl
Kenneth[10], Fannie Lorena[9], Charles Edwin[8],
Daniel Foster[7], William Henry[6], Joseph[5],
Joseph[4], Henry[3], Robert[2], John[1]; Lunstrum:
Carl Kenneth[3], William[2], Peter[1]), b. (twin)
January 17, 1963. (Ref. 1)

1561- <u>Erin Carla</u>[4] <u>Lunstrum</u>, (Wadleigh: Carl
Kenneth[10], Fannie Lorena[9], Charles Edwin[8],
Daniel Foster[7], William Henry[6], Joseph[5],
Joseph[4], Henry[3], Robert[2], John[1]; Lunstrum:
Carl Kenneth[3], William[2], Peter[1]), b. November
20, 1966. (Ref. 1)

Issue of John Philip McKibbin, and 1361- Inez Lorraine (Lunstrum) McKibbin:

1562- John Edward McKibbin, (Wadleigh: Inez Lorraine[10], Fannie Lorena[9], Charles Edwin[8], Daniel Foster[7], William Henry[6], Joseph[5], Joseph[4], Henry[3], Robert[2], John[1]), b. June 15, 1944 in Rochester, Olmstead Co. Minn. m. January 3, 1969 in Sacramento, Sacramento Co., Cal. Shirlee Swanson, b. March 17, 1944 in Livermore, Alameda Co., Cal. (Ref. 1)
    1857 - Killy Ann   1858 - Samuel Alexander

1563- Philip David McKibbin, (Wadleigh: Inez Lorraine[10], Fannie Lorena[9], Charles Edwin[8], Daniel Foster[7], William Henry[6], Joseph[5], Joseph[4], Henry[3], Robert[2], John[1]), b. January 30, 1947 in Sacramento, Sacramento Co., Cal. m. December 22, 1974 in Sacramento, Cal. Katherene Elizabeth Mysing, b. August 16, 1946 in Sacramento, Cal. (Ref. 1)

1564- Steven James McKibbin, (Wadleigh: Inez Lorraine[10], Fannie Lorena[9], Charles Edwin[8], Daniel Foster[7], William Henry[6], Joseph[5], Joseph[4], Henry[3], Robert[2], John[1]), b. January 11, 1949, d. May 25, 1949. died in infancy. (Ref. 1)

1565- Ann Elizabeth McKibbin, (Wadleigh: Inez Lorraine[10], Fannie Lorena[9], Charles Edwin[8], Daniel Foster[7], William Henry[6], Joseph[5], Joseph[4], Henry[3], Robert[2], John[1]), b. February 15, 1950, in Sacramento, Cal. (Ref. 1)

Issue of 1362- Richard Maurice[3] Lunstrum, and Sally Louise (Greenrod) Lunstrum:

1566- Gregory Paul[4] Lunstrum, (Wadleigh: Richard Maurice[10], Fannie Lorena[9], Charles Edwin[8], Daniel Foster[7], William Henry[6],

Joseph[5], Joseph[4], Henry[3], Robert[2], John[1];
Lunstrum: Richard Maurice[3], William[2], Peter[1]),
b. March 25, 1950 in Boise, Ida. (Ref. 1)

1567- Kirk William[4] Lunstrum, (Wadleigh:
Richard Maurice[10], Fannie Lorena[9], Charles
Edwin[8], Daniel Foster[7], William Henry[6],
Joseph[5], Joseph[4], Henry[3], Robert[2], John[1];
Lunstrum: Richard Maurice[3], William[2], Peter[1]),
b. November 15, 1951 in Boise, Ida. (Ref. 1)

1568- Eric Richard[4] Lunstrum, (Wadleigh:
Richard Maurice[10], Fannie Lorena[9], Charles
Edwin[8], Daniel Foster[7], William Henry[6],
Joseph[5], Joseph[4], Henry[3], Robert[2], John[1];
Lunstrum: Richard Maurice[3], William[2], Peter[1]),
b. January 13, 1955 in Seattle, King Co.,
Wash. (Ref. 1)

**Issue of Glen Mahlon Rhodes, and 1363- Lois
(Johnson) Rhodes:**

1569- Glenda Joyce Rhodes, (Wadleigh: Helen
Mary[9], Charles Edwin[8], Daniel Foster[7], William
Henry[6], Joseph[5], Joseph[4], Henry[3], Robert[2],
John[1]), b. March 3, 1937. m. March 4, 1967 at
Edina, Mo. William Bryson Hawkins, b. August
19, 1928 in Deer Ridge, Lewis Co., Mo. (Ref. 1)

1570- Arvid Elmer Rhodes, (Wadleigh: Helen
Mary[9], Charles Edwin[8], Daniel Foster[7], William
Henry[6], Joseph[5], Joseph[4], Henry[3], Robert[2],
John[1]), b. July 7, 1941. (Ref. 1)

1571- Anita Carol Rhodes, (Wadleigh: Helen
Mary[9], Charles Edwin[8], Daniel Foster[7], William
Henry[6], Joseph[5], Joseph[4], Henry[3], Robert[2],
John[1]), b. July 7, 1943. m. September 14, 1964
David Jefferies V, b. May 29, 1937. (Ref. 1)
    1859 - Angela Davon   1860 - David

1572- <u>Connie</u> <u>Fay</u> <u>Rhodes</u>, (Wadleigh: Helen
Mary[9], Charles Edwin[8], Daniel Foster[7], William
Henry[6], Joseph[5], Joseph[4], Henry[3], Robert[2],
John[1]), b. November 7, 1951. m. February 7,
1975 in Liberty, Tex. George Harold Rottinger,
b. December 13, 1945 in Hammonton, Atlantic
Co., N.J. (Ref. 1)
       1861 - Diane Rebecca

**Issue of Roy Chester Wissman and 1367- Ella
Dorothy (Wadleigh) Wissman:**

1573- <u>Richard</u> <u>Leroy</u> <u>Wissman</u>, (Wadleigh: Ella
Dorothy[10], Robert Leroy[9], Charles Edwin[8],
Daniel Foster[7], William Henry[6], Joseph[5],
Joseph[4], Henry[3], Robert[2], John[1]), b. September
12, 1943. m. July 6, 1968 Susan Lynn Stuerke,
b. April 19, 1944. (Ref. 1)
       1862 - Jeffery James

1574- <u>James</u> <u>Joseph</u> <u>Wissman</u>, (Wadleigh: Ella
Dorothy[10], Robert Leroy[9], Charles Edwin[8],
Daniel Foster[7], William Henry[6], Joseph[5],
Joseph[4], Henry[3], Robert[2], John[1]), b. June 25,
1946. m. August 24, 1968 Linda Kaye Petree, b.
March 6, 1949. (Ref. 1)
     1863 - Jason James   1864 - Amy Lynn

1575- <u>Sharon</u> <u>Anne</u> <u>Wissman</u>, (Wadleigh: Ella
Dorothy[10], Robert Leroy[9], Charles Edwin[8],
Daniel Foster[7], William Henry[6], Joseph[5],
Joseph[4], Henry[3], Robert[2], John[1]), b. November
13, 1951. m. November 17, 1974 Steve Allen
Gardner, b. July 20, 1951. (Ref. 1)

**Issue of Herman M. Meisenheimer and 1368-
Hallie Jane (Wadleigh) Meisenheimer:**

1576- <u>Calvin</u> <u>Levi</u> <u>Meisenheimer</u>, (Wadleigh:
Hallie Jane[10], Clarence Levi[9], Charles Edwin[8],

Daniel Foster[7], William Henry[6], Joseph[5],
Joseph[4], Henry[3], Robert[2], John[1]), b. September
19, 1961. (Ref. 1)

1577- <u>Bonnie Elizabeth Meisenheimer</u>, (Wadleigh:
Hallie Jane[10], Clarence Levi[9], Charles Edwin[8],
Daniel Foster[7], William Henry[6], Joseph[5],
Joseph[4], Henry[3], Robert[2], John[1]), b. January
23, 1963. (Ref. 1)

Issue of Terry Benson and 1370- Josephine (Wadleigh) Benson:

1578- <u>Deborah Jane Benson</u>, (Wadleigh:
Josephine[10], Clarence Levi[9], Charles Edwin[8],
Daniel Foster[7], William Henry[6], Joseph[5],
Joseph[4], Henry[3], Robert[2], John[1]), b. April 8,
1956. (Ref. 1)

1579- <u>Paul David Benson</u>, (Wadleigh:
Josephine[10], Clarence Levi[9], Charles Edwin[8],
Daniel Foster[7], William Henry[6], Joseph[5],
Joseph[4], Henry[3], Robert[2], John[1]), b. July 14,
1958. (Ref. 1)

Issue of 1389- Walter Burns Kyd and Linnea Blanche (Lind) Kyd:

1580- <u>John Robert Kyd</u>, (Wadleigh: Walter
Burns[10], Bertha May[9], Everett[8], Daniel Foster[7],
William Henry[6], Joseph[5], Joseph[4], Henry[3],
Robert[2], John[1]), b. December 28, 1936. (Ref. 2)

Issue of Carroll Riley and 1390- Annabel (Kyd) Riley:

1581- <u>Don Albert Riley</u>, (Wadleigh: Anabel[10],
Bertha May[9], Everett[8], Daniel Foster[7], William

Henry[6], Joseph[5], Joseph[4], Henry[3], Robert[2],
John[1]), b. May 3, 1925 in Des Moines, Ia. m.
October 3, 1946 in Des Moines Reva Jean
Shinkle, d. of Mavis Shinkle, b. July 11, 1924
at Hartley, Ia. Both served in U.S. Navy in WW
II. Occ. Artist and Art Salesman. Res. Los
Angeles, Cal. (Ref. 2)
        1865 - Dale Alan   1867 - Mark Kevin
        1866 - Brian Don

**Issue of Harold E. Lang and 1391- Mary Louise
(Kyd) Lang:**

no issue

**Issue of Clifford Minie Hogan and 1392- Alma
Emma (Kyd) Hogan:**

1582- Ramona Elizabeth Hogan, (Wadleigh: Alma
Emma[10], Bertha May[9], Everett[8], Daniel Foster[7],
William Henry[6], Joseph[5], Joseph[4], Henry[3],
Robert[2], John[1]), b. March 29, 1930 at Iowa
Falls, Ia. m. April 4, 1945 in Iowa Falls
James R. Harrison, s. of Clarence Harrison and
Eugenia (McNeal) Harrison, b. January 3, 1922
at Traer, Ia., d. April 14, 1982 at Waterloo,
Ia. Occ. h.- Autobody repair, w.- Nurses Aide.
Res. Traer, Ia. (Ref. 2)
        1868 - Victoria Lee   1870 - Mary E.
        1869 - James R.   1871 - Ricky Joe

1583- Robert Clifford Hogan, (Wadleigh: Alma
Emma[10], Bertha May[9], Everett[8], Daniel Foster[7],
William Henry[6], Joseph[5], Joseph[4], Henry[3],
Robert[2], John[1]), b. October 5, 1932. (Ref. 2)

1584- James Colbert Hogan, (Wadleigh: Alma
Emma[10], Bertha May[9], Everett[8], Daniel Foster[7],
William Henry[6], Joseph[5], Joseph[4], Henry[3],
Robert[2], John[1]), b. April 9, 1934 in Iowa

Falls, Ia. m. October 25, 1969 in Iowa Falls,
Ia. Patricia Elaine Gardner, d. of Everett
Berdette Gardner and Grace Marie (Hoisington)
Gardner, b. April 17, 1945 at Ankeny, Ia. Res.
Iowa Falls, Ia., Chicago, Ill., Texas and
California. (Ref. 2)

1872 - Grace Marie	1875 - Francis Everett
1873 - David James	1876 - Roy Alan
1874 - Alma Emma	1877 - Patrick Walter

1585- Francis Walter Hogan, (Wadleigh: Alma
Emma[10], Bertha May[9], Everett[8], Daniel Foster[7],
William Henry[6], Joseph[5], Joseph[4], Henry[3],
Robert[2], John[1]), b. January 17, 1936 in Iowa
Falls, Ia., d. July 3, 1986 in Omaha, Neb.,
bur. at Iowa Falls. m. 1st March 8, 1953 in
Iowa Falls Minnie May Holman, d. of Lyle P.
Holman and Elsie L. (Endfield) Holman, b. May
17, 1938 at Pisgah, Ia., d. October 15, 1970 at
Iowa Lutheran Hosp., Des. Moines, Ia. m. 2nd
October 6, 1974 in Bellevue, Neb. Linda Kay
Schimp, b. August 8, 1942 at Wichita, Kan.
Occ. Career USAF and Antique dealer and
refinisher. (Ref. 2) 1878 - 1879 by 1st wife
    1878 - Kathleen Diane 1879 - Michael Francis

1586- Gerald Thomas Hogan, (Wadleigh: Alma
Emma[10], Bertha May[9], Everett[8], Daniel Foster[7],
William Henry[6], Joseph[5], Joseph[4], Henry[3],
Robert[2], John[1]), b. November 16 (or 17), 1937
at Iowa Falls, Ia. m. September 16, 1956 in
Iowa Falls Jessie Jean Holman, d. of Lyle P.
Holman and Elsie L. (Endfield) Holman, b.
September 7, 1941 at Moorhead, Ia. Occ.
construction at prestressed concrete plant and
auctioneer. Res. Des Moines and Iowa Falls,
Ia. (Ref. 2)

1880 - Sherri Jean	1882 - Kelly Brian
1881 - Gerald Thomas	

1587- Keith Allen Hogan, (Wadleigh: Alma
Emma[10], Bertha May[9], Everett[8], Daniel Foster[7],
William Henry[6], Joseph[5], Joseph[4], Henry[3],

Robert[2], John[1]), b. March 31, 1939 in Iowa
Falls, Ia. m. December 5, 1977 in Iowa Falls
Joan (Schaper) Knode, d. of John Conrad and
Florence Esther (Rahfeldt) Schaper, b. April
1937. Occ. construction worker. Res. Chicago,
Ill., Tyler, Tex., New Mexico and California.
(Ref. 2)
    1883 - Kendall Donavon

1588- Alma Margaret Hogan, (Wadleigh: Alma
Emma[10], Bertha May[9], Everett[8], Daniel Foster[7],
William Henry[6], Joseph[5], Joseph[4], Henry[3],
Robert[2], John[1]), b. June 14, 1942 in Iowa
Falls, Ia. m. June 3, 1977 in Iowa Falls Dale
Ball, no additional data. Occ. w. shipper with
publisher (Ref. 2)

1589- June Louise Hogan, (Wadleigh: Alma
Emma[10], Bertha May[9], Everett[8], Daniel Foster[7],
William Henry[6], Joseph[5], Joseph[4], Henry[3],
Robert[2], John[1]), b. May 6, 1944 in Iowa Falls,
Ia. m. July 28, 1964 in Eldora, Ia. Ronald M.
Eason, s. of George W. and Margerie Maxine
(King) Eason, b. June 23, 1942 at Iowa Falls.
Res. Iowa Falls, Ia. (Ref. 2)
   1884 - Ronald Eugene   1886 - George Clifford
   1885 - Valarie Maxine

1590- Donald Dean Hogan, (Wadleigh: Alma
Emma[10], Bertha May[9], Everett[8], Daniel Foster[7],
William Henry[6], Joseph[5], Joseph[4], Henry[3],
Robert[2], John[1]), b. June 2, 1946 in Iowa Falls,
Ia. m. December 17, 1967 in Iowa Falls Ruth
Esther Schaper, d. of John Conrad Schaper and
Florence Esther (Rahfeldt) Schaper, b. October
14, 1945 at State Center, Ia. Served in U.S.
Army, Occ. h. Municipal waterworks operator,
w. insurance clerk and medical lab and x-ray
technician. (Ref. 2)
    1887 - Angela Annette 1889 - Nathaniel Lynn
    1888 - David Ray

1591- <u>Robert</u> <u>Allen</u> <u>Hogan</u>, (Wadleigh: Unknown - grandson) raised by Clifford and Alma, b. August 5, 1958. (Ref. 2)

Issue of Albert Edward Upton and 1393- Audrey Belle (Paige) Upton:

1592- <u>Joseph</u> <u>Edward</u> <u>Upton</u>, (Wadleigh: Audrey Belle[10], Hattie Belle[9], Everett[8], Daniel Foster[7], William Henry[6], Joseph[5], Joseph[4], Henry[3], Robert[2], John[1]), b. March 6, 1929 in Green Ridge, Mo. m. December 1, 1964 in Stover, Mo. Cletta Fay (Dority) Braden, no additional data. (Ref. 2)

1593- <u>George</u> <u>LeRoy</u> <u>Upton</u>, (Wadleigh: Audrey Belle[10], Hattie Belle[9], Everett[8], Daniel Foster[7], William Henry[6], Joseph[5], Joseph[4], Henry[3], Robert[2], John[1]), b. November 2, 1935 in Green Ridge, Mo. m. October 12, 1956 in Smithton, Mo. De Laine Griffith, d. of Othel Ivan and Sara Willia Baxter Griffith, b. August 21, 1937 at Smithton. Res. Green Ridge, Warsaw and Smithton, Mo., Dubuque, Garner and Manley, Ia., Sun City, Ariz., Occ. h.-Ariz. State Dept. of Revenue, Land Dept., w.-Ariz. Dept of Economic Security. (Ref. 2)
    1890 - George Kerris 1891 - Kristy DeAnn

1594- <u>Clyde</u> <u>Mervin</u> <u>Upton</u>, (Wadleigh: Audrey Belle[10], Hattie Belle[9], Everett[8], Daniel Foster[7], William Henry[6], Joseph[5], Joseph[4], Henry[3], Robert[2], John[1]), b. October 7, 1943 in Green Ridge, Mo. m. August 3, 1963 in Sedalia, Mo. Betty Lou Logan, d. of Ruben James and Dorothy Viola (Spires) Logan, b. April 26, 1945 at Sedalia Mo. Res. Sedalia and Blackburn, Mo. and Kansas City, Kan., Occ. Mechanic and Body Shop operator, OTR Truck Driver (auto transport). (Ref. 2)
    1892 - James Lee 1893 - Theresa Lynette

1595- Alice Louise Upton, (Wadleigh: Audrey
Belle[10], Hattie Belle[9], Everett[8], Daniel
Foster[7], William Henry[6], Joseph[5], Joseph[4],
Henry[3], Robert[2], John[1]), b. June 19, 1946 in
Sedalia, Mo. m. June 18, 1967 in Green Ridge,
Mo. John Thomas Bronson, Jr., s. of John Thomas
Bronson, Sr. and Marjorie Eloise (Wheeler)
Bronson, b. October 13, 1945 at Sedalia, Mo.
Res. Green Ridge, Mo. (Ref. 2)
     1894 - John Thomas 1895 - Audrey Eloise

**Issue of 1394- Louis Leroy Paige and Mary
Helen (Staats) Paige:**

1596- Marilee Paige, (Wadleigh: Louis Leroy[10],
Hattie Belle[9], Everett[8], Daniel Foster[7],
William Henry[6], Joseph[5], Joseph[4], Henry[3],
Robert[2], John[1]), b. April 14, 1936 in Green
Ridge, Mo. m. December 28, 1958 in Dallas,
Tex. Norman Scott Newkirk Jr., s. of Norman
Scott Newkirk, Sr. and Leona Jane (Allen)
Newkirk, b. October 9, 1932 at Warsaw, Mo.,
div. June 14, 1976. Res. Dallas, Tex. and
Warsaw, Mo. Occ. Bank officer. (Ref. 2)
     1896 - Nick James

1597- Robert LeRoss Paige, (Wadleigh: Louis
Leroy[10], Hattie Belle[9], Everett[8], Daniel
Foster[7], William Henry[6], Joseph[5], Joseph[4],
Henry[3], Robert[2], John[1]), b. August 17, 1942 in
Beaumont, Tex. Served in Viet Nam. (Ref. 2)

**Issue of 1395- Forest Martin Paige and Ruth
Loretta (Howard) Paige:**

1598- Mary Etta Paige, (Wadleigh: Forest
Martin[10], Hattie Belle[9], Everett[8], Daniel
Foster[7], William Henry[6], Joseph[5], Joseph[4],
Henry[3], Robert[2], John[1]), b. March 8, 1939 in
Green Ridge, Mo. m. September 19, 1958 in
Dallas, Tex. Donny Arymol Sosebee, s. of Arymol

Haywood and Ora Mae (Kurklin) Sosebee, b. July
11, 1937 at Lubbock, Tex., d. April 15, 1985 at
Dallas, bur. at Lubbock. Occ. h.-typesetter,
w.- Pre-school teacher.   (Ref. 2)
  1897 - Laurie Anne   1899 - Darren Keith
  1898 - Michael Craig 1900 - Steven Kent

1599- Janet Sue Paige, (Wadleigh: Forest
Martin[10], Hattie Belle[9], Everett[8], Daniel
Foster[7], William Henry[6], Joseph[5], Joseph[4],
Henry[3], Robert[2], John[1]), b. December 7, 1940 in
Green Ridge, Mo. m. 1st June 24, 1960 in
Dallas, Tex. John Baxter Kidd, s. of Leslie and
Helen (Thompson) (Sellars) Kidd, b. July 5,
1940 at Columbia, La., div. December 3, 1967.
m. 2nd October 10, 1970 in Dallas John Charles
English, s. of Leonard Charles and Anna Frances
(Everhart) English, b. February 28, 1940 at
Linton, Ind. Occ. w.- Bank officer, h1.- armed
forces, served in Germany and Viet Nam, h2.-
Carpenter. Res. Dallas Tex., Bamberg, Germany,
and Indianapolis, Ind. (Ref. 2) 1901 - 1902
by 1st husb.
  1901 - John Jay   1902 - James Kyle

1600- Howard Lee Paige, (Wadleigh: Forest
Martin[10], Hattie Belle[9], Everett[8], Daniel
Foster[7], William Henry[6], Joseph[5], Joseph[4],
Henry[3], Robert[2], John[1]), b. April 11, 1942 in
Windsor, Mo. m. 1st July 1, 1962 in Dallas,
Tex. Martha Kay Pennington, d. of Walter Howard
Pennington II, b. October 13,   d. August 1981
at Houston, Tex. div. February 2, 1971 at
Dallas. m. 2nd August 7, 1971 in Richardson,
Tex. Velma Jane (Bowen) Curtis, d. of Ordis and
Linnie Pearl Bowen, b. June 7, 1942 at Durant,
Ok. Res. Arlington, Dallas, and Garland Tex.
and Germantown, Tenn. Occ. Engineer with
Kraft, Inc. Ed. Univ. of Texas/Arlington.
(Ref. 2) 1903 by 1st w. 1904 - 1905 by 2nd w.
  1903 - Allen James   1905 - Kevin Lee
  1904 - Todd Anderson

1601- David Martin Paige, (Wadleigh: Forest
Martin[10], Hattie Belle[9], Everett[8], Daniel
Foster[7], William Henry[6], Joseph[5], Joseph[4],
Henry[3], Robert[2], John[1]), b. March 13, 1952 in
Dallas, Tex.   (Ref. 2)

**Issue of Hoyt Seldon Holley and 1396- Gladys
Lorene (Paige) Holley:**

1602- Gerald Robert Holley, (Wadleigh: Gladys
Lorene[10], Hattie Belle[9], Everett[8], Daniel
Foster[7], William Henry[6], Joseph[5], Joseph[4],
Henry[3], Robert[2], John[1]), b. October 1, 1934 in
Avery, Mo., d. October 1, 1934 in Avery. died
in infancy. (Ref. 2)

1603- Shirley Jean Holley, (Wadleigh: Gladys
Lorene[10], Hattie Belle[9], Everett[8], Daniel
Foster[7], William Henry[6], Joseph[5], Joseph[4],
Henry[3], Robert[2], John[1]), b. January 10, 1936 in
Avery, near Fairfield in Benton Co., Mo. m.
February 19, 1955 in Warsaw, Mo. Robert Eugene
Scott, s. of Ura Erban and Mary Caroline
(Smith) Scott, b. June 13, 1935 at Brownington,
Mo. Res. Independence, Mo. Occ. h.- Regional
Manager for Concrete Products firm. (Ref. 2)
    1906 - Robert Keith   1907 - Timothy Lee

1604- Hoyt Allen Holley, (Wadleigh: Gladys
Lorene[10], Hattie Belle[9], Everett[8], Daniel
Foster[7], William Henry[6], Joseph[5], Joseph[4],
Henry[3], Robert[2], John[1]), b. July 23, 1938 in
Avery, Mo. m. January 28, 1962 in Warsaw, Mo.
Theodora Lee Wise, d. of Theodore Roosevelt and
Viola Blanche (Hainline) Wise, b. January 14,
1941 at Warsaw. Occ. h.- Farmer and official
with Missouri Farmers Assoc. w.- dental
technician and Real Estate. Res. Avery,
Versailles and Warsaw, Mo. (Ref. 2)
    1908 - Russell Allen

1605- <u>Kenneth</u> <u>Carl</u> <u>Holley</u>, (Wadleigh: Gladys
Lorene[10], Hattie Belle[9], Everett[8], Daniel
Foster[7], William Henry[6], Joseph[5], Joseph[4],
Henry[3], Robert[2], John[1]), b. February 4, 1941 in
Avery, Mo. m. June 29, 1965 in Sedalia, Mo.,
Sharon Loyola Paxton, d. of Earl Foster and
Laura Marie (Smith) Paxton, b. December 16,
1944 at Sedalia. Ed. BS in Education from
Southwest Missouri State. Occ. h.- Teacher,
w.- Beautician. Res. Pattonville (St. Louis)
and Grandview (Kansas City), Mo. (Ref. 2)
    1909 - Todd Kenneth   1911 - Shelly Christine
    1910 - Angela Loyola

1606- <u>Betty</u> <u>Ann</u> <u>Holley</u>, (Wadleigh: Gladys
Lorene[10], Hattie Belle[9], Everett[8], Daniel
Foster[7], William Henry[6], Joseph[5], Joseph[4],
Henry[3], Robert[2], John[1]), b. September 2, 1944
in Sedalia, Mo. m. October 23, 1965 in Warsaw,
Mo. Lowell Earnest Cobb, Jr., b. September 2,
1944. Occ. h.- Farmer, w.- Beautician. Res.
Camdenton and Warsaw, Mo.   (Ref. 2)
    1912 - Becky Ann   1913 - Bobbi Lynn

1607- <u>Ruby</u> <u>Belle</u> <u>Holley</u>, (Wadleigh: Gladys
Lorene[10], Hattie Belle[9], Everett[8], Daniel
Foster[7], William Henry[6], Joseph[5], Joseph[4],
Henry[3], Robert[2], John[1]), b. September 6, 1946.
m. June 1, 1968 in Warsaw, Mo. Philip Matthew
Renzulli, s. of Felix Anthony Renzulli of New
York and Genieve Antonette (Maratea) Renzulli
of Mass., b. September 27, 1945 in Springfield,
Mass. ED. h.- BS in Physical Education from
Central Missouri State Univ., w.- BS in
Education from Central Missouri State Univ.
Occ. h.- Postal Inspector, w.- Real Estate
Sales. Res. Warrensburg, Independence, Kansas
City, and Raytown, Mo., Rockville Center N.Y.,
Wichita, Kan. and Chantilly, Va.   (Ref. 2)
    1914 - Damon Mathew   1915 - Kara Marie

Issue of 1397- Charles Earl Paige and Stella Rosenmae (Edmundson) Paige:

1608- <u>Charles Earl Paige, Jr.</u>, (Wadleigh: Charles Earl[10], Hattie Belle[9], Everett[8], Daniel Foster[7], William Henry[6], Joseph[5], Joseph[4], Henry[3], Robert[2], John[1]), b. January 11, 1951 in Columbia, Mo. m. December 19, 1981 in Dallas, Tex. Barbara Jean Berry, d. of Lt. Col. Eugene and Bonita Edna (Baer) Berry, b. July 20, 1956 at Pleasanton, Cal. div. 1984. Ed. h.- BA in Radio and Television from Univ. of Missouri and graduate work at Columbia College of Broadcasting in Chicago. Occ. television news promotion. Res. Columbia, Mo. and Houston and Dallas, Texas. (Ref. 2)

1609- <u>George Leonard Paige</u>, (Wadleigh: Charles Earl[10], Hattie Belle[9], Everett[8], Daniel Foster[7], William Henry[6], Joseph[5], Joseph[4], Henry[3], Robert[2], John[1]), b. September 27, 1953 in Lexington, Mo. Occ. Draftsman. Res. Rogers, Ark. and Dallas Tex.   (Ref. 2)

25, 1954 at Lebanon. Occ. h.- machinist with Boeing Aircraft. Res. Derby, Kan. (Ref. 2)
  1916 - Tricia Ann   1918 - Kathryn Renee
  1917 - John Harold

Issue of 1398- Elmer Wright[10] Wadleigh and Ida Mae (Robinson) Wadleigh:

1611- <u>Carol Lee[11] Wadleigh</u>, (Elmer Wright[10], Louis Henry[9], Everett[8], Daniel Foster[7], William Henry[6], Joseph[5], Joseph[4], Henry[3], Robert[2], John[1]), b. January 19, 1942 in Beaumont, Tex., m. June 16, 1960 in Beaumont Odea V. McNeil, Jr., s. of Odea V. and Odessa (Spurlock) McNeil, b. March 17, 1940 at Berring, Polk Co., Tex. Res. Neches, Texas. (Ref. 2)
  1919 - Russell Glen   1921 - Clinton Wade
  1920 - Teri Lyne   1922 - Robyn Lea

1612- <u>Myrna Kay</u>[11] <u>Wadleigh</u>, (Elmer Wright[10], Louis Henry[9], Everett[8], Daniel Foster[7], William Henry[6], Joseph[5], Joseph[4], Henry[3], Robert[2], John[1]), b. November 18, 1944 in Beaumont, Tex. m. April 1, 1964 in Beaumont Charles Leon Miller, s. of Emmet Daniel and Gevena Marie (Farris) Miller, b. September 2, 1939. Res. Beaumont, Tex. (Ref. 2)

    1923 - Wendi K.   1924 - C. Craig

1613- <u>Lucinda Rae</u>[11] <u>Wadleigh</u>, (Elmer Wright[10], Louis Henry[9], Everett[8], Daniel Foster[7], William Henry[6], Joseph[5], Joseph[4], Henry[3], Robert[2], John[1]), b. September 29, 1950 in Beaumont, Tex. m. 1st June 27, 1969 in Beaumont James Winnfield Bigelow, s. of Elbert Jordon and Viola Mae Bigelow, d. June 28, 1979 at Lake Charles, Calcasieu Par., La., bur. Mimosa Pines Cemetery, Sulphur City, Calcasieu Par., La. m. 2nd July 3, 1980 Robert William Gaudet, Sr., s. of Oscar Girchard and Mary Joyce (Moreau) Gaudet, b. June 16, 1940 at Lake Charles, La. Occ. h1.- Sales, h2.- Sales, w.- Beauty consultant. Res. Lafayette, La. (Ref. 2)

1925 - 1926 by 1st husb.

    1925 - Jeffery Winnfield 1926 - Michael James

Issue of 1398- Elmer Wright[10] Wadleigh and Christine Ann (Prater) (Nobles) Wadleigh:

no issue

Issue of Loy Harris Smith and 1399- Cleo Louise (Wadleigh) Smith:

1614- <u>Juan Loy Smith</u>, (Wadleigh: Cleo Louise[10], Louis Henry[9], Everett[8], Daniel Foster[7], William Henry[6], Joseph[5], Joseph[4], Henry[3], Robert[2], John[1]), b. December 24, 1937 in Green Ridge, Mo. m. April 9, 1961 in Cole Camp, Mo. Gayle Anita Harris, d. of Raymond

Eldridge and Opal Blanche (Stone) Harris, b.
November 8, 1941 in Missouri, div. 1970. Occ.
h.- Real Estate appraisals. Ed. BS in Business
Administration from Central Missouri State
Univ. Res. Independence, Mo. (Ref. 2)
    1927 - Tracey Rene'   1928 - Anita Gay

1615- Errol Louis Smith, (Wadleigh: Cleo
Louise^{10}, Louis Henry^9, Everett^8, Daniel
Foster^7, William Henry^6, Joseph^5, Joseph^4,
Henry^3, Robert^2, John^1), b. January 28, 1944 in
Sedalia, Mo. m. August 4, 1967 in Berkley (St.
Louis), Mo. Karen Sue Griese, d. of Frank Henry
and Edythe Catherine (Wilkinson) Griese, b. May
5, 1945 at St. Louis, Mo. Ed. BS in
Agriculture Economics from Univ. of Missouri at
Columbia. Occ. h.- Regional Manager for
Ralston Purina. Res. St. John, Mo. (Ref. 2)
    1929 - Chad Errol 1930 - Matthew Shane

**Issue of Lee Ezra Templeton and 1400- Mabel
Lucille (Wadleigh) Templeton:**

1616- Sherry Sue Templeton, (Wadleigh: Mabel
Lucille^{10}, Louis Henry^9, Everett^8, Daniel
Foster^7, William Henry^6, Joseph^5, Joseph^4,
Henry^3, Robert^2, John^1), b. January 30, 1947 in
Columbus, Ga. m. 1st 1969 John Hove of
Raytown, Tex. div. 1977. m. 2nd April 21, 1979
in Honolulu, Ha. Terry Lynn Janusz, s. of Casey
and Winifred P. (Uhley) Janusz, b. March 12,
1943 at Omaha, Neb. Ed. BA in Education from
Tulsa Univ. Occ. h1.- lawyer, h2.- Sales, w.-
teacher. Res. Mannheim, W. Germany. (Ref. 2)

1617- April Lyn Templeton, (Wadleigh: Mabel
Lucille^{10}, Louis Henry^9, Everett^8, Daniel
Foster^7, William Henry^6, Joseph^5, Joseph^4,
Henry^3, Robert^2, John^1), b. November 7, 1949 in
Kansas City, Mo. m. March 27, 1971 in Raytown,
Mo. Verne Elston Schanz, Jr., s. of Verne
Elston and Betty Jane (Jackson) Schanz, b.

September 15, 1949 at Carrollton, Mo. Ed.
h.w.- BS in psychology from Tulsa Univ., Occ.
h.- Meat wholesaler, w.- teacher. Res. Kansas
City, Mo. (Ref. 2)
    1931 - Lacey Michelle 1932 - Corey Alan

1618- Oneta Jan Templeton, (Wadleigh: Mabel
Lucille[10], Louis Henry[9], Everett[8], Daniel
Foster[7], William Henry[6], Joseph[5], Joseph[4],
Henry[3], Robert[2], John[1]), b. May 17, 1956 in
Kansas City, Mo. m. April 3, 1982 in Kansas
City Arnold Howard McMann, Jr., s. of Arnold
Howard and June D. (Wheat) McMann, b. November
20, 1953 at Springfield, Ill. Ed. BSW/MSW
(Social Work) from Univ. of Missouri/Columbia.
Occ. h.- Respiratory Therapist, w.- Social
Worker. Res. Kansas City, Mo. (Ref. 2)

1619- Lisa Michele Templeton, (Wadleigh: Mabel
Lucille[10], Louis Henry[9], Everett[8], Daniel
Foster[7], William Henry[6], Joseph[5], Joseph[4],
Henry[3], Robert[2], John[1]), b. March 16, 1962.
Ed. Univ. of Missouri/Columbia and Sorbonne
Univ.-Paris. (Ref. 2)

**Issue of James Wesley Bullard III and 1401-
Iva Lou (Wadleigh) Bullard:**

1620- James Wesley Bullard IV, (Wadleigh: Iva
Lou[10], Louis Henry[9], Everett[8], Daniel Foster[7],
William Henry[6], Joseph[5], Joseph[4], Henry[3],
Robert[2], John[1]), b. October 21, 1943 in
Windsor, Mo. m. April 22, 1967 in Cameron, Mo.
Judith Carmen Ford, d. of Edwin F. and Ruby M.
(Holaday) Ford, b. March 15, 1944 at Jefferson
City, Mo. Ed. BA in biology from Southwest
Missouri State Univ., grad. studies at Menorah
Hosp. and Oral Roberts Univ., Occ. Medical
Technician and Missionary in Algeria. Res.
Springfield, Kansas City and Neosho, Mo.;
Frankfurt, W. Germany; Il Matin, Algeria;
Topeka, Kan.; Subic Bay, Philippines; and

WADLEIGH GENEALOGY   ELEVENTH GENERATION

Glenpool, Okla.   (Ref. 2)
   1933 - James Wesley   1935 - Julieta Holaday
   1934 - Krystal Joy

1621- Rebecca Cheryl Bullard, (Wadleigh: Iva
Lou[10], Louis Henry[9], Everett[8], Daniel Foster[7],
William Henry[6], Joseph[5], Joseph[4], Henry[3],
Robert[2], John[1]), b. November 15, 1946 in Rolla,
Mo. m. July 9, 1966 in Urich, Mo. Stephen
Arthur Smith, s. of William A. and Mary
Elizabeth (Mendenhall) Smith, b. January 4,
1946 at Clinton, Mo. Occ. farmer, Res. Urich,
Mo. (Ref. 2)
      1936 - Stephanie Elise
      1937 - Christopher William

1622- Loring Louis Bullard, (Wadleigh: Iva
Lou[10], Louis Henry[9], Everett[8], Daniel Foster[7],
William Henry[6], Joseph[5], Joseph[4], Henry[3],
Robert[2], John[1]), b. February 26, 1952 in
Washington, Mo. m. February 12, 1982 in Urich,
Mo. Paula Kay Ringer, b. July 22, 1953 at
Carrollton, Mo. Ed. BS in biology from Central
Missouri State Univ. Occ. h.- Sanitarian
(health service), w.- television producer
(commercials). Res. Springfield, Mo. (Ref. 2)

1623- Deborah Carol Bullard, (Wadleigh: Iva
Lou[10], Louis Henry[9], Everett[8], Daniel Foster[7],
William Henry[6], Joseph[5], Joseph[4], Henry[3],
Robert[2], John[1]), b. April 3, 1962 in
Springfield, Mo. m. August 11, 1984 in Urich,
Mo. Kirk Troy Garten, s. of Ted Roy and Mary
(Butterfield) Garten, b. September 20, 1962 at
McPherson, Kan. Ed. h.- student at Central
Missouri State Univ., w.- BS and grad. student
in psychology at Central Missouri State Univ.
Res. Warrensburg, Mo. (Ref. 2)

WADLEIGH - 320

Issue of 1402- Harvey Everett[10] Wadleigh and Shirley Jean (Williams) Wadleigh:

1624- Gregory Scott[11] Wadleigh, (Harvey Everett[10], Louis Henry[9], Everett[8], Daniel Foster[7], William Henry[6], Joseph[5], Joseph[4], Henry[3], Robert[2], John[1]), b. November 19, 1956 in Windsor, Mo. (Ref. 2)

1625- Lori Dawn[11] Wadleigh, (Harvey Everett[10], Louis Henry[9], Everett[8], Daniel Foster[7], William Henry[6], Joseph[5], Joseph[4], Henry[3], Robert[2], John[1]), b. May 26, 1961 in Kansas City, Mo. (Ref. 2)

1626- Douglas Louis[11] Wadleigh, (Harvey Everett[10], Louis Henry[9], Everett[8], Daniel Foster[7], William Henry[6], Joseph[5], Joseph[4], Henry[3], Robert[2], John[1]), b. November 8, 1964 in Kansas City, Mo. (Ref. 2)

Issue of 1404- Norwood Licklider and Charlotte Lynn (Hastings) Licklider:

1627- Alan Benton Licklider, (Wadleigh: Norwood[10], Hazel Carrie[9], Everett[8], Daniel Foster[7], William Henry[6], Joseph[5], Joseph[4], Henry[3], Robert[2], John[1]), b. November 23, 1950 in Denver, Colo. m. March 17, 1974 in Medford, Ore. Margaret Geneva Say, b. November 19, 1952. Ed. BS in Parks and Recreation Management from Oregon State Univ. Occ. retail manager, freelance photographer and Parks and Recreation Director. Res. Bellevue, Wash. (Ref. 2)
    1938 - Ryan Alan   1939 - Geneva Marie

1628- Jane Carrie Licklider, (Wadleigh: Norwood[10], Hazel Carrie[9], Everett[8], Daniel Foster[7], William Henry[6], Joseph[5], Joseph[4], Henry[3], Robert[2], John[1]), b. April 25, 1953 in Seattle, Wash. m. December 22, 1973 in

Medford, Ore. Robin Allen Espasandin, b.
November 24, 1951. Res. Juneau, Alas. (Ref. 2)
  1940 - Paul Alan   1941 - Carrie Lynn

**Issue of John Martin and 1406- Irene
(Wadleigh) Martin:**

1629- <u>Leota Faye Martin</u>, (Wadleigh: Irene[10],
Fred Elmer[9], Henry Libby[8], Daniel Foster[7],
William Henry[6], Joseph[5], Joseph[4], Henry[3],
Robert[2], John[1]), b. September 14, 1941. m.
July 2, 1961 Irvin Diggs, b. October 28, 1939.
(Ref. 1)

1630- <u>Lois Irene Martin</u>, (Wadleigh: Irene[10],
Fred Elmer[9], Henry Libby[8], Daniel Foster[7],
William Henry[6], Joseph[5], Joseph[4], Henry[3],
Robert[2], John[1]), b. June 12, 1945. m. December
19, 1961 Gerry Dunn, b. January 22, 1942.
(Ref. 1)
  1932 - Machele Denise   1933 - Jerry Elmer

**Issue of Theodore French and 1408- Edith
Marie (Wadleigh) French:**

no issue

**Issue of Douglas Hill and 1408- Edith Marie
(Wadleigh) (French) Hill:**

no issue

**Issue of Ralph Daehn and 1409- Myrtle Evelyn
(Wadleigh) Daehn:**

1631- <u>Debra Lynn Daehn</u>, (Wadleigh: Myrtle
Evelyn[10], Fred Elmer[9], Henry Libby[8], Daniel

Foster[7], William Henry[6], Joseph[5], Joseph[4], Henry[3], Robert[2], John[1]), b. May 5, 1953. m. October 15, 1972 Roderick Hathaway, b. April 25, 1952. (Ref. 1)

1632- Charles William Daehn, (Wadleigh: Myrtle Evelyn[10], Fred Elmer[9], Henry Libby[8], Daniel Foster[7], William Henry[6], Joseph[5], Joseph[4], Henry[3], Robert[2], John[1]), b. May 7, 1955. m. September 18, 1976 Vickie Seamans, b. August 25, 1958. (Ref. 1)
        1944 - Corey Ralph

Issue of 1411- Kenneth Herbert[10] Wadleigh and Bea (Peters) Wadleigh:

1633- Deborah Susan[11] Wadleigh, (Kenneth Herbert[10], Arthur Gilbert[9], Henry Libby[8], Daniel Foster[7], William Henry[6], Joseph[5], Joseph[4], Henry[3], Robert[2], John[1]), b. April 6, 1950. (Ref. 1)

1634- Patrice Marie[11] Wadleigh, (Kenneth Herbert[10], Arthur Gilbert[9], Henry Libby[8], Daniel Foster[7], William Henry[6], Joseph[5], Joseph[4], Henry[3], Robert[2], John[1]), b. August 20, 1953. (Ref. 1)

Issue of 1412- Ronald Gale[10] Wadleigh and Phyllis (Harriman) Wadleigh:

1635- Janet Susan[11] Wadleigh, (Ronald Gale[10], Arthur Gilbert[9], Henry Libby[8], Daniel Foster[7], William Henry[6], Joseph[5], Joseph[4], Henry[3], Robert[2], John[1]), b. May 29, 1956. (Ref. 1)

1636- Ronald Gale[11] Wadleigh, (Ronald Gale[10], Arthur Gilbert[9], Henry Libby[8], Daniel Foster[7], William Henry[6], Joseph[5], Joseph[4], Henry[3],

Robert^2, John^1), b. June 20, 1958, d. 1958.
(Ref. 1)

1637- <u>Alan Arthur</u>^{11} Wadleigh, (Ronald Gale^{10},
Arthur Gilbert^9, Henry Libby^8, Daniel Foster^7,
William Henry^6, Joseph^5, Joseph^4, Henry^3,
Robert^2, John^1), b. January 11, 1961. (Ref. 1)

1638- <u>Lois Ann</u>^{11} Wadleigh, (Ronald Gale^{10},
Arthur Gilbert^9, Henry Libby^8, Daniel Foster^7,
William Henry^6, Joseph^5, Joseph^4, Henry^3,
Robert^2, John^1) no data. (Ref. 1)

**Issue of 1413- Woodrow Wilson^{10} Wadleigh and
Ruby Irene (Davis) Wadleigh:**

1639- <u>Nelda Juline</u>^{11} Wadleigh, (Woodrow
Wilson^{10}, Ralph Libby^9, Henry Libby^8, Daniel
Foster^7, William Henry^6, Joseph^5, Joseph^4,
Henry^3, Robert^2, John^1), b. August 25, 1945.
(Ref. 1)

1640- <u>John Curtis</u>^{11} Wadleigh, (Woodrow
Wilson^{10}, Ralph Libby^9, Henry Libby^8, Daniel
Foster^7, William Henry^6, Joseph^5, Joseph^4,
Henry^3, Robert^2, John^1), b. March 13, 1948, d.
March 14, 1948. died in infancy. (Ref. 1)

**Issue of 1415- Charles Elmer^{10} Wadleigh and
Clo (Reed) Wadleigh:**

1641- <u>Francis Marie</u>^{11} Wadleigh, (Charles
Elmer^{10}, Ralph Libby^9, Henry Libby^8, Daniel
Foster^7, William Henry^6, Joseph^5, Joseph^4,
Henry^3, Robert^2, John^1), b. July 6, 1940. m.
January 29, 1961 Harold Hiner, b. June 28,
1938. (Ref. 1)
     1945 - Douglas Harold 1947 - Paula Marie
     1946 - Elizabeth Ann

1642- Charles Vernon[11] Wadleigh, (Charles
Elmer[10], Ralph Libby[9], Henry Libby[8], Daniel
Foster[7], William Henry[6], Joseph[5], Joseph[4],
Henry[3], Robert[2], John[1]), b. August 25, 1943.
m. January 27, 1968 Linda Gertz, b. October 26,
1942. (Ref. 1)
        1948 - Christina Lee   1949 - Vicki

Issue of Jennings Sayre and 1416- Twyla Mae (Wadleigh) Sayre:

1643- William Jennings Sayre, (Wadleigh: Twyla
Mae[10], Ralph Libby[9], Henry Libby[8], Daniel
Foster[7], William Henry[6], Joseph[5], Joseph[4],
Henry[3], Robert[2], John[1]), b. December 22, 1938.
m. April 17, 1959 Betty Elmer, b. April 17,
1941, div. 1968. (Ref. 1)
        1950 - Kevin   1951 - Sandra Mischeele

1644- Louanna Sayre, (Wadleigh: Twyla Mae[10],
Ralph Libby[9], Henry Libby[8], Daniel Foster[7],
William Henry[6], Joseph[5], Joseph[4], Henry[3],
Robert[2], John[1]), b. January 13, 1946. m.
August 12, 1962 Ronald C. Henderson, b. January
20, 1944. (Ref. 1)
        1952 - Ronda Renae

1645- Marilyn Sayre, (Wadleigh: Twyla Mae[10],
Ralph Libby[9], Henry Libby[8], Daniel Foster[7],
William Henry[6], Joseph[5], Joseph[4], Henry[3],
Robert[2], John[1]), b. September 25, 1952. m.
October 23, 1976 Niell Carmichael, b. September
4, 1953. (Ref. 1)

Issue of Marion Barklow and 1417- Helen Alice (Wadleigh) Barklow:

1646- Virginia Sue Barklow, (Wadleigh: Helen
Alice[10], Ralph Libby[9], Henry Libby[8], Daniel
Foster[7], William Henry[6], Joseph[5], Joseph[4],

Henry[3], Robert[2], John[1]), b. January 29, 1947.
(Ref. 1)

1647- Kenneth Rowen Barklow, (Wadleigh: Helen
Alice[10], Ralph Libby[9], Henry Libby[8], Daniel
Foster[7], William Henry[6], Joseph[5], Joseph[4],
Henry[3], Robert[2], John[1]), b. November 2, 1950.
(Ref. 1)

Issue of 1418- Ralph Norman[10] Wadleigh and Susanne (Schmidt) Wadleigh:

1648- Michael Norman[11] Wadleigh, (Ralph
Norman[10], Ralph Libby[9], Henry Libby[8], Daniel
Foster[7], William Henry[6], Joseph[5], Joseph[4],
Henry[3], Robert[2], John[1]), b. June 2, 1963.
(Ref. 1)

1649- Leslie Herbert[11] Wadleigh, (Ralph
Norman[10], Ralph Libby[9], Henry Libby[8], Daniel
Foster[7], William Henry[6], Joseph[5], Joseph[4],
Henry[3], Robert[2], John[1]), b. October 10, 1964.
(Ref. 1)

Issue of Royce B. Clark, Jr. and 1419- Alma Darlene (Wadleigh) Clark:

1650- Michael Royce Clark, (Wadleigh: Alma
Darlene[10], Ralph Libby[9], Henry Libby[8], Daniel
Foster[7], William Henry[6], Joseph[5], Joseph[4],
Henry[3], Robert[2], John[1]), b. November 10, 1954.
m. February 14, 1975 Vicki Louise Hammer, b.
January 18, 1955. (Ref. 1)

1651- Steven Douglas Clark, (Wadleigh: Alma
Darlene[10], Ralph Libby[9], Henry Libby[8], Daniel
Foster[7], William Henry[6], Joseph[5], Joseph[4],
Henry[3], Robert[2], John[1]), b. March 29, 1958, d.
July 1958. died in infancy. (Ref. 1)

1652- <u>Larry Brion Clark</u>, (Wadleigh: Alma Darlene[10], Ralph Libby[9], Henry Libby[8], Daniel Foster[7], William Henry[6], Joseph[5], Joseph[4], Henry[3], Robert[2], John[1]), b. July 24, 1959. (Ref. 1)

1653- <u>Diane Lynette Clark</u>, (Wadleigh: Alma Darlene[10], Ralph Libby[9], Henry Libby[8], Daniel Foster[7], William Henry[6], Joseph[5], Joseph[4], Henry[3], Robert[2], John[1]), b. May 14, 1962. (Ref. 1)

Issue of 1420- Leland Arthur[10] Wadleigh and Dorothy (Andronaco) Wadleigh:

1654- <u>Laura Joanne[11]</u> Wadleigh, (Leland Arthur[10], Ralph Libby[9], Henry Libby[8], Daniel Foster[7], William Henry[6], Joseph[5], Joseph[4], Henry[3], Robert[2], John[1]), b. June 20, 1936. (Ref. 1)

1655- <u>Linda[11]</u> Wadleigh, (Leland Arthur[10], Ralph Libby[9], Henry Libby[8], Daniel Foster[7], William Henry[6], Joseph[5], Joseph[4], Henry[3], Robert[2], John[1]), b. January 4, 1963. (Ref. 1)

Issue of 1421- Lloyd Dale[10] Wadleigh and Linda (Hildebrandt) Wadleigh:

1656- <u>Rachel[11]</u> Wadleigh, (Lloyd Dale[10], Ralph Libby[9], Henry Libby[8], Daniel Foster[7], William Henry[6], Joseph[5], Joseph[4], Henry[3], Robert[2], John[1]), b. March 7, 1970. (Ref. 1)

Issue of Robert LeeRoy Ross, Jr. and 1423-Esther Irene (Wadleigh) Ross:

1657- Irene Marie Ross, (Wadleigh: Esther Irene[10], Joseph Everett[9], Henry Libby[8], Daniel Foster[7], William Henry[6], Joseph[5], Joseph[4], Henry[3], Robert[2], John[1]), b. April 18, 1954. (Ref. 1)

1658- Kerry Lee Ross, (Wadleigh: Esther Irene[10], Joseph Everett[9], Henry Libby[8], Daniel Foster[7], William Henry[6], Joseph[5], Joseph[4], Henry[3], Robert[2], John[1]), b. August 26, 1955. m. March 12, 1966 Steven Earl Geist, b. July 15, 1952. (Ref. 1)

1659- Roberta Lynne Ross, (Wadleigh: Esther Irene[10], Joseph Everett[9], Henry Libby[8], Daniel Foster[7], William Henry[6], Joseph[5], Joseph[4], Henry[3], Robert[2], John[1]), b. October 14, 1954. (Ref. 1)

1660- Robert LeeRoy Ross, III, (Wadleigh: Esther Irene[10], Joseph Everett[9], Henry Libby[8], Daniel Foster[7], William Henry[6], Joseph[5], Joseph[4], Henry[3], Robert[2], John[1]), b. February 8, 1958. (Ref. 1)

1661- Richard Edward Ross, (Wadleigh: Esther Irene[10], Joseph Everett[9], Henry Libby[8], Daniel Foster[7], William Henry[6], Joseph[5], Joseph[4], Henry[3], Robert[2], John[1]), b. September 4, 1959. (Ref. 1)

1662- Craig William Ross, (Wadleigh: Esther Irene[10], Joseph Everett[9], Henry Libby[8], Daniel Foster[7], William Henry[6], Joseph[5], Joseph[4], Henry[3], Robert[2], John[1]), b. August 26, 1961. (Ref. 1)

Issue of Emmett L. Lane and 1424- Vere Louise (Wadleigh) Lane:

1663- <u>Allen Ross Lane</u>, (Wadleigh: Vere
Louise^{10}, Joseph Everett^9, Henry Libby^8, Daniel
Foster^7, William Henry^6, Joseph^5, Joseph^4,
Henry^3, Robert^2, John^1), b. April 3, 1943. m.
March 12, 1966 Cheryl Burton, b. July 11, 1943.
(Ref. 1)

1664- <u>Caren Margaret Lane</u>, (Wadleigh: Vere
Louise^{10}, Joseph Everett^9, Henry Libby^8, Daniel
Foster^7, William Henry^6, Joseph^5, Joseph^4,
Henry^3, Robert^2, John^1), b. November 20, 1944.
m. October 31, 1965 David Onsgard, b. November
26, 1943, d. 1969. (Ref. 1)

1665- <u>Christine Louise Lane</u>, (Wadleigh: Vere
Louise^{10}, Joseph Everett^9, Henry Libby^8, Daniel
Foster^7, William Henry^6, Joseph^5, Joseph^4,
Henry^3, Robert^2, John^1), b. June 22, 1949. m.
November 21, 1969 Russell Law, b. May 3, 1949,
d. 1976. (Ref. 1)

1666- <u>Forrest Emmitt Lane</u>, (Wadleigh: Vere
Louise^{10}, Joseph Everett^9, Henry Libby^8, Daniel
Foster^7, William Henry^6, Joseph^5, Joseph^4,
Henry^3, Robert^2, John^1), b. December 21, 1955.
(Ref. 1)

1667- <u>Murray Wadleigh Lane</u>, (Wadleigh: Vere
Louise^{10}, Joseph Everett^9, Henry Libby^8, Daniel
Foster^7, William Henry^6, Joseph^5, Joseph^4,
Henry^3, Robert^2, John^1), b. January 25, 1958.
(Ref. 1)

1668- <u>Holly Diane Lane</u>, (Wadleigh: Vere
Louise^{10}, Joseph Everett^9, Henry Libby^8, Daniel
Foster^7, William Henry^6, Joseph^5, Joseph^4,
Henry^3, Robert^2, John^1), b. December 29, 1964.
(Ref. 1)

Issue of 1421- Roger Alan[10] Wadleigh and Montine (Pruitt) Wadleigh:

1669- Alan Michael[11] Wadleigh, (Roger Alan[10], Joseph Everett[9], Henry Libby[8], Daniel Foster[7], William Henry[6], Joseph[5], Joseph[4], Henry[3], Robert[2], John[1]), b. June 15, 1954. (Ref. 1)

Issue of 1426- John Richard[10] Wadleigh and Lyndall (Brown) Wadleigh:

1670- Linda Louise[11] Wadleigh, (John Richard[10], Joseph Everett[9], Henry Libby[8], Daniel Foster[7], William Henry[6], Joseph[5], Joseph[4], Henry[3], Robert[2], John[1]), b. April 18, 1959. (Ref. 1)

1671- Sharon Kaye[11] Wadleigh, (John Richard[10], Joseph Everett[9], Henry Libby[8], Daniel Foster[7], William Henry[6], Joseph[5], Joseph[4], Henry[3], Robert[2], John[1]), b. December 31, 1960. (Ref. 1)

1672- John Joseph[11] Wadleigh, (John Richard[10], Joseph Everett[9], Henry Libby[8], Daniel Foster[7], William Henry[6], Joseph[5], Joseph[4], Henry[3], Robert[2], John[1]), b. July 16, 1962. (Ref. 1)

1673- Kenneth Lee[11] Wadleigh, (John Richard[10], Joseph Everett[9], Henry Libby[8], Daniel Foster[7], William Henry[6], Joseph[5], Joseph[4], Henry[3], Robert[2], John[1]), b. December 1, 1965. (Ref. 1)

Issue of Charles Gimer and 1427- Eileen Marie (Wadleigh) Gimer:

1674- Peggy Eileen Gimer, (Wadleigh: Eileen Marie[10], Herbert Calvin[9], Henry Libby[8], Daniel Foster[7], William Henry[6], Joseph[5], Joseph[4], Henry[3], Robert[2], John[1]), b. April 29, 1950. (Ref. 1)

1675- <u>Mary Ellen Gimer</u>, (Wadleigh: Eileen
Marie[10], Herbert Calvin[9], Henry Libby[8], Daniel
Foster[7], William Henry[6], Joseph[5], Joseph[4],
Henry[3], Robert[2], John[1]), b. August 18, 1953.
(Ref. 1)

1676- <u>Robert Charles Gimer</u>, (Wadleigh: Eileen
Marie[10], Herbert Calvin[9], Henry Libby[8], Daniel
Foster[7], William Henry[6], Joseph[5], Joseph[4],
Henry[3], Robert[2], John[1]), b. February 22, 1955.
(Ref. 1)

1677- <u>Kathleen Louise Gimer</u>, (Wadleigh: Eileen
Marie[10], Herbert Calvin[9], Henry Libby[8], Daniel
Foster[7], William Henry[6], Joseph[5], Joseph[4],
Henry[3], Robert[2], John[1]), b. April 12, 1957.
(Ref. 1)

**Issue of 1428- Robert Wilson[10] Wadleigh and
Mary Ann (Fletcher) Wadleigh:**

1678- <u>Patti Ann[11]</u> Wadleigh, (Robert Wilson[10],
Herbert Calvin[9], Henry Libby[8], Daniel Foster[7],
William Henry[6], Joseph[5], Joseph[4], Henry[3],
Robert[2], John[1]), b. February 1, 1958. (Ref. 1)

1679- <u>Robert Mark[11]</u> Wadleigh, (Robert Wilson[10],
Herbert Calvin[9], Henry Libby[8], Daniel Foster[7],
William Henry[6], Joseph[5], Joseph[4], Henry[3],
Robert[2], John[1]), b. April 24, 1960. (Ref. 1)

**Issue of Ernest Klein and 1429- Elva Aldina
(Wadleigh) Klein:**

1680- <u>Elva Myreen Klein</u>, (Wadleigh: Elva
Aldina[10], Harold Brewster[9], Henry Libby[8],
Daniel Foster[7], William Henry[6], Joseph[5],
Joseph[4], Henry[3], Robert[2], John[1]), b. December
14, 1940. m. 1st April 16, 1960 Fred Dowdy, b.

September 15, 1929, div. m. 2nd February 27,
1971 Richard Stroup, b. February 27, 1971.
(Ref. 1)   1953 - 1956 by 1st h.
    1953 - Loren Bean   1955 - Valerie Lynn
    1954 - Denise Eileen 1956 - Scott Douglas

1681- Ernestine Gay Klein, (Wadleigh: Elva
Aldina[10], Harold Brewster[9], Henry Libby[8],
Daniel Foster[7], William Henry[6], Joseph[5],
Joseph[4], Henry[3], Robert[2], John[1]), b. March 9,
1942. m. 1st May 1, 1964 Jerry Wall, b.
January 13, 1940, div. m. 2nd Bobby L.
Waddell, b. December 28, 1942. (Ref. 1) 1957 -
1958 by 1st husb.
   1957 - Keith Darren 1958 - Melita Lanette

1682- Norvyn Bruce Klein, (Wadleigh: Elva
Aldina[10], Harold Brewster[9], Henry Libby[8],
Daniel Foster[7], William Henry[6], Joseph[5],
Joseph[4], Henry[3], Robert[2], John[1]), b. August 14,
1948. m. 1st November 2, 1968 Bonnie Jean
Ferdig, b. December 14, 1948. div. m. 2nd May
24, 1974 Donna Carol Smark, b. April 30, 1949.
(Ref. 1)   1959 by 1st wife, 1960 - 1961 by 2nd
wife.
    1959 - Deanna Marie 1961 - Jeramy Austin
    1960 - Norvyn Michael

**Issue of Wilbur Lewis Springer and 1429- Elva
Aldina (Wadleigh) (Klein) Springer:**

no issue

**Issue of Kenneth Dayton and 1430- Joyce Ellen
(Wadleigh) Dayton:**

1683- Cheryle Ann Dayton, (Wadleigh: Joyce
Ellen[10], Harold Brewster[9], Henry Libby[8], Daniel
Foster[7], William Henry[6], Joseph[5], Joseph[4],
Henry[3], Robert[2], John[1]), b. March 25, 1947. m.

September 2, 1968 Kenneth Kinkel, b. October
29, 1943. (Ref. 1)
    1962 - Kenneth William   1963 - Kevin Allen

1684- Judith Lynne Dayton, (Wadleigh: Joyce
Ellen[10], Harold Brewster[9], Henry Libby[8], Daniel
Foster[7], William Henry[6], Joseph[5], Joseph[4],
Henry[3], Robert[2], John[1]), b. November 23, 1949.
m. November 18, 1969 William Allen Moore, no
additional data. (Ref. 1)
    1964 - Tammy Lynn

1685- Katherine Jeanne Dayton, (Wadleigh:
Joyce Ellen[10], Harold Brewster[9], Henry Libby[8],
Daniel Foster[7], William Henry[6], Joseph[5],
Joseph[4], Henry[3], Robert[2], John[1]), b. June 19,
1951. (Ref. 1)

**Issue of 1432- Calvin Herbert[10] Wadleigh and
Phyllis (LaRoe) (LeKar) Wadleigh:**

1686- Linda Diane[11] Wadleigh, (Calvin
Herbert[10], Harold Brewster[9], Henry Libby[8],
Daniel Foster[7], William Henry[6], Joseph[5],
Joseph[4], Henry[3], Robert[2], John[1]), b. June 18,
1958. m. David Martinez, no additional data.
(Ref. 1)
    1965 - Diana Jo

1687- Steven Calvin[11] Wadleigh, (Calvin
Herbert[10], Harold Brewster[9], Henry Libby[8],
Daniel Foster[7], William Henry[6], Joseph[5],
Joseph[4], Henry[3], Robert[2], John[1]), b. July 8,
1959. (Ref. 1)

1688- Janet Sue[11] Wadleigh, (Calvin Herbert[10],
Harold Brewster[9], Henry Libby[8], Daniel Foster[7],
William Henry[6], Joseph[5], Joseph[4], Henry[3],
Robert[2], John[1]), b. August 2, 1960. (Ref. 1)

1689- <u>Michelle Rae Ann</u>[11] Wadleigh, (Calvin
Herbert[10], Harold Brewster[9], Henry Libby[8],
Daniel Foster[7], William Henry[6], Joseph[5],
Joseph[4], Henry[3], Robert[2], John[1]), b. May 6,
1974. (Ref. 1)

**Issue of 1434- Donald Lee[10] Wadleigh and Mary
Jane (Trueba) Wadleigh:**

1690- <u>Michael John</u>[11] Wadleigh, (Donald Lee[10],
Eugene Henry[9], Henry Libby[8], Daniel Foster[7],
William Henry[6], Joseph[5], Joseph[4], Henry[3],
Robert[2], John[1]), b. February 18, 1957 (Ref. 1)

1691- <u>Mark James</u>[11] Wadleigh, (Donald Lee[10],
Eugene Henry[9], Henry Libby[8], Daniel Foster[7],
William Henry[6], Joseph[5], Joseph[4], Henry[3],
Robert[2], John[1]), b. July 29, 1958. (Ref. 1)

1692- <u>Monica Jill</u>[11] Wadleigh, (Donald Lee[10],
Eugene Henry[9], Henry Libby[8], Daniel Foster[7],
William Henry[6], Joseph[5], Joseph[4], Henry[3],
Robert[2], John[1]), b. November 2, 1959, d. May
30, 1976. died in adolescence. (Ref. 1)

**Issue of 1435- Robert Henry[10] Wadleigh and
Ruth (Hatton) Wadleigh:**

1693- <u>Dale Eugene</u>[11] Wadleigh, (Robert Henry[10],
Eugene Henry[9], Henry Libby[8], Daniel Foster[7],
William Henry[6], Joseph[5], Joseph[4], Henry[3],
Robert[2], John[1]), b. May 2, 1954. m. May 11,
1977 Toni Marble, no additional data. (Ref. 1)

1694- <u>Donna Lee</u>[11] Wadleigh, (Robert Henry[10],
Eugene Henry[9], Henry Libby[8], Daniel Foster[7],
William Henry[6], Joseph[5], Joseph[4], Henry[3],
Robert[2], John[1]), b. August 16, 1955. m. August
17, 1976 Carl Benson, no other data. (Ref. 1)

1695- <u>Barbara Sue</u>[11] <u>Wadleigh</u>, (Robert Henry[10], Eugene Henry[9], Henry Libby[8], Daniel Foster[7], William Henry[6], Joseph[5], Joseph[4], Henry[3], Robert[2], John[1]), b. October 12, 1957. (Ref. 1)

1696- <u>Robert Allen</u>[11] <u>Wadleigh</u>, (Robert Henry[10], Eugene Henry[9], Henry Libby[8], Daniel Foster[7], William Henry[6], Joseph[5], Joseph[4], Henry[3], Robert[2], John[1]), b. August 20, 1959. (Ref. 1)

1697- <u>Nancy Ellen</u>[11] <u>Wadleigh</u>, (Robert Henry[10], Eugene Henry[9], Henry Libby[8], Daniel Foster[7], William Henry[6], Joseph[5], Joseph[4], Henry[3], Robert[2], John[1]), b. February 28, 1965. (Ref. 1)

Issue of 1436- Glen Eugene[10] Wadleigh and Frances (McIntosh) Wadleigh:

1698- <u>Karen Sue</u>[11] <u>Wadleigh</u>, (Glen Eugene[10], Eugene Henry[9], Henry Libby[8], Daniel Foster[7], William Henry[6], Joseph[5], Joseph[4], Henry[3], Robert[2], John[1]), b. August 4, 1951. m. September 26, 1970 Robert Scott Rice, no additional data. (Ref. 1)
        1966 - Rebecca Thayer

1699- <u>Michele Allyn</u>[11] <u>Wadleigh</u>, (Glen Eugene[10], Eugene Henry[9], Henry Libby[8], Daniel Foster[7], William Henry[6], Joseph[5], Joseph[4], Henry[3], Robert[2], John[1]), b. December 3, 1952. m. February 12, 1973 James Sides, b. October 20, 1952. (Ref. 1)
        1967 - Colin James

1700- <u>Debra Frances</u>[11] <u>Wadleigh</u>, (Glen Eugene[10], Eugene Henry[9], Henry Libby[8], Daniel Foster[7], William Henry[6], Joseph[5], Joseph[4], Henry[3], Robert[2], John[1]), b. October 27, 1955. m. October 15, 1974 Charles Baker, b. August 8,

1952. (Ref. 1)
     1968 - Justin Glen

1701- <u>Marianne</u>[11] <u>Wadleigh</u>, (Glen Eugene[10], Eugene Henry[9], Henry Libby[8], Daniel Foster[7], William Henry[6], Joseph[5], Joseph[4], Henry[3], Robert[2], John[1]), b. February 6, 1958. m. September 10, 1977 Philip McNamara, b. July 6, 1957. (Ref. 1)

Issue of Karl Enns and 1437- Mable Leota (Nice) Enns:

1702- <u>Bernice Leota</u> Enns, (Wadleigh: Mable Leota[10], Edna Rose[9], Henry Libby[8], Daniel Foster[7], William Henry[6], Joseph[5], Joseph[4], Henry[3], Robert[2], John[1]), b. October 13, 1934. m. September 6, 1958 Clay Markle, b. October 18, 1932. (Ref. 1)
          1969 - Lynne Anne   1971 - Diane Elise
          1970 - Larry Allen   1972 - Cindy Lee

1703- <u>Vernon Royse</u> Enns, (Wadleigh: Mable Leota[10], Edna Rose[9], Henry Libby[8], Daniel Foster[7], William Henry[6], Joseph[5], Joseph[4], Henry[3], Robert[2], John[1]), b. July 2, 1936. m. July 6, 1958 Sue Long, b. August 24, 1939. (Ref. 1)
          1973 - Kimberly Sue   1975 - Douglas Brent
          1974 - Vicki Lee   1976 - Terri David

1704- <u>Ronald Karl</u> Enns, (Wadleigh: Mable Leota[10], Edna Rose[9], Henry Libby[8], Daniel Foster[7], William Henry[6], Joseph[5], Joseph[4], Henry[3], Robert[2], John[1]), b. August 10, 1938. m. March 15, 1959 Marilyn Kaye Watters, b. August 26, 1940. (Ref. 1)
          1977 - Donnie Ray   1979 - Gary Wayne
          1978 - Kathy Dawn   1980 - Sherri Renee

1705- Kenneth Eugene Enns, (Wadleigh: Mable
Leota[10], Edna Rose[9], Henry Libby[8], Daniel
Foster[7], William Henry[6], Joseph[5], Joseph[4],
Henry[3], Robert[2], John[1]), b. July 12, 1944. m.
August 28, 1970 Karen Sue Seipp, b. March 17,
1949. (Ref. 2)
    1981 - Jeffrey Scott

1706- Karen Faye Enns, (Wadleigh: Mable
Leota[10], Edna Rose[9], Henry Libby[8], Daniel
Foster[7], William Henry[6], Joseph[5], Joseph[4],
Henry[3], Robert[2], John[1]), b. March 28, 1953. m.
June 8, 1974 Michael W. Van Galder, b. April
14, 1953. (Ref. 1)

1707- Carolyn Rose Enns, (Wadleigh: Mable
Leota[10], Edna Rose[9], Henry Libby[8], Daniel
Foster[7], William Henry[6], Joseph[5], Joseph[4],
Henry[3], Robert[2], John[1]), b. May 20, 1958.
(Ref. 1)

**Issue of 1438- Harry Alfred Nice and
Magdalena (Edelman) Nice:**

1708- Stanley Ray Nice, (Wadleigh: Harry
Alfred[10], Edna Rose[9], Henry Libby[8], Daniel
Foster[7], William Henry[6], Joseph[5], Joseph[4],
Henry[3], Robert[2], John[1]), b. November 13, 1944.
m. February 12, 1964 Marjorie Brunk, b. Sep-
tember 4, 1946, d. October 29, 1969. (Ref. 1)
    1982 - Carla Sue   1983 - Kevin Ray

1709- Mary Joyce Nice, (Wadleigh: Harry
Alfred[10], Edna Rose[9], Henry Libby[8], Daniel
Foster[7], William Henry[6], Joseph[5], Joseph[4],
Henry[3], Robert[2], John[1]), b. December 22, 1945.
m. August 22, 1970 Lee Gingerich, b. February
24, 1946. (Ref. 1)
    1984 - Cheryle Ann

1710- <u>Lester</u> <u>Wayne</u> <u>Nice</u>, (Wadleigh: Harry
Alfred[10], Edna Rose[9], Henry Libby[8], Daniel
Foster[7], William Henry[6], Joseph[5], Joseph[4],
Henry[3], Robert[2], John[1]), b. June 2, 1947. m.
June 7, 1968 Linda Birky, b. July 14, 1948.
(Ref. 1)
        1985 - Darrel Jay

1711- <u>Eldon</u> <u>Lee</u> <u>Nice</u>, (Wadleigh: Harry
Alfred[10], Edna Rose[9], Henry Libby[8], Daniel
Foster[7], William Henry[6], Joseph[5], Joseph[4],
Henry[3], Robert[2], John[1]), b. October 21, 1950.
m. November 28, 1970 Linda Burks, b. October
30, 1951. Occ. Minister. (Ref. 1)
   1986 - Jeffrey Lee   1987 - Tamara Michele

1712- <u>James</u> <u>Clifford</u> <u>Nice</u>, (Wadleigh: Harry
Alfred[10], Edna Rose[9], Henry Libby[8], Daniel
Foster[7], William Henry[6], Joseph[5], Joseph[4],
Henry[3], Robert[2], John[1]), b. February 14, 1953.
(Ref. 1)

1713- <u>Esther</u> <u>Rose</u> <u>Nice</u>, (Wadleigh: Harry
Alfred[10], Edna Rose[9], Henry Libby[8], Daniel
Foster[7], William Henry[6], Joseph[5], Joseph[4],
Henry[3], Robert[2], John[1]), b. July 21, 1955, d.
July 22, 1955. died in infancy. (Ref. 1)

1714- <u>Edward</u> <u>Eugene</u> <u>Nice</u>, (Wadleigh: Harry
Alfred[10], Edna Rose[9], Henry Libby[8], Daniel
Foster[7], William Henry[6], Joseph[5], Joseph[4],
Henry[3], Robert[2], John[1]), b. August 10, 1963.
(Ref. 1)

**Issue of Clayton Wolfer and 1439- Ida Rose
(Nice) Wolfer:**

1715- <u>Doris</u> <u>LaVerne</u> <u>Wolfer</u>, (Wadleigh: Ida
Rose[10], Edna Rose[9], Henry Libby[8], Daniel
Foster[7], William Henry[6], Joseph[5], Joseph[4],

Henry^3, Robert^2, John^1), b. August 4, 1938. m.
March 7, 1958 Marion Knox, b. October 27, 1937.
(Ref. 1)
   1988 - Duane Allen   1990 - Larry Leone
   1989 - Steven Louis   1991 - Daryl Vernon

1716- Dianne Joyce Wolfer, (Wadleigh: Ida
Rose^{10}, Edna Rose^9, Henry Libby^8, Daniel
Foster^7, William Henry^6, Joseph^5, Joseph^4,
Henry^3, Robert^2, John^1), b. July 1, 1939. m.
August 14, 1959 Millard Paulus, b. March 16,
1936. (Ref. 1)
   1992 - Marlin Dean   1994 - Leon Daniel
   1993 - Karen Louis   1995 - Janet Marie

1717- Alta Rose Wolfer, (Wadleigh: Ida Rose^{10},
Edna Rose^9, Henry Libby^8, Daniel Foster^7,
William Henry^6, Joseph^5, Joseph^4, Henry^3,
Robert^2, John^1), b. September 27, 1942. m.
December 27, 1965 Kenneth Lee Gerig, b. July 8,
1941. (Ref. 1)
   1996 - Arlan Kent 1998 - Lynette Rose
   1997 - Galen Lewis

1718- Miriam Jean Wolfer, (Wadleigh: Ida
Rose^{10}, Edna Rose^9, Henry Libby^8, Daniel
Foster^7, William Henry^6, Joseph^5, Joseph^4,
Henry^3, Robert^2, John^1), b. April 24, 1948. m.
March 9, 1968 Gary Hooley, b. June 13, 1948.
(Ref. 1)
   1999 - Randell Eric   2000 - Vicky Leigh

1719- Marvin Doyle Wolfer, (Wadleigh: Ida
Rose^{10}, Edna Rose^9, Henry Libby^8, Daniel
Foster^7, William Henry^6, Joseph^5, Joseph^4,
Henry^3, Robert^2, John^1), b. October 11, 1949.
m. March 21, 1970 Louise Weldon, b. November
20, 1950. (Ref. 1)
    2001 - John Phillip   2003 - Brian Heath
    2002 - Monica Ann   2004 - Sue Ann Joy

Issue of 1440- Howard Fred Nice and Luella (Wolfer) Nice:

1720- <u>Marlene Yovonne Nice</u>, (Wadleigh: Howard Fred^{10}, Edna Rose^{9}, Henry Libby^{8}, Daniel Foster^{7}, William Henry^{6}, Joseph^{5}, Joseph^{4}, Henry^{3}, Robert^{2}, John^{1}), b. January 8, 1943. m. June 14, 1964 Stanley Kroff, b. July 6, 1943. (Ref. 1)
    2005 - Jeremy Arthur   2006 - Carrie Heather

1721- <u>Judith Ann Nice</u>, (Wadleigh: Howard Fred^{10}, Edna Rose^{9}, Henry Libby^{8}, Daniel Foster^{7}, William Henry^{6}, Joseph^{5}, Joseph^{4}, Henry^{3}, Robert^{2}, John^{1}), b. July 1, 1944. m. March 20, 1972 Stanley Jones, b. February 23, 1947. (Ref. 1)

1722- <u>Loren Howard Nice</u>, (Wadleigh: Howard Fred^{10}, Edna Rose^{9}, Henry Libby^{8}, Daniel Foster^{7}, William Henry^{6}, Joseph^{5}, Joseph^{4}, Henry^{3}, Robert^{2}, John^{1}), b. January 8, 1948. m. December 16, 1966 Susan Meyers, b. October 20, 1947. (Ref. 1)
    2007 - Teresa Ann   2008 - Mathew Loren

1723- <u>Gary Duane Nice</u>, (Wadleigh: Howard Fred^{10}, Edna Rose^{9}, Henry Libby^{8}, Daniel Foster^{7}, William Henry^{6}, Joseph^{5}, Joseph^{4}, Henry^{3}, Robert^{2}, John^{1}), b. September 28, 1949. m. June 7, 1975 Esther Zook, b. October 4, 1953. (Ref. 1)

1724- <u>Dennis Leone Nice</u>, (Wadleigh: Howard Fred^{10}, Edna Rose^{9}, Henry Libby^{8}, Daniel Foster^{7}, William Henry^{6}, Joseph^{5}, Joseph^{4}, Henry^{3}, Robert^{2}, John^{1}), b. September 22, 1954. m. August 24, 1974 Margaret Stauffer, b. May 15, 1956. (Ref. 1)
    2009 - Angela Michelle   2010 - Christine Dawn

1725- <u>Douglas Dean Nice</u>, (Wadleigh: Howard Fred^{10}, Edna Rose^9, Henry Libby^8, Daniel Foster^7, William Henry^6, Joseph^5, Joseph^4, Henry^3, Robert^2, John^1), b. March 10, 1962. (Ref. 1)

Issue of Robert Coblentz and 1441- Ruth Ellen (Nice) Coblentz:

1726- <u>Freddie LaVerne Coblentz</u>, (Wadleigh: Ruth Ellen^{10}, Edna Rose^9, Henry Libby^8, Daniel Foster^7, William Henry^6, Joseph^5, Joseph^4, Henry^3, Robert^2, John^1), b. May 18, 1944. m. 1st September 19, 1964 Marilyn Ann Blanchard, div. 1966. m. 2nd August 12, 1967 Pamela Stevens, no additional data. (Ref. 1) 2011 by 1st w., 2012 by 2nd w.
        2011 - Kimberly Kae   2012 - Corey Allen

1727- <u>Daniel Keith Coblentz</u>, (Wadleigh: Ruth Ellen^{10}, Edna Rose^9, Henry Libby^8, Daniel Foster^7, William Henry^6, Joseph^5, Joseph^4, Henry^3, Robert^2, John^1), b. October 20, 1945. m. February 21, 1964 Kathleen Vera Shenk, b. April 9, 1945. (Ref. 1)
        2013 - Glynnis Dawn   2014 - Todd Daniel

1728- <u>Patricia Ellen Coblentz</u>, (Wadleigh: Ruth Ellen^{10}, Edna Rose^9, Henry Libby^8, Daniel Foster^7, William Henry^6, Joseph^5, Joseph^4, Henry^3, Robert^2, John^1), b. May 25, 1947. m. March 14, 1970 Wendell Harry Lux, b. June 25, 1948. (Ref. 1)

1729- <u>Thomas Robert Coblentz</u>, (Wadleigh: Ruth Ellen^{10}, Edna Rose^9, Henry Libby^8, Daniel Foster^7, William Henry^6, Joseph^5, Joseph^4, Henry^3, Robert^2, John^1), b. March 12, 1949. (Ref. 1)

1730- Gaylord Ralph Coblentz, (Wadleigh: Ruth Ellen[10], Edna Rose[9], Henry Libby[8], Daniel Foster[7], William Henry[6], Joseph[5], Joseph[4], Henry[3], Robert[2], John[1]), b. September 26, 1952. m. October 31, 1974 Debbie Diane Hendricks, no additional data. (Ref. 1)
        2015 - Brandy Ann

1731- Debra Diane Coblentz, (Wadleigh: Ruth Ellen[10], Edna Rose[9], Henry Libby[8], Daniel Foster[7], William Henry[6], Joseph[5], Joseph[4], Henry[3], Robert[2], John[1]), b. August 27, 1955. m. March 1, 1975 Gary John Sherva, no additional data. (Ref. 1)

Issue of Lynn Wolfer and 1442- Dorothy Mae (Nice) Wolfer:

1732- Lynn Eileen Wolfer, (Wadleigh: Dorothy Mae[10], Edna Rose[9], Henry Libby[8], Daniel Foster[7], William Henry[6], Joseph[5], Joseph[4], Henry[3], Robert[2], John[1]), b. August 31, 1947. m. September 1, 1965 Floyd Eugene Nelson, b. May 9, 1945. (Ref. 1)
        2016 - Karen Lynann   2017 - Tracy Camille

1733- Kathryn Faye Wolfer, (Wadleigh: Dorothy Mae[10], Edna Rose[9], Henry Libby[8], Daniel Foster[7], William Henry[6], Joseph[5], Joseph[4], Henry[3], Robert[2], John[1]), b. September 15, 1949. m. May 2, 1970 Timothy Wayne Zook, b. January 19, 1950. (Ref. 1)
        2018 - Anthony Wayne   2020 - Sheldon Lance
        2019 - Leighton Grant

1734- Ronald Reno Wolfer, (Wadleigh: Dorothy Mae[10], Edna Rose[9], Henry Libby[8], Daniel Foster[7], William Henry[6], Joseph[5], Joseph[4], Henry[3], Robert[2], John[1]), b. May 28, 1951. m. September 15, 1972 Rowene Rae Burkey, b. March 22, 1952. (Ref. 1)
        2021 - Elroy Shad   2022 - Michael William

1735- <u>Beverly Ann Wolfer</u>, (Wadleigh: Dorothy
Mae[10], Edna Rose[9], Henry Libby[8], Daniel
Foster[7], William Henry[6], Joseph[5], Joseph[4],
Henry[3], Robert[2], John[1]), b. September 17, 1963.
(Ref. 1)

1736- <u>Byron Duane Wolfer</u>, (Wadleigh: Dorothy
Mae[10], Edna Rose[9], Henry Libby[8], Daniel
Foster[7], William Henry[6], Joseph[5], Joseph[4],
Henry[3], Robert[2], John[1]), b. December 17, 1963.
(Ref. 1)

**Issue of Theron Edward Killian and 1443-
Gwendolyn Alta (Nice) Killian:**

1737- <u>Barbara Sue Killian</u>, (Wadleigh:
Gwendolyn Alta[10], Edna Rose[9], Henry Libby[8],
Daniel Foster[7], William Henry[6], Joseph[5],
Joseph[4], Henry[3], Robert[2], John[1]), b. October
30, 1951. m. 1st Joe Beauchamp, div. 1970. m.
2nd May 4, 1971 Alvin LeRoy Taylor, b. November
23, 1950. (Ref. 1) 2023 - 2024 by 1st h.,
2025 by 2nd h.
   2023 - Calinia Jo 2025 - Kevin Leroy
   2024 - Michele Deanne

1738- <u>Reno Richard Killian</u>, (Wadleigh:
Gwendolyn Alta[10], Edna Rose[9], Henry Libby[8],
Daniel Foster[7], William Henry[6], Joseph[5],
Joseph[4], Henry[3], Robert[2], John[1]), b. January 3,
1953. m. December 21, 1973 Catherine Camp, b.
April 13, 1955. (Ref. 1)
   2026 - Richard Roy

1739- <u>James Edward Killian</u>, (Wadleigh:
Gwendolyn Alta[10], Edna Rose[9], Henry Libby[8],
Daniel Foster[7], William Henry[6], Joseph[5],
Joseph[4], Henry[3], Robert[2], John[1]), b. April 20,
1958. m. January 25, 1977 Viki Lee Anderson,
b. February 11, 1956. (Ref. 1)

1740- <u>Sandra Marie Killian</u>, (Wadleigh:
Gwendolyn Alta[10], Edna Rose[9], Henry Libby[8],
Daniel Foster[7], William Henry[6], Joseph[5],
Joseph[4], Henry[3], Robert[2], John[1]), b. January
20, 1960. m. March 19, 1976 Jose Manuel
Pedraza, b. March 20, 1953. (Ref. 1)
    2027 - Tanya Lynn

**Issue of 1444- Robert Louis Nice and Fern Amy
(Roth) Nice:**

1741- <u>Linda Luanna Nice</u>, (Wadleigh: Robert
Louis[10], Edna Rose[9], Henry Libby[8], Daniel
Foster[7], William Henry[6], Joseph[5], Joseph[4],
Henry[3], Robert[2], John[1]), b. November 4, 1954.
m. March 15, 1974 Edward J. Ebbs, b. July 19,
1954. (Ref. 1)

1742- <u>Carmen Marie Nice</u>, (Wadleigh: Robert
Louis[10], Edna Rose[9], Henry Libby[8], Daniel
Foster[7], William Henry[6], Joseph[5], Joseph[4],
Henry[3], Robert[2], John[1]), b. June 25, 1957, d.
April 15, 1969. died in adolescence. (Ref. 1)

1743- <u>Julia Rene Nice</u>, (Wadleigh: Robert
Louis[10], Edna Rose[9], Henry Libby[8], Daniel
Foster[7], William Henry[6], Joseph[5], Joseph[4],
Henry[3], Robert[2], John[1]), b. September 26, 1958.
(Ref. 1)

1744- <u>Kendra Lynette Nice</u>, (Wadleigh: Robert
Louis[10], Edna Rose[9], Henry Libby[8], Daniel
Foster[7], William Henry[6], Joseph[5], Joseph[4],
Henry[3], Robert[2], John[1]), b. December 7, 1961.
(Ref. 1)

Issue of Harrison Gray Otis Meyer and 1445-Leona Evalyn (Rector) Meyer:

1745- <u>Laurence Gray Meyer</u>, (Wadleigh: Harrison Gray Otis[10], Mary Emma[9], Henry Libby[8], Daniel Foster[7], William Henry[6], Joseph[5], Joseph[4], Henry[3], Robert[2], John[1]), b. September 20, 1946 in Medford, Jackson Co., Ore. m. June 21, 1969 in Severn Park, Anne Arundel Co., Md. Sharon Marie Katski, b. November 28, 1949 in Anapolis, Anne Arundel Co., Md. (Ref. 1)
    2028 - Lawrence Gray

1746- <u>Charles Edwin Meyer</u>, (Wadleigh: Harrison Gray Otis[10], Mary Emma[9], Henry Libby[8], Daniel Foster[7], William Henry[6], Joseph[5], Joseph[4], Henry[3], Robert[2], John[1]), b. May 15, 1951 in Medford, Jackson Co., Ore. (Ref. 1)

1747- <u>Elizabeth Annette Meyer</u>, (Wadleigh: Harrison Gray Otis[10], Mary Emma[9], Henry Libby[8], Daniel Foster[7], William Henry[6], Joseph[5], Joseph[4], Henry[3], Robert[2], John[1]), b. July 29, 1955 in Medford, Ore. m. January 15, 1977 in Medford, Ore. Kenneth Wayne Joy, b. January 10, 1956 in Oakland, Alameda Co., Cal. (Ref. 1)

1748- <u>Jeffrey Wayne Meyer</u>, (Wadleigh: Harrison Gray Otis[10], Mary Emma[9], Henry Libby[8], Daniel Foster[7], William Henry[6], Joseph[5], Joseph[4], Henry[3], Robert[2], John[1]), b. August 12, 1957 in Medford, Ore., d. August 17, 1970 in Central Point, Ore. died in adolescence. (Ref. 1)

Issue of 1446- John Orland Rector and Netta Rose (Brown) (Lowney) Rector:

no issue

Issue of James Henry Heffler, Jr. and 1447- Velma JoAnn (Rector) Heffler:

1749- <u>Charlene Marie Heffler</u>, (Wadleigh: James Henry[10], Mary Emma[9], Henry Libby[8], Daniel Foster[7], William Henry[6], Joseph[5], Joseph[4], Henry[3], Robert[2], John[1]), b. August 22, 1955 in Portland, Washington Co., Ore. m. July 23, 1972 Bruce Ernest Gilbert, b. November 4, 1947 in Portland, Ore. (Ref. 1)
　　2029 - Brenda K.   2030 - Jeana Marie

1750- <u>James Henry Heffler, III</u>, (Wadleigh: James Henry[10], Mary Emma[9], Henry Libby[8], Daniel Foster[7], William Henry[6], Joseph[5], Joseph[4], Henry[3], Robert[2], John[1]), b. September 6, 1956 in Portland, Ore. (Ref. 1)

1751- <u>Rachel Ann Heffler</u>, (Wadleigh: James Henry[10], Mary Emma[9], Henry Libby[8], Daniel Foster[7], William Henry[6], Joseph[5], Joseph[4], Henry[3], Robert[2], John[1]), b. December 23, 1957 in Portland, Ore. m. July 11, 1975 Terry Eugene Lee, b. May 21, 1953 in Portland, Ore. (Ref. 1)
　　2031 - Shelly Lynn

Issue of William Ray Arnold and 1448- Mary Carol (Rector) Arnold:

1752- <u>Scott William Arnold</u>, (Wadleigh: Mary Carol[10], Mary Emma[9], Henry Libby[8], Daniel Foster[7], William Henry[6], Joseph[5], Joseph[4], Henry[3], Robert[2], John[1]), b. July 10, 1970 in Medford, Ore. (Ref. 1)

Issue of 1470- Richard C.^{9} Smithand Fay E. (Jacques) Smith:

1753- <u>Danny D.</u>^{10} <u>Smith</u>, (Wadleigh: Richard C.^{11}, Fred Linwood^{10}, Isaiah Waldron^9, Henry M.^{8}, Sally^7, Richard^6, Mary^5, Elizabeth^4, Jonathan^3, Joanna^2, John^1) no data. Occ. Geneologist. Res. RFD #5A, Gardiner Maine. (Ref. 49)

Issue of 1479- Philip Winston^{10} Pillsbury and Eleanor (Bellows) Pillsbury:

1754- <u>Philip Winston</u>^{11} <u>Pillsbury, Jr.</u>, (Wadleigh: Philip Winston^{11}, Charles Stinson^{10}, Charles Alfred^9, George Alfred^8, Susanna^7, Benjamin^6, Thomas^5, Benjamin^4, Robert^3, Robert^2, John^1; Pillsbury: Philip Winston^{10}, Charles Stinson^9, Charles Alfred^8, George Alfred^7, John^6, Micajah^5, Caleb^4, Caleb^3, Moses^2, William^1), b. November 20, 1935 in Minneapolis, Minn. (Ref. 50-33)

1755- <u>Henry Adams</u>^{11} <u>Pillsbury</u>, (Wadleigh: Philip Winston^{11}, Charles Stinson^{10}, Charles Alfred^9, George Alfred^8, Susanna^7, Benjamin^6, Thomas^5, Benjamin^4, Robert^3, Robert^2, John^1; Pillsbury: Philip Winston^{10}, Charles Stinson^9, Charles Alfred^8, George Alfred^7, John^6, Micajah^5, Caleb^4, Caleb^3, Moses^2, William^1), b. January 12, 1937 in Chicago, Ill. (Ref. 50-33)

Issue of Oswald Bates Lord and 1480- Mary Stinson (Pillsbury) Lord:

1756- <u>Charles Pillsbury Lord</u>, (Wadleigh: Mary Stinson[11], Charles Stinson[10], Charles Alfred[9], George Alfred[8], Susanna[7], Benjamin[6], Thomas[5], Benjamin[4], Robert[3], Robert[2], John[1]), b. September 28, 1933 in New York, N.Y. (Ref. 50-31)

1757- <u>Richard Lord</u>, (Wadleigh: Mary Stinson[11], Charles Stinson[10], Charles Alfred[9], George Alfred[8], Susanna[7], Benjamin[6], Thomas[5], Benjamin[4], Robert[3], Robert[2], John[1]), b. July 30, 1935 in New York, N.Y., d. October 23, 1935. died in infancy. (Ref. 50-31)

1758- <u>Winston Lord</u>, (Wadleigh: Mary Stinson[11], Charles Stinson[10], Charles Alfred[9], George Alfred[8], Susanna[7], Benjamin[6], Thomas[5], Benjamin[4], Robert[3], Robert[2], John[1]), b. August 14, 1937 in New York, N.Y. (Ref. 50-31)

Issue of Elliott Bates McKee and 1481- Katharine Stevens (Pillsbury) McKee:

1759- <u>Philip Winston McKee</u>, (Wadleigh: Katharine Stevens[11], Charles Stinson[10], Charles Alfred[9], George Alfred[8], Susanna[7], Benjamin[6], Thomas[5], Benjamin[4], Robert[3], Robert[2], John[1]), b. January 20, 1932 in Paris, France. (Ref. 50-31)

1760- <u>Elliott Bates McKee</u>, (Wadleigh: Katharine Stevens[11], Charles Stinson[10], Charles Alfred[9], George Alfred[8], Susanna[7], Benjamin[6], Thomas[5], Benjamin[4], Robert[3], Robert[2], John[1]), b. January 10, 1934 in Mt. Kisco, N.Y. (Ref. 50-31)

Issue of John Austin Becker, Jr., and 1482-
Helen Winston (Pillsbury) Becker:

1761- Katharine Winston Becker, (Wadleigh:
Helen Winston[11], Charles Stinson[10], Charles
Alfred[9], George Alfred[8], Susanna[7], Benjamin[6],
Thomas[5], Benjamin[4], Robert[3], Robert[2], John[1]),
b. December 5, 1933 in Albany, N.Y. (Ref. 50-
32)

1762- Elizabeth Becker, (Wadleigh: Helen
Winston[11], Charles Stinson[10], Charles Alfred[9],
George Alfred[8], Susanna[7], Benjamin[6], Thomas[5],
Benjamin[4], Robert[3], Robert[2], John[1]), b. July
22, 1936 in Albany, N.Y. (Ref. 50-32)

Issue of Charles Edward Veltman and 1489-
Alice Pillsbury (Ayer) Veltman:

1763- Harold Charles Veltman, (Wadleigh: Alice
Pillsbury[11], Harriot Topliff[10], Fred Carleton[9],
George Alfred[8], Susanna[7], Benjamin[6], Thomas[5],
Benjamin[4], Robert[3], Robert[2], John[1]), b.
December 21, 1927. (Ref. 50-30)

1764- Harriot Pillsbury Veltman, (Wadleigh:
Alice Pillsbury[11], Harriot Topliff[10], Fred
Carleton[9], George Alfred[8], Susanna[7], Benjamin[6],
Thomas[5], Benjamin[4], Robert[3], Robert[2], John[1]),
b. April 16, 1931. (Ref. 50-30)

Issue of William Rathbun Hees, Jr. and 1490-
Ann Dana (Ayer) Hees:

1765- William Rathbun Hees, III, (Wadleigh:
Ann Dana[11], Harriot Topliff[10], Fred Carleton[9],
George Alfred[8], Susanna[7], Benjamin[6], Thomas[5],
Benjamin[4], Robert[3], Robert[2], John[1]) no data.
(Ref. 50-30)

WADLEIGH GENEALOGY   TWELFTH GENERATION

Issue of Frederick William Durham and 1504-
Constance Jean (Wadleigh) Durham:

1766- <u>Alison April Durham</u>, (Wadleigh:
Constance Jean[11], William Henry[10], Arthur
Garfield[9], Frank Lawrence[8], William Henry[7],
William Henry[6], Joseph[5], Joseph[4], Henry[3],
Robert[2], John[1]), b. April 21, 1975. (Ref. 2)

1767- <u>Naomi Elizabeth Durham</u>, (Wadleigh:
Constance Jean[11], William Henry[10], Arthur
Garfield[9], Frank Lawrence[8], William Henry[7],
William Henry[6], Joseph[5], Joseph[4], Henry[3],
Robert[2], John[1]), b. July 18, 1980. (Ref. 2)

1768- <u>Michael Wadleigh Durham</u>, (Wadleigh:
Constance Jean[11], William Henry[10], Arthur
Garfield[9], Frank Lawrence[8], William Henry[7],
William Henry[6], Joseph[5], Joseph[4], Henry[3],
Robert[2], John[1]), b. September 3, 1983. (Ref. 2)

Issue of 1509- Donald Elvin[11] Wadleigh and
Cheryl Ann (Roddy) (Palmer) Wadleigh:

1769- <u>Tiffany Ann</u>[12] Wadleigh, (Donald Elvin[11],
Charles Harry[10], Daniel Edward[9], Charles
Edwin[8], Daniel Foster[7], William Henry[6],
Joseph[5], Joseph[4], Henry[3], Robert[2], John[1]), b.
October 20, 1965 in Minneapolis, Minn., (adpt.)
Res. Red Wing, Minn., Elmhurst, Crete,
Kankakee, and Park Forest Ill. and Alexandria,
Va. (Ref. 1, 9)

1770- <u>Shawn Paul</u>[12] Wadleigh, (Donald Elvin[11],
Charles Harry[10], Daniel Edward[9], Charles
Edwin[8], Daniel Foster[7], William Henry[6],
Joseph[5], Joseph[4], Henry[3], Robert[2], John[1]), b.
August 14, 1969 in Edina, Minn., (adpt.) Res.
Red Wing, Minn., Elmhurst, Crete, Carbondale,
Champaign-Urbana and Park Forest, Ill. and
Alexandria, Va. (Ref. 1, 9)

Issue of 1512- David Elmer[11] Wadleigh and Rosalyn (Johnson) Wadleigh:

1771- <u>Amber Rose</u>[12] <u>Wadleigh</u>, (David Elmer[11], Elmer Edward[10], Daniel Edward[9], Charles Edwin[8], Daniel Foster[7], William Henry[6], Joseph[5], Joseph[4], Henry[3], Robert[2], John[1]), b. January 13, 1978 at Mitchell, S.D. (Ref. 1, 9)

Issue of 1513- Dale LeRoy[11] Wadleigh and Bess (Kingsbury) Wadleigh:

1772- <u>Cindy Leigh</u>[12] <u>Wadleigh</u>, (Dale LeRoy[11], Elmer Edward[10], Daniel Edward[9], Charles Edwin[8], Daniel Foster[7], William Henry[6], Joseph[5], Joseph[4], Henry[3], Robert[2], John[1]), b. July 5, 1969. (Ref. 1, 9)

1773- <u>Theressa Ann</u>[12] <u>Wadleigh</u>, (Dale LeRoy[11], Elmer Edward[10], Daniel Edward[9], Charles Edwin[8], Daniel Foster[7], William Henry[6], Joseph[5], Joseph[4], Henry[3], Robert[2], John[1]), b. February 1, 1973. (Ref. 1, 9)

1774- <u>Jeanette</u>[12] <u>Wadleigh</u>, (Dale LeRoy[11], Elmer Edward[10], Daniel Edward[9], Charles Edwin[8], Daniel Foster[7], William Henry[6], Joseph[5], Joseph[4], Henry[3], Robert[2], John[1]), b. August 14, 1975. (Ref. 1, 9)

Issue of 1514- Richard Lee[11] Wadleigh and Karen (Hille) Wadleigh:

1775- <u>Shawn Lee</u>[12] <u>Wadleigh</u>, (Richard Lee[11], Elmer Edward[10], Daniel Edward[9], Charles Edwin[8], Daniel Foster[7], William Henry[6], Joseph[5], Joseph[4], Henry[3], Robert[2], John[1]), b. August 14, 1973. (Ref. 1, 9)

1776- Sarah Louise[12] Wadleigh, (Richard Lee[11], Elmer Edward[10], Daniel Edward[9], Charles Edwin[8], Daniel Foster[7], William Henry[6], Joseph[5], Joseph[4], Henry[3], Robert[2], John[1]), b. March 23, 1977. (Ref. 1, 9)

Issue of 1516- Jerry Keith[11] Wadleigh and Darlene (Stickley) Wadleigh:

1777- Eric Keith[12] Wadleigh, (Jerry Keith[11], Elmer Edward[10], Daniel Edward[9], Charles Edwin[8], Daniel Foster[7], William Henry[6], Joseph[5], Joseph[4], Henry[3], Robert[2], John[1]), b. May 24, 1967. (Ref. 1, 9)

1778- Bryan Keith[12] Wadleigh, (Jerry Keith[11], Elmer Edward[10], Daniel Edward[9], Charles Edwin[8], Daniel Foster[7], William Henry[6], Joseph[5], Joseph[4], Henry[3], Robert[2], John[1]), b. October 13, 1968. (Ref. 1, 9)

1779- Dena May[12] Wadleigh, (Jerry Keith[11], Elmer Edward[10], Daniel Edward[9], Charles Edwin[8], Daniel Foster[7], William Henry[6], Joseph[5], Joseph[4], Henry[3], Robert[2], John[1]), b. August 7, 1971. (Ref. 1, 9)

Issue of 1516- Eugene Edward[11] Wadleigh and Cindy (Jacobson) Wadleigh:

1780- Peggy Lynn[12] Wadleigh, (Eugene Edward[11], Elmer Edward[10], Daniel Edward[9], Charles Edwin[8], Daniel Foster[7], William Henry[6], Joseph[5], Joseph[4], Henry[3], Robert[2], John[1]), b. March 21, 1976. (Ref. 1, 9)

1781- Glen Martin[12] Wadleigh, (Eugene Edward[11], Elmer Edward[10], Daniel Edward[9], Charles Edwin[8], Daniel Foster[7], William Henry[6], Joseph[5],

Joseph[4], Henry[3], Robert[2], John[1]), b. September 17, 1977. (Ref. 1, 9)

Issue of 1517- Lester Edward Schimmel and Violetta Rose (McCrea) Schimmel:

1782- Karla Kay Schimmel, (Wadleigh: Lester Edward[11], Erline Myrtle[10], Daniel Edward[9], Charles Edwin[8], Daniel Foster[7], William Henry[6], Joseph[5], Joseph[4], Henry[3], Robert[2], John[1]), b. April 19, 1964. m. October 8, 1983 Roy Irwin Boone in American Lutheran Church at Milbank, S.D., s. of Stanley and Joanne (Veen) Boone of Milbank, S.D., b. October 1, 1964 at Milbank, S.D. Ed. h.- A.S. in Electronics from Wilmar Vocational, w.- A.S. in Accounting from Wilmar Vocational, Occ. Accountant and Businessman, Res. Wilmar, Minn. (Ref. 1, 9)

1783- Kevin Lester Schimmel, (Wadleigh: Lester Edward[11], Erline Myrtle[10], Daniel Edward[9], Charles Edwin[8], Daniel Foster[7], William Henry[6], Joseph[5], Joseph[4], Henry[3], Robert[2], John[1]), b. October 18, 1968. Occ. Carpenter. (Ref. 1, 9)

Issue of 1518- Robert Daniel[11] Wadleigh and Sandra Kay (Bruer) Wadleigh:

1784- Daniel Edward[12] Wadleigh, (Robert Daniel[11], Robert David[10], Daniel Edward[9], Charles Edwin[8], Daniel Foster[7], William Henry[6], Joseph[5], Joseph[4], Henry[3], Robert[2], John[1]), b. February 4, 1969. (Ref. 1, 9)

1785- Dana[12] Wadleigh, (Robert Daniel[11], Robert David[10], Daniel Edward[9], Charles Edwin[8], Daniel Foster[7], William Henry[6], Joseph[5], Joseph[4], Henry[3], Robert[2], John[1]), b. February 4, 1969. (Ref. 1, 9)

Issue of 1519- Bruce Edward[11] Wadleigh and Nguyen Thi Mai (Law) Wadleigh:

1786- Robert Bruce[12] Wadleigh, (Bruce Edward[11], Robert David[10], Daniel Edward[9], Charles Edwin[8], Daniel Foster[7], William Henry[6], Joseph[5], Joseph[4], Henry[3], Robert[2], John[1]), b. April 16, 1973. (Ref. 1, 9)

1787- Mai Lai[12] Wadleigh, (Bruce Edward[11], Robert David[10], Daniel Edward[9], Charles Edwin[8], Daniel Foster[7], William Henry[6], Joseph[5], Joseph[4], Henry[3], Robert[2], John[1]), b. May 27, 1975. (Ref. 1, 9)

Issue of Richard Allan McMichael and 1520- Susan Kay[11] (Wadleigh) McMichael:

1788- Jason Bradley McMichael, (Wadleigh: Susan Kay[11], Robert David[10], Daniel Edward[9], Charles Edwin[8], Daniel Foster[7], William Henry[6], Joseph[5], Joseph[4], Henry[3], Robert[2], John[1]), b. November 29, 1979. (Ref. 9)

1789- Robert James McMichael, (Wadleigh: Susan Kay[11], Robert David[10], Daniel Edward[9], Charles Edwin[8], Daniel Foster[7], William Henry[6], Joseph[5], Joseph[4], Henry[3], Robert[2], John[1]), b. October 30, 1981. (Ref. 9)

1790- Jessica Marie McMichael, (Wadleigh: Susan Kay[11], Robert David[10], Daniel Edward[9], Charles Edwin[8], Daniel Foster[7], William Henry[6], Joseph[5], Joseph[4], Henry[3], Robert[2], John[1]), b. August 8, 1985 in the Netherlands. (Ref. 9)

Issue of Paul Hendrickson and 1521- Sally Ann
(Cogdill) Hendrickson:

1791- <u>Guy Lee</u> Hendrickson, (Wadleigh: Sally
Ann[11], Ada Margaret[10], Daniel Edward[9], Charles
Edwin[8], Daniel Foster[7], William Henry[6],
Joseph[5], Joseph[4], Henry[3], Robert[2], John[1]), b.
June 23, 1957. Occ. Automotive Dealer in
Yankton, S.D. Ed. USD-Springfield and Hastings
College, Nebr. Res. Hastings and Niobrara,
Nebr. and Springfield and Yankton, S.D. (Ref.
1, 9)

1792- <u>Troy Ernest</u> Hendrickson, (Wadleigh:
Sally Ann[11], Ada Margaret[10], Daniel Edward[9],
Charles Edwin[8], Daniel Foster[7], William Henry[6],
Joseph[5], Joseph[4], Henry[3], Robert[2], John[1]), b.
February 2, 1959 at Kansas City, Mo. m. Donna,
no additional data. Occ. h. Career counseler,
w. teacher both at Flandreau Indian School
S.D., Ed. Univ. of South Dakota-Springfield
and Dakota Wesleyan Univ., Res. Springfield,
Mitchell and Flandreau, S.D. (Ref. 1, 9)
   2032 - Anthony Paul 2033 - Benjamin Thomas

1793- <u>Paula Ann</u> Hendrickson, (Wadleigh: Sally
Ann[11], Ada Margaret[10], Daniel Edward[9], Charles
Edwin[8], Daniel Foster[7], William Henry[6],
Joseph[5], Joseph[4], Henry[3], Robert[2], John[1]), b.
November 9, 1960. m. December 28, 1979 Mr.
Schmaltz, s. of Wendlen Schmaltz and Colleen
(Ellis) Schmaltz, b. November 22, 1961 at
Yankton, S.D. Occ. h. Equipment Manu. w.
Prison Guard. Ed. Univ. of South Dakota-
Springfield. Res. Springfield, S.D. (Ref.
1, 9)
   2034 - Rebecca Ann 2035 - Danielle

Issue of Al Lopez and 1522- Peggy Lou (Cogdill) Lopez:

1794- <u>David (aka: Corey) Dean Lopez</u>, (Wadleigh: Peggy Lou[11], Ada Margaret[10], Daniel Edward[9], Charles Edwin[8], Daniel Foster[7], William Henry[6], Joseph[5], Joseph[4], Henry[3], Robert[2], John[1]), b. August 6, 1960 at Kansas City, Mo. Occ. Carpenter. (Ref. 1, 9)

1795- <u>Aliza Lynn Lopez</u>, (Wadleigh: Peggy Lou[11], Ada Margaret[10], Daniel Edward[9], Charles Edwin[8], Daniel Foster[7], William Henry[6], Joseph[5], Joseph[4], Henry[3], Robert[2], John[1]), b. June 6, 1963 at Riverside, Cal. Occ. Opthamologist (Ref. 1, 9)

1796- <u>Alan Roman Lopez</u>, (Wadleigh: Peggy Lou[11], Ada Margaret[10], Daniel Edward[9], Charles Edwin[8], Daniel Foster[7], William Henry[6], Joseph[5], Joseph[4], Henry[3], Robert[2], John[1]), b. March 10, 1966 at Riverside, Cal. (Ref. 1, 9)

Issue of Jerome Staples and 1523- Connie Kay (Cogdill) Staples:

1797- <u>Jay Dean Staples</u>, (Wadleigh: Connie Kay[11], Ada Margaret[10], Daniel Edward[9], Charles Edwin[8], Daniel Foster[7], William Henry[6], Joseph[5], Joseph[4], Henry[3], Robert[2], John[1]), b. April 7, 1970 at Bassett, Neb. (Ref. 1, 9)

1798- <u>Jeffery Dean Staples</u>, (Wadleigh: Connie Kay[11], Ada Margaret[10], Daniel Edward[9], Charles Edwin[8], Daniel Foster[7], William Henry[6], Joseph[5], Joseph[4], Henry[3], Robert[2], John[1]), b. August 18, 1972 at Neligh Neb. (Ref. 1, 9)

1799- <u>Jody Lee Staples</u>, (Wadleigh: Connie Kay[11], Ada Margaret[10], Daniel Edward[9], Charles

Edwin[8], Daniel Foster[7], William Henry[6], Joseph[5], Joseph[4], Henry[3], Robert[2], John[1]), b. February 11, 1974 at Neligh Neb. (Ref. 1, 9)

1800- <u>Jonathan Jerome Staples</u>, (Wadleigh: Connie Kay[11], Ada Margaret[10], Daniel Edward[9], Charles Edwin[8], Daniel Foster[7], William Henry[6], Joseph[5], Joseph[4], Henry[3], Robert[2], John[1]), b. April 12, 1982 at Gregory, S.D. (Ref. 9)

Issue of Rocco Minino, Jr. and 1524- Anita Louise (Cogdill) Minino:

1801- <u>Amy Louise Minino</u>, (Wadleigh: Anita Louise[11], Ada Margaret[10], Daniel Edward[9], Charles Edwin[8], Daniel Foster[7], William Henry[6], Joseph[5], Joseph[4], Henry[3], Robert[2], John[1]), b. October 14, 1974. (Ref. 1, 9)

1802- <u>Lori Lynn Minino</u>, (Wadleigh: Anita Louise[11], Ada Margaret[10], Daniel Edward[9], Charles Edwin[8], Daniel Foster[7], William Henry[6], Joseph[5], Joseph[4], Henry[3], Robert[2], John[1]), b. September, 23, 1976. (Ref. 9)

1803- <u>Rocco Minino, III</u>, (Wadleigh: Anita Louise[11], Ada Margaret[10], Daniel Edward[9], Charles Edwin[8], Daniel Foster[7], William Henry[6], Joseph[5], Joseph[4], Henry[3], Robert[2], John[1]), b. November 2, 1979. (Ref. 9)

Issue of 1525- Gifford Lane Cogdill and Amy (Benson) Cogdill:

1804- <u>Christopher Cogdill</u>, (Wadleigh: Gifford Lane[11], Ada Margaret[10], Daniel Edward[9], Charles Edwin[8], Daniel Foster[7], William Henry[6], Joseph[5], Joseph[4], Henry[3], Robert[2], John[1]), b. October 4, 1982. (Ref. 9)

1805- <u>Chris</u> <u>Joy</u> <u>Cogdill</u>, (Wadleigh: Gifford Lane[11], Ada Margaret[10], Daniel Edward[9], Charles Edwin[8], Daniel Foster[7], William Henry[6], Joseph[5], Joseph[4], Henry[3], Robert[2], John[1]), b. May 28, 1984. (Ref. 9)

Issue of 1526- Ronald Lee Taylor and Gloria Jean Taylor:

1806- <u>Michael</u> <u>Scott</u> <u>Taylor</u>, (Wadleigh: Ronald Lee[11], Alta Beatrice[10], Daniel Edward[9], Charles Edwin[8], Daniel Foster[7], William Henry[6], Joseph[5], Joseph[4], Henry[3], Robert[2], John[1]), b. September 16, 1966. (Ref. 1, 9)

Issue of 1526- Ronald Lee Taylor and Carol Jean (Myers) Taylor:

1807- <u>Mark</u> <u>Myers</u> <u>Taylor</u>, (Wadleigh: Ronald Lee[11], Alta Beatrice[10], Daniel Edward[9], Charles Edwin[8], Daniel Foster[7], William Henry[6], Joseph[5], Joseph[4], Henry[3], Robert[2], John[1]), b. 1968, (adpt.) (Ref. 9)

1808- <u>Michael</u> <u>Myers</u> <u>Taylor</u>, (Wadleigh: Ronald Lee[11], Alta Beatrice[10], Daniel Edward[9], Charles Edwin[8], Daniel Foster[7], William Henry[6], Joseph[5], Joseph[4], Henry[3], Robert[2], John[1]), b. 1970, (adpt.) (Ref. 9)

1809- <u>Marty</u> <u>Myers</u> <u>Taylor</u>, (Wadleigh: Ronald Lee[11], Alta Beatrice[10], Daniel Edward[9], Charles Edwin[8], Daniel Foster[7], William Henry[6], Joseph[5], Joseph[4], Henry[3], Robert[2], John[1]), b. 1972, (adpt.) (Ref. 9)

WADLEIGH GENEALOGY   TWELFTH GENERATION

Issue of 1527- Larry Eugene Taylor and Stephanie (Dethlought) Taylor:

1810- Megan Ashley Taylor, (Wadleigh: Larry Eugene[11], Alta Beatrice[10], Daniel Edward[9], Charles Edwin[8], Daniel Foster[7], William Henry[6], Joseph[5], Joseph[4], Henry[3], Robert[2], John[1]), b. October 20, 1981. (Ref. 9)

Issue of Raymond Dowell and 1528- Elizabeth Ann (Taylor) Dowell:

1811- Jason Alexandria Dowell, (Wadleigh: Elizabeth Ann[11], Alta Beatrice[10], Daniel Edward[9], Charles Edwin[8], Daniel Foster[7], William Henry[6], Joseph[5], Joseph[4], Henry[3], Robert[2], John[1]), b. October 14, 1980. (Ref. 9)

1812- Adam Edward Dowell, (Wadleigh: Elizabeth Ann[11], Alta Beatrice[10], Daniel Edward[9], Charles Edwin[8], Daniel Foster[7], William Henry[6], Joseph[5], Joseph[4], Henry[3], Robert[2], John[1]), b. April 26, 1987. (Ref. 9)

Issue of Allen Peterson and 1529- Roxe Lea (Gusso) Peterson:

1813- Troy Allen Peterson, (Wadleigh: Roxe Lea[11], Ida Ilene[10], Daniel Edward[9], Charles Edwin[8], Daniel Foster[7], William Henry[6], Joseph[5], Joseph[4], Henry[3], Robert[2], John[1]), b. September 2, 1967. (Ref. 1, 9)

1814- Tonya Lee Peterson, (Wadleigh: Roxe Lea[11], Ida Ilene[10], Daniel Edward[9], Charles Edwin[8], Daniel Foster[7], William Henry[6], Joseph[5], Joseph[4], Henry[3], Robert[2], John[1]), b. February 26, 1972. (Ref. 1, 9)

1815- <u>Tiffany Lynn Peterson</u>, (Wadleigh: Roxe
Lea[11], Ida Ilene[10], Daniel Edward[9], Charles
Edwin[8], Daniel Foster[7], William Henry[6],
Joseph[5], Joseph[4], Henry[3], Robert[2], John[1]), b.
October 29, 1978. (Ref. 1, 9)

**Issue of 1530- Rodney Brock Gusso and Carol
(Lindner) Gusso:**

1816- <u>Gregory Edward Gusso</u>, (Wadleigh: Rodney
Brock[11], Ida Ilene[10], Daniel Edward[9], Charles
Edwin[8], Daniel Foster[7], William Henry[6],
Joseph[5], Joseph[4], Henry[3], Robert[2], John[1]), b.
June 30, 1971. (Ref. 1, 9)

1817- <u>Robert Charles Gusso</u>, (Wadleigh: Rodney
Brock[11], Ida Ilene[10], Daniel Edward[9], Charles
Edwin[8], Daniel Foster[7], William Henry[6],
Joseph[5], Joseph[4], Henry[3], Robert[2], John[1]), b.
December 2, 1973. (Ref. 1, 9)

1818- <u>Susan Gusso</u>, (Wadleigh: Rodney Brock[11],
Ida Ilene[10], Daniel Edward[9], Charles Edwin[8],
Daniel Foster[7], William Henry[6], Joseph[5],
Joseph[4], Henry[3], Robert[2], John[1]), b. January
29, 1980. (Ref. 9)

**Issue of Arlyn Wadsworth and 1531- Rochelle
Ilene (Gusso) Wadsworth:**

1819- <u>Craig Arnold Wadsworth</u>, (Wadleigh:
Rochelle Ilene[11], Ida Ilene[10], Daniel Edward[9],
Charles Edwin[8], Daniel Foster[7], William Henry[6],
Joseph[5], Joseph[4], Henry[3], Robert[2], John[1]), b.
September 8, 1974. (Ref. 1, 9)

1820- <u>Chris Arlyn Wadsworth</u>, (Wadleigh:
Rochelle Ilene[11], Ida Ilene[10], Daniel Edward[9],
Charles Edwin[8], Daniel Foster[7], William Henry[6],

Joseph[5], Joseph[4], Henry[3], Robert[2], John[1]), b.
October 9, 1977. (Ref. 1, 9)

Issue of Phillip Brooks and 1532- Renea Pauline (Gusso) Brooks:

1821- Eric Steven Brooks, (Wadleigh: Renea
Pauline[11], Ida Ilene[10], Daniel Edward[9], Charles
Edwin[8], Daniel Foster[7], William Henry[6],
Joseph[5], Joseph[4], Henry[3], Robert[2], John[1]), b.
April 19, 1976. (Ref. 1, 9)

1822- Kelly Ilene Brooks, (Wadleigh: Renea
Pauline[11], Ida Ilene[10], Daniel Edward[9], Charles
Edwin[8], Daniel Foster[7], William Henry[6],
Joseph[5], Joseph[4], Henry[3], Robert[2], John[1]), b.
September 24, 1978. (Ref. 9)

1823- Johanna Brooks, (Wadleigh: Renea
Pauline[11], Ida Ilene[10], Daniel Edward[9], Charles
Edwin[8], Daniel Foster[7], William Henry[6],
Joseph[5], Joseph[4], Henry[3], Robert[2], John[1]), b.
May 13, 1986. (Ref. 9)

Issue of 1533- William Greg Paul and Mary Kathryn (McKamie) Paul:

1824- Michele Renee Paul, (Wadleigh: William
Greg[11], Mary Lorene[10], Nettie Florence[9],
Charles Edwin[8], Daniel Foster[7], William Henry[6],
Joseph[5], Joseph[4], Henry[3], Robert[2], John[1]), b.
May 14, 1974. (Ref. 1)

Issue of 1534- George Colbert Johnson and Jacque (Chambers) Johnson:

1825- James Richard Colbert Johnson,
(Wadleigh: George Colbert[11], Hazel Caroline[10],

Nettie Florence[9], Charles Edwin[8], Daniel
Foster[7], William Henry[6], Joseph[5], Joseph[4],
Henry[3], Robert[2], John[1]), b. October 5, 1960.
(Ref. 1)

Issue of Gary Louis Turner and 1536- Caroline Kay (Johnson) Turner:

1826- Chera Leigh Turner, (Wadleigh: Caroline
Kay[11], Hazel Caroline[10], Nettie Florence[9],
Charles Edwin[8], Daniel Foster[7], William Henry[6],
Joseph[5], Joseph[4], Henry[3], Robert[2], John[1]), b.
May 16, 1960. (Ref. 1)

1827- Jona Lynn Turner, (Wadleigh: Caroline
Kay[11], Hazel Caroline[10], Nettie Florence[9],
Charles Edwin[8], Daniel Foster[7], William Henry[6],
Joseph[5], Joseph[4], Henry[3], Robert[2], John[1]), b.
October 6, 1961. (Ref. 1)

1828- Gregory Alan Turner, (Wadleigh: Caroline
Kay[11], Hazel Caroline[10], Nettie Florence[9],
Charles Edwin[8], Daniel Foster[7], William Henry[6],
Joseph[5], Joseph[4], Henry[3], Robert[2], John[1]), b.
October 18, 1963. (Ref. 1)

Issue of 1537- Stanley Ray Bell and Ann (Thompson) Bell:

1829- Karen Alice Bell, (Wadleigh: Stanley
Ray[11], Howard Charles[10], Nettie Florence[9],
Charles Edwin[8], Daniel Foster[7], William Henry[6],
Joseph[5], Joseph[4], Henry[3], Robert[2], John[1]), b.
June 10, 1972. (Ref. 1)

Issue of 1538- Daniel Robert Bell and Susan
Lee (Guthrie) Bell:

1830- Erin Lee Bell, (Wadleigh: Daniel
Robert[11], Howard Charles[10], Nettie Florence[9],
Charles Edwin[8], Daniel Foster[7], William Henry[6],
Joseph[5], Joseph[4], Henry[3], Robert[2], John[1]), b.
March 6, 1975. (Ref. 1)

Issue of James Daugherty and 1539- Arvilla
D.[11] (Wadleigh) Daugherty:

1831- James Paul Daugherty, (Wadleigh: Arvilla
D.[11], Paul Edward[10], James Augustus[9], Charles
Edwin[8], Daniel Foster[7], William Henry[6],
Joseph[5], Joseph[4], Henry[3], Robert[2], John[1]), b.
January 7, 1959. (Ref. 1)

1832- Christopher Lee Daugherty, (Wadleigh:
Arvilla D.[11], Paul Edward[10], James Augustus[9],
Charles Edwin[8], Daniel Foster[7], William Henry[6],
Joseph[5], Joseph[4], Henry[3], Robert[2], John[1]), b.
January 11, 1961. (Ref. 1)

Issue of Duke Collins and 1539- Arvilla D.[11]
(Wadleigh) (Daugherty) Collins:

1833- Susan Elaine Collins, (Wadleigh: Arvilla
D.[11], Paul Edward[10], James Augustus[9], Charles
Edwin[8], Daniel Foster[7], William Henry[6],
Joseph[5], Joseph[4], Henry[3], Robert[2], John[1]), b.
December 18, 1968 (twin). (Ref. 1)

1834- Sandra Jean Collins, (Wadleigh: Arvilla
D.[11], Paul Edward[10], James Augustus[9], Charles
Edwin[8], Daniel Foster[7], William Henry[6],
Joseph[5], Joseph[4], Henry[3], Robert[2], John[1]), b.
December 18, 1968 (twin). (Ref. 1)

Issue of John Holmberg and 1540- Karen Jean[11] (Wadleigh) Holmberg:

1835- John Scott Holmberg, (Wadleigh: Karen Jean[11], Paul Edward[10], James Augustus[9], Charles Edwin[8], Daniel Foster[7], William Henry[6], Joseph[5], Joseph[4], Henry[3], Robert[2], John[1]), b. September 11, 1963. (Ref. 1)

1836- Jeannie Marie Holmberg, (Wadleigh: Karen Jean[11], Paul Edward[10], James Augustus[9], Charles Edwin[8], Daniel Foster[7], William Henry[6], Joseph[5], Joseph[4], Henry[3], Robert[2], John[1]), b. October 6, 1965. (Ref. 1)

1837- Jeanette Rene Holmberg, (Wadleigh: Karen Jean[11], Paul Edward[10], James Augustus[9], Charles Edwin[8], Daniel Foster[7], William Henry[6], Joseph[5], Joseph[4], Henry[3], Robert[2], John[1]), b. October 13, 1967. (Ref. 1)

1838- Jennifer Lynn Holmberg, (Wadleigh: Karen Jean[11], Paul Edward[10], James Augustus[9], Charles Edwin[8], Daniel Foster[7], William Henry[6], Joseph[5], Joseph[4], Henry[3], Robert[2], John[1]), b. September 27, 1970. (Ref. 1)

Issue of 1541- Charles Edward[11] Wadleigh and Judith Kay (Gardner) Wadleigh:

1839- Michael Edward[12] Wadleigh, (Charles Edward[11], Omer Basil[10], James Augustus[9], Charles Edwin[8], Daniel Foster[7], William Henry[6], Joseph[5], Joseph[4], Henry[3], Robert[2], John[1]), b. August 15, 1964. (Ref. 1)

1840- Michelle Rene[12] Wadleigh, (Charles Edward[11], Omer Basil[10], James Augustus[9], Charles Edwin[8], Daniel Foster[7], William Henry[6], Joseph[5], Joseph[4], Henry[3], Robert[2], John[1]), b. August 5, 1966. (Ref. 1)

Issue of 1543- Roger Basil[11] Wadleigh and Minnie Bell (Gardner) Wadleigh:

1841- Tara Leanne[12] Wadleigh, (Roger Basil[11], Omer Basil[10], James Augustus[9], Charles Edwin[8], Daniel Foster[7], William Henry[6], Joseph[5], Joseph[4], Henry[3], Robert[2], John[1]), b. October 31, 1970. (Ref. 1)

1842- Susann Augusta[12] Wadleigh, (Roger Basil[11], Omer Basil[10], James Augustus[9], Charles Edwin[8], Daniel Foster[7], William Henry[6], Joseph[5], Joseph[4], Henry[3], Robert[2], John[1]), b. January 10, 1973. (Ref. 1)

Issue of William Wayne Campbell and 1543- Twyla Ann[11] (Wadleigh) Campbell:

1843- Kelly Wayne Campbell, (Wadleigh: Twyla Ann[11], Omer Basil[10], James Augustus[9], Charles Edwin[8], Daniel Foster[7], William Henry[6], Joseph[5], Joseph[4], Henry[3], Robert[2], John[1]), b. February 23, 1971. (Ref. 1)

Issue of 1544- William Bruce[4] Lunstrum and Valerie Josephine (Kroll) Lunstrum:

1844- Bryan Ross[5] Lunstrum, (Wadleigh: William Bruce[11], Mervyn Wayne[10], Fannie Lorena[9], Charles Edwin[8], Daniel Foster[7], William Henry[6], Joseph[5], Joseph[4], Henry[3], Robert[2], John[1]; Lunstrum: William Bruce[4], Mervyn Wayne[3], William[2], Peter[1]), b. April 17, 1962 at Laurel, Prince Georges Co. Md. (Ref. 1)

1845- Megan Beth[5] Lunstrum, (Wadleigh: William Bruce[11], Mervyn Wayne[10], Fannie Lorena[9], Charles Edwin[8], Daniel Foster[7], William Henry[6], Joseph[5], Joseph[4], Henry[3], Robert[2], John[1]; Lunstrum: William Bruce[4], Mervyn Wayne[3],

William[2], Peter[1]), b. June 10, 1965 at Colorado
Springs, El Paso Co., Colo. (Ref. 1)

Issue of 1546- Ralph David[4] Lunstrum and Kandy Robb (Cameron) Lunstrum:

1846- Lorene Sue[5] Lunstrum, (Wadleigh: Ralph
David[11], Mervyn Wayne[10], Fannie Lorena[9],
Charles Edwin[8], Daniel Foster[7], William Henry[6],
Joseph[5], Joseph[4], Henry[3], Robert[2], John[1];
Lunstrum: Ralph David[4], Mervyn Wayne[3],
William[2], Peter[1]), b. March 6, 1966 at Salt
Lake City, Lake Co., Ut. (Ref. 1)

Issue of Alan James Skille and 1547- Margaret Paige[4] (Lunstrum) Skille:

1847- Keith Alan Skille, (Wadleigh: Margaret
Paige[11], Mervyn Wayne[10], Fannie Lorena[9],
Charles Edwin[8], Daniel Foster[7], William Henry[6],
Joseph[5], Joseph[4], Henry[3], Robert[2], John[1]), b.
June 8, 1963 at Vallejo, Solano Co., Cal.
(Ref. 1)

1848- Margit Christine Skille, (Wadleigh:
Margaret Paige[11], Mervyn Wayne[10], Fannie
Lorena[9], Charles Edwin[8], Daniel Foster[7],
William Henry[6], Joseph[5], Joseph[4], Henry[3],
Robert[2], John[1]), b. February 1, 1966 at
Charleston, Charleston Co., S.C. (Ref. 1)

Issue of James Petty and 1548- Susan Beth[4] (Lunstrum) Petty:

1849- Valarie Jo Petty, (Wadleigh: Susan
Beth[11], Fordyce Wilbur[10], Fannie Lorena[9],
Charles Edwin[8], Daniel Foster[7], William Henry[6],
Joseph[5], Joseph[4], Henry[3], Robert[2], John[1]), b.
September 24, 1965 at Boise, Ida. (Ref. 1)

1850- <u>Dana Joanne Petty</u>, (Wadleigh: Susan
Beth[11], Fordyce Wilbur[10], Fannie Lorena[9],
Charles Edwin[8], Daniel Foster[7], William Henry[6],
Joseph[5], Joseph[4], Henry[3], Robert[2], John[1]), b.
December 15, 1967, at Boise, Ida. (Ref. 1)

**Issue of 1549- Carl Kenneth[4] Lunstrum and
Madeline Elizabeth (Kane) Lunstrum:**

1851- <u>Sarah Kristine[5] Lunstrum</u>, (Wadleigh:
Carl Kenneth[11], Carl Kenneth[10], Fannie Lorena[9],
Charles Edwin[8], Daniel Foster[7], William Henry[6],
Joseph[5], Joseph[4], Henry[3], Robert[2], John[1];
Lunstrum: Carl Kenneth[4], Carl Kenneth[3],
William[2], Peter[1]), b. November 30, 1968 at
Nampa, Canyon Co., Ida. (Ref. 1)

1852- <u>Amy Kathleen[5] Lunstrum</u>, (Wadleigh: Carl
Kenneth[11], Carl Kenneth[10], Fannie Lorena[9],
Charles Edwin[8], Daniel Foster[7], William Henry[6],
Joseph[5], Joseph[4], Henry[3], Robert[2], John[1];
Lunstrum: Carl Kenneth[4], Carl Kenneth[3],
William[2], Peter[1]), b. August 5, 1970, at Nampa,
Canyon Co., Ida. (Ref. 1)

1853- <u>Casey Matthew[5] Lunstrum</u>, (Wadleigh:
Carl Kenneth[11], Carl Kenneth[10], Fannie Lorena[9],
Charles Edwin[8], Daniel Foster[7], William Henry[6],
Joseph[5], Joseph[4], Henry[3], Robert[2], John[1];
Lunstrum: Carl Kenneth[4], Carl Kenneth[3],
William[2], Peter[1]), b. April 21, 1972, at Nampa,
Canyon Co., Ida. (Ref. 1)

1854- <u>Kristen Patrick[5] Lunstrum</u>, (Wadleigh:
Carl Kenneth[11], Carl Kenneth[10], Fannie Lorena[9],
Charles Edwin[8], Daniel Foster[7], William Henry[6],
Joseph[5], Joseph[4], Henry[3], Robert[2], John[1];
Lunstrum: Carl Kenneth[4], Carl Kenneth[3],
William[2], Peter[1]), b. August 1975, at Nampa,
Canyon Co., Ida. (Ref. 1)

WADLEIGH GENEALOGY   TWELFTH GENERATION

Issue of 1550- James Peter[4] Lunstrum and Patricia Jane (Godschalx) Lunstrum:

1855- Eric Godschalx[5] Lunstrum, (Wadleigh:
James Peter[11], Carl Kenneth[10], Fannie Lorena[9],
Charles Edwin[8], Daniel Foster[7], William Henry[6],
Joseph[5], Joseph[4], Henry[3], Robert[2], John[1];
Lunstrum: James Peter[4], Carl Kenneth[3],
William[2], Peter[1]), b. May 6, 1973 at Boise, Ada
Co., Ida. (Ref. 1)

1856- Elizabeth Mary[5] Lunstrum, (Wadleigh:
James Peter[11], Carl Kenneth[10], Fannie Lorena[9],
Charles Edwin[8], Daniel Foster[7], William Henry[6],
Joseph[5], Joseph[4], Henry[3], Robert[2], John[1];
Lunstrum: James Peter[4], Carl Kenneth[3],
William[2], Peter[1]), b. April 25, 1974 at Boise,
Ada Co., Ida. (Ref. 1)

Issue of 1562- John Edward McKibbin and Shirlee (Swanson) McKibbin:

1857- Killy Ann McKibbin, (Wadleigh: John
Edward[11], Inez Lorraine[10], Fannie Lorena[9],
Charles Edwin[8], Daniel Foster[7], William Henry[6],
Joseph[5], Joseph[4], Henry[3], Robert[2], John[1]), b.
July 3, 1969 at Sacramento, Sacramento Co.,
Cal. (Ref. 1)

1858- Samuel Alexander McKibbin, (Wadleigh:
John Edward[11], Inez Lorraine[10], Fannie Lorena[9],
Charles Edwin[8], Daniel Foster[7], William Henry[6],
Joseph[5], Joseph[4], Henry[3], Robert[2], John[1]), b.
August 31, 1972 at Sacramento, Sacramento Co.,
Cal. (Ref. 1)

Issue of David Jefferies, V, and 1571- Anita Carol (Rhodes) Jefferies:

1859- <u>Angela Davon Jefferies</u>, (Wadleigh: Anita Carol[11], Lois[10], Helen Mary[9], Charles Edwin[8], Daniel Foster[7], William Henry[6], Joseph[5], Joseph[4], Henry[3], Robert[2], John[1]), b. April 28, 1965 at Wichita, Sedgwick Co., Kan. (Ref. 1)

1860- <u>David Jefferies, VI</u>, (Wadleigh: Anita Carol[11], Lois[10], Helen Mary[9], Charles Edwin[8], Daniel Foster[7], William Henry[6], Joseph[5], Joseph[4], Henry[3], Robert[2], John[1]), b. January 8, 1969. (Ref. 1)

Issue of George Harold Rottinger and 1572- Connie Fay (Rhodes) Rottinger:

1861- <u>Diane Rebecca Rottinger</u>, (Wadleigh: Connie Fay[11], Lois[10], Helen Mary[9], Charles Edwin[8], Daniel Foster[7], William Henry[6], Joseph[5], Joseph[4], Henry[3], Robert[2], John[1]), b. November 17, 1976 in Harris Co., Tex. (Ref. 1)

Issue of 1573- Richard Leroy Wissman and Susan Lynn (Stuerke) Wissman:

1862- <u>Jeffery James Wissman</u>, (Wadleigh: Richard Leroy[11], Ella Dorothy[10], Robert Leroy[9], Charles Edwin[8], Daniel Foster[7], William Henry[6], Joseph[5], Joseph[4], Henry[3], Robert[2], John[1]), b. November 25, 1969. (Ref. 1)

Issue of 1574- James Joseph Wissman and Linda Kaye (Petree) Wissman:

1863- <u>Jason James Wissman</u>, (Wadleigh: James Joseph[11], Ella Dorothy[10], Robert Leroy[9], Charles Edwin[8], Daniel Foster[7], William Henry[6],

Joseph[5], Joseph[4], Henry[3], Robert[2], John[1]), b. May 18, 1973. (Ref. 1)

1864- Amy Lynn Wissman, (Wadleigh: James Joseph[11], Ella Dorothy[10], Robert Leroy[9], Charles Edwin[8], Daniel Foster[7], William Henry[6], Joseph[5], Joseph[4], Henry[3], Robert[2], John[1]), b. August 22, 1975. (Ref. 1)

Issue of 1581- Don Albert Riley and Reva Jean (Shinkle) Riley:

1865- Dale Alan Riley, (Wadleigh: Don Albert[11], Annabel[10], Bertha May[9], Everett[8], Daniel Foster[7], William Henry[6], Joseph[5], Joseph[4], Henry[3], Robert[2], John[1]), b. December 17, 1947 at Des Moines, Ia., d. October 25, 1978 at Los Angeles, Cal. from motorcycle accident. (Ref. 2)

1866- Brian Don Riley, (Wadleigh: Don Albert[11], Annabel[10], Bertha May[9], Everett[8], Daniel Foster[7], William Henry[6], Joseph[5], Joseph[4], Henry[3], Robert[2], John[1]), b. May 14, 1950 at Des Moines, Ia. m. June 10, 1972 at Los Angles, Cal. Pamela Ann Cramer, no additional data. (Ref. 2)

1867- Mark Kevin Riley, (Wadleigh: Don Albert[11], Annabel[10], Bertha May[9], Everett[8], Daniel Foster[7], William Henry[6], Joseph[5], Joseph[4], Henry[3], Robert[2], John[1]), b. July 24, 1961. (Ref. 2)

Issue of James R. Harrison and 1582- Ramona Elizabeth (Hogan) Harrison:

1868- Victoria Lee Harrison, (Wadleigh: Don Albert[11], Annabel[10], Bertha May[9], Everett[8],

Daniel Foster[7], William Henry[6], Joseph[5], Joseph[4], Henry[3], Robert[2], John[1]), b. April 19, 1946 at Iowa Falls, Ia. m. 1966 in S.C. Hayes L. Lomax, div. no additional data. (Ref. 2)

1869- James R. Harrison, Jr., (Wadleigh: Don Albert[11], Annabel[10], Bertha May[9], Everett[8], Daniel Foster[7], William Henry[6], Joseph[5], Joseph[4], Henry[3], Robert[2], John[1]), b. May 6, 1947 at Waterloo, Ia. m. February 21, 1970 at Traer, Ia. Betty A. Karpisek, no additional data. (Ref. 2)

1870- Mary E. Harrison, (Wadleigh: Don Albert[11], Annabel[10], Bertha May[9], Everett[8], Daniel Foster[7], William Henry[6], Joseph[5], Joseph[4], Henry[3], Robert[2], John[1]), b. March 6, 1949 at Iowa City, Ia. m. 1st February 1969 at Douglas, Ga. John Patton, div. m. 2nd August 1977 Lon Smith, div. no additional data. (Ref. 2)

1871- Ricky Joe Harrison, (Wadleigh: Don Albert[11], Annabel[10], Bertha May[9], Everett[8], Daniel Foster[7], William Henry[6], Joseph[5], Joseph[4], Henry[3], Robert[2], John[1]), b. April 7, 1950 at Waterloo, Ia., d. October 18, 1974 at Waterloo. did not marry. (Ref. 2)

Issue of 1584- James Colbert Hogan and Patricia Elaine (Gardner) Hogan:

1872- Grace Marie Hogan, (Wadleigh: James Colbert[11], Alma Emma[10], Bertha May[9], Everett[8], Daniel Foster[7], William Henry[6], Joseph[5], Joseph[4], Henry[3], Robert[2], John[1]), b. August 14, 1959 at Iowa City, Ia. m. September 20, 1978 at San Diego, Cal. Donald R. Dowling, no additional data. Occ. h.-w. U.S. Navy. (Ref. 2)

1873- David James Hogan, (Wadleigh: James
Colbert[11], Alma Emma[10], Bertha May[9], Everett[8],
Daniel Foster[7], William Henry[6], Joseph[5],
Joseph[4], Henry[3], Robert[2], John[1]), b. February
25, 1968 at Iowa City, Ia. (Ref. 2)

1874- Alma Emma Hogan, (Wadleigh: James
Colbert[11], Alma Emma[10], Bertha May[9], Everett[8],
Daniel Foster[7], William Henry[6], Joseph[5],
Joseph[4], Henry[3], Robert[2], John[1]), b. September
1970 at Oak Park, Ill. (Ref. 2)

1875- Francis Everett Hogan, (Wadleigh: James
Colbert[11], Alma Emma[10], Bertha May[9], Everett[8],
Daniel Foster[7], William Henry[6], Joseph[5],
Joseph[4], Henry[3], Robert[2], John[1]), b. January
25, 1972 at Chicago, Ill. (Ref. 2)

1876- Roy Alan Hogan, (Wadleigh: James
Colbert[11], Alma Emma[10], Bertha May[9], Everett[8],
Daniel Foster[7], William Henry[6], Joseph[5],
Joseph[4], Henry[3], Robert[2], John[1]), b. February
10, 1977 at Chicago, Ill. (Ref. 2)

1877- Patrick Walter Hogan, (Wadleigh: James
Colbert[11], Alma Emma[10], Bertha May[9], Everett[8],
Daniel Foster[7], William Henry[6], Joseph[5],
Joseph[4], Henry[3], Robert[2], John[1]), b. January
20, 1978 at Chicago, Ill. (Ref. 2)

**Issue of 1585- Francis Walter Hogan and
Minnie May (Holman) Hogan:**

1878- Kathleen Diane Hogan, (Wadleigh: Francis
Walter[11], Alma Emma[10], Bertha May[9], Everett[8],
Daniel Foster[7], William Henry[6], Joseph[5],
Joseph[4], Henry[3], Robert[2], John[1]), b. September
2, 1960 at Iowa Falls, Ia. m. May 23, 1981 at
Bellevue, Neb. Craig Steven Pendergast, no
additional data. Occ. h. Student-business, w.
Student-drafting. (Ref. 2)

1879- <u>Michael Francis Hogan</u>, (Wadleigh: Francis Walter[11], Alma Emma[10], Bertha May[9], Everett[8], Daniel Foster[7], William Henry[6], Joseph[5], Joseph[4], Henry[3], Robert[2], John[1]), b. July 30, 1962 at Iowa Falls, Ia. (Ref. 2)

Issue of 1585- Francis Walter Hogan and Linda Kay (Schimp) Hogan:

no issue

Issue of 1586- Gerald Thomas Hogan and Jessie Jean (Holman) Hogan:

1880- <u>Sherri Jean Hogan</u>, (Wadleigh: Gerald Thomas[11], Alma Emma[10], Bertha May[9], Everett[8], Daniel Foster[7], William Henry[6], Joseph[5], Joseph[4], Henry[3], Robert[2], John[1]), b. February 26, 1958 at Iowa Falls, Ia. m. June 11, 1977 at Iowa Falls Rex A. Meyer, no data. (Ref. 2)

1881- <u>Gerald Thomas Hogan, Jr.</u>, (Wadleigh: Gerald Thomas[11], Alma Emma[10], Bertha May[9], Everett[8], Daniel Foster[7], William Henry[6], Joseph[5], Joseph[4], Henry[3], Robert[2], John[1]), b. January 4, 1961 at Iowa Falls, Ia. Occ. Student in Arizona. (Ref. 2)

1882- <u>Kelly Brian Hogan</u>, (Wadleigh: Gerald Thomas[11], Alma Emma[10], Bertha May[9], Everett[8], Daniel Foster[7], William Henry[6], Joseph[5], Joseph[4], Henry[3], Robert[2], John[1]), b. September 23, 1962 at Iowa Falls, Ia. m. April 30, 1983 at Altoona, Ia. Kelli Karla Cory, no additional data. (Ref. 2)

Issue of 1587- Keith Allen Hogan and Joan (Schaper) (Knode) Hogan:

1883- Kendall Donavon Hogan, (Wadleigh: Keith Allen[11], Alma Emma[10], Bertha May[9], Everett[8], Daniel Foster[7], William Henry[6], Joseph[5], Joseph[4], Henry[3], Robert[2], John[1]), b. March 5, 1978. (Ref. 2)

Issue of Ronald M. Eason and 1589- June Louise (Hogan) Eason:

1884- Ronald Eugene Eason, (Wadleigh: June Louise[11], Alma Emma[10], Bertha May[9], Everett[8], Daniel Foster[7], William Henry[6], Joseph[5], Joseph[4], Henry[3], Robert[2], John[1]), b. May 7, 1960 at Iowa City, Ia. m. June 5, at Eldora, Ia. Debra S. Schuller, no additional data. (Ref. 2)

1885- Valerie Maxine Eason, (Wadleigh: June Louise[11], Alma Emma[10], Bertha May[9], Everett[8], Daniel Foster[7], William Henry[6], Joseph[5], Joseph[4], Henry[3], Robert[2], John[1]), b. April 23, 1965 in San Fernando Valley, Cal. (Ref. 2)

1886- George Clifford Eason, (Wadleigh: June Louise[11], Alma Emma[10], Bertha May[9], Everett[8], Daniel Foster[7], William Henry[6], Joseph[5], Joseph[4], Henry[3], Robert[2], John[1]), b. December 7, 1976 at Iowa Falls, Ia. (Ref. 2)

Issue of 1591- Donald Dean Hogan and Ruth Esther (Schaper) Hogan:

1887- Angela Annette Hogan, (Wadleigh: Donald Dean[11], Alma Emma[10], Bertha May[9], Everett[8], Daniel Foster[7], William Henry[6], Joseph[5], Joseph[4], Henry[3], Robert[2], John[1]), b. October 3, 1968 at Iowa Falls, Ia. (Ref. 2)

1888- David Ray Hogan, (Wadleigh: Donald
Dean[11], Alma Emma[10], Bertha May[9], Everett[8],
Daniel Foster[7], William Henry[6], Joseph[5],
Joseph[4], Henry[3], Robert[2], John[1]), b. February
7, 1970 at Iowa Falls, Ia. (Ref. 2)

1889- Nathaniel Lynn Hogan, (Wadleigh: Donald
Dean[11], Alma Emma[10], Bertha May[9], Everett[8],
Daniel Foster[7], William Henry[6], Joseph[5],
Joseph[4], Henry[3], Robert[2], John[1]), b. December
17, 1974 at Iowa Falls, Ia. (Ref. 2)

**Issue of 1593- George LeRoy Upton and De
Laine (Griffith) Upton:**

1890- George Kerris Upton, (Wadleigh: George
LeRoy[11], Audrey Belle[10], Hattie Belle[9],
Everett[8], Daniel Foster[7], William Henry[6],
Joseph[5], Joseph[4], Henry[3], Robert[2], John[1]), b.
January 31, 1958 at Windsor, Mo. (Ref. 2)

1891- Kristy De Ann Upton, (Wadleigh: George
LeRoy[11], Audrey Belle[10], Hattie Belle[9],
Everett[8], Daniel Foster[7], William Henry[6],
Joseph[5], Joseph[4], Henry[3], Robert[2], John[1]), b.
August 23, 1961 at Windsor, Mo. m. July 18,
1981 at Garner, Ia. Mark Dean Goodale, s. of
William Goodale and Veronica (Thieson) Goodale,
b. June 30, 1960 in Mitchell Co., Ia. Res.
Ames, Ia. (Ref. 2)

**Issue of 1594- Clyde Mervin Upton and Betty
Lou (Logan) Upton:**

1892- James Lee Upton, (Wadleigh: Clyde
Mervin[11], Audrey Belle[10], Hattie Belle[9],
Everett[8], Daniel Foster[7], William Henry[6],
Joseph[5], Joseph[4], Henry[3], Robert[2], John[1]), b.
January 22, 1965 at Windsor, Mo. (Ref. 2)

1893- <u>Theresa</u> <u>Lynette</u> <u>Upton</u>, (Wadleigh: Clyde Mervin[11], Audrey Belle[10], Hattie Belle[9], Everett[8], Daniel Foster[7], William Henry[6], Joseph[5], Joseph[4], Henry[3], Robert[2], John[1]), b. December 10, 1969, at Windsor, Mo. (Ref. 2)

Issue of John Thomas Bronson, Jr. and 1595- Alice Louise (Upton) Bronson:

1894- <u>John</u> <u>Thomas</u> <u>Bronson,</u> <u>III</u>, (Wadleigh: John Thomas[11], Audrey Belle[10], Hattie Belle[9], Everett[8], Daniel Foster[7], William Henry[6], Joseph[5], Joseph[4], Henry[3], Robert[2], John[1]), b. October 2, 1968 at Windsor, Mo. (Ref. 2)

1895- <u>Audrey</u> <u>Eloise</u> <u>Bronson</u>, (Wadleigh: John Thomas[11], Audrey Belle[10], Hattie Belle[9], Everett[8], Daniel Foster[7], William Henry[6], Joseph[5], Joseph[4], Henry[3], Robert[2], John[1]), b. December 24, 1973 at Sedalia, Mo. (Ref. 2)

Issue of Norman Scott Newkirk, Jr. and 1596- Marilee (Paige) Newkirk:

1896- <u>Nick</u> <u>James</u> <u>Newkirk</u>, (Wadleigh: Norman Scott[11], Audrey Belle[10], Hattie Belle[9], Everett[8], Daniel Foster[7], William Henry[6], Joseph[5], Joseph[4], Henry[3], Robert[2], John[1]), b. November 26, 1968 at Macks Creek, Mo. (Ref. 2)

Issue of Donny Arymol Sosebee and 1598- Mary Etta (Paige) Sosebee:

1897- <u>Laurie</u> <u>Anne</u> <u>Sosebee</u>, (Wadleigh: Donny Arymol[11], Audrey Belle[10], Hattie Belle[9], Everett[8], Daniel Foster[7], William Henry[6], Joseph[5], Joseph[4], Henry[3], Robert[2], John[1]), b. May 22, 1960 at Dallas, Tex. m. January 2, 1982 at Dallas, Gordon James Ball, s. of James

Boyd Ball and Charmian Coe Ball, b. April 8,
1956 at Odessa, Tex. Ed. w.- BS in Business
Administration and Accounting from Texas Tech.
Univ. h.- BS in Construction Engineering
Technology and Architecture from Texas Tech.
Univ. Occ. w.- CPA with accounting firm, h.-
Engineer/Estimator. Res. Casper Wyo. and
Dallas and Mesquite, Tex. (Ref. 2)

1898- Michael Craig Sosebee, (Wadleigh: Donny
Arymol[11], Audrey Belle[10], Hattie Belle[9],
Everett[8], Daniel Foster[7], William Henry[6],
Joseph[5], Joseph[4], Henry[3], Robert[2], John[1]), b.
August 28, 1961 at Dallas, Tex. (Ref. 2)

1899- Darren Keith Sosebee, (Wadleigh: Donny
Arymol[11], Audrey Belle[10], Hattie Belle[9],
Everett[8], Daniel Foster[7], William Henry[6],
Joseph[5], Joseph[4], Henry[3], Robert[2], John[1]), b.
December 21, 1967 (twin) at Dallas, Tex. (Ref.
2)

1900- Steven Kent Sosebee, (Wadleigh: Donny
Arymol[11], Audrey Belle[10], Hattie Belle[9],
Everett[8], Daniel Foster[7], William Henry[6],
Joseph[5], Joseph[4], Henry[3], Robert[2], John[1]), b.
December 21, 1967 (twin) at Dallas, Tex. (Ref.
2)

**Issue of John Baxter Kidd and 1599- Janet Sue
(Paige) Kidd:**

1901- John Jay (Kidd) English, (Wadleigh:
Janet Sue[11], Forest Martin[10], Hattie Belle[9],
Everett[8], Daniel Foster[7], William Henry[6],
Joseph[5], Joseph[4], Henry[3], Robert[2], John[1]), b.
April 20, 1964 at Wurtzburg, Germany, adpt. by
John Charles English in 1971. m. October 5,
1985 at Indianapolis, Ind. Brenda Jo Paton, no
additional data. (Ref. 2)

1902- <u>James Kyle (Kidd) English</u>, (Wadleigh:
Janet Sue[11], Forest Martin[10], Hattie Belle[9],
Everett[8], Daniel Foster[7], William Henry[6],
Joseph[5], Joseph[4], Henry[3], Robert[2], John[1]), b.
January 7, 1966 at Nuremburg, Germany, adpt. by
John Charles English in 1971. (Ref. 2)

**Issue of John Charles English and 1599- Janet
Sue (Paige) (Kidd) English:**

no issue.

**Issue of 1600- Howard Lee Paige and Martha
Kay (Pennington) Paige:**

1903- <u>Allen James Paige</u>, (Wadleigh: Howard
Lee[11], Forest Martin[10], Hattie Belle[9],
Everett[8], Daniel Foster[7], William Henry[6],
Joseph[5], Joseph[4], Henry[3], Robert[2], John[1]), b.
June 18, 1964 at Dallas, Tex. (Ref. 2)

**Issue of 1600- Howard Lee Paige and Velma
Jane (Bowen) (Curtis) Paige:**

1904- <u>Todd Anderson (Curtis) Paige</u>, (Wadleigh:
Howard Lee[11], Forest Martin[10], Hattie Belle[9],
Everett[8], Daniel Foster[7], William Henry[6],
Joseph[5], Joseph[4], Henry[3], Robert[2], John[1]), b.
January 11, 1968 at Dallas, Tex., adpt. by
Howard Lee Paige. (Ref. 2)

1905- <u>Kevin Lee Paige</u>, (Wadleigh: Howard
Lee[11], Forest Martin[10], Hattie Belle[9],
Everett[8], Daniel Foster[7], William Henry[6],
Joseph[5], Joseph[4], Henry[3], Robert[2], John[1]), b.
February 18, 1974 at Irving, Tex. (Ref. 2)

Issue of Robert Eugene Scott and 1603-Shirley Jean (Holley) Scott:

1906- Robert Keith Scott, (Wadleigh: Shirley Jean[11], Gladys Lorene[10], Hattie Belle[9], Everett[8], Daniel Foster[7], William Henry[6], Joseph[5], Joseph[4], Henry[3], Robert[2], John[1]), b. August 16, 1955 in Independence, Mo. m. August 20, 1983 at Kansas City, Kan. Catherine Elizabeth Wright, d. of Robert L. Wright and Jo Ann (O'Brien) Wright, no additional data. Res. Independence, Mo., (Ref. 2)

1907- Timothy Lee Scott, (Wadleigh: Shirley Jean[11], Gladys Lorene[10], Hattie Belle[9], Everett[8], Daniel Foster[7], William Henry[6], Joseph[5], Joseph[4], Henry[3], Robert[2], John[1]), b. July 19, 1962 at Independence, Mo. (Ref. 2)

Issue of 1604- Hoyt Allen Holley and Theodora Lee (Wise) Holley:

1908- Russell Allen Holley, (Wadleigh: Hoyt Allen[11], Gladys Lorene[10], Hattie Belle[9], Everett[8], Daniel Foster[7], William Henry[6], Joseph[5], Joseph[4], Henry[3], Robert[2], John[1]), b. July 6, 1966 at Sedalia, Mo. (Ref. 2)

Issue of 1605- Kenneth Carl Holley and Sharon Loyola (Paxton) Holley:

1909- Todd Kenneth Holley, (Wadleigh: Kenneth Carl[11], Gladys Lorene[10], Hattie Belle[9], Everett[8], Daniel Foster[7], William Henry[6], Joseph[5], Joseph[4], Henry[3], Robert[2], John[1]), b. December 8, 1966 at St. Charles, Mo. (Ref. 2)

1910- Angela Loyola Holley, (Wadleigh: Kenneth Carl[11], Gladys Lorene[10], Hattie Belle[9], Everett[8], Daniel Foster[7], William Henry[6],

Joseph[5], Joseph[4], Henry[3], Robert[2], John[1]), b.
October 30, 1969 at Kansas City, Mo. (Ref. 2)

1911- Shelly Christine Holley, (Wadleigh:
Kenneth Carl[11], Gladys Lorene[10], Hattie Belle[9],
Everett[8], Daniel Foster[7], William Henry[6],
Joseph[5], Joseph[4], Henry[3], Robert[2], John[1]), b.
September 17, 1972 at Kansas City, Mo. (Ref. 2)

Issue of Lowell Earnest Cobb, Jr. and 1606-Betty Ann (Holley) Cobb:

1912- Becky Ann Cobb, (Wadleigh: Betty Ann[11],
Gladys Lorene[10], Hattie Belle[9], Everett[8],
Daniel Foster[7], William Henry[6], Joseph[5],
Joseph[4], Henry[3], Robert[2], John[1]), b. June 17,
1968 at Sedalia, Mo. (Ref. 2)

1913- Bobbi Lynn Cobb, (Wadleigh: Betty
Ann[11], Gladys Lorene[10], Hattie Belle[9],
Everett[8], Daniel Foster[7], William Henry[6],
Joseph[5], Joseph[4], Henry[3], Robert[2], John[1]), b.
September 24, 1970 at Sedalia, Mo., d. January
4, 1979 at Warsaw, Mo., bur. at Shawnee
Cemetery, Warsaw, Mo. died in childhood.
(Ref. 2)

Issue of Philip Matthew Renzulli and 1607-Ruby Belle (Holley) Renzulli:

1914- Damon Mathew Renzulli, (Wadleigh: Ruby
Belle[11], Gladys Lorene[10], Hattie Belle[9],
Everett[8], Daniel Foster[7], William Henry[6],
Joseph[5], Joseph[4], Henry[3], Robert[2], John[1]), b.
September 14, 1972 at Rockville Center, Long
Island, N.Y. (Ref. 2)

1915- Kara Marie Renzulli, (Wadleigh: Ruby
Belle[11], Gladys Lorene[10], Hattie Belle[9],

Everett[8], Daniel Foster[7], William Henry[6], Joseph[5], Joseph[4], Henry[3], Robert[2], John[1]), b. October 20, 1975 at Rockville Center, Long Island, N.Y. (Ref. 2)

Issue of 1608- Charles Earl Paige, Jr. and Barbara Jean (Berry) Paige:

no issue

Issue of Harold Hause Duffey, Jr. and 1610- Patricia Ann (Paige) Duffey:

1916- Tricia Ann Duffey, (Wadleigh: Patricia Ann[11], Charles Earl[10], Hattie Belle[9], Everett[8], Daniel Foster[7], William Henry[6], Joseph[5], Joseph[4], Henry[3], Robert[2], John[1]), b. September 18, 1974 at Wichita, Kan. (Ref. 2)

1917- John Harold Duffey, (Wadleigh: Patricia Ann[11], Charles Earl[10], Hattie Belle[9], Everett[8], Daniel Foster[7], William Henry[6], Joseph[5], Joseph[4], Henry[3], Robert[2], John[1]), b. June 9, 1980 at Wichita, Kan. (Ref. 2)

1918- Kathryn Renee Duffey, (Wadleigh: Patricia Ann[11], Charles Earl[10], Hattie Belle[9], Everett[8], Daniel Foster[7], William Henry[6], Joseph[5], Joseph[4], Henry[3], Robert[2], John[1]), b. April 25, 1983 at Wichita, Kan. (Ref. 2)

Issue of Odea V. McNeil, Jr. and 1611- Carol Lee[11] (Wadleigh) McNeil:

1919- Russell Glen McNeil, (Wadleigh: Carol Lee[11], Elmer Wright[10], Louis Henry[9], Everett[8], Daniel Foster[7], William Henry[6], Joseph[5], Joseph[4], Henry[3], Robert[2], John[1]), b. July 25,

1961 at Beaumont, Tex., m. August 24, 1985 at
Neterland, Tex. Tammy McGowan, no additional
data. (Ref. 2)

1920- Teri Lyne McNeil, (Wadleigh: Carol
Lee[11], Elmer Wright[10], Louis Henry[9], Everett[8],
Daniel Foster[7], William Henry[6], Joseph[5],
Joseph[4], Henry[3], Robert[2], John[1]), b. August 25,
1964 at Beaumont, Tex., m. February 24, 1984
at Groves, Tex. Danny Jim Norton, s. of Herbert
Carl Norton and Dorothy Serrette Norton, b.
April 2, 1965 at Port Arthur, Tex., Occ. h.-
with Gulf States Utilities, w.- travel agent.
Res. Bridge City, Tex. (Ref. 2)

1921- Clinton Wade McNeil, (Wadleigh: Carol
Lee[11], Elmer Wright[10], Louis Henry[9], Everett[8],
Daniel Foster[7], William Henry[6], Joseph[5],
Joseph[4], Henry[3], Robert[2], John[1]), b. December
29, 1966 at Beaumont, Tex., d. August 17, 1984
at Port Neches, Tex. died in adolescence.
(Ref. 2)

1922- Robyn Lee McNeil, (Wadleigh: Carol
Lee[11], Elmer Wright[10], Louis Henry[9], Everett[8],
Daniel Foster[7], William Henry[6], Joseph[5],
Joseph[4], Henry[3], Robert[2], John[1]), b. February
10, 1971 at Beaumont, Tex. (Ref. 2)

**Issue of Charles Leon Miller and 1612- Myrna
Kay[11] (Wadleigh) Miller:**

1923- Wendi K. Miller, (Wadleigh: Myrna Kay[11],
Elmer Wright[10], Louis Henry[9], Everett[8], Daniel
Foster[7], William Henry[6], Joseph[5], Joseph[4],
Henry[3], Robert[2], John[1]), b. January 8, 1965 at
Beaumont, Tex. (Ref. 2)

1924- C. Craig Miller, (Wadleigh: Myrna Kay[11],
Elmer Wright[10], Louis Henry[9], Everett[8], Daniel

Foster[7], William Henry[6], Joseph[5], Joseph[4],
Henry[3], Robert[2], John[1]), b. September 6, 1967
at Beaumont, Tex. (Ref. 2)

**Issue of James Winnfield Bigelow and 1613-
Lucinda Rae[11] (Wadleigh) Bigelow:**

1925- <u>Jeffery</u> <u>Winnfield</u> (Bigelow) <u>Gaudet</u>,
(Wadleigh: Lucinda Rae[11], Elmer Wright[10],
Louis Henry[9], Everett[8], Daniel Foster[7], William
Henry[6], Joseph[5], Joseph[4], Henry[3], Robert[2],
John[1]), b. August 18, 1971 at Sulphur City,
Calcasieu Par., La., adpt. November 1980 by
Robert William Gaudet. (Ref. 2)

1926- <u>Michael</u> <u>James</u> (Bigelow) <u>Gaudet</u>,
(Wadleigh: Lucinda Rae[11], Elmer Wright[10],
Louis Henry[9], Everett[8], Daniel Foster[7], William
Henry[6], Joseph[5], Joseph[4], Henry[3], Robert[2],
John[1]), b. March 1, 1976 at Sulphur City,
Calcasieu Par., La., adpt. November 1980 by
Robert William Gaudet. (Ref. 2)

**Issue of Robert William Gaudet, Sr. and 1613-
Lucinda Rae[11] (Wadleigh) (Bigelow) Gaudet:**

no issue

**Issue of 1615- Juan Loy Smith and Gayle Anita
(Harris) Smith:**

1927- <u>Tracy</u> <u>Rene'</u> <u>Smith</u>, (Wadleigh: Juan
Loy[11], Cleo Louise[10], Louis Henry[9], Everett[8],
Daniel Foster[7], William Henry[6], Joseph[5],
Joseph[4], Henry[3], Robert[2], John[1]), b. September
6, 1961 at Independence, Mo., m. July 6,
1985 at Independence Jack D. Floyd, s. of
Tommie Floyd and Gerta Floyd. no additional
data. Res. Orlando, Fla. (Ref. 2)

1928- Anita Gay Smith, (Wadleigh: Juan Loy[11], Cleo Louise[10], Louis Henry[9], Everett[8], Daniel Foster[7], William Henry[6], Joseph[5], Joseph[4], Henry[3], Robert[2], John[1]), b. August 7, 1965 at Independence, Mo. (Ref. 2)

Issue of 1615- Errol Louis Smith and Karen Sue (Griese) Smith:

1929- Chad Errol Smith, (Wadleigh: Errol Louis[11], Cleo Louise[10], Louis Henry[9], Everett[8], Daniel Foster[7], William Henry[6], Joseph[5], Joseph[4], Henry[3], Robert[2], John[1]), b. February 29, 1968 at Town and Country, Mo. (Ref. 2)

1930- Matthew Shane Smith, (Wadleigh: Errol Louis[11], Cleo Louise[10], Louis Henry[9], Everett[8], Daniel Foster[7], William Henry[6], Joseph[5], Joseph[4], Henry[3], Robert[2], John[1]), b. August 16, 1971 at Town and Country, Mo. (Ref. 2)

Issue of John Hove and 1616- Sherry Sue (Templeton) Hove:

no issue

Issue of Terry Lynn Janusz and 1616- Sherry Sue (Templeton) (Hove) Janusz:

no issue

Issue of Verne Elston Schanz, Jr. and 1617- April Lyn (Templeton) Schanz:

1931- Lacey Michelle Schanz, (Wadleigh: April Lyn[11], Mabel Lucille[10], Louis Henry[9], Everett[8], Daniel Foster[7], William Henry[6], Joseph[5], Joseph[4], Henry[3], Robert[2], John[1]), b. October 7, 1978 at Kansas City, Mo. (Ref. 2)

1932- <u>Corey Alan Schanz</u>, (Wadleigh: April
Lyn[11], Mabel Lucille[10], Louis Henry[9], Everett[8],
Daniel Foster[7], William Henry[6], Joseph[5],
Joseph[4], Henry[3], Robert[2], John[1]), b. April 26,
1983 at Kansas City, Mo. (Ref. 2)

**Issue of Arnold Howard McMann, Jr. and 1618-
Oneta Jan (Templeton) McMann:**

no issue

**Issue of 1620- James Wesley Bullard, IV and
Judith Carmen (Ford) Bullard:**

1933- <u>James Wesley Bullard, V</u>, (Wadleigh:
James Wesley[11], Iva Lou[10], Louis Henry[9],
Everett[8], Daniel Foster[7], William Henry[6],
Joseph[5], Joseph[4], Henry[3], Robert[2], John[1]), b.
December 14, 1970 at Neosho, Mo. (Ref. 2)

1934- <u>Krystal Joy Bullard</u>, (Wadleigh: James
Wesley[11], Iva Lou[10], Louis Henry[9], Everett[8],
Daniel Foster[7], William Henry[6], Joseph[5],
Joseph[4], Henry[3], Robert[2], John[1]), b. March 27,
1973 at St. Joseph, Mo. (Ref. 2)

1935- <u>Julieta Holaday Bullard</u>, (Wadleigh:
James Wesley[11], Iva Lou[10], Louis Henry[9],
Everett[8], Daniel Foster[7], William Henry[6],
Joseph[5], Joseph[4], Henry[3], Robert[2], John[1]), b.
March 19, 1977 at Angeles City, Philippines.
(Ref. 2)

**Issue of Stephen Arthur Smith and 1621-
Rebecca Cheryl (Bullard) Smith:**

1936- <u>Stephanie Elise Smith</u>, (Wadleigh:
Rebecca Cheryl[11], Iva Lou[10], Louis Henry[9],
Everett[8], Daniel Foster[7], William Henry[6],

Joseph[5], Joseph[4], Henry[3], Robert[2], John[1]), b. February 16, 1968 at Rantoul, Ill. (Ref. 2)

1937- <u>Christopher William Smith</u>, (Wadleigh: Rebecca Cheryl[11], Iva Lou[10], Louis Henry[9], Everett[8], Daniel Foster[7], William Henry[6], Joseph[5], Joseph[4], Henry[3], Robert[2], John[1]), b. December 3, 1970 at Tucson, Ariz. (Ref. 2)

Issue of 1622- Loring Louis Bullard and Paula Kay (Ringer) Bullard:

no issue

Issue of Kirk Troy Garten and 1623- Deborah Carol (Bullard) Garten:

no issue

Issue of 1627- Alan Benton Licklider and Margaret Geneva (Say) Licklider:

1938- <u>Ryan Alan Licklider</u>, (Wadleigh: Alan Benton[11], Norwood[10], Hazel Carrie[9], Everett[8], Daniel Foster[7], William Henry[6], Joseph[5], Joseph[4], Henry[3], Robert[2], John[1]), b. September 21, 1981 at Bend, Ore. (Ref. 2)

1939- <u>Geneva Marie Licklider</u>, (Wadleigh: Alan Benton[11], Norwood[10], Hazel Carrie[9], Everett[8], Daniel Foster[7], William Henry[6], Joseph[5], Joseph[4], Henry[3], Robert[2], John[1]), b. May 25, 1983 at Bellevue, Wash. (Ref. 2)

Issue of Robin Allen Espasandin and 1628- Jane Carrie (Licklider) Espasandin:

1940- <u>Paul Alan Espasandin</u>, (Wadleigh: Jane Carrie[11], Norwood[10], Hazel Carrie[9], Everett[8],

Daniel Foster[7], William Henry[6], Joseph[5], Joseph[4], Henry[3], Robert[2], John[1]), b. May 3, 1978 at Bellevue, Wash. (Ref. 2)

1941- Carrie Lynn Espasandin, (Wadleigh: Jane Carrie[11], Norwood[10], Hazel Carrie[9], Everett[8], Daniel Foster[7], William Henry[6], Joseph[5], Joseph[4], Henry[3], Robert[2], John[1]), b. April 27, 1982 at Bellevue, Wash. (Ref. 2)

Issue of Gerry Dunn and 1630- Lois Irene (Martin) Dunn:

1942- Machele Denise Dunn, (Wadleigh: Lois Irene[11], Irene[10], Fred Elmer[9], Henry Libby[8], Daniel Foster[7], William Henry[6], Joseph[5], Joseph[4], Henry[3], Robert[2], John[1]), b. July 3, 1962. (Ref. 1)

1943- Jerry Elmer Dunn, (Wadleigh: Lois Irene[11], Irene[10], Fred Elmer[9], Henry Libby[8], Daniel Foster[7], William Henry[6], Joseph[5], Joseph[4], Henry[3], Robert[2], John[1]), b. October 3, 1963. (Ref. 1)

Issue of 1632- Charles William Daehn and Vickie (Seamans) Daehn:

1944- Cory Ralph Daehn, (Wadleigh: Charles William[11], Myrtle Evelyn[10], Fred Elmer[9], Henry Libby[8], Daniel Foster[7], William Henry[6], Joseph[5], Joseph[4], Henry[3], Robert[2], John[1]), b. July 6, 1977. (Ref. 1)

Issue of Harold Hiner and 1641- Francis Marie[11] (Wadleigh) Hiner:

1945- Douglas Harold Hiner, (Wadleigh: Charles Elmer[10], Ralph Libby[9], Henry Libby[8], Daniel Foster[7], William Henry[6], Joseph[5], Joseph[4], Henry[3], Robert[2], John[1]), b. February 21, 1962. (Ref. 1)

1946- Elizabeth Ann Hiner, (Wadleigh: Charles Elmer[10], Ralph Libby[9], Henry Libby[8], Daniel Foster[7], William Henry[6], Joseph[5], Joseph[4], Henry[3], Robert[2], John[1]), b. September 24, 1963. (Ref. 1)

1947- Paula Marie Hiner, (Wadleigh: Charles Elmer[10], Ralph Libby[9], Henry Libby[8], Daniel Foster[7], William Henry[6], Joseph[5], Joseph[4], Henry[3], Robert[2], John[1]), b. January 21, 1965. (Ref. 1)

Issue of 1642- Charles Vernon[11] Wadleigh and Linda (Gertz) Wadleigh:

1948- Christina Lee[12] Wadleigh, (Charles Vernon[11], Charles Elmer[10], Ralph Libby[9], Henry Libby[8], Daniel Foster[7], William Henry[6], Joseph[5], Joseph[4], Henry[3], Robert[2], John[1]), b. June 1. (Ref. 1)

1949- Vicki[12] Wadleigh, (Charles Vernon[11], Charles Elmer[10], Ralph Libby[9], Henry Libby[8], Daniel Foster[7], William Henry[6], Joseph[5], Joseph[4], Henry[3], Robert[2], John[1]), b. October 9, 1972. (Ref. 1)

Issue of 1643- William Jennings Sayre and Betty (Elmer) Sayre:

1950- Kevin Sayre, (Wadleigh: William Jennings[11], Twyla Mae[10], Ralph Libby[9], Henry Libby[8], Daniel Foster[7], William Henry[6], Joseph[5], Joseph[4], Henry[3], Robert[2], John[1]), b. April 7, 1960. (Ref. 1)

1951- Sandra Mischeele Sayre, (Wadleigh: William Jennings[11], Twyla Mae[10], Ralph Libby[9], Henry Libby[8], Daniel Foster[7], William Henry[6], Joseph[5], Joseph[4], Henry[3], Robert[2], John[1]), b. September 10, 1963. (Ref. 1)

Issue of Ronald C. Henderson and 1644- Louanna (Sayre) Henderson:

1952- Ronda Renae Henderson, (Wadleigh: Louanna[11], Twyla Mae[10], Ralph Libby[9], Henry Libby[8], Daniel Foster[7], William Henry[6], Joseph[5], Joseph[4], Henry[3], Robert[2], John[1]), b. May 19, 1967. (Ref. 1)

Issue of Fred Dowdy and 1680- Elva Myreen (Klein) Dowdy:

1953- Loren Bean Dowdy, (Wadleigh: Elva Myreen[11], Elva Aldina[10], Harold Brewster[9], Henry Libby[8], Daniel Foster[7], William Henry[6], Joseph[5], Joseph[4], Henry[3], Robert[2], John[1]), b. February 25, 1959. (Ref. 1)

1954- Denise Eileen Dowdy, (Wadleigh: Elva Myreen[11], Elva Aldina[10], Harold Brewster[9], Henry Libby[8], Daniel Foster[7], William Henry[6], Joseph[5], Joseph[4], Henry[3], Robert[2], John[1]), b. July 22, 1961. (Ref. 1)

1955- Valerie Lynn Dowdy, (Wadleigh: Elva Myreen[11], Elva Aldina[10], Harold Brewster[9], Henry Libby[8], Daniel Foster[7], William Henry[6], Joseph[5], Joseph[4], Henry[3], Robert[2], John[1]), b. July 20, 1962. (Ref. 1)

1956- Scott Douglas Dowdy, (Wadleigh: Elva Myreen[11], Elva Aldina[10], Harold Brewster[9], Henry Libby[8], Daniel Foster[7], William Henry[6], Joseph[5], Joseph[4], Henry[3], Robert[2], John[1]), b. June 10, 1964. (Ref. 1)

Issue of Richard Stroup and 1680- Elva Myreen (Klein) (Dowdy) Stroup:

no issue

Issue of Jerry Wall and 1682- Ernestine Gay (Klein) Wall:

1957- Keith Darren Wall, (Wadleigh: Ernestine Gay[11], Elva Aldina[10], Harold Brewster[9], Henry Libby[8], Daniel Foster[7], William Henry[6], Joseph[5], Joseph[4], Henry[3], Robert[2], John[1]), b. March 10, 1966. (Ref. 1)

1958- Melita Lanette Wall, (Wadleigh: Ernestine Gay[11], Elva Aldina[10], Harold Brewster[9], Henry Libby[8], Daniel Foster[7], William Henry[6], Joseph[5], Joseph[4], Henry[3], Robert[2], John[1]), b. September 14, 1968. (Ref. 1)

Issue of Bobby L. Waddell and 1681- Ernestine Gay (Klein) (Wall) Waddell:

no issue

Issue of 1682- Norvyn Bruce Klein and Bonnie Jean (Ferdig) Klein:

1959- Deanna Marie Klein, (Wadleigh: Norvyn Bruce[11], Elva Aldina[10], Harold Brewster[9], Henry Libby[8], Daniel Foster[7], William Henry[6], Joseph[5], Joseph[4], Henry[3], Robert[2], John[1]), b. July 9, 1969. (Ref. 1)

Issue of 1682- Norvyn Bruce Klein and Donna Carol (Smark) Klein:

1960- Norvyn Michael Klein, (Wadleigh: Norvyn Bruce[11], Elva Aldina[10], Harold Brewster[9], Henry Libby[8], Daniel Foster[7], William Henry[6], Joseph[5], Joseph[4], Henry[3], Robert[2], John[1]), b. September 1, 1974. (Ref. 1)

1961- Jeremy Austin Klein, (Wadleigh: Norvyn Bruce[11], Elva Aldina[10], Harold Brewster[9], Henry Libby[8], Daniel Foster[7], William Henry[6], Joseph[5], Joseph[4], Henry[3], Robert[2], John[1]), b. April 22, 1976. (Ref. 1)

Issue of Kenneth Kinkel and 1683- Cheryle Ann (Dayton) Kinkel:

1962- Kenneth William Kinkel, (Wadleigh: Cheryle Ann[11], Joyce Ellen[10], Harold Brewster[9], Henry Libby[8], Daniel Foster[7], William Henry[6], Joseph[5], Joseph[4], Henry[3], Robert[2], John[1]), b. October 2, 1971. (Ref. 1)

1963- Kevin Allen Kinkel, (Wadleigh: Cheryle Ann[11], Joyce Ellen[10], Harold Brewster[9], Henry Libby[8], Daniel Foster[7], William Henry[6], Joseph[5], Joseph[4], Henry[3], Robert[2], John[1]), b. March 18, 1977. (Ref. 1)

Issue of William Allen Moore and 1684- Judith Lynne (Dayton) Moore:

1964- Tammy Lynn Moore, (Wadleigh: Judith Lynne[11], Joyce Ellen[10], Harold Brewster[9], Henry Libby[8], Daniel Foster[7], William Henry[6], Joseph[5], Joseph[4], Henry[3], Robert[2], John[1]), b. June 10, 1975. (Ref. 1)

Issue of David Martinez and 1686- Linda Diane[11] (Wadleigh) Martinez:

1965- Diana Jo Martinez, (Wadleigh: Linda Diane[11], Calvin Herbert[10], Harold Brewster[9], Henry Libby[8], Daniel Foster[7], William Henry[6], Joseph[5], Joseph[4], Henry[3], Robert[2], John[1]), b. December 18, 1975. (Ref. 1)

Issue of Robert Scott Rice and 1698- Karen Sue[11] (Wadleigh) Rice:

1966- Rebecca Thayer Rice, (Wadleigh: Karen Sue[11], Glen Eugene[10], Eugene Henry[9], Henry Libby[8], Daniel Foster[7], William Henry[6], Joseph[5], Joseph[4], Henry[3], Robert[2], John[1]), b. June 4, 1975. (Ref. 1)

Issue of James Sides and 1699- Michele Allyn[11] (Wadleigh) Sides:

1967- Colin James Sides, (Wadleigh: Michele Allyn[11], Glen Eugene[10], Eugene Henry[9], Henry Libby[8], Daniel Foster[7], William Henry[6], Joseph[5], Joseph[4], Henry[3], Robert[2], John[1]), b. October 30, 1973. (Ref. 1)

Issue of Charles Baker and 1700- Debra Frances[11] (Wadleigh) Baker:

1968- <u>Justin Glen Baker</u>, (Wadleigh: Debra Frances[11], Glen Eugene[10], Eugene Henry[9], Henry Libby[8], Daniel Foster[7], William Henry[6], Joseph[5], Joseph[4], Henry[3], Robert[2], John[1]), b. January 10, 1977. (Ref. 1)

Issue of Clay Markle and 1702- Bernice Leota (Enns) Markle:

1969- <u>Lynne Anne Markle</u>, (Wadleigh: Bernice Leota[11], Mable Leota[10], Edna Rose[9], Henry Libby[8], Daniel Foster[7], William Henry[6], Joseph[5], Joseph[4], Henry[3], Robert[2], John[1]), b. April 24, 1959. (Ref. 1)

1970- <u>Larry Allen Markle</u>, (Wadleigh: Bernice Leota[11], Mable Leota[10], Edna Rose[9], Henry Libby[8], Daniel Foster[7], William Henry[6], Joseph[5], Joseph[4], Henry[3], Robert[2], John[1]), b. July 16, 1960. (Ref. 1)

1971- <u>Diane Elise Markle</u>, (Wadleigh: Bernice Leota[11], Mable Leota[10], Edna Rose[9], Henry Libby[8], Daniel Foster[7], William Henry[6], Joseph[5], Joseph[4], Henry[3], Robert[2], John[1]), b. February 19, 1967. (Ref. 1)

1972- <u>Cindy Lee Markle</u>, (Wadleigh: Bernice Leota[11], Mable Leota[10], Edna Rose[9], Henry Libby[8], Daniel Foster[7], William Henry[6], Joseph[5], Joseph[4], Henry[3], Robert[2], John[1]), b. January 12, 1969. (Ref. 1)

Issue of 1703- Vernon Royse Enns and Sue (Long) Enns:

1973- Kimberly Sue Enns, (Wadleigh: Vernon Royse[11], Mable Leota[10], Edna Rose[9], Henry Libby[8], Daniel Foster[7], William Henry[6], Joseph[5], Joseph[4], Henry[3], Robert[2], John[1]), b. December 1, 1960. (Ref. 1)

1974- Vicki Lee Enns, (Wadleigh: Vernon Royse[11], Mable Leota[10], Edna Rose[9], Henry Libby[8], Daniel Foster[7], William Henry[6], Joseph[5], Joseph[4], Henry[3], Robert[2], John[1]), b. July 25, 1962. (Ref. 1)

1975- Douglas Brent Enns, (Wadleigh: Vernon Royse[11], Mable Leota[10], Edna Rose[9], Henry Libby[8], Daniel Foster[7], William Henry[6], Joseph[5], Joseph[4], Henry[3], Robert[2], John[1]), b. May 20, 1965. (Ref. 1)

1976- Terri David Enns, (Wadleigh: Vernon Royse[11], Mable Leota[10], Edna Rose[9], Henry Libby[8], Daniel Foster[7], William Henry[6], Joseph[5], Joseph[4], Henry[3], Robert[2], John[1]), b. August 9, 1970. (Ref. 1)

Issue of 1704- Ronald Karl Enns and Marilyn Kaye (Watters) Enns:

1977- Donnie Ray Enns, (Wadleigh: Ronald Karl[11], Mable Leota[10], Edna Rose[9], Henry Libby[8], Daniel Foster[7], William Henry[6], Joseph[5], Joseph[4], Henry[3], Robert[2], John[1]), b. January 15, 1960. (Ref. 1)

1978- Kathy Dawn Enns, (Wadleigh: Ronald Karl[11], Mable Leota[10], Edna Rose[9], Henry Libby[8], Daniel Foster[7], William Henry[6], Joseph[5], Joseph[4], Henry[3], Robert[2], John[1]), b. June 23, 1961. (Ref. 1)

1979- Gary Wayne Enns, (Wadleigh: Ronald Karl[11], Mable Leota[10], Edna Rose[9], Henry Libby[8], Daniel Foster[7], William Henry[6], Joseph[5], Joseph[4], Henry[3], Robert[2], John[1]), b. July 25, 1962. (Ref. 1)

1980- Sherri Ranee Enns, (Wadleigh: Ronald Karl[11], Mable Leota[10], Edna Rose[9], Henry Libby[8], Daniel Foster[7], William Henry[6], Joseph[5], Joseph[4], Henry[3], Robert[2], John[1]), b. May 29, 1969. (Ref. 1)

Issue of 1705- Kenneth Eugene Enns and Karen Sue (Seipp) Enns:

1981- Jeffrey Scott Enns, (Wadleigh: Kenneth Eugene[11], Mable Leota[10], Edna Rose[9], Henry Libby[8], Daniel Foster[7], William Henry[6], Joseph[5], Joseph[4], Henry[3], Robert[2], John[1]), b. February 10, 1977 (adpt.) (Ref. 1)

Issue of 1708- Stanley Ray Nice and Marjorie (Brunk) Nice:

1982- Carla Sue Nice, (Wadleigh: Stanley Ray[11], Harry Alfred[10], Edna Rose[9], Henry Libby[8], Daniel Foster[7], William Henry[6], Joseph[5], Joseph[4], Henry[3], Robert[2], John[1]), b. July 29, 1964. (Ref. 1)

1983- Kevin Ray Nice, (Wadleigh: Stanley Ray[11], Harry Alfred[10], Edna Rose[9], Henry Libby[8], Daniel Foster[7], William Henry[6], Joseph[5], Joseph[4], Henry[3], Robert[2], John[1]), b. March 14, 1967. (Ref. 1)

Issue of Lee Gingerich and 1709- Mary Joyce (Nice) Gingerich:

1984- Cheryle Ann Gingerich, (Wadleigh: Mary Joyce[11], Harry Alfred[10], Edna Rose[9], Henry Libby[8], Daniel Foster[7], William Henry[6], Joseph[5], Joseph[4], Henry[3], Robert[2], John[1]), b. November 2, 1974. (Ref. 1)

Issue of 1711- Lester Wayne Nice and Linda (Birky) Nice:

1985- Darrel Jay Nice, (Wadleigh: Lester Wayne[11], Harry Alfred[10], Edna Rose[9], Henry Libby[8], Daniel Foster[7], William Henry[6], Joseph[5], Joseph[4], Henry[3], Robert[2], John[1]), b. September 14, 1968. (Ref. 1)

Issue of 1711- Eldon Lee Nice and Linda (Burks) Nice:

1986- Jeffrey Lee Nice, (Wadleigh: Eldon Lee[11], Harry Alfred[10], Edna Rose[9], Henry Libby[8], Daniel Foster[7], William Henry[6], Joseph[5], Joseph[4], Henry[3], Robert[2], John[1]), b. August 11, 1974. (Ref. 1)

1987- Tamara Michele Nice, (Wadleigh: Eldon Lee[11], Harry Alfred[10], Edna Rose[9], Henry Libby[8], Daniel Foster[7], William Henry[6], Joseph[5], Joseph[4], Henry[3], Robert[2], John[1]), b. June 20, 1977. (Ref. 1)

Issue of Marion Knox and 1715- Doris LaVerne (Wolfer) Knox:

1988- Duane Allen Knox, (Wadleigh: Doris LaVerne[11], Ida Rose[10], Edna Rose[9], Henry Libby[8], Daniel Foster[7], William Henry[6],

Joseph[5], Joseph[4], Henry[3], Robert[2], John[1]), b. June 1, 1960. (Ref. 1)

1989- <u>Steven Louis Knox</u>, (Wadleigh: Doris LaVerne[11], Ida Rose[10], Edna Rose[9], Henry Libby[8], Daniel Foster[7], William Henry[6], Joseph[5], Joseph[4], Henry[3], Robert[2], John[1]), b. April 15, 1962. (Ref. 1)

1990- <u>Larry Leone Knox</u>, (Wadleigh: Doris LaVerne[11], Ida Rose[10], Edna Rose[9], Henry Libby[8], Daniel Foster[7], William Henry[6], Joseph[5], Joseph[4], Henry[3], Robert[2], John[1]), b. March 26, 1963. (Ref. 1)

1991- <u>Daryl Vernon Knox</u>, (Wadleigh: Doris LaVerne[11], Ida Rose[10], Edna Rose[9], Henry Libby[8], Daniel Foster[7], William Henry[6], Joseph[5], Joseph[4], Henry[3], Robert[2], John[1]), b. May 31, 1974. (Ref. 1)

Issue of Millard Paulus and 1716- Dianne Joyce (Wolfer) Paulus:

1992- <u>Marlin Dean Paulus</u>, (Wadleigh: Dianne Joyce[11], Ida Rose[10], Edna Rose[9], Henry Libby[8], Daniel Foster[7], William Henry[6], Joseph[5], Joseph[4], Henry[3], Robert[2], John[1]), b. May 3, 1961. (Ref. 1)

1993- <u>Karen Louis Paulus</u>, (Wadleigh: Dianne Joyce[11], Ida Rose[10], Edna Rose[9], Henry Libby[8], Daniel Foster[7], William Henry[6], Joseph[5], Joseph[4], Henry[3], Robert[2], John[1]), b. October 15, 1962. (Ref. 1)

1994- <u>Leon Daniel Paulus</u>, (Wadleigh: Dianne Joyce[11], Ida Rose[10], Edna Rose[9], Henry Libby[8], Daniel Foster[7], William Henry[6], Joseph[5],

Joseph[4], Henry[3], Robert[2], John[1]), b. April 24, 1964. (Ref. 1)

1995- Janet Marie Paulus, (Wadleigh: Dianne Joyce[11], Ida Rose[10], Edna Rose[9], Henry Libby[8], Daniel Foster[7], William Henry[6], Joseph[5], Joseph[4], Henry[3], Robert[2], John[1]), b. May 17, 1965. (Ref. 1)

Issue of Kenneth Lee Gerig and 1717- Alta Rose (Wolfer) Gerig:

1996- Arlan Kent Gerig, (Wadleigh: Kenneth Lee[11], Ida Rose[10], Edna Rose[9], Henry Libby[8], Daniel Foster[7], William Henry[6], Joseph[5], Joseph[4], Henry[3], Robert[2], John[1]), b. October 28, 1966. (Ref. 1)

1997- Galen Lewis Gerig, (Wadleigh: Kenneth Lee[11], Ida Rose[10], Edna Rose[9], Henry Libby[8], Daniel Foster[7], William Henry[6], Joseph[5], Joseph[4], Henry[3], Robert[2], John[1]), b. April 24, 1969. (Ref. 1)

1998- Lynette Rose Gerig, (Wadleigh: Kenneth Lee[11], Ida Rose[10], Edna Rose[9], Henry Libby[8], Daniel Foster[7], William Henry[6], Joseph[5], Joseph[4], Henry[3], Robert[2], John[1]), b. July 30, 1975. (Ref. 1)

Issue of Gary Hooley and 1718- Miriam Jean (Wolfer) Hooley:

1999- Randall Eric Hooley, (Wadleigh: Miriam Jean[11], Ida Rose[10], Edna Rose[9], Henry Libby[8], Daniel Foster[7], William Henry[6], Joseph[5], Joseph[4], Henry[3], Robert[2], John[1]), b. July 26, 1971. (Ref. 1)

2000- <u>Vicky Leigh Hooley</u>, (Wadleigh: Miriam Jean[11], Ida Rose[10], Edna Rose[9], Henry Libby[8], Daniel Foster[7], William Henry[6], Joseph[5], Joseph[4], Henry[3], Robert[2], John[1]), b. September 13, 1974. (Ref. 1)

Issue of 1719- Marvin Doyle Wolfer and Louise (Weldon) Wolfer:

2001- <u>John Phillip Wolfer</u>, (Wadleigh: Marvin Doyle[11], Ida Rose[10], Edna Rose[9], Henry Libby[8], Daniel Foster[7], William Henry[6], Joseph[5], Joseph[4], Henry[3], Robert[2], John[1]), b. October 24, 1971. (Ref. 1)

2002- <u>Monica Ann Wolfer</u>, (Wadleigh: Marvin Doyle[11], Ida Rose[10], Edna Rose[9], Henry Libby[8], Daniel Foster[7], William Henry[6], Joseph[5], Joseph[4], Henry[3], Robert[2], John[1]), b. August 29, 1972. (Ref. 1)

2003- <u>Brian Heath Wolfer</u>, (Wadleigh: Marvin Doyle[11], Ida Rose[10], Edna Rose[9], Henry Libby[8], Daniel Foster[7], William Henry[6], Joseph[5], Joseph[4], Henry[3], Robert[2], John[1]), b. October 7, 1974. (Ref. 1)

2004- <u>Sue Ann Joy Wolfer</u>, (Wadleigh: Marvin Doyle[11], Ida Rose[10], Edna Rose[9], Henry Libby[8], Daniel Foster[7], William Henry[6], Joseph[5], Joseph[4], Henry[3], Robert[2], John[1]), b. May 23, 1977. (Ref. 1)

Issue of Stanley Kroff and 1720- Marlene Yovonne (Nice) Kroff:

2005- <u>Jeremy Arthur Kroff</u>, (Wadleigh: Marlene Yavonne[11], Howard Fred[10], Edna Rose[9], Henry Libby[8], Daniel Foster[7], William Henry[6],

Joseph[5], Joseph[4], Henry[3], Robert[2], John[1]), b.
March 17, 1969. (Ref. 1)

2006- <u>Carrie Heather Kroff</u>, (Wadleigh: Marlene
Yavonne[11], Howard Fred[10], Edna Rose[9], Henry
Libby[8], Daniel Foster[7], William Henry[6],
Joseph[5], Joseph[4], Henry[3], Robert[2], John[1]), b.
January 21, 1972. (Ref. 1)

**Issue of 1722- Loren Howard Nice and Susan
(Meyers) Nice:**

2007- <u>Teresa Ann Nice</u>, (Wadleigh: Loren
Howard[11], Howard Fred[10], Edna Rose[9], Henry
Libby[8], Daniel Foster[7], William Henry[6],
Joseph[5], Joseph[4], Henry[3], Robert[2], John[1]), b.
June 19, 1967. (Ref. 1)

2008- <u>Mathew Loren Nice</u>, (Wadleigh: Loren
Howard[11], Howard Fred[10], Edna Rose[9], Henry
Libby[8], Daniel Foster[7], William Henry[6],
Joseph[5], Joseph[4], Henry[3], Robert[2], John[1]), b.
August 18, 1971. (Ref. 1)

**Issue of 1724- Dennis Leone Nice and Margaret
(Stauffer) Nice:**

2009- <u>Angela Michelle Nice</u>, (Wadleigh: Dennis
Leone[11], Howard Fred[10], Edna Rose[9], Henry
Libby[8], Daniel Foster[7], William Henry[6],
Joseph[5], Joseph[4], Henry[3], Robert[2], John[1]), b.
December 13, 1975. (Ref. 1)

2010- <u>Christine Dawn Nice</u>, (Wadleigh: Dennis
Leone[11], Howard Fred[10], Edna Rose[9], Henry
Libby[8], Daniel Foster[7], William Henry[6],
Joseph[5], Joseph[4], Henry[3], Robert[2], John[1]), b.
June 26, 1977. (Ref. 1)

Issue of 1726- Freddie LaVerne Coblentz and
Marilyn Ann (Blanchard) Coblentz:

2011- Kimberly Kae Coblentz, (Wadleigh:
Freddie LaVerne[11], Ruth Ellen[10], Edna Rose[9],
Henry Libby[8], Daniel Foster[7], William Henry[6],
Joseph[5], Joseph[4], Henry[3], Robert[2], John[1]), b.
June 29, 1965. (Ref. 1)

Issue of 1726- Freddie LaVerne Coblentz and
Pamela (Stevens) Coblentz:

2012- Cory Allen Coblentz, (Wadleigh: Freddie
LaVerne[11], Ruth Ellen[10], Edna Rose[9], Henry
Libby[8], Daniel Foster[7], William Henry[6],
Joseph[5], Joseph[4], Henry[3], Robert[2], John[1]), b.
September 13, 1971. (Ref. 1)

Issue of 1727- Daniel Keith Coblentz and
Kathleen Vera (Shenk) Coblentz:

2013- Glynnis Dawn Coblentz, (Wadleigh: Daniel
Keith[11], Ruth Ellen[10], Edna Rose[9], Henry
Libby[8], Daniel Foster[7], William Henry[6],
Joseph[5], Joseph[4], Henry[3], Robert[2], John[1]), b.
April 7, 1965. (Ref. 1)

2014- Todd Daniel Coblentz, (Wadleigh: Daniel
Keith[11], Ruth Ellen[10], Edna Rose[9], Henry
Libby[8], Daniel Foster[7], William Henry[6],
Joseph[5], Joseph[4], Henry[3], Robert[2], John[1]), b.
March 22, 1968. (Ref. 1)

Issue of 1730- Gaylord Ralph Coblentz and
Debbie Diane (Hendricks) Coblentz:

2015- Brandy Ann Coblentz, (Wadleigh: Gaylord
Ralph[11], Ruth Ellen[10], Edna Rose[9], Henry
Libby[8], Daniel Foster[7], William Henry[6],

Joseph[5], Joseph[4], Henry[3], Robert[2], John[1]), b.
September 23, 1976. (Ref. 1)

Issue of Floyd Eugene Nelson and 1732- Lynn Eileen (Wolfer) Nelson:

2016- Karen Lynann Nelson, (Wadleigh: Floyd
Eugene[11], Ruth Ellen[10], Edna Rose[9], Henry
Libby[8], Daniel Foster[7], William Henry[6],
Joseph[5], Joseph[4], Henry[3], Robert[2], John[1]), b.
July 4, 1971 (adpt.) (Ref. 1)

2017- Tracy Camille Nelson, (Wadleigh: Floyd
Eugene[11], Ruth Ellen[10], Edna Rose[9], Henry
Libby[8], Daniel Foster[7], William Henry[6],
Joseph[5], Joseph[4], Henry[3], Robert[2], John[1]), b.
February 11, 1974, (adpt.) (Ref. 1)

Issue of Timothy Wayne Zook and 1733- Kathryn Faye (Wolfer) Zook:

2018- Anthony Wayne Zook, (Wadleigh: Kathryn
Faye[11], Ruth Ellen[10], Edna Rose[9], Henry Libby[8],
Daniel Foster[7], William Henry[6], Joseph[5],
Joseph[4], Henry[3], Robert[2], John[1]), b. May 19,
1971. (Ref. 1)

2019- Leighton Grant Zook, (Wadleigh: Kathryn
Faye[11], Ruth Ellen[10], Edna Rose[9], Henry Libby[8],
Daniel Foster[7], William Henry[6], Joseph[5],
Joseph[4], Henry[3], Robert[2], John[1]), b. December
5, 1972. (Ref. 1)

2020- Sheldon Lance Zook, (Wadleigh: Kathryn
Faye[11], Ruth Ellen[10], Edna Rose[9], Henry Libby[8],
Daniel Foster[7], William Henry[6], Joseph[5],
Joseph[4], Henry[3], Robert[2], John[1]), b. March 1,
1976. (Ref. 1)

WADLEIGH GENEALOGY   TWELFTH GENERATION

Issue of 1734- Ronald Reno Wolfer and Rowene Rae (Burkey) Wolfer:

2021- Elroy Shad Wolfer, (Wadleigh: Ronald Reno[11], Dorothy Mae[10], Edna Rose[9], Henry Libby[8], Daniel Foster[7], William Henry[6], Joseph[5], Joseph[4], Henry[3], Robert[2], John[1]), b. July 14, 1974. (Ref. 1)

2022- Michael William Wolfer, (Wadleigh: Ronald Reno[11], Dorothy Mae[10], Edna Rose[9], Henry Libby[8], Daniel Foster[7], William Henry[6], Joseph[5], Joseph[4], Henry[3], Robert[2], John[1]), b. April 1, 1976. (Ref. 1)

Issue of Joe Beauchamp and 1737- Barbara Sue (Killian) Beauchamp:

2023- Calinia Jo Beauchamp, (Wadleigh: Barbara Sue[11], Gwendolyn Alta[10], Edna Rose[9], Henry Libby[8], Daniel Foster[7], William Henry[6], Joseph[5], Joseph[4], Henry[3], Robert[2], John[1]), b. December 18, 1968. (Ref. 1)

2024- Michele Deanne Beauchamp, (Wadleigh: Barbara Sue[11], Gwendolyn Alta[10], Edna Rose[9], Henry Libby[8], Daniel Foster[7], William Henry[6], Joseph[5], Joseph[4], Henry[3], Robert[2], John[1]), b. February 28, 1970. (Ref. 1)

Issue of Alvin LeRoy Taylor and 1737- Barbara Sue (Killian) (Beauchamp) Taylor:

2025- Kevin LeRoy Taylor, (Wadleigh: Barbara Sue[11], Gwendolyn Alta[10], Edna Rose[9], Henry Libby[8], Daniel Foster[7], William Henry[6], Joseph[5], Joseph[4], Henry[3], Robert[2], John[1]), b. September 6, 1971 (Ref. 1)

Issue of 1738- Reno Richard Killian and Catherine (Camp) Killian:

2026- Richard Roy Killian, (Wadleigh: Reno Richard[11], Gwendolyn Alta[10], Edna Rose[9], Henry Libby[8], Daniel Foster[7], William Henry[6], Joseph[5], Joseph[4], Henry[3], Robert[2], John[1]), b. March 22, 1974. (Ref. 1)

Issue of Jose Manuel Pedraza and 1740- Sandra Marie (Killian) Pedraza:

2027- Tanya Lynn Killian, (Wadleigh: Sandra Marie[11], Gwendolyn Alta[10], Edna Rose[9], Henry Libby[8], Daniel Foster[7], William Henry[6], Joseph[5], Joseph[4], Henry[3], Robert[2], John[1]), b. May 23, 1974. (Ref. 1)

Issue of 1745- Laurence Gray Meyer and Sharon Marie (Katski) Meyer:

2028- Lawrence Gray Meyer, (Wadleigh: Laurence Gray[11], Leona Evelyn[10], Mary Emma[9], Henry Libby[8], Daniel Foster[7], William Henry[6], Joseph[5], Joseph[4], Henry[3], Robert[2], John[1]), b. April 24, 1976 at Medford, Jackson Co., Ore. (Ref. 1)

Issue of Bruce Ernest Gilbert and 1749- Charlene Marie (Heffler) Gilbert:

2029- Brenda K. Gilbert, (Wadleigh: Charlene Marie[11], Velma JoAnne[10], Mary Emma[9], Henry Libby[8], Daniel Foster[7], William Henry[6], Joseph[5], Joseph[4], Henry[3], Robert[2], John[1]), b. September 6, 1971 at Portland, Ore. (Ref. 1)

2030- Jeana Marie Gilbert, (Wadleigh: Charlene Marie[11], Velma JoAnne[10], Mary Emma[9], Henry

Libby^8, Daniel Foster^7, William Henry^6, Joseph^5, Joseph^4, Henry^3, Robert^2, John^1), b. September 28, 1974, at Portland, Ore. (Ref. 1)

Issue of Terry Eugene Lee and 1751- Rachel Ann (Heffler) Lee:

2031- <u>Shelly Lynn Lee</u>, (Wadleigh; Rachel Ann^{11}, Velma JoAnne^{10}, Mary Emma^9, Henry Libby^8, Daniel Foster^7, William Henry^6, Joseph^5, Joseph^4, Henry^3, Robert^2, John^1)b. January 8, 1976 at Portland, Ore. (Ref. 1)

Issue of 1792- Troy Ernest Hendrickson and Donna Hendrickson:

2032- <u>Anthony Paul Hendrickson</u>, (Wadleigh: Troy Ernest[12], Sally Ann[11], Ada Margaret[10], Daniel Edward[9], Charles Edwin[8], Daniel Foster[7], William Henry[6], Joseph[5], Joseph[4], Henry[3], Robert[2], John[1]), b. November 10, 1983 at Flandreau, S.D. (Ref. 9)

2033- <u>Benjamin Thomas Hendrickson</u>, (Wadleigh: Troy Ernest[12], Sally Ann[11], Ada Margaret[10], Daniel Edward[9], Charles Edwin[8], Daniel Foster[7], William Henry[6], Joseph[5], Joseph[4], Henry[3], Robert[2], John[1]), b. April 14, 1988 at Flandreau, S.D. (Ref. 9)

Issue of Mr. Schmaltz and 1793- Paula Ann (Hendrickson) Schmaltz:

2034- <u>Rebecca Ann Schmaltz</u>, (Wadleigh: Paula Ann[12], Sally Ann[11], Ada Margaret[10], Daniel Edward[9], Charles Edwin[8], Daniel Foster[7], William Henry[6], Joseph[5], Joseph[4], Henry[3], Robert[2], John[1]), b. August 17, 1979 at Springfield, S.D. (Ref. 9)

2035- <u>Danielle Schmaltz</u>, (Wadleigh: Paula Ann[12], Sally Ann[11], Ada Margaret[10], Daniel Edward[9], Charles Edwin[8], Daniel Foster[7], William Henry[6], Joseph[5], Joseph[4], Henry[3], Robert[2], John[1]), b. January 23, 1983 at Springfield, S.D. (Ref. 9)

INDEX OF DIRECT DECENDANTS

- A -

Arnold
  Scott William, 346
Ayer
  Alice Pillsbury, 284
  Ann Dana, 284

- B -

Badger
  Benjamin E., 145
  Estella, 196
  Gertrude, 196
  Walter, 197
  William, 145, 196
Baker
  Justin Glen, 393
Baldwin
  Bill, 257
  Clifford, 257
Bardwell
  Beatrice Pillsbury,
    284
  Robert Daniels, 285
Barklow
  Kenneth Rowen, 326
  Virginia Sue, 325
Batchelder
  Abigail, 36
  Benjamin, 37
  Daniel, 36
  Deborah, 36
  Elizabeth, 35
  Eunice, 37
  Hannah, 36
  John, 35
  Joshua, 35
  Mary, 35

Batchelder (cont.)
  Nathan, 36
  Ruth, 36
Bean
  Daniel, 130
  Hannah, 131
  William, 130
Beauchamp
  Calinia Jo, 403
  Michele Deanne, 403
Becker
  Elizabeth, 349
  Katharine Winston,
    349
Bell
  Bernice Nelva, 252
  Daniel Robert, 298
  Erin Lee, 363
  Hazel Caroline, 252
  Howard Charles, 252
  Karen Alice, 362
  Mary Lorene, 252
  Stanley Ray, 298
Benson
  Deborah Jane, 307
  Paul David, 307
Bigelow
  Jeffery Winnfield,
    383
  Michael James, 383
Boyce
  Ira Wadleigh, 119
  Jesse Wadleigh, 177
  Reuben, 119
  Ruth Fairbanks, 119
Bronson
  Audrey Eloise, 376
  John Thomas, 376
Brooks
  Eric Steven, 361

Coblentz (cont.)
  Gaylord Ralph, 342
  Glynnis Dawn, 401
  Kimberly Kae, 401
  Patricia Ellen, 341
  Thomas Robert, 341
  Todd Daniel, 401
Coffin
  Mary, 70
  Sarah, 70
Cogdill
  Anita Louise, 294
  Chris Joy, 358
  Christopher, 357
  Connie Kay, 293
  Gifford Lane, 294
  Peggy Lou, 293
  Sally Ann, 293
Colby
  Charles, 144
  Elizabeth, 144
  Fred, 195
  Nathan, 195
  Sarah, 195
  Walter, 144
Collins
  Sandra Jean, 363
  Susan Elaine, 363
Comings
  Bertha, 245
  Joseph T., 245
Cram
  Abigail, 11
  Argentine, 11
  Benjamin, 14
  Elizabeth, 37
  John, 14
  Jonathan, 14
  Mary, 15
  Nehemiah, 37
  Wadleigh, 14
Cummings
  Alfred Pillsbury, 188
  Charles E., 188
Currier
  Abigail, 118
  Anna, 47
  Benjamin, 80
  David, 48, 76
  Dorothy, 46-47

Currier (cont.)
  Elizabeth, 76
  Ezekiel, 46
  George, 234
  Hannah, 48
  Jacob, 77
  James, 77
  Molly, 48
  Moses, 77
  Nathaniel, 76, 231
  Samuel, 46
  Susanna, 48, 77
  Thomas, 78
Curtis
  Todd Anderson, 378

- D -

Daehn
  Charles William, 323
  Cory Ralph, 387
  Debra Lynn, 322
Daugherty
  Christopher Lee, 363
  James Paul, 363
Davis
  Elenor, 55
  John, 56
  Jonathan, 55
  Juda, 55
  Phinehas, 56
Dayton
  Cheryle Ann, 332
  Judith Lynne, 333
  Katherine Jeanne, 333
Dearborn
  Ada Estelle, 277
  Arthur Burton, 277
Dodge
  Edward W., 139
  Jennie Greeley, 192
  Sarah Williams, 139
  Susan Maria, 192
  Thomas W., 139
Dolloff
  Betty, 74
  David, 74
  John, 74
  Richard, 42
  Ruth, 74

Gove (cont.)
  Frank, 158
Graves
  Bertie M., 233
  Clarence D., 232
  David Haslem, 177
  James, 81
  John, 118
  John Ernest, 232
  Leonie, 232
  Mary Louise Holt, 279
  Victor Morse, 233
Greeley
  Alwin W., 202
  Emily, 202
  George E., 203
  Josiah Bartlett, 202
Green
  Henry, 207
  Herbert W., 207
Guest
  Elizabeth, 123
  Marcia Ann, 123
  Sarah, 123
Gusso
  Gregory Edward, 360
  Renea Pauline, 296
  Robert Charles, 360
  Rochelle Ilene, 296
  Rodney Brock, 296
  Roxe Lea, 295
  Susan, 360

        - H -

Harrison
  James R., 371
  Mary E., 371
  Ricky Joe, 371
  Victoria Lee, 370
Hees
  William Rathbun, 349
Heffler
  Charlene Marie, 346
  James Henry, 346
Henderson
  Ronda Renae, 389
Hendrickson
  Anthony Paul, 406
  Benjamin Thomas, 406

Hendrickson (cont.)
  Guy Lee, 355
  Paula Ann, 355
  Troy Ernest, 355
Hiner
  Douglas Harold, 388
  Elizabeth Ann, 388
  Paula Marie, 388
Hogan
  Alma Emma, 372
  Alma Margaret, 310
  Angela Annette, 374
  David James, 372
  David Ray, 375
  Donald Dean, 310
  Francis Everett, 372
  Francis Walter, 309
  Gerald Thomas, 309,
    373
  Grace Marie, 371
  James Colbert, 308
  June Louise, 310
  Kathleen Diane, 372
  Keith Allen, 309
  Kelly Brian, 373
  Kendall Donavon, 374
  Michael Francis, 373
  Nathaniel Lynn, 375
  Patrick Walter, 372
  Ramona Elizabeth, 308
  Robert Allen, 311
  Robert Clifford, 308
  Roy Alan, 372
  Sherri Jean, 373
Holley
  Angela Loyola, 379
  Betty Ann, 315
  Gerald Robert, 314
  Hoyt Allen, 314
  Kenneth Carl, 315
  Ruby Belle, 315
  Russell Allen, 379
  Shelly Christine, 380
  Shirley Jean, 314
  Todd Kenneth, 379
Holmberg
  Jeanette Renee, 364
  Jeannie Marie, 364
  Jennifer Lynn, 364
  John Scott, 364

Tilton (cont.)
  Henry, 243
  Herbert Abel, 201
  Jean Louise, 287
  Joseph A., 201
  Levi Benson, 200
  Lewis Blake, 244
  Nathan, 151
  Philip Nathan, 243
Townsend
  Sarah, 192
Turner
  Chera Leigh, 362
  Gregory Alan, 362
  Jona Lynn, 362

- U -

Upton
  Alice Louise, 312
  Clyde Mervin, 311
  George Kerris, 375
  George LeRoy, 311
  James Lee, 375
  Joseph Edward, 311
  Kristy De Ann, 375
  Theresa Lynette, 376

- V -

Veltman
  Harold Charles, 349
  Harriot Pillsbury,
    349

- W -

Wadleigh
  Aaron, 59
  Abbie Jane, 157
  Abbie Smith, 234
  Abby Elizabeth, 179
  Abel, 29
  Abigail, 8, 10, 15,
    23, 49, 127, 136,
    171
  Abraham, 61
  Achsah, 60, 161
  Ada Margaret, 173,
    251

Wadleigh (cont.)
  Adams, 29, 54, 122
  Addie, 185
  Adelaide Phillips,
    190
  Adeline, 138
  Adrines, 122
  Alan Arthur, 324
  Alan Michael, 330
  Albert P., 234
  Albert Prescott, 168,
    230
  Albra, 51, 70
  Alice, 9
  Alice C., 143
  Alice H., 208
  Alma Edna, 215
  Alma Darlene, 268
  Alonzo, 169, 183
  Alonzo K., 184
  Alta Beatrice, 251
  Alwin C., 153
  Amanda, 132
  Amasa, 131
  Amber Rose, 351
  Andrew J., 125
  Ann Eliza, 153
  Anna, 33, 34, 78, 216
  Anna Marshall, 155
  Anna T., 170
  Anna W., 121
  Anne, 50, 65
  Annie, 63
  Annie Fogg, 224
  Annie W., 222
  Arthur Albert, 278
  Arthur Edison, 186
  Arthur Garfield, 206
  Arthur Gilbert, 217
  Arthur Milton, 266
  Arvilla D., 298
  Asa, 108
  Augusta, 139
  Bainbridge, 142
  Barbara Sue, 335
  Benjamin, 9, 16, 27,
    30, 38, 49, 51-52,
    56, 62, 79, 90,
    106, 120, 124,
    133, 233

Wadleigh (cont.)
Ebenezer, 21, 22, 88, 90
Eben Pearson, 129
Ebenezer Eastman, 137
Ebenezer Stevens, 137
Edith, 204
Edith Marie, 266
Edna Blanche, 180
Edna Rose, 218
Edward, 32, 80
Edward F., 172
Eileen Marie, 270
Eleanor, 49
Eleazer, 80
Electa, 175
Elen, 144
Elener, 80
Elijah, 67, 78, 117
Eliphalet, 86, 89-90, 131
Elisha, 72, 114
Elisha B., 116
Eliza, 113, 115
Eliza Ann, 124, 147
Eliza A., 185
Eliza B., 234
Eliza F., 116
Elizabeth, 16, 22, 50, 61, 65, 78, 84, 87, 92, 122, 146
Elizabeth Malcher, 164
Elkins, 190
Ella Dorothy, 255
Ellen Foster, 155
Ellery Channing, 152
Elmer Albert, 229
Elmer Edward, 249
Elmer Ernest, 237
Elmer Wright, 262
Elsa M., 279
Elva Aldina, 270
Elwell, 147
Emery Leland, 104
Emily H., 142
Emma Josephine, 173
Emma R., 176

Wadleigh (cont.)
Enoch, 29, 69, 84, 113
Enoch Hunt, 120
Enos Dole, 63
Ephriam, 9, 55, 59, 85, 87, 128, 137
Ephriam S., 121
Erastus, 132
Eric Keith, 352
Erline Myrtle, 250
Ernest W., 174
Erwin Walter, 249
Esther, 162
Esther Irene, 269
Ethelinda, 128
Eugene Edward, 291
Eugene Henry, 218
Eunice, 110
Eve J., 228
Everett, 157
Everett Frederick, 143
Everlyn Bridgeman, 276
Ezekiel, 87
Fannie, 168, 222
Fannie Lorena, 210
Florence A., 235
Florence Emma, 216
Frances M., 208
Frances Mason, 246
Frances Wentworth, 114
Francis Marie, 324
Frank A., 235
Frank Eugene, 236, 275
Frank H., 173
Frank H. Newell, 162 223
Frank Lawrence, 155
Frank Leland, 247
Frank Otis, 202
Frank Weston, 230
Franklin Adams, 141
Fred, 174
Fred Burley, 227
Fred Elmer, 216
Fred James, 278

Wadleigh (cont.)
  Love, 31
  Lovey, 61
  Lucinda, 143
  Lucinda Mary, 214
  Lucinda Rae, 317
  Lucy, 169
  Lucy Jane, 155
  Luke, 93
  Luther, 132
  Luther Jethro, 224
  Lydia, 38, 61, 128,
    131, 143
  Lydia Dustin, 163
  Lydia F., 133
  Maaura, 157
  Mabel Ellen, 231
  Mabel Lucille, 263
  Mabelle Lane, 207
  Mae Warren, 181
  Mahala, 116
  Mahitable, 83
  Mai Lai, 354
  Malinda, 143
  Maranda, 166
  Marcia, 30
  Maria, 185
  Marianne, 336
  Marion Inez, 237
  Mark, 101, 153
  Mark James, 334
  Mark John, 150
  Mark W., 244
  Martha, 15, 60
  Martha Abby, 228
  Martha Ellen, 168
  Martha Jane, 142, 143
  Martha O., 228
  Maurice Colman, 275
  Mary, 1, 3, 7, 16,
    21-23, 28, 30, 34,
    39, 50-51, 60-61,
    63, 66-67, 78, 80,
    92, 115, 126, 128,
    137, 151, 161
  Mary Ann, 67, 117,
    124, 199, 228
  Mary A., 160
  Mary Ellen, 170
  Mary Elvira, 185

Wadleigh (cont.)
  Mary Emma, 219
  Mary Etta, 231
  Mary Jane, 120, 171
  Mary Louisa, 179
  Mary Love, 222
  Mary Mason, 165
  Mary Mianda, 183
  Mary N., 184
  Mary Percy, 227
  Mary Rice, 114
  May Helene, 186
  Mehitible, 89
  Melissa, 169
  Melissa Colby, 169
  Melvin Clarence, 204
  Meriable, 30
  Merriam, 50
  Michael Edward, 364
  Michael John, 334
  Michael Norman, 326
  Michele Allyn, 335
  Michelle Rae Ann, 334
  Michelle Rene, 364
  Mildred E., 280
  Milton, 132
  Milton B., 185
  Mina Beulah, 237
  Minnie Cora, 173
  Miriam, 50, 140, 242
  Molly, 110
  Molly Blake, 164
  Monica Jill, 334
  Moses, 21, 23, 29,
    59, 62, 82, 85,
    88, 175
  Moses C., 176
  Myrna Kay, 317
  Myrtle Evelyn, 266
  Myrtle May Williams,
    219
  M. Louisa, 126
  Nancy, 60, 87, 99,
    107, 109, 146,
    151, 171
  Nancy Currier, 96
  Nancy Ellen, 335
  Nancy Morrill, 167
  Nathan B., 107
  Nathaniel, 72

Wadleigh (cont.)
  Simon Hayes, 111
  Smith Glidden, 190
  Steven Calvin, 333
  Steven Erwin, 289
  Stephen G., 112
  Sophronia, 123
  Susan A., 119
  Susan Dole, 96
  Susan Elizabeth, 222
  Susan Kay, 292
  Susan W., 154, 235
  Susann Augusta, 365
  Susanna, 59, 91, 100, 125
  Sylvia, 138
  Tara Leanne, 365
  Taylor, 92
  Theodosia B., 119
  Theophilus, 37, 65
  Theressa Ann, 351
  Tiffany Ann, 350
  Thomas, 16, 31, 52, 58, 92, 93, 140
  Thomas H., 138
  Thomas Miles, 91
  Twyla Ann, 299
  Twyla Mae, 267
  Vere Louise, 269
  Vicki, 388
  Viola, 183
  Virginia Francis, 287
  Walter Emory, 209
  Walter Kendall, 226
  Walter Luther, 278
  Walter L., 244
  Walter Raymond, 265
  Warren, 163
  Washington Irving, 225
  William, 6, 22, 27, 28, 68, 83, 85, 113, 115, 124
  William Augustus, 227
  William Frank, 200
  William Henry, 66, 103, 246
  William H., 160, 171
  William Otis, 288
  William P., 112

Wadleigh (cont.)
  William S., 171
  William Young, 186
  Willie, 182
  Woodrow Wilson, 267
Wadley
  David Richard, 97
  Dole, 98
  George, 148
  George Dole, 148
  John Dole, 147
  John Everingham, 148
  Lydia Colcord, 97
  Loring Reynolds, 148
  Mary Millen, 147
  Moses, 97
  Rebecca Everingham, 148
  Satura Dole, 97
  Sara Pierce, 148
  Sarah Lois, 147
  William Morrill, 96
  William Oconius, 147
Wadsworth
  Chris Arlyn, 360
  Craig Arnold, 360
Walkup
  Thelma, 265
Wall
  Keith Darren, 390
  Melita Lanette, 390
Webster
  Eliza, 127
  Hannah, 127
  Mary Ann, 127
Williams
  George T., 182
Willis
  Claire W., 212
  Clara Martha, 212
  Elmer Pierre, 211
  Estella Pearl, 211
  Fred, 212
  Jessie Irene, 211
Wissman
  Amy Lynn, 370
  James Joseph, 306
  Jason James, 369
  Jeffery James, 369
  Richard Leroy, 306

Colorado (cont.)
  LaJunta, 217
  Montrose, 261
  Nomte Vista, 218
  Otero Cty., 158, 217,
    267
  Rio Grande Cty., 218
  Sugar City, 158
  Weld Cty., 274
Columbia College of
    Broadcasting, 316
Connecticut
  Bridgeport, 223, 277
  Guilford, 282
  Newbury, 26
  New Haven, 282
  New London, 187

       - D -

Dakota Wesleyan Univ.,
    291, 355
Dana Farber Cancer
Institute, 288
Dartmouth Univ., 133,
    187
D.C.
  Washington, 133, 282

       - E -

England
  Bristol, 1, 2
  Excester, 2
  Lincolnshire, 157
  London, 292

       - F -

Flandreau Indian
    School, 355
Florida
  Carrabelle, 233
  Gainesville, 233
  Jacksonville, 289
  Orlando, 383

Florida (cont.)
  Titusville, 219
France
  Paris, 282, 319, 348

       - G -

Georgetown Univ., 133
Georgia, 98
  Atlanta, 262-263
  Augusta, 97
  Bolingbroke, 96-97
  Columbus, 318
  Douglas, 371
  Dublin, 232
  Great Hill Planta-
    tion, 96-97
  Oakland, 147-148
  Pikes Peak Planta-
    tion, 148
  Savannah, 96-97, 148
    284
  Screvens Cty., 148
  Washington Cty., 147
    148
Germany
  Bamberg, 313
  Frankfurt, 319
  Mannheim, 318
  Nuremburg, 378
  Wurtzburg, 377
Grace College, 294

       - H -

Hastings College, 355
Hawaii
  Honolulu, 318
Holland, 14
  Amsterdam, 284
Hungary
  Gyoma, 297
Huron College, 292

       - I -

B - 2

- O -

Ohio
  Bridgeport, 148
  Hamilton Cty., 157
  Plainsville, 57
  Preble Cty., 157
Oklahoma
  Durant, 313
  Glenpool, 320
  Yukon, 287
Oral Roberts Univ., 319
Oregon
  Astoria, 277, 301,
    225
  Bend, 386
  Central Point, 345
  Clatsop Cty., 301
  Jackson Cty., 219,
    274, 345, 404
  Medford, 219, 265,
    274, 321-322, 345,
    404
  Portland, 274, 346,
    404-405
  Vale, 218
  Washington Cty., 274,
    346
Oregon State Univ., 321

- P -

Pennsylvania
  Philadelphia, 71, 114
Philippines
  Angeles City, 385
  Subic Bay, 319
Princeton Univ., 282

- R -

Rhode Island
  Cape Brenton, 24
  Providence, 158
  Providence Cty., 158

- S -

Scotland, 206
  Edinburgh, 52
Smith College, 281-282
Sorbonne Univ. of
    Paris, 319
South Carolina, 371
  Charleston, 366
  Charleston Cty., 366
South Dakota
  Alpena, 249
  Brookings, 296
  Butler, 250, 291
  Clark, 250
  Clark Cty., 209, 249-
    251
  Crocker, 209
  Davison Cty., 184
  Day Cty., 291
  Flandreau, 355, 406
  Grant Cty., 291
  Gregory, 294, 357
  Hot Springs, 250, 292
  Keystone, 290
  Kilborn Twp., 291
  Lennox, 249, 289
  Milbank, 353
  Mitchell, 239, 290-
    291, 294, 351, 355
  Mt. Marty College,
    292
  Mt. Vernon, 184, 249-
    250, 290-291
  Rapid City, 289-291
  Raymond, 209
  Redfield, 289
  Runningwater, 251,
    293
  Sioux Falls, 177
  Spearfish, 292
  Springfield, 293-294,
    355, 406
  Twin Brooks, 291
  Volin, 249
  Watertown, 209
  Watertown, 251, 295-
    296
  Webster, 291

INDEX OF FAMILY NAMES

Bradbury, 15
Bradley, 169
Bragdon, 17, 41
Bretton, 275
Brewster, 71, 114, 156, 158, 208, 217
Bricket, 228
Bridgeman, 223, 276
Brigham, 184, 237
Bronson, 312, 376
Brooks, 144, 296, 361
Brown, 10-11, 34-35, 64, 76, 98-99, 125, 149, 151, 200, 208, 213, 221, 247-248, 258-259, 269, 274-275, 284, 330, 345
Bruer, 292, 353
Brunk, 337, 395
Buffum, 38, 66
Bullard, 264, 319-320, 385-386
Bullock, 101, 153
Burbank, 71-72, 114
Buren, 275
Burkey, 342, 403
Burks, 338, 396
Burley, 113, 162, 165, 227
Burnham, 56, 141, 193-194
Burton, 329
Buswell, 91, 110, 136
Butterfield, 320

- C -

Call, 100, 150
Calley, 169
Cameron, 300, 366
Camp, 343, 404
Campbell, 299, 365
Canney, 172
Capehart, 148, 198
Capen, 199
Carleton, 134, 186
Carlton, 126, 180
Carmichael, 325
Carr, 88-89, 130

Carroll, 191, 195, 241-242
Carson, 79
Carter, 12
Caruthers, 8
Case, 264
Cass, 109
Cawley, 110
Chadwick, 131
Challis, 132
Chambers, 297, 361
Champlin, 138
Chapman, 69, 113
Chase, 33, 48, 66, 76, 110, 154, 166, 183, 201, 204-206, 236, 243, 245
Chatterton, 106, 161
Chellis, 185
Cheney, 139-140, 192
Chute, 169
Cilly, 61
Clark, 34, 95, 97, 268, 282, 326-327
Clement, 144, 195
Clifford, 49, 83, 101
Cloud, 160
Clough, 8-9, 30-31, 49, 79
Cobb, 217, 268, 315, 380
Coblentz, 273, 341-342, 401
Coffin, 18, 39, 41, 70, 127
Cogdill, 251, 293-294, 355-358
Colbert, 252
Colburn, 92
Colby, 52, 82, 94, 127, 144, 195, 235
Colcord, 39, 62, 96
Cole, 105, 160, 231
Collins, 298, 363
Comings, 205, 245
Connor, 9, 35, 236, 280
Cook, 187, 239
Cooke, 177, 232
Corbett, 244, 287
Corliss, 129, 181

Lundberg, 182, 236
Lunstrum, 210, 253-254,
   300-305, 365-368
Lunt, 26
Lux, 341

- M -

MacBean, 24
MaCoy, 199
Magoon, 15
Mallon, 103
Maloon, 113, 173
Maratea, 315
Marble, 334
Markle, 336, 393
Marsh, 9, 92, 104
Marston, 2, 8, 13-14,
   38, 67, 90, 107, 131,
   141, 193
Martin, 50, 216, 265,
   322, 387
Martinez, 333, 392
Mason, 118, 177
Masters, 103, 155
McCampbell, 157, 212-
   213, 219, 257-258
McClinch, 222
McCloon, 189
McCrea, 291, 353
McCrilliss, 161, 222
McDavitt, 207, 247
McGowan, 382
McIntosh, 272, 335
McKamie, 297, 361
McKee, 282, 348
McKibbin, 254, 304, 368
McKinley, 246
McKnight, 283
McMann, 319, 385
McMichael, 292, 354
McNamara, 336
McNeal, 308
McNeil, 316, 381-382
McQuesten, 130
McWayne, 191
Meadow, 244
Mebane, 233
Meininger, 297

Meisenheimer, 256, 306-
   307
Melcher, 4, 37, 64, 99,
   150, 198-199, 242
Mendenhall, 320
Mercer, 13
Mellon, 155
Merrill, 222, 276
Merrow, 234
Meyer, 274, 345, 373,
   404
Meyers, 340, 400
Miles, 43, 57, 91, 297
Miller, 317, 382
Mills, 1, 5, 17
Minino, 294, 357
Moody, 10
Moor, 119
Moore, 40, 115, 170,
   231, 333, 392
Moreau, 317
Morgan, 169, 230
Morrill, 8, 24-28, 42-
   47, 49, 51-53, 63,
   69, 75-76, 78, 86,
   113, 124, 126-127,
   137, 154, 179, 203
Morrill-Wiggin, 203
Morris, 219
Morrison, 108, 168,
   229, 276, 286
Morse, 177
Moulton, 13, 56, 204
Mugridge, 56
Mullin, 160, 221
Myers, 260, 294, 358
Mysing, 304

- N -

Nason, 241
Neal, 68, 72, 106, 109,
   112, 170-172
Nealley, 106
Nelson, 3, 9, 342, 402
Newell, 115
Newkirk, 312, 376
Newman, 250, 293

Smark, 332, 391
Smith, 1, 5, 9, 12, 15,
  17, 30, 33-34, 37,
  41, 61-62, 70-71, 74,
  78, 106, 117, 124,
  137, 166, 177, 181,
  190, 211, 224, 232,
  234, 256, 263, 277,
  279, 314-315, 317-
  318, 320, 347, 371,
  383-386
Snow, 229
Snyder, 189, 241, 286
Sosebee, 312, 376-377
Sousley, 294
Spires, 311
Springer, 270, 332
Spurlock, 316
Staats, 261, 312
Stall, 165
Stanyan, 15
Staples, 293, 356-357
Stauffer, 340, 400
Sterns, 25
Stetzel, 214, 261
Stevens, 7, 10, 17-18,
  24, 26, 31-32, 41,
  50, 59, 62, 77, 95,
  183, 238, 262, 341,
  401
Stevenson, 241, 286
Stickley, 290, 352
Stiles, 170, 230
Stinson, 187, 238
Stockbridge, 66, 103
Stokes, 114, 174
Stone, 196, 318
Stoner, 254, 301
Storer, 19
Strickrod, 220
Stroup, 332, 390
Stuerke, 306, 369
Sturgis, 239
Sutherland, 235, 279
Swain, 10, 33, 163, 175
Swanson, 304, 368
Sweatt, 60, 61
Sweeney, 245
Swerngin, 211, 256
Swett, 83, 84, 121, 122

- T -

Taggart, 191
Talkelm, 218, 271
Tarr, 96
Taylor, 108, 164, 205,
  211, 245-246, 251,
  294-295, 343, 358-
  359, 403
Templeton, 263, 318-
  319, 384-385
Tessier, 287
Thieson, 375
Thing, 2, 5-7, 17-20,
  24, 41
Thomas, 163-164, 195,
  224,   226, 253
Thompson, 41, 70, 116,
  264, 298, 313, 362
Thorne, 175
Thurston, 39
Tiffany, 242
Tilton, 4, 11-12, 44,
  96, 100, 109, 150-
  151, 165, 171, 200-
  201, 206, 226,
  243-244, 287
Tipping, 2
Titcomb, 85, 124
Toothaker, 232, 279
Towle, 90
Townsend, 140, 192
Tracy, 148
Treworgie, 4
Treworgye, 6
Trueba, 271, 334
Trumbull, 195
Tuck, 13, 99
Tucker, 26, 128
Turner, 89, 293, 297,
  362
Tuxbury, 86, 125
Tyers, 27, 48

- U -

Uhley, 318

- Y -

York, 243
Yorke, 125
Young, 2, 7, 18, 24,
    42, 133, 186, 271

- Z -

Zook, 340, 342, 402

WADLEIGH CHRONICLE

REFERENCES

1. The Descendants of Edwin Flavel Brewster, 1822-1911 by William Keven Armstrong, Copyright 1978 William Keven Armstrong, Gateway Press, Baltimore, LCCCN 78-55483.

2. The Wadleighs of New England by Rosenmae Paige, August 1983, Manuscript.

3. The Everett Wadleigh Family and Related Families by Charles E. and Rosenmae Paige, 1984, Manuscript.

4. The Old Families of Salisbury and Amesbury Massachusetts by David W. Hoyt, Providence, R.I., 1897; Reprint: New England History Press, Somersworth NH, 1981, ISBN 0-89725-026-5, LCCCN 81-83877.

5. Dauntless Dunn compiled by the Early Settlers, 1970, Hardbound public domain.

6. Lennox, 60th Anniversary Edition, Sixty Years of Progress, 1879-1939 compiled by the Jubilee Directors, Lennox Independent, Lennox SD.

7. Lennox thru 75 Years, Diamond Jubilee, 1897-1954 compiled by the Jubilee Directors, Lennox Independent, Lennox SD.

8. Lennox through 100 Years, 1879-1979, A Century of Progress compiled by the Jubilee Directors, Lennox Independent, Lennox SD.

9. Contemporary Family Records compiled by Donald E. Wadleigh, Park Forest, Ill. and Alma C. Wadleigh, Lennox, S. D.

10. Geneological Dictionary of New England, compiled by Savage. (in 4 vol.)

11. The New England Historical and Genealogical Register, Vol. CXXXII, July 1978.

12. Burke's American Families with British Ancestry, Excerpted from "Burke's Genealogical and Heraldic History of the Landed Gentry, 16th Edition", ISBN 0-8063-0662-9, Genealogical Publishing Co., Baltimore, 1977.

13. Geneological History of the Mayflower Families, Geneological Press, Baltimore, MD.

14. The History of Lincoln County, South Dakota, Copyright 1985, Pine Hill Press, Freeman, S.D.

15. Saco Valley Settlements and Families, by G.T. Ridlon, Pub. 1969 by Tuttle, Orig. pub. 1895 Portland Me.

16. The Libby Family in America, 1602-1881, by Charles T. Libby, Pub. 1882.

17. History of New London, Connecticut, by Frances Manwaring Caulkins, 1895, Pub. H.D. Utley of Press of the Day Publishing Co., New London, Ct.

18. Memorial History of Hampstead, N.H., by Harriette Elizabeth Noyes, Vol. 2.

19. History of the Town of Duxbury, Mass. with Genealogical Registers, by Justin Winsor, 1849, Crosby & Nichols, Washington Street, Boston, Mass.

20. A Memorial History of Hampstead, New Hampshire, by Harriette Eliza Noyes, 1903, George G. Reed, Boston, Mass.

21. The History of Kensington, N. H., by Rev. Roland D. Sawyer, 1946, Knowlton & McLeary Co., Farmington, Maine.

22. History of Scituate Masssachusetts, from
its Settlement to 1831, by Samuel Deane, 1831,
James Loring, Pub., Boston, Mass.

23. History of the Town of Exeter, New
Hampshire, by Charles H. Bell, 1888, J. E.
Farwell & Co., Boston, Mass.

24. See S9.

25. History of Sutton, N.H., by Mrs. Augusta
Harvey Worton, Republican Press Assn., Concord,
N.H., 1890.

26. Old Kittery and Her Families, compiled by
Everett S. Stackpole, 1981.

27. Exeter, New Hampshire, 1888-1988, by Nancy
Carnegie Merrill, 1988, Peter E. Randall, Pub.,
Portsmouth, N.H.

28. A Catalogue of the names of the First
Puritan Settlers of the Colony of Connecticut,
comp. by R. R. Hinman, 1968, Genealogical
Publishing Company, Baltimore.

29. Descendants of Thomas Gleason of
Watertown, Mass. 1607-1909, compiled by John B.
White and L. M. Wilson, 1909.

30. History of the Town of Hampton Falls, New
Hampshire, 1640-1900, by Warren Brown, 1900,
John B. Clark Co, Manchester, N.H.

31. History of Hampton Falls, Vol. II, 1900-
1917, by Warren Brown, 1918, The Rumford Press,
Concord, N.H.

32. Plucker-Witte Genealogy, 1989, by Eleanor
Skoog, 1989, manuscript.

33. John Lee of Farmington, Hartford Co.,
Conn. and his Decendants, Second Edition,
compl. by Leonard Lee and Sarah Fiske Lee,
(First Edition by Sarah Marsh Lee), 1897, publ.

"Lee Assn." Republican-Record Book Print,
Meriden, Conn.

34. Supplement to John Lee of Farmington,
Hartford Co., Conn. and his Decendants, compl.
by Leonard Lee, 1900, publ. "Lee Assn."
Republican-Record Book Print, Meriden, Conn.

35. The Story of the Gilmans and a Gilman
Genealogy of the Descendants of Edward Gilman
of Hingham, England, 1550-1950, by Constance Le
Neve Gilman Ames, Yakima Washington.

36. The Ancestry of William Gilman Maguire of
Sanford, Maine by William and Beulah Maguire,
Completed by Martin H. Jewett, manuscript,
1978, Library of Congress #78-55796.

37. Colonial Families of the U.S.A., Vol. 5.,
by George Norberry Mackenzie, Genealogical
Publishing, Baltimore. Library of Congress
#66-18423.

38. Genealogical Dictionary of Maine and New
Hampshire, by Sybil Noyes, Charles Thornton
Libby, and Walter Goodwin Davis, Genealogical
Publishing, Baltimore, 1976. (Originally pub.
in five parts, Portland, Me. 1928-1939)

39. The Ladd Family of Piscataquis County,
Maine, compiled by Mrs. Joseph H. Garrity, West
Palm Beach, Fla., 1974. (Manuscript)

40. A Geneological and Biographical Record of
that Branch of the Family of Gilman Descended
from the Honorable John Gilman of Exeter, N.H.,
Compiled by Arthur Gilman, Pub. J. Munsell,
Albany, 1863.

41. History of Hingham, Mass, The Genealogies,
by George Lincoln, (from Correspondence from
Robert B. Fearing of Schenectady, NY), 1893.

42. Mayflower Families Through Five
Generations in three volumes, Ed. by Lucy Mary
Kellogg, General Society of Mayflower

Descendants, 1975.

43. <u>Charles E. Wadleigh and Hannah M. Wadleigh</u>, Military records, death certificates and pension records.

44. <u>Biographical Directory of the United States Congress, 1774-1971</u>, compiled by Kennedy, U.S.G.P.O. Stock # 5271-0249, 1971.

45. <u>School District Clerk's Record</u>, Spring Valley School District, Clark, S.D., Daniel E. Wadleigh, Clerk, 1915-1920.

46. <u>Genealogy of the Gilman Family in England and America traced in the line of the Hon. John Gilman, of Exeter, N.H.</u>, by Arthur Gilman of Glynllyn, J. Munsell, 78 State Street, Albany, 1864.

47. <u>Piscataqua Pioneers, 1623-1775, Register of Members and Ancestors</u>, Edited by John Scales, A.M., Dover, N.H., 1919.

48. <u>The Old Logg House by the Bridge</u>, by Robbins Paxson Gilman,

49. <u>Genealogy of Edward Gilman</u>, compiled by Danny D. Smith, R.F.D. #5A, Gardiner, Maine, 04345, 20 May 1982.

50. <u>Ancestry of Charles Stinson Pillsbury and John Sargent Pillsbury</u>, by Mary Lovering Holman, 2 vol., 1938.

51. <u>History of the Descendants of Elder John Strong of Northampton, Mass.</u>, by Benjamin W. Dwight, 2 vol., Joel Munsell, Albany, 1871.

52. Contemporary Family Records compiled by William Kevin Armstrong, Ekalaka, Mont.

53. Contemporary Family Records compiled by Mary Brewster Stapp, Huntsville, Ala.

54. Contemporary Family Records compiled by

Jack Lipka, Montague, Mich.

55.   History of Brome County Quebec, from the
Date of Grants of Land Therein to the Present
Time, by Rev. Ernest M. Taylor, M.A., Vol. I,
John Lovell & Son, Limited, Montreal, 1908.

56.   Contemporary Family Records compiled by
Phillip Wadleigh, Marietta, Ga.

SECONDARY SOURCES

S1.   Correspondence: Mrs. Betty B. Messier,
Box 35, Coventry Conn. 06328, dated April 17,
1990.

S2.   Correspondence: A. F. Dixon, 42 Laurel
Drive, Oakdale Conn. 06370, dated February 16,
1990, incl 5 pages and one chart.

S3.   Charts compiled by Ruth Smith Painter,
17814 Jug St., Burton, OH 44021, dated Apr. 27,
1990.

S4.   Correspondence: Robert G. Holt, 48
Deerfield Drive, P.O. Box 739, Montpelier VT
05602, dated February 19, 1990 incl 10 Family
Records and 2 charts; and Correspodence dated
March 25, 1990 with 12 Records.

S5.   Correspondence: Lorraine R. Taylor, 1674
Woodland Drive, Provo, UT 84604, dated February
23, 1990 incl IGI data.

S6.   Correspondence: M. Faith Kent, P.O. Box
374, Lancaster, N.H., 03584, dated February 17,
1990.

S7.   Correspondence: Beryl Berry Brown, 11
Parkside Ave. Brattleboro, VT 05301, with 2
charts, 9 Family Records sheets (text), and
1958 letter from Ms. Smith of Kingston-upon-
Surrey.

S8.   Biography of Nathan Birdseye Williston by
Prof. Williston Walker, a one-page excerpt of a
manuscript located by the archivist of Williston Northampton School and confirmed indepen-
dently in correspondence dated February 23,
1989 from Warren D. Buchanan of Connecticut
Coordinated Genesearch.

S9.   Correspondence Carol A. Burke, 20 Beech
St. Richmond, Me. referencing Me. Provincial
Records II:75, Mt. Vernon Me. Village Records,

Salisbury Ma. Village Records, mss. on file at
N.H. Hist. Soc. by John S. Wadleigh of Amesbury
and Kensington, and the Mary Lovering Holman
papers at the N.E.H.G.S.